Chronicling Cultures

Chronicling Cultures
Long-Term Field Research in Anthropology

Edited by Robert V. Kemper and Anya Peterson Royce

ALTAMIRA
PRESS

A Division of Rowman & Littlefield Publishers, Inc.
Walnut Creek • Lanham • New York • Oxford

ALTAMIRA PRESS
A Division of Rowman & Littlefield Publishers, Inc.
1630 North Main Street, #367
Walnut Creek, CA 94596
www.altamirapress.com

Rowman & Littlefield Publishers, Inc.
4720 Boston Way
Lanham, MD 20706

12 Hid's Copse Road
Cumnor Hill, Oxford OX2 9JJ, England

British Library Cataloguing in Publication Information Available

Library of Congress Cataloging-in-Publication Data

Chronicling cultures : long-term field research in anthropology / edited by Robert V. Kemper and Anya Peterson Royce.
    p. cm.
Includes bibliographical references and index.
ISBN 0-7591-0193-0 (cloth : alk. paper) — ISBN 0-7591-0194-9 (pbk. : alk. paper)
    1. Anthropology—Field work. 2. Anthropology—Research. I. Kemper, Robert V., 1945- II. Royce, Anya Peterson.

GN33.3.F53 C57 2002
301'.07'2—dc21
                                                            2001053564

Printed in the United States of America

♾™ The paper used in this publication meets the minimum requirements of American National Standard for Information Sciences—Permanence of Paper for Printed Library Materials, ANSI/NISO Z39.48-1992.

CONTENTS

PREFACE

Like its subject matter, this volume has been a long-term enterprise. In the early 1970s, George Foster, Elizabeth Colson, and Thayer Scudder recognized that their field research projects in Tzintzuntzan, Mexico, and in Gwembe, Zambia—though quite different in their origins, theoretical orientations, and goals—had numerous common features simply because the projects involved repeated visits to the same communities over a long period of time. This recognition led them to approach Lita Osmundsen (then president of the Wenner-Gren Foundation for Anthropological Research) about organizing a conference at Burg Wartenstein, Austria, to bring together social anthropologists from different traditions to explore the implications of long-term research. The results of the Burg Wartenstein conference were summarized in a report in the journal *Current Anthropology* (Colson et al. 1976) and in a volume entitled *Long-Term Field Research in Social Anthropology* (Foster et al. 1979), which contained the revised versions of the papers discussed at the conference.

That volume was divided into four parts to reflect the diversity of the field research projects presented. Part I, "Long-Term Research in Historical Perspective," contained chapters by Louise Lamphere on fieldwork among the Navajo from Clyde Kluckhohn through the Lake Powell Project of the mid-1970s; by the Mexican anthropologist Alfonso Villa Rojas (who died in 1998, at age 91) on his fieldwork in the Mayan region of Mexico; by William Mangin (now retired as professor emeritus at Syracuse University) on the Vicos Project in highland Peru, from its inception by Allan Holmberg through the Peace Corps era; and by Tamás Hofer (currently, director of the Ethnographic Museum in Budapest) on his collaborative work with Edit Fél in the peasant community of Átány in their native Hungary. Part II, "General Ethnographic Studies," included reports by M. J. Meggitt (now retired as professor emeritus at Queens College in New York City) on his fieldwork among the Enga of Papua New Guinea; by Leopold Pospisil (currently professor emeritus of anthropology at Yale University and curator emeritus at the Peabody Museum; see Pospisil 1995) on his research among the Tirolean peasants of Obernberg, Austria; by June Helm (currently professor emerita at the University of Iowa; see Helm 2001) on her research among the

Dogrib and other Dene peoples in Canada's Northwest Territories; and by Foster on his first thirty years in Tzintzuntzan. Part III, "Problem-Oriented Studies," featured chapters by Kemper on the beginnings of his research among migrants from Tzintzuntzan in Mexico City; by T. Scarlett Epstein on her revisits to two villages in Mysore in south India; by Scudder and Colson on their research in Gwembe; and by Hussein Fahim (see Fahim 1981, 1982) on his experiences as an Egyptian anthropologist working in a Nubian village. Part IV, "Team Projects," chronicled two of the best-known large-scale projects in contemporary social anthropology—the Harvard Chiapas Project, examined by Evon Z. Vogt, and the Kalahari Research Project, analyzed by Richard B. Lee.

Then, in 1991, Colson and Kemper organized a follow-up session on "Theoretical and Methodological Flexibility in Long-Term Field Research in Social Anthropology" for the annual meeting of the American Anthropological Association (AAA) held in Chicago. From the original Burg Wartenstein group, Scudder, Lee (now with Megan Biesele as co-presenter), Foster, and Kemper reported on their continuing work in Gwembe, among the !Kung San, and in Tzintzuntzan, respectively. Other participants in the Chicago session included Thomas Headland and Janet Headland (1997), who discussed their three decades of research among the Agta hunter-gatherers in the Philippines; Susan Wadley (1994; cf. Wiser and Wiser 2000), who talked about the work of the missionaries William and Charlotte Wiser and other researchers (including herself) in the north Indian village of Karimpur since 1925; Karen Hansen (1989, 2000), who examined issues of time, space, and gender in her urban fieldwork in Zambia; Conrad Kottak (1986, 1999), who compared his longitudinal projects in Arembepe, Brazil, and Ivato, Madagascar; Gloria Rudolf (1999), who considered the strengths and weaknesses of long-term participant observation based on her fieldwork in Panama; and Ronald Waterbury (1989), who reported on his research in the Valley of Oaxaca, Mexico, since 1965. George Collier, who has studied land-use practices and politics for more than thirty years (Collier and Quaratiello 1994) in Chiapas, Mexico, served as discussant for the session.

In response to the very positive reaction to this session, Kemper began to organize a new volume on long-term field research, with the intent of combining contributions updated from the 1979 book with papers presented at Chicago. Unfortunately, because of the death of one contributor, the retirements of others, and the changing career demands of several others, it proved difficult to assemble an appropriate set of contributions, and plans for publication languished.

In 1997, Kemper collaborated with Anya Peterson Royce, a longtime colleague, in writing about ethical issues for social anthropologists in Mexico, based on their respective long-term experiences in Tzintzuntzan and in Juchitán (Kemper and Royce 1997; Royce and Kemper 1998). Their commentary generated considerable interest and helped to revive the idea of doing a new volume on long-term field research. In 1998, with funding from the Andrew Mellon Foundation, Kemper began to work with Doug White and his Swiss colleague Eric

Widmer in a social network approach to analyzing the long-term Tzintzuntzan data sets. White previously had collaborated with Scudder and Colson on their Gwembe materials and is involved with several other long-term projects, including the writing of a major monograph with Ulla Johansen about her long-term ethnographic research among nomads in Turkey.

In 1999, another AAA session was planned, this time focused on the question of "passing the mantle" in long-term projects. Sponsored by the Association of Senior Anthropologists and attended by an overflow crowd, the session provided an interactive discussion among anthropologists involved in the Gwembe and Tzintzuntzan projects. On the Gwembe side of the table, Colson, Scudder, Rhonda Gillett-Netting, Sam Clark, and Lisa Cliggett were present; on the Tzintzuntzan side of the table, Kemper, Stanley Brandes, Scott Anderson, and Peter Cahn were present. Unfortunately, Bennett Siamwiza and George and Mary Foster were unable to attend. Royce led the session, guiding the panelists and audience through what all agreed was one of the most enjoyable and enthusiastic AAA sessions in years.

These activities culminated in an invitation from Mitchell Allen, publisher of AltaMira Press, to assemble a volume on long-term field research. The twelve chapters included here represent the old and the new, spanning the continuum from Foster, who has been working in Tzintzuntzan since 1945, to Cahn, who first went to Tzintzuntzan in 1998 and completed his dissertation in 2001. Aside from Cliggett and Cahn, whose chapters consider long-term fieldwork from the perspective of younger scholars, the rest of the authors have spent more than thirty years doing research in their respective field sites. Perhaps Cliggett and Cahn will prepare another collection of long-term studies in 2025, marking the fiftieth anniversary of the original gathering at Burg Wartenstein.

As always, the preparation of an edited volume is possible only through the dedication of many individuals, a number of whom are acknowledged in the appropriate chapters. First, we give thanks to the diverse funding agencies and many individuals—anonymous peer reviewers, professional critics and colleagues, friends, parents, spouses, children, and grandchildren—who have facilitated and tolerated our fieldwork at great distances for so many years. Their support would be meaningless without the long-term collaboration of thousands of persons in our diverse field sites around the globe. We are fortunate to count as friend and family some very special individuals without whom our field experiences could not have followed the long-term trajectories reported in this volume.

We gratefully acknowledge the excellent editorial work of Dr. Julie Adkins, whose remarkable eye and sense of grace are reflected throughout the pages of this volume. In addition, we want to thank Ronald R. Royce for his assistance with matters of linguistic notation and other subtle elements of the editorial art. Additional acknowledgments appear at the beginning of the notes sections of particular chapters.

PREFACE

We—indeed, anthropologists around the globe—owe a great debt to three individuals who have been the guiding spirits behind the first long-term field research volume, the conferences, and this collection. Elizabeth Colson, George M. Foster, and Thayer Scudder have shaped anthropology, especially as a field dedicated to sustained ethnographic research, through their research and writing, through their nurturing of students, and through their efforts to improve people's lives and to create more humane and effective development policies. This volume represents another example of how they have passed the mantle to a younger generation.

Finally, we wish to give special recognition to the late Lita Osmundsen, whose enthusiasm for all forms of anthropological research put an entire generation of students and professionals in her debt—and into the field. In her memory, all royalties from the sale of this volume will be given to the Wenner-Gren Foundation to further its research program.

References Cited

Collier, George A. and Elizabeth Lowery Quaratiello
(1994) *Basta! Land and the Zapatista Rebellion in Chiapas*. Oakland, CA: Institute for Food and Development Policy.

Colson, Elizabeth, George M. Foster, Thayer Scudder, and Robert V. Kemper
(1976) "Long-term research in social anthropology." *Current Anthropology* 17(3):494–496.

Fahim, Hussein M.
(1981) *Dams, People and Development: The Aswan High Dam Case*. New York: Pergamon Press.
(1982) *Indigenous Anthropology in Non-Western Countries*. Durham: Carolina Academic Press.

Foster, George M., Thayer Scudder, Elizabeth Colson, and Robert V. Kemper [editors]
(1979) *Long-Term Field Research in Social Anthropology*. New York: Academic Press.

Hansen, Karen Tranberg
(1989) *Distant Companions: Servants and Employers in Zambia, 1900–1985*. Ithaca, NY: Cornell University Press.
(2000) Salaula: *The World of Secondhand Clothing and Zambia*. Chicago: University of Chicago Press.

Headland, Thomas N. and Janet D. Headland
(1997) "Limitation of human rights, land exclusion, and tribal extinction: The Agta Negritos of the Philippines." *Human Organization* 56(1):79–90.

Helm, June
(2001) *The People of Denendeh: Ethnohistory of the Indians of Canada's Northwest Territories*. Iowa City: University of Iowa Press.

Kemper, Robert V. and Anya Peterson Royce
(1997) "Ethical issues for social anthropologists in Mexico: A North American perspective." *Human Organization* 56(4):479–483.

Kottak, Conrad P.
(1986) *Madagascar: Society and History.* Durham: Carolina Academic Press.
(1999) *Assault on Paradise: Social Change in a Brazilian Village.* Third edition. New York: McGraw-Hill.

Pospisil, Leopold
(1995) *Obernberg: A Quantitative Analysis of a Tirolean Peasant Economy.* Memoirs Volume 24. New Haven: Connecticut Academy of Arts and Sciences.

Royce, Anya Peterson and Robert V. Kemper
(1998) "Finding a footing on the moral high ground: Connections, interventions, and more ethical implications." *Human Organization* 57(3):328–330.

Rudolf, Gloria
(1999) *Panama's Poor: Victims, Agents, and Historymakers.* Gainesville: University of Florida Press.

Wadley, Susan S.
(1994) *Struggling with Destiny in Karimpur, 1925–1984.* Berkeley: University of California Press.

Waterbury, Ronald
(1989) "Embroidery for tourists: A contemporary putting-out system in Oaxaca, Mexico." Pp. 243–271 in Annette Weiner and Jane Schneider (editors), *Cloth and Human Experience.* Washington, D.C.: Smithsonian Institution Press.

Wiser, William H. and Charlotte Viall Wiser
(2000) *Behind Mud Walls: Seventy-Five Years in a North Indian Village.* Updated and expanded edition, with chapters by Susan S. Wadley. Berkeley: University of California Press.

LONG-TERM FIELD RESEARCH: METAPHORS, PARADIGMS, AND THEMES

Anya Peterson Royce and Robert V. Kemper

The uniqueness of anthropology lies in its commitment to a tradition of field-based research, the source of our ethnographic description. From that social and cultural description, we derive theories of human behavior and gain perspectives on human understanding. Ethnography, while grounded in the specific, refers to the general and does so in a dialectical fashion.

A radical shift in anthropological method resulted from Bronislaw Malinowski's Trobriand Islands field research, carried out in three expeditions between 1914 and 1920. Malinowski's was *not* the first field research,[1] but it did provide the model for intensive immersion over extended periods that anthropology has claimed as its hallmark for most of the twentieth century. As Stocking (1983:93) has observed:

> It involved a shift in the primary locus of investigation, from the deck of the mission ship or the verandah of the mission station to the teeming center of the village, and a corresponding shift in the conception of the ethnographer's role, from that of inquirer to that of participant "in a way" in village life. It also required a shift in theoretical orientation. . . . And, finally, it required not only enactment but embodiment—or precisely the sort of mythic transformation Malinowski provided.

A. L. Epstein (1967:xii) wrote perceptively of the difference between what Malinowski did as a result of direct observation in contrast to his predecessors: "Malinowski did not write descriptions at the level of culture, custom, ritual, and belief. He dealt instead with how people grew up in a society of a particular culture, and how they used and rebelled against that culture."

Malinowski (1922:3) himself drew a distinction between observations and inferences, maintaining that the researcher had to be careful to mark which was which in writing for others' consumption: "Only such ethnographic sources are of unquestionable scientific value, in which we can clearly draw the line between . . . the results of direct observation and of native statements and interpretations, and . . . the inferences of the author, based on his common sense and psychological insight."

Malinowski was very much in the naturalist field science tradition, as is acknowledged by his dedication of his monograph about the Trobriands fieldwork, *Argonauts of the Western Pacific*, to his mentor, Seligman.[2]

Guiding Metaphors and Disciplinary Paradigms

That what he observed in the field might be affected by his training, experience, theoretical orientation, or personality was not a concern of Malinowski's. Instead, we must turn to Clyde Kluckhohn, an American anthropologist dedicated to long-term field research, for an early articulation of this reflexive notion. Kluckhohn drew attention to it in 1939, supporting his own discussion with a statement by Alfred North Whitehead: "And the first point to remember is that the observational order is invariably interpreted in terms of the concepts supplied by the conceptual order" (cited in Kluckhohn 1939:331).

In 1986, Edward Bruner spoke to this point in his examination of changing modes of discourse about American Indians. According to Brüner (1986:4), social scientists writing in the 1930s and 1940s about social change saw the present as "disorganization, the past as glorious, and the future as assimilation." In contrast, Bruner observed that, in the discourse of the 1980s, "the present is viewed as a resistance movement, the past as exploitation, the future as ethnic resurgence." Laurel Richardson's (1988:202) concept of "implicit guiding metaphor"—meaning the dominant ways we think about people and problems that derive from the historical, political, and social contexts in which we work—is exactly what Bruner articulated with his examples. As a science, anthropology is not immune to its own guiding metaphors.

By the 1940s, anthropology was distinguished by fieldwork, by a methodology that gathers evidence through participant observation and that tries to separate data from inference, and by the acknowledgment that researchers' observations are colored by who they are and by what paradigms are shaping the field at the moment. Anthropologists did not, however, assume a consistently diachronic approach, believing rather that cultures could be described either in a past "traditional" state or in a "contemporary" state that had reached equilibrium through the process of acculturation (Redfield, Linton, and Herskovits 1936).

Acknowledgment that not all societies necessarily strived toward equilibrium, nor did they all enjoy a healthy state in which all of their elements contributed toward a smoothly functioning society, emerged from the changing contexts in which anthropologists found themselves working during and after World War II (cf. Lewis 1951; Redfield 1950). Disintegrating empires in Africa and Asia left anything but smoothly functioning societies (cf. Gluckman 1956; Mandelbaum 1970). Perhaps as an antidote to the chaotic state of the world at large, small-scale communities—understood as dynamic, strategizing entities responding to both external and internal events—gradually became the focus of ethnographic observation and analysis. For many anthropologists, the "bounded" community described in the "ethnographic present" became a cherished fiction, even though it rarely corresponded to anything observable in the real world. As Clifford Geertz (1962:7) remarked in a critical review of studies of peasant life, "Is not the intensive study of very small, territorially localized groups of people apt to be as misleading as enlightening so far as the comprehension of a complex society is concerned?"

This analytical framework and the problems associated with it, especially in the genre of peasant studies that became so popular in the 1950s and 1960s (cf. Potter, Diaz, and Foster 1967), may have been an artifact of how and by whom fieldwork was done. Doctoral students cutting their professional teeth, as it were, on a description of the "other," spent from a year to two years in the field, usually in a suitably exotic location (Gupta and Ferguson 1997:8), eventually returning "home" to write a dissertation which subsequently might be published as yet another community-level case study.

First Fieldwork

First-time fieldworkers often struggle to find clean lines and consistency in what they encounter. Often, the result is to commit what Whitehead (1967:58) called "the fallacy of misplaced concreteness." Confronted with a bewildering array of customs, values, behaviors, and settings, and armed with a set of hypotheses, fieldworkers tried to retain control by fixing attention on the accessible—that is, on what people are willing to share and what may be observed. We try to minimize conflicts among phenomena observed as well as between phenomena and hypotheses, explaining them, when forced to, either as part of a long-term process of reconciliation or as exceptions. We seldom see them as providing surges of energy that jolt us out of the "drowse of the accustomed," to borrow Robert Penn Warren's wonderful phrase. Neophyte fieldworkers rarely are comfortable with the dynamism and unpredictability of ethnographic situations. Swinging between the drowse of the accustomed and the chaos of the unexpected, researchers feel a need to restrain and contain. We may not leave out all the wildness and unpredictability, but, when we return home from the field, often we write in ways that "tame." Any work that claims to interpret human lives must acknowledge and recognize the uneven terrain of every individual life.

Perhaps all new fieldworkers should take to heart what Lévi-Strauss (1968:349) described as the mandate of anthropology: "to bear testimony to future generations of the ingeniousness, diversity, and imagination of our species."

Long-Term Field Research

Returning to the field changes how anthropologists see and what they accept. Multiple visits to the same field site make it difficult to ignore the pace of the everyday and the staccato bursts of the extraordinary. In a session on "Passing the Mantle" at the 1999 American Anthropological Association annual meeting, Elizabeth Colson commented about the benefits of long-term field research: "It's a chance of facing my own failures of understanding, and at the same time learning, getting deeper in, and seeing that things are always changing and therefore that I am living as they are, in the stream of time."

Long-term field research—of whatever type it may be, from its beginnings with Clyde Kluckhohn's Ramah Navajo Project and the Robert Redfield–Alfonso Villa Rojas collaboration among the Maya in Yucatán to the ongoing studies represented in this volume—has changed the face of anthropology. It has held up both *change* and *persistence* to be regular features of human society and has revealed the complexity of both. It has made us sensitive to ethical issues and responsibilities in ways impossible to grasp from single-visit ethnography (Kemper and Royce 1997; Royce and Kemper 1998). It has contributed in major ways to the fields of development and applied anthropology. It has promoted multidisciplinary approaches, as well as embracing the participation of local and national scholars. It has brought new research questions to our agenda and pioneered new methodologies. It has acknowledged that such involvement over time transforms anthropologists, and so has anticipated the whole debate over the role of anthropologists and the impact of anthropology on the societies being studied. In short, it has changed the nature of the field. The editors of *Long-Term Field Research in Social Anthropology* anticipated this, saying that perhaps this approach to field research would prove as revolutionary as that of Malinowski (Foster et al. 1979:6).

Types of Long-Term Research

A long span of time during which anthropologists work in the same place or with the same people—broken by other obligations such as teaching, writing, and soliciting new sources of funding—represents a minimal definition of long-term research.[3] Within this lies considerable variation—in length of time, in original impetus, in goals, in the time between field trips, and in the composition of the research personnel. Long-term research has its own dynamic; at different times, it takes on different configurations and goals. Work that begins with a single researcher or a couple (Pendleton, Epstein, Johansen, Royce) subsequently may involve students, colleagues, and local scholars. Extended beyond the original researcher, the work may be handed over to those who have been collaborators or may be restarted by entirely new researchers. Sometimes restudies (Epstein) become ongoing, collaborative projects. Shifts in large-scale longitudinal research projects (as described by Lamphere, Lee and Biesele, and Vogt) may represent shifts in the field itself. The two examples of multigenerational projects (Gwembe and Tzintzuntzan) presented in this volume did not begin with that goal of "passing the mantle" but they are now in that process. Further, the initial impetus for each was different—Gwembe resulted from a request to examine the near- and intermediate-term impacts of resettlement because of the Kariba Dam; Tzintzuntzan was conceived initially as a short-term training opportunity for students.

Some long-term studies, especially those with a clearly delineated problem focus or with predetermined funding levels, may have prescribed time limits; other projects may have no logical endpoint. For example, if researchers decided to examine the impact of a new school (or a new clinic, etc.) being built in a community, how long would be long enough to study its impact? One possible ethnographic approach would be to follow the school graduates (or persons treated at the clinic, etc.) and then compare their subsequent careers with those of persons growing up in the community who make no use of the school (or clinic, etc.). But for "how long"? And "how many" annual cohorts should be studied to measure impact?

Because the human condition is open ended, our research designs also need to be open ended. The "typical" year of dissertation fieldwork may, in fact, not be typical at all. Floods, political revolutions, El Niño, currency devaluations, and a hundred other natural and human events always transform a "typical" year into an unusual year. Indeed, a "typical" year does not exist at all; it is as much a myth as is the "bounded" community. Therefore, we look beyond a single year because we are interested in real life, as real people enjoy it, struggle with it, and survive it— year after year, and then decade upon decade. Our willingness to go beyond a "typical" year is a measure of our commitment to see life on its own terms instead of through our external assumptions (and external funding). To do otherwise is to impose ourselves on the flow of life and knowingly to reduce our chances of comprehending the story of the people and their place(s) in that life.

Settings

It may be an effect of the times—the 1950s and 1960s—when most of the long-term projects in this volume were started, but the "communities" in question all involved geographically recognizable places, whether the singular locations of a nucleated settlement such as Tzintzuntzan, the dispersed settlements surrounding the Zinacantan ceremonial center, or the multiple grazing places of the Turkish nomads or multiple watering holes of the Ju/'hoansi-!Kung. All of these field sites represented "natural" communities; not one was located in an "institutional" setting such as schools, hospitals, churches, prisons, or governmental agencies. All of the field sites initially were located in non-Western settings (depending on how the Navajo case is interpreted) although, after thirty years, the effects of relocation and migration have placed some people beyond their original communities and into Western settings.

The late 1950s through the 1960s have been referred to by a number of senior anthropologists as a "golden age" for American anthropology. There were substantial funds available from the government and from private foundations to pursue all kinds of fieldwork at considerable distances, especially in the context of the hundreds of "foreign-area" studies centers created in those days. Funds also were available to enable graduate students to spend one year or more (the intensive Malinowski model of fieldwork) in a self-selected field site. By contrast, today, research funds for ethnography seem to be much more difficult to obtain. In the current budgetary environment, no funding source, whether private foundation or the National Science Foundation (NSF), is able to cache resources for projects intended to last for decades. The administrative time frame is simply too shortsighted. Many anthropologists seem to be willing to tolerate the mismatch between short-term funding cycles and long-term fieldwork plans.

In some other fields, however, special arrangements have been made to deal with longitudinal research. For example, the LTER (Long-Term Ecological

Research) network has been in existence since 1980. Sixteen LTER sites in North America receive grant support through NSF, with funding renewable every six years. According to an outside evaluation panel, LTER's "unique strength" is "its ability to study ecological phenomena over years, even decades." LTER is a favorite among ecologists because of its long-term vision and stable funding, although some scholars feel that LTER scientists need to do a better job of comparing data across sites and must overcome a fragmented approach to the human role in environmental change (Stone 1993:334–335).

Just imagine that anthropologists were successful in lobbying Congress and the NSF to create and fund a similar network of designated Long-Term *Ethnographic* Research sites, not just in North America but around the globe. Of course, the lack of comparability of data gathered from site to site in the ecological network would appear to be inconsequential next to the extreme diversity of information collected in long-term ethnographic fieldwork, for even the conceptual categories vary from culture to culture in ways that ecologists could only imagine.

Reading the current tables of contents of standard anthropological journals or strolling through the book exhibits at the annual meeting of the American Anthropological Association, we all see how much the profession has changed in a generation. Anthropologists no longer focus exclusively on the "other," but instead are carrying out fieldwork "at home" (Jackson 1987) and everywhere else in the world, on topics that go far beyond the traditional categories found in museum catalogues or in the numbered codes in the *Outline of Cultural Materials*. Will we ever have long-term studies of affluent urban enclaves such as Highland Park in the middle of Dallas or Beverly Hills in the midst of Los Angeles? Will someone do follow-up studies on Tally's Corner (Liebow 1967) or in the Appalachian Valley (Hicks 1976)?

As we move into the twenty-first century, many ethnographic studies of "institutional settings" are being carried out here and abroad. The question is: How many will go beyond their immediate, short-term project goals and be transformed into longitudinal research projects? Is it possible that, thirty years from now, a quite different collection of long-term ethnographic studies might be published? Might it contain studies on the life cycle of halfway houses for persons with HIV/AIDS? How about investigations of the different effects of bilingual education, English as a Second Language programs, and language immersion programs? What of reports on the intergenerational integration of guest workers in the European Union? And would any of the dozens of current studies on homelessness in U.S. cities be sustained for a generation? Obviously, the list is almost endless of the short-term, synchronic studies that might be extended and transformed into long-term research projects. However, this would require a change in the culture of funding agencies as well as a reorientation in the values of many anthropologists who happily move from one-shot study to one-shot study (cf. Wacaster and Firestone 1978).

Another setting that influences long-term studies is that of the academy, where nearly all longitudinal ethnographic projects are now based, and are likely to continue to be based. Given that the projects reported in this volume began long before human subjects committees and institutional review boards came into existence, it is fair to ask: Would these projects have been "approved" if they had had to go through these review procedures decades ago? As the projects have continued into the present, the anthropologists involved have had to submit information about their projects to obtain continuing funding from granting agencies. Once approved, do long-term projects have an easier time gaining institutional approval the next time, and again after that? Might there be a competitive advantage for those submitting proposals for restudies or for continuing studies? Answering such questions requires saying more about our academic and institutional cultures than most of us are willing to admit.

Organization of This Volume

The chapters in this volume are arranged primarily on the basis of personnel and project size. Part I focuses on research projects that began with one individual (or a married couple) and have developed over the decades to include collaborations with others. Royce, Epstein, and Pendleton have all involved students and colleagues in their projects, often with different disciplinary backgrounds, and have increasingly collaborated with local and national personnel. All have been involved in consulting with local people and with representatives of national-level institutions, both governmental and academic. Johansen and White's work represents an unusually innovative collaboration, involving the application of new computer-enhanced genealogical methodologies to an extensive longitudinal database. White explains his interest in Johansen's project in this way: "Although Johansen characterizes her fieldwork as a typical 'loner' study, it was the systematic character of the long-term data and genealogies that later attracted me to ask new questions about her materials on social organization, leadership, and the adaptation in nomad life ways."

Part II presents three large-scale, long-term ethnographic enterprises. The earliest includes fieldwork with the Navajo that began in 1936 with Kluckhohn's Ramah Project. Herself a participant since the early 1960s, Lamphere documents the four phases of this work since its inception. In 1957, Vogt began his research in Chiapas very modestly—with himself, one graduate student, and a Land Rover—but this soon blossomed into the Harvard Chiapas Project, well known not only for its prodigious ethnographic production, but also as a training site for well over a hundred graduate and undergraduate anthropology students. In the final chapter of part II, Lee and Biesele describe the work with the Ju/'hoansi-!Kung begun in the 1950s by the Marshalls, then continued by Lee and DeVore beginning in the 1960s. The research has been virtually continuous since that time, involving dozens of researchers who have published some of the most significant research on hunter-gatherer populations. All three chapters in Part II speak to the issue of continuity past the current generation, suggesting that the long-term trend is toward collaboration and sharing direction with the peoples themselves.

Part III includes essays by representatives of the different generations of participants in two well-known multigenerational projects: Gwembe and Tzintzuntzan. While other longitudinal projects in parts I and II have continued past the initial fieldworkers, the leaders of the Gwembe and Tzintzuntzan projects have been *intentional* about selecting and training those who follow them in these projects. Scudder and Colson and Foster also have established guidelines for the consistent collection of "minimal core data," including the use of detailed maps, censuses, and regular surveys to update the situation of households and their members, not only in the base communities but also among thousands of migrants. What Gwembe fieldworkers call the "checklist" has its Tzintzuntzan equivalent in the "master file"—in both cases a fieldworker can carry around a notebook with detailed data on several thousand persons.

The anthropologists who began and nurtured the Gwembe and Tzintzuntzan projects also have been *intentional* about addressing the many practical and ethical concerns of gathering, analyzing, caring for, and sharing large data sets. They have considerable wisdom to offer regarding current issues surrounding protection of human subjects, confidentiality, and privacy rights, as seen from the perspective of dealing with change and continuity for some fifty years. Not surprisingly, they also recognize the importance of planning for contingencies in dynamic and possibly conflict-laden field situations. They are sensitive to the problems associated with trying (and failing) to predict the future for the people in the communities where they have spent so many years as participant observers.

Those who have been elected to receive "the mantle" in these multigenerational projects have assumed significant responsibilities to the people in the field sites and to the profession. Cliggett, Kemper, and Cahn speak frankly of their concerns, as well as their appreciation for those who have gone ahead of them. Students contemplating fieldwork in a field site already worked by another ethnographer can learn many valuable lessons from the second and third generations of the Gwembe and Tzintzuntzan projects.

Taken together, the twelve chapters in this volume help us to appreciate the practical demands of managing long-term projects, as well as to evaluate the potential theoretical and methodological contributions that arise from systematically observing and participating in human communities for a generation and more. In these chapters, we learn about the benefits and the difficulties associated with the ethnographic enterprise, far beyond the ritual of "one year in the field." The authors—from those with more than half a century of fieldwork experience to those just beginning their careers—contribute a special perspective to the never-ending dialogue about how we, as anthropologists, learn to see and understand cultural diversity across space and time.

Themes

Despite the different settings, time periods, initial goals, and configurations of personnel, a number of common themes emerge from these essays, many with major implications for anthropological theories, methods, and ethics.

Working across Shifts in the Political Landscape

One of the most insistent issues in anthropology today has been the position of anthropology vis-à-vis colonialism, the "other," voice, and representation (Fox 1991; Gupta and Ferguson 1997; Geertz 2000). Much of the discussion occurs in the realm of the general and the abstract. The contribution of long-term field research is that ethnographers live the aftermath of empire, live the effects of shifting political institutions, live the dismantling and creation of nation-states. Long-term researchers live through these shifts alongside people themselves and so are able to appreciate both the events and the responses. Sharing the lives of people who become friends, surrogate family, and collaborators makes the category of "other" impossible to maintain. Finally, the dynamic of this kind of research includes more rather than fewer voices as years pass, and the ethnographer's representation is one of several; indeed, it may be part of a composite reached jointly with the represented. The long-term researcher cannot ignore these issues and remain in the field. The issues themselves become more nuanced when one sees them across changing contexts and through time. Scudder and Colson speak eloquently to this point: "A long-term study is likely to diminish the roseate hues in which so much of ethnographic description is couched. At the same time, the people who are the focus of the study become more the product of their own history and less the exemplars of universal cultural patterns."

Pendleton, working in Namibia, describes the many shifts in political contexts that have framed his research: "I have seen the people and the place change over the years from the influence of apartheid, through the run-up to independence, and on to the post-independence era." Lee and Biesele and their collaborators witnessed the removal of the Ju/'hoansi to reserves and then the gradual migration of some of their young people to the cities, where they disappeared into the city. But they also have seen the emerging convergence between the Ju agenda and perspectives of development agencies and scholars. The so-called crisis in hunter-gatherer studies seems to allow, some say, only two positions—either the Ju/'hoansi must be maintained in a kind of pristine Arcadianism or they must be maintained as wards of an assimilating state. The truth of their situation lies somewhere between these two extremes, but this truth is only visible by virtue of having lived one's ethnography across the changes.

Development Stances: Observers, Active Partners, Advocates

Long-term studies give ethnographers multiple opportunities for strategizing with and advocating for the peoples with whom they work. On a continuum from "observers" to "active partners" to "advocates," where are they most comfortable and from which position do they act? Does this change over time? From situation to situation?

The ethnographers represented in part I are clear examples of a shift from observer to active partner and, in some instances and in some cases, to advocate. It is important here to remind ourselves that we never abandon the stance of observer; doing so robs our interpretations and recommendations of validity because they then are based on opinion and reaction. As Geertz (2000:39) suggests, we are always seeing society as an object and experiencing it as a subject.

Although Epstein's original research topic was economic development, she did not actively pursue its implications until her return. Then, she says, she realized the importance of working out the policy implications of her findings and translating them into action-oriented programs to improve the lot of the poorest in the societies she studied. Pendleton's initial interest lay in the inequalities of the social system under apartheid. Now it is about change, development, and using anthropology to train, teach, and work on issues of community empowerment. Royce's involvement has shaped itself on the Zapotec model of *binni guendabianni*, a knowledgeable person willing to use that knowledge to benefit the community. She works through the Casa de la Cultura on programs to educate young Zapotec about their cultural legacy and, at their request, responds to the work of journalists and filmmakers who caricature Zapotec culture. Her first monograph (Royce 1975) was reprinted in 1990 as part of a series of the one hundred most important books on Mexico's indigenous peoples, thereby giving it a broader impact in policy discussions.

Large-scale projects, such as those described by Lamphere involving the Navajo, show a similar trajectory. Kluckhohn's Ramah Project was intended as a study of the socialization of Navajo children. What Lamphere calls "Anglo research interest and commitment to a scientific paradigm" continued to determine Navajo studies through the 1980s. Because of the proliferation of Navajo institutions such as Diné College—especially the Historic Preservation Department—and their interest in defining and doing research, the ethnographic agenda has shifted to include applied research associated with cultural resource management, historic preservation, repatriation, and policy-related issues such as aging, diabetes, drinking, and relocation.

Colson and Scudder began their Gwembe study at the request of the Rhodes-Livingstone Institute to look at the long-term consequences of resettlement on people soon to be uprooted by the building of the Kariba Dam. It went well past the original parameters, in terms of both time and problem, and has had enormous policy implications not only for Zambia but, by virtue of what their "Relocation Theory" tells us, for resettlement projects anywhere in the world. As a result of their work and considerable experience with Gwembe, the Zambian government, and international development agencies, they are forceful and blunt in their conclusions: "Involuntary community resettlement is *never* an appropriate development strategy."

Lee and Biesele and their collaborators have been active partners with the Ju/'hoansi in helping to present themselves and to improve their economic and social status. Biesele was director for a time of the Nyae Nyae Ju/'hoansi Development Foundation of Namibia, which arose in response to some Ju/'hoansis' desire to rid themselves of the poverty and passivity of being welfare recipients. Much of the strategy has to do with land rights and traditional systems of land tenure. Biesele and her colleagues also have turned their attention to the problem of education, creating the Village Schools Project in 1990. Lee and Biesele, the Marshalls, and others associated with these two long-term projects have found ways to be both researchers and advocates. As Lee and Biesele argue:

> Becoming an "advocate" or "intervenor" clearly alters the work of anthropologists; but given the stakes, what was the option? To the anticipated charge of conventional science that such intervention creates epistemological distortion, we would argue that knowledge produced in a situation where people are fully involved may be different, but no less important. If anything, it is clearer and more vital.

A different form of being an "active partner" with the people occurred in June 2000, when the long-awaited translation into Spanish of Foster's original monograph (Foster and Ospina 1948) about Tzintzuntzan finally became available to the public.[4] This translation, *Los Hijos del Imperio* (Foster and Ospina 2000), may have a significant impact on Tzintzuntzan's growing awareness of itself as heir to a great civilization, in large measure prompted by the attention and commitment of Foster, his colleagues and students, and their students over more than half a century.

Patterns of Growth and Migration

The great time depth of long-term studies offers a distinctive opportunity to witness growth and shifting configurations of communities as modern technologies and economies enter people's lives. Without doubt, large-scale movements of labor from labor-rich economies to labor-poor ones, and movements of displaced persons from homelands to temporary "homes," make migrations, relocations, and diaspora increasingly permanent features of today's world. The commitment to see these movements across space *and time* makes far richer understanding possible.

For many of us, the growth of the communities in which we do fieldwork has been a factor in how we approach our tasks and what we learn from the way communities grow. Pendleton began working in Katutura in 1968 when it had a population of about 20,000. In 1997, it had grown to 70,000. Juchitán's 1971 population was 26,000. Royce's latest estimate puts it at 90,000. On a smaller scale, Tzintzuntzan's "core" population grew from 1,231 in 1945 to 3,346 in 2000. In these cases, tracing the development of new settlements may provide insights into class and ethnic distinctions, perceptions of what it means to be "resident" or "migrant" (or somewhere in between), and relationships across sections of the community.

Epstein notes the complicated relationship between caste and class that has developed in Wangala and Dalena, especially as evidenced by settlement patterns. From the time (1957) of Johansen's first fieldwork with the Aydĭnlĭ, the population of Turkey went from 25 million to about 65 million in 1995. As a result of her experiences with these nomadic people, she recognizes that "what such dry numbers mean to the self-consciousness of people can really be understood only through the experience of long-term fieldwork." In their collaboration, Johansen and White examine and explain the changing patterns of population mobility and social organization through network analysis based on genealogical reconstructions combined with oral histories.

Resettlement accounts for the change of "home" for the Gwembe. Following the consequences of that involuntary move led Scudder and Colson to formulate "Relocation Theory." Reverberations of the original scattering still can be seen in Cliggett's work, a generation later. Resettlement also characterizes many events in the history of the Ju/'hoansi. What we learn from the intimate and enduring involvement with these ethnographic instances is that the reality *lived by the people* bears very little resemblance to the simplistic notions of government bureaucrats, development officials, and policymakers. But even in these disparate circumstances, we can observe and learn about the toughness, persistence, and imagination of those who are uprooted.

Migration poses another strategy used by those who would better their lives or the lives of those they hold dear. There is little question that long-term observation allows researchers to recognize and document motivations, strategies, processes, and consequences in a way simply not possible over the short term. In 1969, Kemper began his dissertation research on the adaptation of Tzintzuntzan migrants in Mexico City and, since then, he and his field assistants (many of them Tzintzuntzeños themselves) have followed the people from their community to dozens of locations in Mexico and the United States. In examining their social and economic strategies, he has come to appreciate their active agency in the face of unfavorable national and international structures. The *compadrazgo* (co-godparenthood) and a strong sense of community (reflected in their *comunidad indígena*), rooted in their Indian past and subsequent colonial experiences, continue to be vital both among the migrants and in Tzintzuntzan itself. An "extended community" is forming that may permit this community to weather political-economic storms that have overwhelmed other rural places in Mexico and around the globe. Without long-term fieldwork, we would be unable to see and learn from their experiences.

The Provisional Nature of Knowledge

One of the positive qualities of longitudinal research, and its negative side as well, is that it is always a "work in progress" (cf. Hart, Pilling, and Goodale 1988; Hinshaw 1975; Read 1986). Johansen notes that the passage of even a few years can lead to a change in perspective about what is happening in people's lives. Scudder and Colson propose that publications in longitudinal studies are always interim reports. Epstein and Foster analyze their predictions and sort them into failures and successes. Royce's first published effort to answer the question of how the Isthmus Zapotec sustained a dynamic identity as Zapotec—while being successful economically and politically within the larger Mexican context—focused on historic, economic, and political factors. This was not incorrect, but provided only a partial explanation. Fuller understanding came to Royce only after she saw people acting in everyday and extraordinary ways over decades—thus showing her how to separate what is fundamental from what is ephemeral.

Researchers—especially those on a university tenure track—publish many short, focused pieces of research, not putting off making their analyses available until they are "absolutely certain." This is a "plus" for the field because it provides information and ideas for discussion and comparison. We frequently need to correct, add to, or otherwise tinker with earlier conclusions (cf. Sanjek 1990). Having to analyze data for an article or a paper presentation at professional meetings means coming to grips with what we know and do not know, seeing the missing pieces, making the connections, fitting the parts into a larger whole. In this process, we can recognize wrong-headed approaches or interpretations. Data analyzed in this fashion allow us to ask new questions. Accepting the provisional state of our knowledge, and acting nevertheless, also allows us to recognize more easily the influence of theoretical fashions, funding preferences, and implicit guiding metaphors (cf. Garbett 1967; Richardson 1988). As Scudder noted at the 1999 AAA session on "Passing the Mantle," we find out increasingly how our models of sociocultural systems go wrong.

Impact on the People and Their Cultures

Whether in the short term or in the long term, ethnographers have a wide range of "impacts" on the people and their cultures, ranging from specific instances of material benefit to more subtle but no less vital examples of psychological and emotional impact.

Foster speaks for all the generations of the Tzintzuntzan project when he says that their attention over so many years has given the people a sense of pride and a feeling that they must be something special, that Tzintzuntzan is no ordinary town. Scudder, Colson, and the new generations of the Gwembe project provide a sense of continuity for people who live in a world of increasing discontinuities. In both places, people come with questions about their own lives, knowing that an essential but forgotten birth date is recorded in the ethnographer's notebook.

Epstein echoes experiences that many of us have had when she writes of her meeting with an old village friend, now nearly blind, on her return to Wangala: "When I approached him he fumbled with his hands reaching out to touch me; when I took his hands in mine, he said quietly and with great dignity: 'Now that

I know that you are still alive and have come back to see me again I can die in peace,' which made me feel very small indeed."

Johansen's stories of the delight of people when she brought photographs, mounted a slide show with a battery-operated projector, or brought copies of publications are common for many of us—and point to a dual function we ethnographers can serve. One is to be unofficial historians for the cultures in which we work, not only because of all the archival, ethnohistorical, and sometimes archaeological data we routinely seek and then preserve, but also because of the thirty-five to sixty-plus years of "history" represented by our own fieldwork. This is not an insignificant contribution, particularly if some of the key artifacts, documents, and photographs are provided to local or regional libraries, museums, schools, and town governments. The other function is, as Foster has said, that our work adds value to the peoples' lives. We may rightly say that their lives have value without us but, in the face of state and national powers which structure their futures, our ethnographic interests and our professional voices can make a difference.

Material benefits come in many forms and we all participate in ways helpful and appropriate. Wages for field assistants, compensation for informants, gifts that are part of being a reciprocating member of the community, even funds to help with medical expenses, school fees and books, building projects, and so forth are standard, if not unproblematic. Still, we know that our reciprocity never reaches the level of the benefits we receive during our professional lives. Consider the experience of Mandy Rudge, who recently completed a Ph.D. dissertation in Karimpur, India, a community studied by ethnographers for some seventy-five years (Wiser and Wiser 2000). After describing the "discontent" of some villagers (particularly the very poor) with the "help" they were able to get from ethnographers who come to Karimpur, Rudge (1998:20) concludes:

> We should remember that without our research participants' generosity, their profound hospitality, and their willingness to share their lives, the discipline of anthropology would not exist. What constitutes reciprocity in a given research situation needs to be more fully explored but it is clear that, if the people of Karimpur bear any similarity to other people who have been researched, then reciprocity is a key issue in the work that we do.

Some researchers also have founded or facilitated community assistance organizations, including those documented in their chapters by Lee and Biesele, Pendleton, and Lamphere. Other fieldworkers contribute indirectly to their communities by sharing ethnographic knowledge with policymakers, even if they do not always act upon it.

Finally, all of us, through our publications, many in the local language, influence the ways in which people see themselves and the ways in which they are perceived by those who have some control over their lives. Some of us have experienced having our work be the subject of school assignments or regional seminars, a kind of accountability becoming more and more common and appropriate. When we are interviewed by members of the print or electronic media, what we say can have a significant impact on the people with whom we have labored for so long. The omnipresence of the Internet means that whatever we have written may be available on a computer at a local Internet café down the street or in the next town, readily accessible to government officials or to anyone else interested in the people and places we frequent.

The Impact of Long-Term Fieldwork on Ethnographers

We are transformed by our years in the field. Most of us do not anticipate this, any more than we expect to spend half our lives or more in another culture. There is the simple matter of growing up—most of us come of age in the field, then grow old in it, if we are lucky. We also mature as professional anthropologists in the process (cf. Parkin 2000:95–100).

We do not grow up in our field cultures as we do in our own; in fact, we are under the illusion in our first piece of fieldwork that we are fully trained, mature professionals. If we have sense enough to be humbled by that first experience, we can learn a great deal both about the cultures in which we choose to work and about how to be competent ethnographers. Our "teachers" are the people with whom we work who, for the most part, are remarkably patient. As Geertz has observed, in the field we have to live as members of a community and we learn to think and analyze. Our hosts help us to do both—they keep our social bumblings to a minimum at the same time that they instruct us in all the domains of their lives that we need to understand in our roles as anthropologists. But, of course, these domains are not neat, tidy, and separate. Royce acknowledges this reality in these words: "One of the ways in which we begin to learn in the field context, which makes us different from other social science disciplines, is simply having to take care of the business of living . . . settling in brings you into contact with a whole range of individuals and institutions."

Teachers also include other fieldworkers, especially in those projects that function as teams. Cliggett speaks of the personal ramifications of both when she says that Zambia really is a second home because of responsibilities and relationships, and, like other homes, one both loves and resents the obligations. She goes on to say that her second family is *not* her Zambian friends and assistants, but rather the project team.

Foster is eloquent about the relationship that he and his wife Mary forged with Doña Micaela, who died on the same day that they were returning from Tzintzuntzan to the United States after a fiesta in her home to celebrate the publication of *Los Hijos del Imperio*: "For me, the coincidence of the book publication and Micaela's death marks the end of a long and very special era. With the ethnological mantle passed to Kemper, Brandes, and Cahn, research in Tzintzuntzan surely will go on for decades to come, but for all those who ever knew Doña Mica it can never be quite the same."

Gathering, Analyzing, and Sharing Data

All of the long-term studies reported in this volume began long before computers of any kind—much less portable notebook computers that can be carried in an ethnographer's backpack into the field—were available for processing, analyzing, retrieving, and storing vast amounts of data, both quantitative and qualitative. As a consequence, all of us with thirty or more years of field data have faced (and continue to deal with) issues of converting information on paper into formats amenable to computer manipulation. In many cases, the cost of data conversion is greater than the cost of the original fieldwork! Because the work involved is more complex and demanding than appears at first glance, student assistants generally do not fare well in such data-conversion projects.

No single solution is available to meet all of our ethnographic needs and desires, but time is on our side. Data that could not be handled a decade ago now can be handled fairly well by the current generation of relational database programs and analytical/statistical programs available for personal computers. In the long term, our special needs as ethnographers *can* be met by continually improving and increasingly less expensive computer systems, but we will need to become more competent in managing data to take good advantage of these opportunities. For example, after an earlier period of frustration (in trying to computerize the Gwembe Tonga materials), the collaborative efforts by White are beginning to yield significant rewards—as demonstrated by his work with Johansen to analyze her longitudinal kinship and political leadership data through White's sophisticated mathematical social network software. In conjunction with Eric Widmer, a young and intrepid demographer, White has begun a similar collaboration with Kemper and the Tzintzuntzan project, focusing initially on building a multigenerational social network model (similar to that which he already constructed for the Turkish nomads) based on the data available from the six ethnographic censuses taken from 1945 to 2000.

The problem of gathering, analyzing, and sharing data is by no means unique to long-term studies (cf. Moran 1995), but the need to gather information systematically across several decades does present special challenges to ethnographers, whether working alone or in teams. For instance, if a fieldworker wants to gather comparable data on the age of persons in a population, it is important to know that the "standard" intervals for age cohorts are 0–4, 5–9, 10–14, 15–19, and so forth. Of course, this problem does not plague only anthropologists. The U.S. Census has changed how it treats "Hispanic" populations throughout the twentieth century; as a result, truly comparable data are not available on what is soon to be the largest minority population in the country. In a similar fashion, ethnographers must be attentive to definitions of key terms (e.g., *household*), the coding of variables (e.g., age cohorts), and the construction of scales (e.g., standard of living). For example, working from a 100 percent census of Tzintzuntzan households in 1945, Foster constructed a simple ten-point "level of living" scale. In 1960, items were added to form a twenty-point scale. In subsequent censuses,

some items were dropped as they fell out of use and others added as new consumer goods appeared among the village households. The scale grew to thirty
points for 1970 and 1980, then to forty points in 1990, and finally to fifty points
for 2000. These changes in the level of living scale over six censuses reflect the
openness necessary to track changing economic circumstances in the community
and among migrant households.

Special problems related to what some of us have called "minimum core data"
are distinctive to long-term field research. At the 1975 Wenner-Gren Conference
on Long-Term Field Research, and in response to the stimulus provided by Epstein's presentation of her work in two Mysore villages, the participants agreed
that a "standardization of minimum core data" was highly desirable if ethnographers had any hopes of doing useful cross-cultural longitudinal studies. Although
some anthropologists seem to have determined that any sort of cross-cultural
studies, much less longitudinal ones, are ethnographically problematic (cf. Van
Maanen 1995), other anthropologists are still committed to the possibility that
certain data are sufficiently common to the human condition that they should be
gathered systematically on a regular basis over years and decades (cf. Lewis
1955:276–277). Such data should include "maps, vital statistics, census material
(including marital and parental status, social and residential units of affiliation,
occupations, education, and religion); resource base (minimal descriptive data on
ecological and economic categories); and sociopolitical differentiation" (Foster et
al. 1979:333).

One of the challenges embedded in a long-term effort to gather a significant body of core data (as through a decennial census or biennial community
surveys) is that the gathering of such data is not only time-consuming, but also
takes on a life of its own. A commitment to gathering some semblance of minimum core data from the outset of any project likely to become a long-term project would be ideal, but specific fieldwork situations—especially institutional settings such as hospitals, schools, or prisons—might not permit this. Again, as the
1975 Wenner-Gren conference participants concluded:

> A high degree of openness in orientation should be retained; otherwise, the in-
> vestigator may not see, let alone investigate, the types of shifts in emphasis in hu-
> man affairs and beliefs that can be expected to occur within the contemporary
> world. Important as core data are, their collection should not dominate research,
> nor interfere with the exploration of new topics. (Foster et al. 1979:334)

Another special problem of dealing with longitudinal data sets is unavoid-
able. To put the problem in a few words: people leave, people die, and new people come into a community either through birth or by migration. What this
means is that, over the long term, ethnographers studying a "community" are going to be dealing with different individuals (and households) at different times.
The community is the same, but its membership varies. An alternative approach

would involve selecting a sample of the community (or institutional) population and then following this "panel" of individuals or households across time and space (if they move). Few ethnographers have addressed directly the problem of who our respondents are and how "representative" they are of the broader universe (community or institutional setting) that is being studied (cf. Bernard 1994, 1998).

Even with such methodological problems, long-term ethnographic studies still offer more positive possibilities than does short-term research. A short-term investigation is subject to static models of culture and therefore represents a "compromise" rather than a best choice for understanding the human condition as process. As Menard (1991:68) has concluded, after a careful analysis of longitudinal research as a social science methodology:

> The conclusion is inescapable . . . that for the description and analysis of dynamic change processes, longitudinal research is ultimately indispensable. It is also the case that longitudinal research can, in principle, do much that cross-sectional research cannot, but that there is little or nothing that cross-sectional research can, in principle, do that longitudinal research cannot.

Ethical Issues

Not unexpectedly, long-term field research raises special problems and issues with regard to ethics. Long-term fieldwork also highlights and exaggerates the ordinary ethical issues that emerge in other types of fieldwork. As a discipline, we have our Principles of Professional Responsibility to provide good general guidelines for ethical behavior. We also know that in honoring one principle we may violate another; sometimes, there is no perfect resolution of an ethical dilemma, only less-bad choices (cf. Fluehr-Lobban 1991).

Four special circumstances of long-term fieldwork include the implications of advocacy, of distortions in the local prestige system, of intimate involvement in domestic units and their problems, and of unanticipated negative effects on cultural values. The continuum of stances from observer to active partner to advocate carries with it a concomitant range of ethical choices and dilemmas. Especially for ethnographers who move into active partner and advocacy roles, the potential increases for conflict with regional and national institutions, funding agencies, assistance organizations, and local factions. Moreover, once a fieldworker steps into an advocacy role, it is impossible to step back and claim the impartial role of observer.

All of the cultures in which we do fieldwork have their own systems of status and prestige. We become factors in those systems when we speak with one person or group or family rather than with another, and much more so when we hire certain individuals (and not others) to help us. The smaller the community, the more effect we can have. Foster speaks directly to this when he says that there are negative implications to giving substantial help to just a few people.

In a moving story about the career of a Navajo man who began as an "informant" in the time of Kluckhohn's Ramah Project, Blanchard (1977:69) concludes:

> It may be that traditional anthropological field techniques lead inevitably to the creation of well-trained informants who because of their involvement in the science find it difficult to retain a realistic perspective on either past or present. However, this does not lessen the responsibility of the fieldworker in attempting to eliminate the ill effects of an intensive anthropologist-informant relationship.

The Harvard Chiapas Project has, over the years, employed local persons who, as a result, have been able to move faster through the cargo system and, in general, have greatly improved their economic situations compared to that of their neighbors. In a case similar to that of the Navajo informant described by Blanchard, Vogt mentions one worker who became dependent on them and the project.

Cliggett raised an important consideration in her comments at the 1999 AAA session on "Passing the Mantle." As projects continue and questions and technologies change, the local individuals who have been long-term workers may not continue to be the best informants for new configurations of research questions. What are our long-term obligations to them?

Domestic units shape themselves over generations and this is how we experience them at home and in the field. Our initial friends grow old and die; their children also grow up and become old; new generations come along. Our relations with succeeding generations are different, yet we remain related in everyone's reckoning. Problems are different, and means of resolving them change as well. Ethnographers become elders to whom, in most societies, one goes with problems both emotional and material. We find ourselves having to suggest resolutions of problems in ways that were not expected early in our fieldwork careers. Because we know more, we are expected to be able to deal with problems in culturally appropriate ways. In our first years in the field, we often are called upon to mediate, but then it is because of our status as "outsiders" perceived either as being impartial or as having more power, or both.

Ethnographers, by virtue of personality or experience, manage to move back and forth between "homes," with a minimum of invidious comparison. This may not be the case with people whose homes we share when we are in the field. Trips to our homes, the accoutrements of research that we bring into the field, the way we dress, the gifts we share—all these invite comparison. Much of the time these comparisons take the form of acknowledging that ways of living *are* different. Sometimes, the ethnographer's culture suffers by the comparison. But sometimes people may feel less well off or more provincial in comparison. Often these are individuals who are somehow marginalized in their own communities.

Ordinary ethical issues in short-term fieldwork may be exacerbated over the long term. These issues include importunities or outright interference by bureaucrats or government officials who may want to exploit the ethnographer's data and breach confidences.

In some cases, we are invited to do research in a specific area or on a particular problem by local hosts. In most cases, we have had some exchange with host institutions or government representatives about our proposed research. We may have few further interactions with our official hosts, or we may be asked to make our data available. The ethical implications of such a situation are obvious and serious. One of the first questions is: Whose data are they? There will be different answers depending upon where the ethnographer stands. There is the question of confidentiality of information and protecting the people with whom we work. Questions of our institutional relationships, future funding, and access to the field site are weighty, and not easily dismissed. Our actions also will have a bearing on other researchers, whether currently in the field or hoping to come in the future. The more time one spends at a given field location, the more likely it is that these matters will arise. Being proactive, in the sense of having identified host country institutions to serve as repositories for ethnographic materials, is the best and most appropriate strategy, as demonstrated in the cases reported by Scudder and Colson, Pendleton, Epstein, and others.

Concern for confidentiality follows from the preceding discussion. Protecting informants is an ethical obligation from the first day of fieldwork; it simply becomes more significant as research continues for years and decades. Mechanisms and controls need to be put in place to keep data confidential and out of the wrong hands. For example, the Gwembe project uses diaries kept by local persons, and these are sources of excellent ethnographic information. Eventually, the transcriptions of these diaries could go to archives in Zambia, but for now such access to the material would be disruptive and even dangerous to the people in the sample communities. Eventually, some provision must be made for safekeeping data after those who gathered it are no longer around.

Teams of researchers, especially multidisciplinary investigators, create special ethical problems, for they may not share the same principles of professional responsibility. Teams of fieldworkers may be harder for local populations to absorb, especially if the community is small and conservative. This is why Foster is known for the "Tzintzuntzan" project rather than the "Ihuatzio" project—his team was too large when it arrived in Ihuatzio and found that the local people were not willing to put up with so many strangers, even strangers with lovely letters of introduction from all of the appropriate government agencies. Multidisciplinary research is more difficult to explain to the local people because of its inherent diversity. Ethnographers and agronomists, for instance, deal with farmers in very different ways.

In some ways, ethical issues in long-term research are like the challenges of family life. The more intimate the relationships and the mutual knowledge, the greater the potential for disagreement. At the same time, such intimacy allows more opportunities and more avenues for resolving conflicts. As Ken Wilson

(1993:198) points out in thinking about the ethics of fieldwork, "fieldwork is for life"—and this is truer yet for long-term fieldwork that does, indeed, last a lifetime, both for the ethnographers involved and for the people and places being studied.

Conclusion

Fieldwork is the defining feature of social and cultural anthropology. It and the ethnography that results endure long past the theoretical insights attached to particular schools or individuals (Geertz 1988:4). As Colson commented at the 1999 AAA session on "Passing the Mantle," long-term fieldwork forces an anthropologist to think about human relations and the way in which human beings live their lives.

It may be that anthropology is distinctive because of the institution of fieldwork. Geertz (2000:39) writes about the results:

> It does not permit any significant separation of the occupational and extra-occupational spheres of one's life . . . one must see society as an object and experience it as a subject. Everything anyone says, everything anyone does, even the mere physical setting, has both to form the substance of one's personal existence and to be taken as the grist for one's analytical mill. . . . In the field, the anthropologist has to learn to live and think at the same time.

The craft, the discipline of anthropology, takes us beyond the retelling of individual stories and community stories. Those are almost never told in obvious ways. They are told in the daily acts of sharing, committing, negotiating, balancing the idiosyncratic personalities of people with the work of the community. They are told in the rituals surrounding important points in people's lives and in communal celebrations. They are told in the process of finding a place and an identity within larger, impersonal, sometimes hostile contexts. They are told in the many references to the past—the community of memory that acts as a guide for present and future action. They are embedded in the language itself.

The power of anthropology to tell those stories comes from the experience of the ethnographers over years, sometimes lifetimes, of living and sharing the lives of the storytellers. The implications of that commitment, on both sides, are told compellingly in this volume. We have the accumulated wisdom, although we still think of these stories as being "works in progress," derived from the field research that gives us an appreciation of the strength and ingenuity of our fellow humans. Lee and Biesele speak for many ethnographers in their description of the Ju/'hoansi as "living embodiments of alternative modes of life that deserve to exist even in this hard-bitten, post-modern age," offering "hope that ecological and cultural diversity still has a place on this planet."

Robert Coles's 1993 book, *Call to Service*, documents his participation in the beginning of the civil rights movement in the United States. There he writes about what he calls the "exit option." His point is that all those who would be involved in the lives of other people and other communities always have the option of going home at the end of the day. While he was not writing about ethnographers, his is a useful cautionary statement for us. The remarkable characteristic of long-term field research in general and cases described in these pages is that ethnographers who opt for the long-term solution do not elect the "exit option." Our lives and those who have invited us into theirs are linked. When one strand of the web of relationship is touched, the whole of it trembles. Our experience is at once fragile and tough. This knowledge makes us humble; and the longer we remain, the more humble we become.

Notes

1. In the British tradition, the Torres Straits Expedition and the works of Alfred Cort Haddon, Charles G. Seligman, W. H. R. Rivers, and others had that honor; in the tradition of American Indian studies, short-term fieldwork had been carried out before World War I by James Mooney, Alice Fletcher, Frank Cushing, James Dorsey, and others through such agencies as the Bureau of American Ethnology and the U.S. National Museum. Franz Boas (Columbia University and American Museum of Natural History) had done fieldwork among the peoples of the Northwest Coast, and Alfred L. Kroeber (University of California) had done extensive surveys among California Indians (cf. Stocking 1983; Hallowell 1960).

2. At the centennial celebrations of the London School of Economics, Sir Raymond Firth, recipient of the first Ph.D. given in anthropology in 1927, paid tribute to Professor Seligman for his emphasis on fieldwork. Firth recalled a favorite Seligman saying: "Fieldwork is to Anthropology what the blood of the martyrs is to the Church" (Knight 1995:22).

3. The criteria for determining what constitutes a "long-term" or "longitudinal" study are by no means agreed upon in anthropology or in the social sciences. In a comprehensive inventory of more than 250 longitudinal studies concerned with human development, Young, Savola, and Phelps (1991:5) used four criteria for inclusion: "(1) They are prospectively longitudinal in the sense that the investigators collected information during at least two time points, and preferably three, across a span of at least one year; (2) they have an attrition rate for the original sample that is low enough to maintain the longitudinal quality of the study; (3) they have extensive information on the sample, involving multiple measures, preference across more than one domain of behavior; (4) they are currently active or, if inactive, either have plans for reactivation or have data available (or that could be made available) for secondary analyses by other investigators." Clearly, these criteria are very different from those we have used for inclusion in the present volume—in which all of the projects have endured for at least thirty-three years!

4. In the agreement with El Colegio de Michoacán for translation and publication of Foster's monograph, it was arranged that complimentary copies of *Los Hijos del Imperio* would be provided for distribution to the approximately seven hundred households in Tzintzuntzan, as well as to migrant families living outside of their home community.

References

Bernard, H. Russell
(1994) *Research Methods in Anthropology*. Second edition. Walnut Creek, CA: Alta-Mira Press.

Bernard, H. Russell [editor]
(1998) *Handbook of Methods in Cultural Anthropology*. Walnut Creek, CA: AltaMira Press.

Blanchard, Kendall
(1977) "The expanded responsibilities of long term informant relationships." *Human Organization* 36(1):66–69.

Bruner, Edward
(1986) "Ethnography as narrative." Pp. 139–155 in Victor Turner and Edward Bruner (editors), *The Anthropology of Experience*. Champaign-Urbana: University of Illinois Press.

Coles, Robert
(1993) *The Call of Service*. Boston: Houghton Mifflin.

Epstein, A. L. [editor]
(1967) *The Craft of Social Anthropology*. London: Tavistock.

Fluehr-Lobban, Carolyn
(1991) *Ethics and the Profession of Anthropology: Dialogue for a New Era*. Philadelphia: University of Pennsylvania Press.

Foster, George and Gabriel Ospina
(1948) *Empire's Children: The People of Tzintzuntzan*. Smithsonian Institution, Institute of Social Anthropology, Publication No. 6. México, D.F.: Imprenta Nuevo Mundo.
(2000) *Los Hijos del Imperio: La Gente de Tzintzuntzan*. (Translation of Foster and Ospina 1948). Zamora: El Colegio de Michoacán.

Foster, George M., Thayer Scudder, Elizabeth Colson, and Robert V. Kemper [editors]
(1979) *Long-Term Field Research in Social Anthropology*. New York: Academic Press.

Fox, Richard [editor]
(1991) *Recapturing Anthropology*. Santa Fe: School of American Research Press.

Garbett, G. K.
(1967) "The restudy as a technique for the examination of social change." Pp. 116–132 in D. G. Jongmans and P. C. W. Gutkind (editors), *Anthropologists in the Field*. Assen: Van Gorcum.

Geertz, Clifford
(1962) "Studies in peasant life: Community and society." Pp. 1–41 in Bernard J. Siegel (editor), *Biennial Review of Anthropology 1961*. Stanford: Stanford University Press.

(1988) *Works and Lives.* Stanford: Stanford University Press.
(2000) *Available Light.* Princeton: Princeton University Press.

Gluckman, Max
(1956) *Custom and Conflict in Africa.* Oxford: Blackwell.

Gupta, Akhil and James Ferguson [editors]
(1997) *Anthropological Locations.* Berkeley: University of California Press.

Hallowell, A. Irving
(1960) "The beginnings of anthropology in America." Pp. 1–96 in Frederica De-Laguna (editor), *Selected Papers from the American Anthropologist, 1888–1920.* Evanston, IL: Row, Peterson.

Hart, C. W. M., Arnold R. Pilling, and Jane C. Goodale
(1988) *The Tiwi of North Australia.* Third edition. Fort Worth: Holt, Rinehart and Winston.

Hicks, George L.
(1976) *Appalachian Valley.* New York: Holt, Rinehart and Winston.

Hinshaw, Robert E.
(1975) *Panajachel: A Guatemalan Town in Thirty-Year Perspective.* Pittsburgh: University of Pittsburgh Press.

Jackson, Anthony
(1987) *Anthropology at Home.* London and New York: Tavistock.

Kemper, Robert V. and Anya Peterson Royce
(1997) "Ethical issues for social anthropologists in Mexico: A North American perspective." *Human Organization* 56(4):479–483.

Kluckhohn, Clyde
(1939) "The place of theory in anthropological studies." *Philosophy of Science* 6(3):328–344.

Knight, John
(1995) "LSE's double century." *Anthropology Today* 11(5):22–23.

Lévi-Strauss, Claude
(1968) "The concept of primitiveness." Pp. 349–354 in Richard Lee and Irven DeVore (editors), *Man the Hunter.* Chicago: Aldine.

Lewis, Oscar
(1951) *Life in a Mexican Village: Tepoztlán Revisited.* Urbana: University of Illinois Press.
(1955) "Comparisons in cultural anthropology." Pp. 259–292 in William L. Thomas, Jr. (editor), *Yearbook of Anthropology—1955.* New York: Wenner-Gren Foundation for Anthropological Research, Inc.

Liebow, Elliott
(1967) *Tally's Corner: A Study of Negro Streetcorner Men.* Boston: Little, Brown.

Malinowski, Bronislaw
(1922) *Argonauts of the Western Pacific: An Account of Native Enterprise and Adventure in the Archipelagoes of Melanesian New Guinea.* New York: E. P. Dutton & Co.

Mandelbaum, David G.
(1970) *Society in India.* 2 vols. Berkeley: University of California Press.

Menard, Scott
(1991) *Longitudinal Research.* (Quantitative Applications in the Social Sciences, No. 76). Newbury Park, CA: Sage Publications.

Moran, Emilio [editor]
(1995) *The Comparative Analysis of Human Societies: Toward Common Standards for Data Collection and Reporting.* Boulder, CO: Lynn Rienner Publishers.

Parkin, David
(2000) "Templates, evocations, and the long-term fieldworker." Pp. 91–108 in Paul Dresch, Wendy James, and David Parkin (editors), *Anthropologists in a Wider World.* New York and Oxford: Berghahn Books.

Potter, Jack M., May N. Diaz, and George M. Foster [editors]
(1967) *Peasant Society: A Reader.* Boston: Little, Brown.

Read, Kenneth
(1986) *Return to the High Valley: Coming Full Circle.* Berkeley: University of California Press.

Redfield, Robert
(1950) *A Village that Chose Progress: Chan Kom Revisited.* Chicago: University of Chicago Press.

Redfield, Robert, Ralph Linton, and Melville J. Herskovits
(1936) "A memorandum for the study of acculturation." *American Anthropologist* 38:149–152.

Richardson, Laurel
(1988). "The collective story: Postmodernism and the writing of sociology." *Sociological Focus* 21:199–207.

Royce, Anya Peterson
(1975) *Prestigio y Afiliación en una Comunidad Urbana: Juchitán, Oaxaca.* México, D.F.: Instituto Nacional Indigenista. (reprinted 1990 in: Colección Presencias, Dirección General de Publicaciones del Consejo Nacional para la Cultura y las Artes/ INI).

Royce, Anya Peterson and Robert V. Kemper
(1998) "Finding a footing on the moral high ground: Connections, interventions, and more ethical implications." *Human Organization* 57(3):328–330.

Rudge, Mandy
(1998) "Karimpur exchange." *Anthropology Today* 14(3):20.

Sanjek, Roger
(1990) *Fieldnotes: The Makings of Anthropology.* Ithaca: Cornell University Press.

Stocking, George W., Jr.
(1983) "The ethnographer's magic: Fieldwork in British anthropology from Tylor to Malinowski." Pp. 70–120 in George W. Stocking (editor), *Observers Observed: Essays on Ethnographic Fieldwork.* (History of Anthropology, Volume 1.) Madison: University of Wisconsin Press.

Stone, Richard
(1993) "Long-term NSF network urged to broaden scope." *Science* 262(13):334–335.

Van Maanen, John [editor]
(1995) *Representation in Ethnography.* Thousand Oaks, CA: Sage Publications.

Wacaster, C. Thompson and William A. Firestone
(1978) "The promise and problems of long-term, continuous fieldwork." *Human Organization* 37(3):269–275.

Whitehead, Alfred North
(1967) *Science and the Modern World.* New York: Free Press.

Wilson, Ken
(1993) "Thinking about the ethics of fieldwork." Pp. 179–199 in Stephen Devereux and John Hoddinott (editors), *Fieldwork in Developing Countries.* Boulder, CO: Lynn Rienner Publishers.

Wiser, William and Charlotte Wiser
(2000) *Behind Mud Walls: Seventy-five Years in a North Indian Village.* Updated and expanded edition, with chapters by Susan S. Wadley. Berkeley: University of California Press

Young, Copeland H., Kristen L. Savola, and Erin Phelps
(1991) *Inventory of Longitudinal Studies in the Social Sciences.* Newbury Park, CA: Sage Publications.

Part I

RESTUDIES AND REVISITS:
STYLES OF COLLABORATIVE RESEARCH

In most cases, social and cultural anthropologists do their first major field research for their dissertations. They usually go on to publish several scholarly articles and a monograph based on that initial work. And then, for the rest of their professional lives, most turn away from that "first fieldwork" (Anderson 1990) in order to pursue other opportunities. On the balancing scale of our career goals, many of us seem content to limit the potential contribution of our first fieldwork in exchange for the intellectual tug of other themes at other places.

An alternative model, and one being weighed carefully by more scholars these days, emphasizes building on that first fieldwork to enhance its contributions. Because of the substantial initial investment in establishing rapport, in learning a field language, and so forth, more anthropologists have begun to think of field research as a long-term commitment rather than a one-shot enterprise. Some continue to develop our relationships with the first fieldwork community for a lifetime, to the point that our self-definitions—as anthropologists and as persons—become intertwined with that community.

The relationship of social and cultural anthropologists with field sites typically begins with one fieldworker and one field site—the case common to dissertation research and to the chapters in part I. Later, after surviving their rite of passage through individual fieldwork, anthropologists may elect to establish and maintain relationships with multiple field communities, either sequentially or simultaneously. Occasionally, as seen in the chapters in part II, multiple fieldworkers do research in a single community, either all at once in teams or in different combinations at different periods. In a few instances, as in the cases of Gwembe and Tzintzuntzan discussed in part III, multiple fieldworkers extend across anthropological generations.

Most anthropologists develop intensive relationships with several communities during our careers, but typically just one at a time. In long-term ethnographic studies we do not abandon our first community, but seek opportunities to sustain the relationship through restudies from time to time. Some anthropologists carry out fieldwork, whether short term or long term, in several sites and make only occasional revisits to their first community. A small number become so committed to long-term fieldwork that they always see a return visit to the community of their first fieldwork as the first option when applying for research grants or sabbatical leaves. The experiences of the authors in this volume suggest that opportunities to do research in other places offer valuable comparative insights that can help our understanding of the long-term field situation.

As fieldworkers, anthropologists do not interact with their communities in the sterile setting of a laboratory (cf. Howell 1990). We are not chemists or geneticists. We live in the field with our whole being, often with spouse, children, or partner (cf. Cassell 1987; Flinn, Marshall, and Armstrong 1997; Markowitz and Ashkenazi 1999). And we recognize, explicitly in our professional ethics codes, that the scientific production involved in fieldwork is a collaborative enterprise implicating both fieldworkers and the persons in the communities in which the research takes place.

The anthropologists—Anya Peterson Royce, Wade Pendleton, T. Scarlett Epstein, and Ulla Johansen—who discuss their long-term experiences here all began research in their respective field sites for their first fieldwork. They had no prior commitment or immediate inspiration that led them to contemplate doing long-term field research among those communities. The immediate demand of completing a dissertation focused them on the here and now rather than on the future.

So what happened to convert their initial short-term experiences into long-term involvements with those communities? By attending to their individual situations, perhaps we can see how they came to become long-term participants in their respective communities and how their relationships have been sustained during long and productive professional careers. In the process, some common patterns emerge that might apply to other cases of long-term field research begun by individual ethnographers.

Royce did her dissertation fieldwork in the provincial city of Juchitán, Mexico, during 1971–1972, after preliminary encounters with the Juchitecos in 1967 and 1968. She returned in summer 1974 to do research in the parish archives. She recalls her decision to return in these words, "I knew that coming back was important as an indication of my commitment, not simply as an anthropologist but also as someone prepared to assume her share of obligations to the community." Her monograph on Juchitán was published the following year in Mexico City (Royce 1975). In the long term, her commitment to doing *continuing* studies in Juchitán can be measured by her return visits in summer 1978, summer 1980, summer 1981, summer 1982 (with an anthropological colleague and a group of five students), summer 1989, and at least once a year since 1991 (except for 1995). She has maintained this program of relatively frequent return visits even though she spent a number of years as a university administrator and also has conducted research in other settings related to her interests in ethnicity, dance, performance, and virtuosity. Especially significant for Royce is her sense that the project has become a collaboration with local Zapotec. In her chapter she acknowledges that she is "learning to see, learning to listen"—and, in the process of some thirty-five years of participating in the Juchitán community, has made a long-term commitment to the common good.

Pendleton carried out his dissertation research in Katutura, a suburb of Windhoek, capital of Namibia (then South West Africa), for eighteen months during 1968–1969. He had the opportunity to be at the University of Witwatersrand in Johannesburg, South Africa, in 1970–1971 and then at the University of Cape Town in 1972–1973. Before and after each of these assignments, he managed to return to Katutura for brief periods to gather additional data, but when his book was published (Pendleton 1974), it was banned in South Africa. As a result, he was unable to obtain a visa to return to the field until 1987, when he did two months of fieldwork during a sabbatical. Since then, Pendleton has been able to be in Namibia—and to be in direct contact with the Katutura community—for nine months during 1988–1990, for twenty-four months during 1991–1993, for thirty-six months during 1996–1998, and for six months in 2001. The results of these revisits are reflected in numerous publications about Katutura (e.g., Pendleton 1994), as well as other studies, many coauthored with colleagues in Namibia, about diverse social issues of national significance (Frayne and Pendleton 1998; Pendleton and LeBeau 1992). By 2002, he plans to retire from his academic post in the United States and settle permanently in Namibia.

In effect, Pendleton's experiences with the community of Katutura represent a case of interrupted long-term ethnography. He certainly would have continued his visits to Namibia if he had been granted visas; instead, he lost fifteen years and could only find out about events in Katutura through local persons who could get information out to him despite the prevailing restrictions imposed by South Africa. Now free to be in Namibia on a regular basis, he looks forward to a continuing commitment to this long-term project. In conjunction with his colleagues in Namibia, he hopes to conduct a survey of Katutura every five years and to continue doing participant observation and collecting case studies on a regular basis. As he says at the end of his chapter, "How did this happen? I think the answer for me is that I found a niche where anthropology and social science had a purpose and use, and I did also." What Pendleton has found to be an effective strategy—namely, collaborating on large-scale applied social science projects as a way to fund his own long-term ethnographic project—assumes that anthropologists can spend long periods in or near their field sites. For anthropologists with field sites close at hand, Pendleton's strategy sounds very attractive.

Epstein was first in the field in Mysore, South India, during 1954–1956. There she did research in two rural communities, to which she gave the pseudonyms "Wangala" and "Dalena." Her monograph (Epstein 1962) on these communities appeared several years after she had returned to Manchester to complete her dissertation. In remembering those days, she writes, "I hoped that some day I would be able to restudy Wangala and Dalena, but because of financial constraints I saw little chance of being able to do so." Because of communication problems

3

of language and distance, she soon lost touch altogether with her village friends, eventually changing her regional focus to the Pacific and going to New Guinea for fieldwork. Then, quite unexpectedly, she received an opportunity to revisit these two Mysore villages in 1970 as part of a community development project led by a German sociologist. As a result of that collaborative restudy, she was able to update her earlier monograph (Epstein 1973). She has been able to revisit South India on several occasions since 1970 and always has made a point of visiting the two villages—even though she had insufficient time to conduct "serious" fieldwork. Then, in 1996, she attended an "unforgettable" farewell function laying the foundation for a library building that the people of Wangala had decided to build in her name. Subsequently, she published in India a monograph (Epstein, Suryana-Rayana, and Thinme-Gowda 1998) based on her forty years in the two villages. In addition, she participated in a film project through a German anthropological institute about the history of community development efforts in the two villages. Thus, her involvement with the Mysore villages has been limited to a small number of opportunistic revisits, not always planned in advance and not always within her own frame of control.

On the basis of these admittedly intermittent visits, she offers an assessment of her predictions—incorrect and correct—about how these communities have changed since the mid-1950s. She looks at her "incorrect" predictions about what has happened in education, in technology, and in politics; and she examines her "correct" predictions about population growth, gender matters, and caste/class relations. In overall terms, she sees that, while one community was caught up in a process she calls "village introversion," the other became committed to "village extroversion." In sum, within the limits imposed by her intermittent restudies, along with information obtained through her German and south Indian collaborators, Epstein has been able to show that the two villages seem to be following different paths to the future.

After having done a museum-based Ph.D. dissertation on the Yakuts of Siberia, Johansen visited the Aydınlı nomads in Turkey during 1956, then returned for her first fieldwork during 1957–1958. She went back to the field for short periods in 1964 and in 1970, as she continued to pursue a proper understanding of the genealogical history of these nomads. Subsequently, she revisited the nomads in 1982, 1989, and 1995. Then, in 1997, she began an unusual collaboration with Doug White, an American anthropologist who had come to Germany on a fellowship to do social network analysis on a completely different data set. Because White had worked previously with Colson and Scudder on their Gwembe data, he was aware of the possibilities inherent in long-term data sets for doing sophisticated genealogical analyses.

In their collaboration, Johansen and White have advanced long-term studies into another domain. Their jointly authored chapter—distinctively presented as a dialogue—is devoted primarily to discussing their collaboration rather than to tracing in detail the trajectory of Johansen's fieldwork among the Aydınlı. Together, they offer many insights into the costs and benefits of long-term research as well as those associated with collaborative endeavors. Their collaboration demonstrates the significant advantages of having the original fieldworker available as a guide to field notes and kinship charts, unlike the problems encountered in trying to interpret—in Clyde Kluckhohn's absence—the ethnographic materials gathered in the Ramah Project (see Lamphere, in this volume).

When we look for common patterns among these four cases, we discover that the anthropologists have manifested a wide range of continuing involvement with these first fieldwork communities. In different ways, all these anthropologists have developed and sustained a measure of personal commitment to their communities, whether understood as places or peoples. In several cases, they even have been taken in as members of extended families and have taken on the responsibilities for speaking on behalf of the community when they are requested to do so.

Perhaps the most significant common features of these projects is the shift from individual research to collaborative efforts with other scholars and institutions, whether based locally, nationally, or internationally. While some anthropologists manage to carry out long-term ethnographic research projects completely on their own, this seems more typical of restudies than of continuing studies (cf. McCurdy 2000; Rubenstein 2000). The better known (especially through the initial monograph and other publications) the community, the more likely that other scholars will be interested in carrying out research in that place or among that people. In this way, first fieldwork done individually is expanded into different forms of collaborative research.

A common feature in these studies is an awareness of how cultures are sustained in the face of changes. All of the communities have endured significant changes during the past four decades, especially as transformations in the world political economy have come to the local level. Yet, the anthropologists are able to see firsthand the continuities across the generations, to see the decisions affecting the flow of power from father to son, from mother to daughter. To document change and continuity, each of these anthropologists has focused systematically on certain features of community life. For example, over the decades, Royce has taken more than four thousand photographs to mark the changes in Juchitán and its residents, while Johansen has recorded some 1,300 persons into a master kinship "scroll" which covers 412 marriages dating back to the year 1785.

None of these fieldworkers began with a plan to do long-term research in their communities. But, as these chapters indicate, virtually any field study—whether among nomads or sedentary populations, whether in rural areas or in cities—offers the possibility of becoming a long-term study. Accordingly, all of us—whether graduate students planning first fieldwork or seasoned professionals contemplating work in yet another field site—should be aware that the community we study might, someday by someone possibly unknown to us or to the community, become the object of restudy. We should all prepare to become a Robert Redfield (1930) to an unknown Oscar Lewis (1951).

PART I

References Cited

Anderson, Barbara Gallatin
(1990) *First Fieldwork: The Misadventures of an Anthropologist.* Prospect Heights, IL: Waveland Press.

Cassell, Joan [editor]
(1987) *Children in the Field: Anthropological Experiences.* Philadelphia: Temple University Press.

Epstein, T. Scarlett
(1962) *Economic Development and Social Change in South India.* Manchester: Manchester University Press.
(1973) *South India, Yesterday, Today, and Tomorrow: Mysore Villages Revisited.* New York: Holmes and Meier.

Epstein, T. Scarlett, A. P. Suryana-Rayana, and T. Thinme-Gowda
(1998) *Village Voices—40 Years of Rural Transformation in South India.* New Delhi: Sage Publications.

Flinn, Julianna, Leslie Marshall, and Jocelyn Armstrong [editors]
(1997) *Fieldwork and Families: New Models for Ethnographic Research.* Honolulu: University of Hawaii Press.

Frayne, Bruce and Wade Pendleton
(1998) *Report of the Findings of the 5th Nation Public Opinion Survey for Namibia.* Social Sciences Division, Multi-Disciplinary Research Centre, Research Report No. 34. Windhoek: University of Namibia.

Howell, Nancy
(1990) *Surviving Fieldwork: A Report of the Advisory Panel on Health and Safety in Fieldwork.* Special Publication No. 26. Washington, D.C.: American Anthropological Association.

Lewis, Oscar
(1951) *Life in a Mexican Village: Tepoztlán Restudied.* Urbana: University of Illinois Press.

Markowitz, Fran and Michael Ashkenazi
(1999) *Sex, Sexuality, and the Anthropologist.* Urbana and Chicago: University of Illinois Press.

McCurdy, David
(2000) "A tribal village in changing India." *General Anthropology* 6(2):1, 12–13.

Pendleton, Wade
(1974) *Katutura: A Place Where We Do Not Stay. The Social Structure and Social Relationships of People in an African Township in South West Africa.* San Diego: San Diego State University Press.

(1994) *Katutura: A Place Where We Stay. Life in a Post-Apartheid Township in Namibia: Katutura Before and Now.* Windhoek: Gamsberg Macmillan.

Pendleton, Wade and Debbie LeBeau

(1992) *Socio-Economic Analysis of Radio Listener Attitudes in Namibia.* A consultancy report prepared for the Namibian Broadcasting Corporation. Windhoek: Namibian Institute of Social and Economic Research.

Redfield, Robert

(1930) *Tepoztlán: A Mexican Village. A Study of Folk Life.* Chicago: University of Chicago Press.

Royce, Anya Peterson

(1975) *Prestigio y Afiliación en una Comunidad Urbana: Juchitán, Oaxaca.* (Serie de Antropología Social No. 37) México, D.F.: Instituto Nacional Indigenista.

Rubenstein, Hymie

(2000) "Continuity and change in a Caribbean community." *General Anthropology* 7(1):1, 4–7.

CHAPTER ONE
LEARNING TO SEE, LEARNING TO LISTEN: THIRTY-FIVE YEARS OF FIELDWORK WITH THE ISTHMUS ZAPOTEC

Anya Peterson Royce

Prologue

It was a brilliant, cloudless July day in 1967, the second Lunes del Cerro Guelaguetza on the hilltop outside Oaxaca City. I had arrived with the first buses
sometime just after dawn. I had a seat for the performance, but it was not reserved. Now it was just past noon; the sun had several hours ago gone from being pleasantly warming to unremittingly searing; the dances that are the purpose
of this event had lost their interest with the repetition of a limited technical repertoire; I had bruises from the melee that accompanied the end of every delegation's
performance, the crowd going wild trying to snag the gifts that were thrown. One
more delegation, I thought, then the professional company that would perform
the Danza de la Pluma, then I could push my way onto one of the buses returning to the plaza and collapse in my monk's cell of a hotel room.

The entrance music blared, dragging me back to the obligations of fieldwork.
As the dancers gradually filled the stage, I knew that this last group, the Zapotec delegation from Juchitán de Zaragoza, was unlike anything I had seen before in villages
or on the Bellas Artes stage. Dressed in *traje de lujo*, the women wearing the starched
white headdress, *bidaani quichi'*, the men the tall, pointed sombrero *charro veinti-
cuatro*, the dancers were splendid, full of grace and authority. In all that they did, from
placing the lacquered gourds, *xiga gueta*, at the side of the stage, to dancing the un-
derstated *sones*, to acknowledging the admiration of the crowd, they displayed that
kind of assurance that comes from knowing who one is. Neither a false snobbery nor
an ingratiating demeanor, their carriage and character were formal, grave, yet gracious. Now I know it for the Zapotec sense of occasion that characterizes many public and semiprivate events. It acknowledges the gravity and importance of the work,
dxiiña', of sustaining community, the work of being Zapotec. I did not understand
its import then but I knew that I wanted to know more about these people.

In this first entry into the field, I was supported by a Ford Foundation scholarship that provided undergraduates an opportunity to do independent research
anywhere in Latin America. I was interested in the problem of how and whether
dance is transformed when it moves from village to stage. Mexico had a fine company, the Ballet Folklórico de México, that performed a range of indigenous and

La familia Pineda, wedding in Oaxaca, 1999. Photo by Enrique Lemus.

Spanish-derived dances; I had been a professionally trained dancer and I was fluent in Spanish. I spent six weeks during the summer of 1967 working with the Ballet Folklórico in Mexico City, learning the repertoire, watching rehearsals and performances, interviewing its director, Amalia Hernández. I then watched and filmed dance in small villages along the Veracruz coast, having chosen that style because of the technical demands that made it inherently interesting. From there I went to Oaxaca, the state with the highest percentage of indigenous peoples, for the annual presentation of music and dance, the Guelaguetza, where I could see nine or ten different dance traditions all in one place. That choice, which made me aware of the Zapotec of Juchitán, has had consequences that I could never have foreseen. It eliminated for me the possibility of working with any other people and it demanded attention to the whole arena of identity (Royce 1982), persistence, cultural innovation. Dance would be a part of that, but only a small part (cf. Royce 1974, 1977, 1992; Royce and Seeger 1987, 1997).[1]

I returned to Juchitán in the summer of 1968 to see the two *velas* that dominate the month of August, the Vela Agosto and the Vela San Jacinto. I was intrigued enough by what I had seen the preceding summer to want to see the Zapotec in their own setting. *Velas* are one of the defining features of Juchiteco community. A year of planning by women's and men's *mesas directivas* and the sponsors, *los mayordomos*, culminates in processions and parades, Catholic masses, daytime fiestas, exchanges of ritual paraphernalia and food, and an all-night dance. Each *vela* involves many Juchitecos, women and men, young and old, and, like other activities, constitutes people's *dxiiña'* or work.

9

The Vela Agosto, while sharing the same elements as other *velas*, includes a group and a set of activities unique to the contemporary scene. The group is the *mbyo'xho'*, ancient ones, men and boys who chase and threaten the watchers lined up for the parade and then perform the only extant noncouple dance in Juchitán in the courtyard of the parish church.

We—my husband, Ronald R. Royce, and I—were welcomed by the people of both *velas* and were also the objects of much curiosity on the part of children and young people. Movie cameras were not that common then, so the camera, in addition to our obvious foreignness, made us the center of constantly shifting and pressing crowds of children and the occasional drunk. I was embarrassed and mortified but never fearful.

The occasion of *velas* is a good time to begin one's introduction to Juchitán and the Juchitecos. *Velas* are times of public display. The Zapotec are justifiably proud of this tradition and so consider it reasonable that outsiders would want to observe and photograph it. Strangers are also invited to participate as much or as little as they wish. I may have felt uncomfortably visible but they were not uncomfortable at all with me.

The breakdown of our heretofore reliable Volkswagen caused us to stay long past our planned time in the isthmus. Despite the stress of having no car, of rapidly depleting our financial resources, of wondering whether we would ever see home again, and of learning the ropes of car repair, the longer we stayed, the more committed we became to doing further fieldwork here. Quite simply, the people were extraordinarily gracious and the culture a vibrant one.

Learning to Learn: Dissertation Fieldwork

My next field trip to Juchitán did not take place until 1971. The three years between visits were spent in learning all I could about Mexico, the Isthmus Zapotec, and anthropology in general. The problem I had defined for my doctoral dissertation was that of a Zapotec persistent identity. How and why have the Isthmus Zapotec, particularly those of Juchitán, been able to maintain and develop a Zapotec identity; indeed, move freely between a Zapotec identity and a Mexican, even international, identity, where other groups have not? As an indigenous people in a country where Indians are almost exclusively members of the lower class, the Isthmus Zapotec are a remarkable success story. Indeed, from the vantage point of thirty-five years, fundamental elements of Isthmus Zapotec culture, such as the language, are even more visible and embedded in people's lives than ever before.

I proposed some answers to these questions in my book, *Prestigio y Afiliación en una Comunidad Urbana: Juchitán, Oaxaca* (Royce 1975, 1990), in the form of the factors of relative isolation at critical junctures, a sense of opposition, and economic prosperity based on control of land, investment capital, and entrepreneurial ability. Those were not wrong but they were incomplete. In looking at the ways in which they were incomplete, we can learn about the ethnographic process and find affirmation of the utility of long-term field research.

In that first year of immersion between September 1971 and September 1972, my husband and I shared the field. Our complementary sets of expertise molded the shape and content of what we understood. Even two sets of expertise, however, could not diminish the experience of too much detail and too little context that characterizes all first fieldwork. Having worked to refine a problem, you are then put in the position of unrefining its boundaries because you do not know what will prove to be significant. In one of my early letters from the field to Elizabeth Colson, my dissertation director, I seem to have identified this problem: "I am hesitant about sending you my field notes thus far because nothing seems to fit together in any meaningful way. I write notes one day only to find them contradicted the next. It is also difficult to abstract things into categories when I am not sure how the whole goes together" (November 17, 1971).

Her reply to me was judicious and certainly the best advice for any neophyte in the field:

> You say you don't know what to put down because what you hear one day is contradicted by what you hear the next. The only good rule is to put it down—you then put down the next thing you hear. In the end you sort it out and you know what things you misunderstood, where you were deliberately misled (which is interesting), and where the variations come because of the sources of the information. Don't wait to write until you are sure you know! (December 23, 1971)

My first year of field notes are crammed with bits and pieces, observations, snatches of conversations, extracts from local newspapers and radio broadcasts— I wrote down everything whether it made any sense to me or not. Walking through an exhibit of Delacroix's work just recently, I came across a paragraph from his journals that struck me because of the extraordinary parallels with fieldwork: "I didn't begin to do anything passable in my trip to Africa until the moment I had sufficiently forgotten small details and so remembered the striking and poetic side of things for my picture; up to that point I was pursued by the love of exactitude which the majority of people mistake for truth."

It made such an impression because I am just now discovering some of the fundamental truths that underlie Zapotec culture and so finding a context for much that had remained interesting small details. What is crucial to remember here is that Delacroix filled dozens of sketchbooks on his trips, recording the small details without which we never see the poetic or striking side of things. Field notes serve the same purpose. And the recording of them requires tremendous discipline and faith.

One of the ways in which we begin to learn in the field context, which makes us different from other social science disciplines, is simply having to take care of the business of living—finding a place to live, getting an address, arranging for a bank account or other means of handling finances, introducing yourself to local authorities. Settling in brings you into contact with a whole range of individuals and institutions. You have no choice but to deal with them, and, in the process, you learn. In the case of the Isthmus Zapotec, these situations are also the ones in which people manipulate each other, display statuses, and negotiate relative standing. Extremely frustrating, bewildering, and ego bruising, they teach you a great deal about the give and take of real life. As such they are an extremely important antidote to another characteristic of first fieldwork, the tendency to smooth out the bumpy roads in human life, to fill our writing with normative statements as if they were unconnected to living persons and unaffected by human will. Kenneth Read (1965:ix), author of *The High Valley*, laments this style of presentation:

> Why . . . is so much anthropological writing so antiseptic, so devoid of anything that brings a people to life? There they are, pinned like butterflies in a glass case, with the difference, however, that we often cannot tell what color these specimens are; and we are never shown them in flight, never see them soar or die except in generalities.

It took two months to find a house, get a bank account, open a post office box, establish ourselves with both sacred and secular authorities, and acquire a linguistic informant. It was also the last two months of a particularly contentious election for municipal president. Looking back, that election taught me more about Juchitán and fieldwork than any other single event of that first year.

Learning about Identity: The Election

Mexico's dominant party, the Partido Revolucionario Institucional, PRI, was being challenged by an upstart PPS, Partido Popular Socialista. Here is a brief summary from one of my letters to Colson regarding the situation four days before the election:

> The principal contestants for president are Manuel Musalem Santiago (Tarú) and Esteban Peralta Jimenez; the former PPS and the latter PRI. The contest is evidently as bitter as it is because the PPS faction broke off from PRI because they did not want another president forced upon Juchitán by PRI. . . . The entire history of Juchitán is full of active resistance to any attempt at outside control. This is the first time that PRI has been seriously challenged in this area. . . . The challengers have a charismatic leader in the person of Tarú—he is young, handsome and a man of the people. He gives fiery, eloquent speeches in Zapotec and holds the crowd's attention for longer than is normal here. He is evidently tri-lingual in Spanish, Zapotec, and Arabic [he does not speak Arabic, as I later discovered]. His appeal is based upon the fact that he is a Juchiteco. His Arabic heritage [Lebanese] is kept very much in the background and I suspect that it

would be a disadvantage to his campaign. I have already encountered one person—a PRIista—who said scornfully that he was not a Zapotec. He evidently qualifies as a Juchiteco which seems to be the most important qualification. Peralta is a party man, rather grey in comparison but I suspect that he will be the next president. The election will, however, have long-lasting consequences regardless of the outcome because it has caused splits in some of the major families of Juchitán. (November 17, 1971)

I am surprised that I understood as much as I did of what was going on. Part of my understanding I can attribute to a growing friendship with those who have become my sister and my mother, Delia Ramírez Fuentes and her mother Rosinda Fuentes de Ramírez (now viuda de Ramírez, widow). That family was part of the larger, old, important Pineda family, well connected and in a position to know much about local politics. Another part I attribute to a very good, gossipy weekly newspaper, *El Satélite*, that ran nonstop stories on the election. Part, finally, resulted from one of those accidents that characterize fieldwork. One of my all-cotton, multipocketed field outfits was the color of the PPS party. When I was seen, and I was always highly visible, observing one of the big PPS campaign parades wearing that dress, everyone assumed that I was a supporter and I had immediate access to Tarú.

Even so, I was mistaken in several areas. Most important, perhaps, and most understandable, was that Tarú was not the PPS candidate. His brother-in-law was the candidate of record. In the election proper, PPS evidently gained enough votes to win but the state government canceled the election, declaring widespread fraud, and appointed an interim municipal government headed by Tarú, the popular candidate who was not officially a candidate. It was a significant step for the PRI-controlled state government to take because, for all intents and purposes, it acknowledged PRI's defeat. I think it set the scene for the emergence of the COCEI (Coalición de Campesinos y Estudiantes del Istmo) in the late 1970s, a populist party that later gained national prominence with its support of presidential candidate Cuauhtemoc Cárdenas, who ran officially as the PRD candidate.

What I learned about fieldwork is that the Zapotec, even in the middle of a heated election, were flexible and tolerant enough of individual variation that, with reasonable social skills and a willingness to be a participant in the social maneuvering, you were forgiven faux pas and included as a potential member of the community. In the anxiety and arrogance of dissertation fieldwork, I believed that I was always being judged and that something I might do inadvertently could alienate me from the community. I learned too that, while passionate about politics, the Zapotec also regard an individual's political identity as changeable and only one of many identities. Finally, I learned that the Zapotec are quite understanding of human frailty. Even the most abhorrent transgression of Juchiteco moral codes is viewed within the lifelong behavior of the individual and attempts at reconciliation will be made before reaching any final judgment.

13

I did not articulate it for many years, but what all of this behavior pointed toward was the notion of *guendalisaa,* or creating community through a sense of kinship and common purpose. This was a crucial missing part of my answer to the question of Zapotec persistence. All of the other pieces were essential because, without them, the supporting context for persistence would not have existed. But in the absence of the fundamental value of community and one's active responsibility toward it, the fate of Juchitán would have been similar to so many other indigenous communities.

Why Zapotec persistence rather than accommodation to a Mexican national identity? Even with the historical, economic, and demographic factors in their favor, and with the value of community, the question remains, given all the essential elements for success, why be Zapotec?

It was clear that first year that the language was one of the most important symbols of how Juchitecos thought about themselves. In simple demographic terms, 88 percent of the population of Juchitán (whose total population was then a little more than 26,000) were speakers of Isthmus Zapotec, most bilingual with Spanish but some monolingual. This was a striking contrast with Tehuantepec, the other large city of the isthmus, which had less than 1 percent Zapotec speakers, most of whom were concentrated in the quarter of San Blas, historically related to Juchitán. Tarú's success in the political realm had a great deal to do with his fluency in Zapotec and his decision to use it almost exclusively in speechmaking. There was a publication featuring articles about Juchitán and Zapotec history, occasional short stories and poems, some of which were in Zapotec. Begun in the 1930s under the title *Neza* ("Road"), it was now published under the title *Neza Cubi* ("New Road"). The New Testament was also available in Isthmus Zapotec, the work of the Summer Institute of Linguistics (SIL) and Velma Pickett.

Learning Zapotec

Learning the Zapotec language seemed to be a priority for my husband and me both. We visited Virginia Embrey, Velma Pickett's colleague in SIL. Vicky, as she was known in Juchitán, was still living there, doing linguistic work. She suggested a linguistic informant, a twelve-year-old boy from Cheguigo, one of the two most monolingual sections of Juchitán. José Luis, "Huish," spoke only Zapotec at home but knew some Spanish from school, and he was happy to work after school each day for about an hour. He would come by the house and I would elicit Zapotec based on the elicitation schemes designed by my husband, a linguistic anthropologist. I both recorded the sessions and wrote them down, filling a great many tapes and notebooks. That was to provide the basis for developing a grammar of Isthmus Zapotec (Ronald R. Royce, mss.) and has been invaluable to me in my more recent examination of ideas about death, dying, illness, and health.

In terms of fieldwork techniques, using a young boy as a linguistic informant had many more advantages than disadvantages. Huish was infinitely patient in repeating words and phrases, clearly more patient than I often was. He would also not hesitate to correct me. The difficulties with adult informants are that they get bored and they are sometimes prevented by notions of politeness from making corrections. The only real disadvantage was Huish's age and limited experience. Some of what I elicited then was for him hypothetical; for other material, he simply did not yet have the vocabulary.

However minimal my ability in Zapotec was, any effort I made was rewarded disproportionately. My first essays were in the market—you can get by quite handily with nouns and numbers, and aside from potential and, to them, hysterically funny confusion between "sister" (female speaker), "snake," and "fish," words which differ only by tone and vowel length, you can sound convincing. It is the nature of learning a field language that you initially have a much greater passive knowledge than a productive one. I could begin to understand conversations, even questions directed toward me. The frustration lay in being unable to respond or participate. Fortunately or unfortunately, I was fluent in Spanish so I always had the option of using it when Zapotec was beyond me.

I was found by a person, Dr. Esteban Pineda López, who wanted to trade Zapotec for English lessons. He taught English at the Tecnológico and wanted to improve his accent. I was the pupil in Zapotec while Ron taught him English. Unlike Huish, Don Esteban was not patient, and unlike most Zapotec, he was an authoritarian. Why was I so slow? Why was I so lazy? Why couldn't I understand such a simple language? Ron was kinder to him than he to me. Don Esteban had little respect for Zapotec, thinking that it held people back from realizing their potential, and he forced Zapotec grammar into the framework of Spanish. By spending so much time with him, I learned a great deal about those rare Zapotec who want to become Mexican and about how hard a process it is.

Learning about Juchitán: A Third Way

I acquired a field assistant about midway through the year. Roberto Guerra Chiñas was a *muxe'* (member of the Zapotec third gender) of about seventeen. He was a friend of Delia's aunt, Antonia Ramírez de Fuentes, whose household shared the compound with Delia. Chiñas and I had a conversation one afternoon when we were both visiting the compound and we decided to see how he would be as an assistant. Put simply, he was extraordinary. He was very methodical, very observant, had a phenomenal memory, and was fluent in Zapotec and Spanish. Moreover, because he belonged to a liminal category, *muxe'*, he had access to all social classes and genders. He lived in Saltillo, the other most monolingual section of Juchitán, also across the river but south rather than west. He began coming by the house on a daily basis.

My problem was how best to use him since I had not set out to find a field assistant. We began by having him tell me about everything he had done the preceding day, including when conversations took place in Zapotec and when they happened in Spanish. We often did not move beyond this recounting, so rich was

15

it. Moreover, we touched on issues I would not have thought of raising. In one conversation, for example, he spoke about taking cigarettes to a friend who was in jail, so I learned how the political and judicial systems work. Because of Chiñas, I began to know in real terms about the lives of those who live in Saltillo. Less affluent, less schooled, land-poor farmers, for-hire fishermen, some hammockmakers, theirs was a life considerably different from that of residents of the center of the city. The oldest boy, Chiñas was the provider and protector of the family. His mother and the older girls made and sold tortillas but the father frequently drank up the earnings. I became a kind of unofficial godmother to Chiñas's youngest sister, for whom he had high hopes. He saw to it that she finished school. Since then, she has married and has two children, kind of second-generation godchildren to me.

Working with Chiñas, I saw the class system in action. I was also introduced to the world of *muxe'*. There was nothing in the literature about them, but clearly they were a long-established group in Juchitán. The Spanish gloss for *muxe'* is *afeminado*, but a closer match for who they are would be the North American Indian institution of the *berdache*. Many are identified or self-identified as *muxe'* before puberty or shortly thereafter. Traditionally, they dominated the occupations of designing and embroidering the Zapotec woman's *traje* (outfit made up of a blouse [*bidaani*] and a long gathered skirt [*bizuudi'*]), making the paper decorations for parades and *vela* festivities, making a particular kind of festive bread, and making the pottery figurines known as *tanguyu'*. By 1971, they had expanded into other occupations, primarily white-collar clerical positions. For twenty years now, Chiñas has been the assistant manager of a shoe store in a locally owned chain. Although I did not know it then, the *mbyo'xho'* of the Vela Agosto have, from time to time, included *muxe'*. The role of *muxe'* has been slowly changing; in some ways they are becoming more like homosexual cultures elsewhere. Carnival time has always been an opportunity for cross-dressing and outrageous behavior. Now there are beauty pageants in which all the contestants are cross-dressed *muxe'*.

On the other hand, *muxe'* have become more of a presence in traditional Zapotec modes. There are at least two *vela* societies composed of *muxe'*. The *regada* (parade) of one of these in December 1997 was significant for its attention to those parts of *regadas* that are the most Zapotec, hence least changeable if your goal is to keep to tradition. While the *capitana* (parade queen) was a homosexual from northern Mexico who dressed in Zapotec woman's formal costume and the "women" on the floats were cross-dressed *muxe'*, the young girls who march carrying decorated candles were young girls, the sponsoring *mayordomos* were a heterosexual married couple, and the older women who carry vases of flowers were married women. I do not know what to do with the basketball team, "Las Intrépidas Baila Conmigo" (the dance-with-me intrepid ones), composed entirely of *muxe'*. Whatever their particular style, *muxe'* are not set apart from the rest of Juchitán society. They range across social classes; they hold a variety of occupations, traditionally *muxe'* and otherwise; they have male and female friends who

16

are not *muxe'*. They are judged in the same way that any other Juchiteco is judged, in terms of the strength of their active commitment to the community.

Learning about Identity: The Wedding

Why Zapotec? On February 12, 1971, about midway through the year I was invited to a wedding, which I later realized illustrated how people felt about being Zapotec. The wedding of Dr. Fernando Benítez's son to a young woman from Oaxaca City had taken place in Oaxaca the week before with many Juchitecos attending. The Benítez family, however, wanted a local celebration and so condensed the normal four days into one. I was, by this time, occasionally being invited to fiestas on my own rather than as a friend of Rosinda's and Delia's. This was one of those times; I had been invited by the madrina of the *cantaritos* (godmother of the decorated ceramic pots) who was a distant cousin of Rosinda's. The guests were an assortment of local businesspeople, politicians (Tarú among them), the medical profession, many from the local Lebanese families—people who, while not primarily from the old families, knew and valued Zapotec customs.

The mother of the groom had requested that women wear *enagua* (Zapotec dress but not the most formal). Most of the women came in *bizuudi' olan*, the long, full, gathered skirt of flowered material with a nine-inch white lace ruffle at the bottom. A few wore the skirt without the ruffle. Two women wore *bizuudi' renda*, the older style wrapped skirt almost never seen anymore in Juchitán. Both women were wearing it incorrectly wrapped—they had simply wrapped it around them, leaving one end hanging down the side. The correct way (and the only comfortable one) is to stand in the middle of the length and bring both ends to the center so that you have a kick pleat in the front. The only woman wearing the full formal velvet embroidered outfit was the bride. Perhaps 15 out of the 150 women wore *vestido*, a term denoting Western-style dress, myself among them.

There were surprises in the music provided as well. Three groups played—a modern band (mostly brass and percussion), a Zapotec band with the addition of a marimba, and a flute and drum duo (*pito y tambor*). Just as I had never seen wrapped skirts worn at weddings, neither had I heard flute and drum at such festivities. In subsequent years, I have seen wrapped skirts only once for a wedding, these worn by the bridesmaids (incorrectly wrapped!), and I have never heard flute and drum at another wedding. The wedding dance began with *sones*, traditional Zapotec dances. Another difference in the direction of an older tradition came in the dancing of "*La Tortuga*," a dance that mimes the gathering of turtle eggs at the edge of the beach and one rarely done at weddings. It was danced by María Luisa Musalem, the matriarch of one of the Lebanese families, and her female partner.

The only people dancing were women whether the dances were *sones* or modern Latin dances or called dances. Men participated only in the *Mediu xhiga*, the dance in which the object is to break everyone else's clay pot while keeping yours intact. Here, the bride had to dance, even though she was not from the isthmus and had never danced a *son*.

17

The food was plentiful and traditional—shellfish; turtle eggs; stuffed, batter-dipped, and fried chiles; tamales; and all kinds of local cheese. Beer never seemed to run out and bottles of brandy made the rounds almost continuously. The whole event was a very deliberate display of Zapotec identity, even to including items not normally part of weddings—the "Tortuga," the flute and drum, the wearing of the wrapped skirt. At the same time, more modern items appeared in greater abundance as well—the modern band and a full range of dances, crustless chicken sandwiches on white bread (*pan Bimbo*), brandy. The request for women to wear *enagua* was unusual, too. There was much discussion about my coming in Western dress. Most thought I should have worn Zapotec dress as a display of unity in the face of "outsiders" (*dxu* and *wada'*), in this case, the bride and her family. It was in the articulation of this that I realized how important it was for the Benítez family members and their friends to demonstrate the superiority and range of Zapotec tradition, hence those unusual elements. At the same time, they wanted to show that they were affluent and "cultured" enough to compete in the Mexican arena, hence the abundance of modern elements. The ability and resource base to move between identities is a very strong value for the Juchitecos. Had I realized this, I might have reconsidered what I wore. Out of a convoluted reasoning process, based ultimately on a sense of loyalty to Rosinda, who was not going (whether or not she was invited was never made clear), I did not want to make this my debut in *traje*. The higher loyalty, of course, would have been to the Zapotec community.

Learning about Persistence

Why Zapotec? It is an ancient civilization with an active literature. In its current form (mostly crafted in the late nineteenth century with the exception of the language), it is a very costly identity and therefore competitive in the identity market. Its core of *guendalisaa* values the contributions of individuals to the common good, thus ensuring the strategy of moving into new arenas as those develop. Being Zapotec does not restrict one; rather, being Zapotec means that you are open to new ways of accomplishing a healthier and stronger community. It is an identity that is flexible, that can grow and respond to a rapidly changing world; and, in a mestizo-dominated nation, it is singular (cf. Royce 1982, 1993; Royce and Kemper n.d.).

In the first half of the year, my days had grown increasingly crowded as we accumulated language teachers, field assistants, and friends. The walk from our house to the market was six long blocks each way. To go to Rosinda's compound added another three. In the beginning when you want to believe yourself busy but often, in fact, are making busywork for yourself because you do not have the kinds of social obligations that members of the community have, you miss events because you do not have a network; you hesitate to "drop in" because you are afraid you will be disturbing people and besides your Zapotec is not good enough yet, and all the rest, a good long walk is a way of filling time and seeming productive.

When your social obligations multiply so that you visit more people more often and go to more events and therefore write more notes, you need to save time. After four months, my schedule had me making the round trip to the market every morning with an additional trip or stop at Tere's butcher shop and a daily round trip to Rosinda's compound. Working with Huish and Don Esteban took another hour or two a day; writing notes added another three or four hours. Then came all the other things—attending fiestas such as baptisms, weddings, *quinceaños* (a girl's fifteenth birthday), birthdays, *velas*, Christmas *posadas* (visits to houses over the nine days preceding Christmas), visiting new friends and acquaintances, collecting material in the municipal archives, doing a number of small-scale surveys, reading the five or six local weekly papers, listening to the local radio station, visiting the church and doing favors for the priest (recording the Mass in English, for example), visiting the Zeitlins, North American archaeologists who came to Juchitán about four months after we did.

We needed to find a more centrally located house. After a month or so of talking about this necessity with Rosinda and her relatives and friends, we were told about a house only two blocks from the market and three from Rosinda. It was a lovely old-style, high-beamed-ceiling house with a large walled garden. The only negative was that it belonged to a woman who was a midwife and a pawnbroker. We frequently would be awakened in the middle of the night by an hysterical husband who needed the midwife or might get a knock at almost any hour from someone desperate to pawn something. Otherwise, it was ideal. It was in the block fronting on the Calvario chapel and so we became "members" of the Vela Calvario, yet another network.

Now to my daily schedule was added the work with Chiñas, another two hours, and occasionally with other individuals with specialized knowledge. I was also invited to give a paper at a roundtable sponsored by the Roman Catholic Diocese to be held in Tehuantepec. It was the talk that, in 1980, was elaborated and published in two of the local newspapers, "Breve Resúmen de la Historia Económica y Social de Juchitán, Oaxaca." I also had agreed to present papers at the CORD (Committee on Research in Dance) conference in Tucson, Arizona. One of those papers forced me to analyze what I knew about Zapotec dance, "Dance as an Indicator of Social Class and Identity in Juchitán, Oaxaca" (1974). While these were time-consuming obligations, they were also wonderful opportunities to look at all the disparate bits of material I had gathered and to try to make some sense out of them. This is a luxury that we usually have only after returning from the field. Giving a paper in Spanish to a regional audience, while terrifying, was also important in establishing myself as a professional and one who was willing to be a participant in the scholarly life of the region and the nation.

Into this already crowded schedule came the *vela* season of May. Eight *velas*, each four days of festivities, occur back to back during the first half of May. School is suspended; businesses operate on a reduced schedule; the whole city orients itself toward *velas*. Locals, aside from young people who go to all the dances

19

as a way of dating, would normally attend their own *vela* and perhaps one other. As an anthropologist, I felt that I had to see them all. I was aided immeasurably in my attempt at documentation by the custom, then fairly new, of having the important parts of one's *vela* broadcast over the local radio station. When it became clear that it was physically impossible to attend everything, I took extensive notes from the radio broadcasts and relied on anyone I could find who had attended for additional impressions. In the last ten years, many Juchitecos have begun making a videotaped record of their *vela* or other important events. Those are clearly invaluable sources for the ethnographer.

I was away from Juchitán twice during that year, once for ten days at the CORD Tucson conference and then for several days in July when we went to the Guelaguetza in Oaxaca. Those absences did not diminish my local obligations. By August, I had reached the point of exhaustion and helplessness reflected in this letter to Colson:

> You were right when you said that a year was a good length of time for fieldwork. Any temptations I have had to stay longer have been overcome by an ever-expanding network of social obligations. It has become increasingly difficult to stay at home and work without offending people. I have also become more resentful of their demands on my time, probably as a result of familiarity, more work, and the terrible summer weather. We have had no rain for almost a month and the wind has returned with temperatures in the high 90s during the day and the high 80s at night. (August 4, 1971)

Even so, leaving six weeks later was a wrenching experience. It is no easier now. At the end of that first year, I had experienced most of what would later help me understand the driving force behind Zapotec persistence—*guendalisaa*. In fact, my increasingly onerous obligations were part and parcel of that active commitment to community.

Learning to Be Family: Returning to the Field

I returned to Juchitán in the summer of 1974 to do some work in the archives of San Vicente Ferrer, the parish church. This time I was alone and had arranged to stay with Rosinda and her family. It was a significant change from having been there with a husband, living in our own house. To be there initially as a couple was important because it established me as a married woman, hence a member of a particular social category. It is this category of individuals, especially those whose children are grown, on whom the obligations of community weigh most heavily. It proved to be optimal for learning what is fundamental to Zapotec culture. Living in our own house also gave me the luxury of time off-stage, out of public view. When I moved into the bedroom that had been allocated to me in Rosinda's wing of the compound (shared by three extended families), I realized that it was centrally located just off the kitchen and next to Delia. I also quickly learned that, while rooms had doors, they were never shut. I was in the middle of people all the time. I always thought I needed space and time away from people but clearly this was not going to be possible. I grew more comfortable with it over the summer although being sick with an audience of sympathetic people was almost more than I could bear. It did establish me in a different set of relationships, increasingly more familial and increasingly more intimate. Living with the family, I was witness to private behaviors, tensions, and conflicts that had remained hidden during the first year. Indeed, I was a participant in some of these conflicted situations. While they were stressful, I was also grateful for being treated as part of the family. I knew that coming back was important as an indication of my commitment, not simply as an anthropologist but also as someone prepared to assume her share of obligations to the community.

It was during this summer that I became closer to Na Berta Fuentes Pineda, Rosinda's mother and the matriarch of the compound. We would sit in the kitchen peeling, slicing, grinding ingredients for the *comida* (main meal of the day) and she would tell me stories, talk about the family, recount a dream she may have had the previous night, evaluate different women's performance as dancers. I got better and better at remembering long conversations because interrupting Berta to get a notebook or even to jot down notes lost that particular thread. She told marvelous shaggy dog stories and also was masterful at the Zapotec game of risqué punning, a province of older, married women at the expense of men of all ages and statuses. I remember Berta's delight when I managed my first pun in the form of a riddle.

Berta was an extraordinary dancer and was pleased to find such an apt pupil. In the middle of a conversation or meal preparation, if a *son* came on the radio we would be up and dancing. Whenever there was a disagreement about the way a *son* should be danced, Berta was the final authority. In one memorable disagreement that erupted in the rehearsals for the Guelaguetza, I marveled at Berta's tactic of helping people reach a consensus rather than simply laying down the law, which she could easily have done. I learned in this instance, and from being close to her, that confrontation is not a valued mode of behavior for Zapotec, that they prefer incorporating people rather than isolating them, that individuals may differ but are still good people. Social relationships matter and the Zapotec spend a lot of time making them work. Again, it is upon older women that the heaviest responsibility lies.

My work doing an inventory of the parish archives generated a lot of interest. Juchitecos are interested in their history and know a fair amount about it. This was a new source for them. The parish records were amazingly complete, with baptismal and marriage records going back to 1743. Death records began much later and were sporadic. Only a few registries were unreadable from worm damage and burnthrough. Because Juchitán was on the periphery of the Mexican Revolution, it did not see the wholesale destruction of records so common in other more central locations. I left a copy of the inventory I made that summer in the parish office and have subsequently made copies available to parish priests, most recently to Father Arturo Francisco Herrera González, the current parish priest. Unfortunately, almost half the registries have disappeared, lost in the various moves of offices.

Learning to See the Past

On the basis of that inventory, I proposed research for the summer of 1978 on the topic of fertility and social structure. That summer was to be a pilot study, with my colleague Della Collins Cook, a bioanthropologist, examining the earliest of the parish records. We were interested in any patterning of births, any discernable seasonality. Cook and I spent most of that summer laboriously copying baptismal records for the years between 1743 and 1800. Cook was also interested in the *muxe'* and began interviewing some of them.

It was a summer of political unrest. Several "foreigners" had been arrested and taken away mysteriously. My family were concerned enough to have provided me with a letter from the municipal president saying that I was a welcome guest in Juchitán and that my work benefited the city. I have to confess to some nervousness even though the parish church was next to Rosinda's compound, sharing a common wall, in fact. I was known in the city as the author of the book on Juchitán that was required reading for students at ITRI (Instituto Tecnológico del Istmo). I chose to publish it in Spanish in Mexico so that it would be available to the people of Juchitán but I did not anticipate generations of teenagers having to memorize it for examinations.

I acquired a namesake partly on the basis of that book. Rogelio Santiago Cruz had been in his teens in 1971 and came to me looking for work. I introduced him to the Zeitlins, who hired him to help in the cleaning and labeling of potsherds. It gave him the background, the knowledge of English, and the confidence to continue his schooling so that he became the director of computing services at ITRI. He named his second daughter after me and, when asked her name, she would point to a copy of my book and say that she was Anya Peterson Royce.

In the summer of 1980 I returned again, drawn by some of the patterns Cook and I discovered in the early records about marriage and godparent relations and a social class structure that was discernible in the eighteenth century. I spent a lot of time talking with individuals about marriage choices, choice of godparents, particularly baptismal sponsors, and the relative importance of economic as opposed to social factors. It was a topic about which people liked to talk. In trade for their observations, I often was asked to compare today's patterns with those I was seeing in the earliest records. Again, there was a lively intellectual curiosity in historical patterns, especially those that could be connected to ancestors.

This was the summer I collected data on ownership of gold jewelry as a form of liquid capital. I was trusted enough for all the women in the compound to let me weigh their jewelry. We also talked about ownership of land and the strategies of long-term and short-term investments (see Royce 1981). This kind of study would not have been possible earlier in my relationship with Juchitán. The Casa de la Cultura or *Lidxi Guendabianni* (House of Culture) was developing by now into an important cultural institution. Although it was a political plum, its directors continued the work of publishing in the Zapotec language. *Guchachi reza* ("The Split Iguana") joined *Neza* as a literary and cultural journal. Exhibits of artwork occupied two salons while there was a very large room devoted to the archaeological past of the region. A library housed important materials on the isthmus and was always filled with young people. Finally, there was an auditorium for lectures and small performing groups. One of those summers, I gave a performance of dances from Veracruz and the isthmus with a cousin of Mayella's husband who taught folk dance in Veracruz (Mayella is Delia's cousin). More recently, I have given lectures illustrated with slides and have given a book of photographs to which I add photos each time I visit. My idea is to leave a kind of ongoing visual record.

Learning to See the Present

My husband had done all the photography during 1971 to 1972 when we were both in Juchitán. Since I began returning alone, I took up the task of photographing the city and its inhabitants. My strategy was to photograph everything that was new since my last visit, to revisit old structures and places that had changed, to photograph every sign and example of graffiti that used Zapotec, to document all the wall paintings and decorations (more recently, carved trees), and, gradually, to photograph people. I now have a thirty-five-year record of the city and its people. Recently, I struck up an acquaintance with the artist who owns the small shop under the central bandstand that sells Zapotec tape cassettes and CDs, books, and artwork. I told him I had photographs of the bandstand over the last thirty-five years, and he was thrilled to have copies. The bandstand is of more than passing interest because it was the focal point for political rallies and a famous hunger strike of Juchiteca women. During one short period, it also had a lovely welcoming slogan painted on it in Zapotec.

I was initially shy about photographing people—my problem, not theirs—so I started with the children. After a long hiatus with no young children, the compound in the 1980s had two new babies: Mayella's and Diego's first child, Daniella; and Vicente's (Mayella's older brother) and Gloria's first daughter, Karime. It was interesting to see how much the presence of these two enlivened the compound. Mayella and Vicente both had their own homes but spent a large part of the day in the family compound where everyone took turns lavishing love on the babies. Other children came and now include the daughter of my cousin Cesar, who was five when I first began working in Juchitán.

I also began photographing the older women, *las tías* (the aunts) as they were called, because they were getting on in years. I had taken a particularly nice one of Tía Rosa, Berta's sister, and, on the first anniversary of her death (September 1991), I took color photocopies to Juchitán, rolled them up and tied them with a ribbon that had Rosa's name on it, and gave them to family members who came to the mass. Now whenever I bring a particularly nice photo of someone, they joke about using it on the altar when they die (*lú bidó'*, literally, "face of the altar").

Learning to Teach: Taking Students to Juchitán

By virtue of my talking about the Zapotec in classes and my husband offering Zapotec as a language, students, both undergraduate and graduate, had begun expressing an interest in doing research in Juchitán. In the summer of 1981, I laid the groundwork for a project that could involve a team of investigators and in the summer of 1982, Della Cook and I took a group of students to the field. They all knew Spanish, in varying degrees of fluency, and all had also had some Zapotec. The idea was that we would all work on the common project, "Comparative Household Economic Strategies," funded by a collaborative grant from the Midwestern Universities Consortium on International Affairs Women in Development. Then each student would pursue the research for her own thesis.

With the help of my Juchiteco family, we found a house to rent, just across the park from my family and from the parish church and one block from the market and the central plaza. There were seven of us, all women. I had been reluctant to bring men into the field because of the always-volatile political climate. Men, because of the roles they play, are more likely to be in contexts where political quarrels erupt.

None of the students had had any field experience; indeed, with one exception, none had been in a developing country. In spite of all the preparation, they were initially very uncomfortable, psychologically and physically. In Mexico City, the poverty next to affluence bothered them; the miles of garbage piled up on the highway median bothered them; the sight of individuals with harelips or club feet (things that are cosmetically repaired in the United States and so are seldom visible) bothered them.

The physical discomforts began with the twelve-hour bus ride to Juchitán. It is always difficult, even though the buses are relatively new and comfortable. Juchitán's climate is extremely stressful. From April through October, daytime temperatures range from the high eighties to the low hundreds, while falling to the nineties at night. The heat comes with high humidity. From October to the end of March is the season of the *nortes*, dry winds that blow from the gulf to the Pacific, whipping great clouds of dust and sand through the streets. During these windstorms, the temperature may fall as low as the low seventies. Mosquitoes carrying dengue fever and tiny biting flies plague anyone foolhardy enough to venture out unprotected by insect repellent. Our first two weeks in Juchitán were further aggravated by work on the municipal electrical system, which meant that the electricity was shut off every night from 8 P.M. to 6 A.M. This meant that there was no water during those hours since the water was pumped by the electric plant. Della and I and the oldest student, who had been on many archaeological digs with her husband, had already experienced all of this and we tried to prepare the students. In comparison to many field situations, we did well—we had electricity and running water most of the time.

One of the problems for most of the group was having to plan ahead, filling buckets of water, putting on insect repellent and sun block, things that were unnecessary at home. Another source of difficulty was resolved less quickly because none of us recognized it in the beginning. By the summer of this excursion, I had already had thirteen years of working in Juchitán. I was comfortable with the people and they with me. I felt more "at home," more myself, in fact, in Juchitán. The students were uneasy with this person they did not know; I was not the same as I was in Bloomington. They were also struggling to gain acceptance and my ease was difficult for them. In comparison with their own situation, it made them feel inadequate and unloved. For my own part, I have to say that I was overly protective of my own relationship with Juchitecos and probably overly concerned about possible negative effects the students might have. These are not uncommon reactions and I write about them here in the hope that it might be helpful to those planning collaborative research. I am not certain what finally prompted it, but we did have a conversation in which all of these sentiments surfaced. In the aftermath, we were able to deal much more effectively with common problems and with each other.

Each of the students stayed in Juchitán into the following year in households that we had found for them during the summer. The results include two Ph.D. dissertations, one on the hammock-making industry, the other on flower symbolism in Zapotec writing, dress, decorative art, and ritual; a master's thesis on midwifery and the role of medicinal plants in women's health; and an undergraduate honors thesis on pottery as a cottage industry. The latter won the prize given by the College of Arts and Sciences in 1982 for the best thesis in the social and behavioral sciences.

Learning to Mourn

In May of 1982, I received a telegram telling me of Na Berta's death. I had not known either of my own grandmothers, and Berta had become that for me. I could not get to Juchitán for the funeral—in the best of circumstances, it takes twenty-four hours, so we decided that I would come for the Forty Day Mass for the Dead. In those days of waiting, I tried to sort out my feelings and roles while I mourned alone. I had been there for other deaths but this was the first that touched me so directly. How did I balance my mourning as part of the family with my identity as an anthropologist? It was as family that I was going. In the early hours of dawn when I arrived and Rosinda held me, both of us crying, I felt as if I had come home; I was family.

25

Later that morning, as we sat in the room with the altar for Berta, receiving mourners, Delia began telling me about Berta's last days and the funeral. Then she stopped, looked at me, and asked, "Where is your notebook?" Puzzled but obedient, I went to fetch it and had it nearby for the rest of the week's activities. I realized later that personal and professional roles do not have the same degree of separateness that they do here. For my Zapotec family and friends, my being an anthropologist is simply the way in which I contribute to the community. I help tell their story in a way they have come to trust. Were I a medical doctor, my contributions would lie in that arena. The decisive point is making a commitment to the community. Until that happens, you are welcome as a guest; afterward your obligations are the same as any nonresident Zapotec.

Two changes happened at almost the same time that caused a seven-year hiatus in my work in Juchitán. The first was a Guggenheim Fellowship to do a comparative study of classical ballet and mime. That took me to Poland, France, and Italy and resulted in a book published in 1984 and unrelated to anything Zapotec, *Movement and Meaning: Creativity and Interpretation in Ballet and Mime*, and several subsequent publications on the Italian commedia dell'arte. The other change was a major administrative appointment at Indiana University. Between pursuing a major scholarly interest in the structure of the performing arts and the obligations of higher administration, I did not make what had become annual research trips to Mexico.

Learning Wisdom

In 1989, I returned, and, with the exception of 1990 and 1995, have been in Juchitán every year, sometimes making more than one trip. I have continued to document change, photographing many of the same parts of the city so that there is a record of new or remodeled buildings, businesses, schools, and chapels as well as slogans and murals that decorate the streets. A phenomenon that began about ten years ago is the carving of dead or dying trees by local artists, most of which is quite extraordinary. I have also photographed the expansion of the city as new *colonias* (suburbs) spring up and new industrial areas fill open space at the margins. New generations of Juchitecos are the subject of photographs, too, especially but not exclusively those in my own family.

The topics to which I have devoted the last ten years have included local politics and its interaction with regional and national parties and agendas, the system of *velas* (Royce 1992), the aesthetic dimension that runs throughout Isthmus Zapotec culture, and the nature of illness and health. As others have noted, you can, by virtue of long involvement and increasing familiarity, collect data much more efficiently and in shorter periods of time. My work has been aided immensely by the collaboration of my Zapotec sister, Delia Ramírez Fuentes. Knowing what my particular research interests are, she collects materials—publications of the *Lidxi Guendabianni* (House of Culture) or books available at the yearly

book fair, examples of art, photographs taken by family members, documents issued by the parish church, and so forth, and saves them for my visits. She has introduced me to healers working in Juchitán and, for one-time events that happen
when I am not there, she will take extensive notes. Our discussions, as I analyze
data, have been invaluable.

The fact that I am known as someone with an ongoing commitment to
Juchitán has made it possible to examine areas that would have been off-limits in
the beginning. In 1989, for example, I interviewed seven of the leading politicians
in the city, two or more hours each of very open and personal statements, all of
which were tape recorded.

Other topics, the aesthetics of ordinary and extraordinary life, the underly-
ing notion of community (*guendalisaa*), and the centrality of "balance" that runs
through all aspects of Zapotec culture, require the understanding and insight that
come only with long-term fieldwork. Part of this insight derives from an increasing degree of comfort with the Zapotec language and part of it comes from participating and observing everyday and extraordinary events over many years. You
begin to understand what matters and what is ephemeral.

The question that initially drew me to Juchitán—how the people sustain a
vibrant and distinctive identity—still colors all the other research questions I take
up. Now I can go beyond the historic, economic, and political factors to those that
answer not only the how but more importantly the why. Bedrock values, such as
relationships based on mutual respect, on "crafting" everything one does or says,
on achieving balance in one's life, and finally on the respect for wisdom—*guendabianni*, literally, "enlightenment"—have shaped the Zapotec responses to the positive economic and political events that have characterized their history. But you
cannot understand these values except in the actions of people—one demonstrates respect or balance or community or wisdom rather than talking about it.
So, there is a delicate process of seeing people in action over many years, of seeing similar or different responses to situations or people, that is the only key to
recognizing the existence of these values. Once you "see" these values, you understand them as critical factors that shape behavior in virtually every sphere, from
politics to health to making pottery or writing poetry.

Zapotec identity, by most measures, is stronger and more evident now than
it was in 1967 when I first encountered the people of Juchitán. There are more
ongoing publications in Zapotec; more radio and television programs in the language; more efforts on the part of the *Lidxi Guendabianni* and the municipal
government to support Zapotec language and "customs"; more locally sponsored
conferences on Zapotec history and culture; more young artists, painters, poets,
and musicians who base their work on Zapotec tradition; and more interest on
the part of ordinary Juchitecos to participate in the celebration of their identity.
The current director of the *Lidxi Guendabianni* has been working now for several years on the ancient system of Zapotec numbering and mathematics. He
gave a lecture on his work to a packed audience, which included a number of

farmers and fishermen who still use this very old system. A former director, also a linguist, has established a series of workshops on the Zapotec language as well as an outreach program to bring literacy in Zapotec to those whose native spoken language it is.

If we try to explain the reasons for the tenacity of Zapotec ways of being, one obvious explanation would be the multiple strands that reach into all aspects of Zapotec life and which cannot be abstracted. It is this dense, multivalent, flexible sense of identity that sustains the nature of the Zapotec culture. And it is the sense that identity only exists in actions that gives it its strength.

The thirty-five years I have spent living and doing fieldwork with the Isthmus Zapotec, the data I have collected, the analyses I have made have all been essential to coming to my present state of understanding. So have all the ways in which we try to interpret the cultures in which we work for those who do not know them—academic papers, conference presentations, and the classes and seminars that we teach. In all these activities, I have had to come to grips with Zapotec culture in such a way as to make it comprehensible for others. In fact, much of what I have learned about the nature and significance of community comes from teaching about it. My understanding has also grown by conversations with my Zapotec family and friends. In a more formal way, I send drafts of what I am writing to Delia, who commands not only Zapotec and Spanish but also English. She has a complete set of everything I have published as does the *Lidxi Guendabianni*.

Learning Community

One of the more contentious issues in American anthropology in general has been the question of voice—whose voice is privileged? Who speaks for whom? We all have to come to terms with this. What I hear from family and friends and from those Juchitecos who have read my work is that I bring an important perspective as a scholar and as someone who cares about them. My uncle said in response to my question about the propriety of my giving a lecture in the *Lidxi Guendabianni* this coming year, "You are and you are not one of us. You belong here but you also have a home in your own country. Because of that and your training, you see Juchitán in ways that are important for us to hear. At the same time, what you say makes sense to us."

I could not do better than that were I to talk about the impact of my research and that of my students on the people of Juchitán. He was also referring, however, to the importance of someone speaking to those in power in Mexico and beyond about who they are.

Increasingly, I have a more local and active impact in that I am a resource and a sounding board for young Zapotec intellectuals, social scientists, linguists, and theologians. Many bring their work and ideas to me and we talk about them. I have the advantage of thirty-five years of my own research as well as access to the work of earlier ethnographers. This kind of "teaching" requires tact and honesty, but it is worth the effort. Not only is it a personal responsibility but it is a way of helping ensure future scholarship. Were I to make a prediction about the next generation of scholars of Isthmus Zapotec culture, it would be that most will be Isthmus Zapotec. All the signs are there now and I am glad to be able to take part in this development as a facilitator.

Learning Balance

I am fortunate in that my family understands and values my work so they do everything to facilitate it. I have been able to spend the kind of time with them that satisfies us while I am also able to do the research I came to do. I do make more frequent, shorter visits to attend family events—funerals, weddings, commemorations, and so forth. The other pull away from my Zapotec research comes from other research interests—the anthropology of dance and performing arts as well as interest in American Indian and Latino cultures. And there are also the increasing responsibilities as you move from graduate student to senior scholar.

While growing older has generally benefited me in terms of my own standing in Juchitán, it has had one disadvantage. I am less tolerant of the heat than I used to be, so, while summers would be an ideal time for me to be there, I go at other, less convenient times simply because of the summer heat.

As I have discussed previously, some matters simply require time and many field trips before you even "see" them and certainly before you understand them. Especially true here are those values that explain the "why" of Zapotec culture. I have grown more competent in Zapotec culture at the same time as I have grown up in my own culture and as a scholar. Last, I have been loved and sustained both as a person and as a scholar by my Zapotec community. And we have achieved a kind of balance in our mutual respect and aid that has helped us grow.

In October 1999, I went again to Juchitán. The first stop was in Oaxaca City for the wedding of my cousin, Enrique Lemus Fuentes, who was six years old when I first met him in 1971. He was marrying a young woman from D.F. His family, my family, came from Juchitán, Oaxaca, and D.F. for the celebration, though I got the prize for coming the longest distance. All of the women brought their finest *traje de lujo* and their gold *alajas* (jewelry). We also brought a hairdresser to do everyone's hair in the elaborate style with ribbons and flowers. And last, we brought the Santa Cecilia band from Juchitán so that we could dance *sones*, and especially the *mediu xiga*, without which it would not be a wedding. Many of us were staying at a downtown hotel and when we stepped outside in Zapotec dress, we attracted the stares of everyone. I am accustomed to being in Juchitán where the Zapotec are the majority and found it an odd sensation to be a curiosity. The non-Zapotec wedding guests found us exotic, too. My Juchitán family was serene through it all and it made me aware of how comfortable and confident they are with their identity. I have not achieved that kind of confidence and perhaps this may be the lot of the anthropologist.

Returning with the family to Juchitán, I entered into the nine-day cycle of prayers for the soul of Ta Chu, Jesus Ramírez Fuentes, my Zapotec father, whose second All Souls' Day celebration this was. As the week went on, the pace of preparation picked up for building the home altar, *xandu'*, and making sure the tamales and bread would be ready. At the same time, I was working on the speech I was to give Friday evening at the *Lidxi Guendabianni*. I was nervous, having accepted the invitation to speak about thirty-five years experience in Juchitán, speaking to a Zapotec audience about themselves and their city. I had brought some eighty-five slides with me, a tiny number out of the thousands I have taken over the years, in order to show changes and continuities. The title, *Imágenes de Juchitán: El Proyecto Etnográfico 1967–1999*, reflected the multiple focus of what I wanted to say. I wanted to talk about how much the city has changed, its demography and its face, but I also wanted to emphasize the persistent values that have sustained its fundamental Zapotec nature. Finally, I wanted to talk about how anthropologists, in particular this anthropologist, work. The latter is important because Juchitán has continued to be the object of journalists and film crews looking for some exotic subject matter that will catch the attention of readers and viewers. *Elle* magazine published an irresponsible article several years ago about the "sexually promiscuous" and "domineering" women of Juchitán, based on a set of highly selected "interviews." The most recent invasion is that of a Japanese film crew who paid a whirlwind visit to the city and then returned to film the *muxe'* during one of their *velas*. In both these cases and in many more, the purpose was to give the public a taste of the exotic. No thought was given to the way in which any of these single attributes may fit into the whole. Being brought into the public view in this way hurts, and the Zapotec, being the hospitable, civilized people they are, have no defense. It was important for me to talk about what I see are my responsibilities and how I have come to understand what I do.

Delia and I worked on the final draft until I put it aside Thursday afternoon so that we could organize the altar-flower-buying strategies. Friday night we went to the *Lidxi Guendabianni* and watched the audience grow until it filled the auditorium—family, friends, artists, musicians, writers, old, young, people interested in their city. I was grateful for their interest and attention, and, at the end, for their sustaining words of thanks: "*para una mujer que sabe ver con los ojos del corazón a mi pueblo*" ("for a woman who knows how to see my people with the eyes of her heart").

Being an Interpreter

Now, in the summer of 2001, I am working on three projects that continue my association with Juchitán and its people. One is a book, *The Isthmus Zapotec: Art and Artful Lives*, which examines three core values—wisdom, balance, and community—that comprise an aesthetic governing both the arts for which the Zapotec are well known, and the events, large and small, of everyday life. Artfulness and intentionality are embedded in the very fabric of Zapotec culture but it is only now that I understand that. Much of my understanding comes, of course, from the many years of working in Juchitán. Some of it has been shaped, however, by the research I have pursued in the nature of the performing arts, and, in turn, the artistry involved in ethnography.

A second is an exhibit of photographs representing thirty-five years of the lives of Juchitecos. The photographs will come from the more than three thousand slides that document change and areas of persistence for the city and its people. The photographs will remain in the *Lidxi Guendabianni* after the exhibit as part of its permanent collection.

The third, still very much in the beginning stages, is a trilingual edition (Zapotec, Spanish, and English) of some of the poetry of Juchiteco poet Enedino Jiménez. I have translated ten of his poems from Zapotec into English but more selection and translation are in order.

Collaboration is at the heart of all this work, with lectures, with conversations with small groups and individuals, and by making drafts of the work available for comment, all important ways of hearing as many voices and opinions as possible. Fortunately, I will be able to spend the month of February 2002 in Juchitán, listening and responding.

We play a pivotal role in interpreting a culture to itself and to others (Kemper and Royce 1997; Royce and Kemper n.d., 1998). That role engenders keen ethical obligations. This is true for ethnographers no matter how long or short their involvement may be. The role and all its attendant responsibilities do acquire weight and complexity with long-term commitment. You understand subtleties that escape notice early on; you and your hosts assume more vulnerable relationships with each other; as your own status in the profession grows so does your ability to mediate and to speak; you may become an authoritative voice both internally and externally. This latter, in Zapotec, a *binni guendabianni*, a wise or enlightened person, means not only being a repository of wisdom and knowledge but also having the willingness to use it for the good of the community and to be transformed by it. This is very far from the experience of even the most good-hearted fledgling ethnographer, and it is legitimate to ask whether or not we would take that first step knowing this possibility.

Ta Feli, the healer who is a special friend, said to me once that I was like a hummingbird, flying from one place to another, never lighting anywhere, never settling in a home. It may be true. What is true is that I am no longer "homesick." In my first long field stay, I longed for "home." Then, as my visits to Juchitán became more frequent, I longed for Juchitán whenever I was not there. Now I am "at home" wherever I am, but know it is only momentary.

Ta Feli, along with other friends and family, has identified particular qualities I can contribute to the larger community. Every Zapotec has them and, when you make a commitment to *guendalisaa*, you agree to use them for the common good. I am not asked to do extraordinary things. I am asked to view Juchitán with the eyes of my heart, to turn my particular kind of wisdom to enlighten, to speak the truth, to come back. My contributions are valued; my shortcomings forgiven. What more could one want?

Notes

To the generations of Juchitecos who have been my family, friends, and teachers— *diuxquixe pe laatu.*

1. The history of scholarly interest in Juchitán and, more broadly, in the Zapotec of the Isthmus of Tehuantepec is an interesting one. Before my own research, the most recent comprehensive work had been reported by Miguel Covarrubias (1946) in his well-known book, *Mexico South: The Isthmus of Tehuantepec.* While the cultural persistence of the Zapotec as a people is what drew me to Juchitán in the 1960s, I also was intrigued by the lack of attention to their situation since Covarrubias. Since the time of my initial involvement in Juchitán, other scholars have done research there or elsewhere in the isthmus, drawn by the distinctive features that make the Isthmus Zapotec stand apart from other indigenous groups and from Mexicans at large. For example, Beverly López Chiñas (1973) wrote about gender in nearby Tehuantepec, especially the barrio of San Blas, while Leigh Binford (1985) was attracted by the issues of land tenure, social classes, and political conflict. Two political scientists—Howard Campbell (1994; Campbell et al. 1993) and Jeffrey Rubin (1997)—have written about the unusual political climate in Juchitán, centering around the Coalición de Campesinos y Estudiantes del Istmo (COCEI) movement. While we know of each other's work, we have not worked collaboratively nor as a team.

References Cited

Binford, Leigh
(1985) "Political conflict and land tenure in the Mexican Isthmus of Tehuantepec." *Journal of Latin American Studies* 17:179–200.

Campbell, Howard
(1994) *Zapotec Renaissance: Ethnic Politics and Cultural Revivalism in Southern Mexico.* Albuquerque: University of New Mexico Press.

Campbell, Howard, Leigh Binford, Miguel Bartolomé, and Alicia Barnabas
(1993) *Zapotec Struggles: Histories, Politics, and Representations from Juchitán, Oaxaca.* Washington, D.C.: Smithsonian Institution.

Chiñas, Beverly L.
(1973) *The Isthmus Zapotecs: Women's Roles in Cultural Contexts.* New York: Holt, Rinehart and Winston.

Covarrubias, Miguel
(1946) *Mexico South: The Isthmus of Tehuantepec.* New York: Alfred A. Knopf.

Kemper, Robert V. and Anya Peterson Royce
(1997) "Ethical issues for social anthropologists in Mexico: A North American perspective." *Human Organization* 56 (4):479–483.

Read, Kenneth
(1965) *The High Valley*. New York: Charles Scribner's Sons.

Royce, Anya Peterson
(1974) "Dance as an indicator of social class and identity in Juchitán, Oaxaca," *CORD Research Annual VI*. New York: Committee on Research in Dance.
(1975) *Prestigio y Afiliación en una Comunidad Urbana: Juchitán, Oaxaca*. (Serie de Antropología Social No. 37) México, D.F.: Instituto Nacional Indigenista.
(1977) *The Anthropology of Dance*. Bloomington: Indiana University Press.
(1980) "Breve resúmen de la historia económica y social de Juchitán, Oaxaca," *El Satélite* (August) and *Noticias, Voz, y Imagen del Istmo* (August).
(1981) "Isthmus Zapotec households: Economic responses to scarcity and abundance," *Urban Anthropology* 10(3):269–286.
(1982) *Ethnic Identity: Strategies of Diversity*. Bloomington: Indiana University Press.
(1990) *Prestigio y Afiliación en una Comunidad Urbana: Juchitán, Oaxaca*. Mexico, D.F.: Colección Presencias, Dirección General de Publicaciones del Consejo Nacional para la Cultura y las Artes/INI. [reprint of 1975 INI edition]
(1992) "Music, dance, and fiesta: Definitions of Isthmus Zapotec community." *Latin American Anthropology Review* 3:51–60.
(1993) "Ethnicity, nationalism, and the role of the intellectual," Pp. 103–122 in Judith D. Toland (editor), *Ethnicity and the State*. Political and Legal Anthropology Vol. 9. New Brunswick, NJ: Transaction Press.

Royce, Anya Peterson and Robert V. Kemper
(n.d.) "Who is an Indian in Mexico? Perceptions and Performances." Unpublished manuscript.
(1998) "Finding a footing on the moral high ground: Connections, interventions, and more ethical implications." *Human Organization* 57(3):328–330.

Royce, Anya Peterson and Anthony Seeger
(1987) "Music, dance, and drama." Pp. 201–214 in Jack W. Hopkins (editor), *Latin America: Perspectives on a Region*. New York: Holmes & Meier Publishers.
(1997) "Music, dance, and drama: An anthropological perspective." Pp. 226–239 in Jack W. Hopkins (editor), *Latin America: Perspectives on a Region*. Second Edition. New York: Holmes & Meier Publishers.

Rubin, Jeffrey W.
(1997) *Decentering the Regime: Ethnicity, Radicalism, and Democracy in Juchitán, Mexico*. Durham, NC, and London: Duke University Press.

CHAPTER TWO

KATUTURA AND NAMIBIA:
THE PEOPLE, THE PLACE, AND THE FIELDWORK
Wade Pendleton

Introduction

My Namibian research did not start out as a long-term project but it has certainly turned out that way. It began in 1967 and still continues (see table 2.1). After the initial fieldwork in the 1960s and early 1970s, I was denied a visa to enter either Namibia or South Africa by the South African government. For thirteen years I did not visit the country, and I thought I might never be able to return. However, since 1987 I have been in Namibia almost every year, sometimes for extended stays of over two years each. In December 2000, I moved to Windhoek, capital of Namibia, where I am planning to live after my retirement from teaching in 2002.

The Katutura project is both about the people who live in this township located in suburban Windhoek and about the place itself. For me, the place has taken on an identity of its own because of my long interest in its development. I have seen the people and the place change over the years from being under the influence of apartheid, through the run-up to independence, and on to the postindependence era; from being "ruled" by South Africa to having a black majority democratic government. My involvement with Namibia has also changed to include, in addition to Katutura, projects throughout Namibia and the southern Africa region and to include applied anthropology/social science. My long-term fieldwork is not about a specific culture; it is about a place, the people who live there, and my involvement with both.

My Namibian experiences, both professional and personal, have profoundly shaped my life. I began the Katutura project as a "loner," but in the 1990s I have had lots of company from colleagues and friends. I owe a debt to the Namibians and to anthropology, and I have tried to make a few installments on that debt in recent years by teaching sociology and anthropology at the University of Namibia, training and mentoring Namibians, and working on a number of applied research projects at the university's research institute.

Walking home after getting married in Old Katutura. Photo by Wade Pendleton.

The Katutura Research

Description of the Research Site

Namibia is sparsely populated, with about 1.6 million people who are not evenly distributed around the country (UNDP 1997:20). The uneven distribution is due in part to regional inequalities in development, environmental conditions, and political history. About 60 percent of the population lives in the rural north, which makes up only about 15 percent of the land area of the country. Dependent primarily on communal subsistence farming, they are Bantu-speaking peoples, including the Owambo (living in the four north-central regions generally called the four Os), the five Kavango groups, and the two major Caprivi groups.[1]

The rural north is separated from central Namibia by a "veterinary" cordon fence that prevents livestock from entering the central part of the country. This fence was also the boundary demarcating the northern limit of white settler occupation. White settlers, primarily Afrikaners and Germans, own most of the commercial farming area in central Namibia, which occupies about 40 percent of the country's land but only 9 percent of the population, including Namibian farmworkers and their families. On some of the most marginal land in the country are found the rural central communal areas, making up about 20 percent of the land and occupied by about 6 percent of the population: the southern communal area (home to the Nama), the eastern communal areas (home to the Herero), and the western communal areas (home to the Damara). The Herero speak a Bantu language and the Nama and Damara speak a non-Bantu click language. About 25 percent of the national population lives in towns primarily in central Namibia, with almost 40 percent of the urban population concentrated in Windhoek and Katutura.

Table 2.1. Dates of Research/Visits to Katutura and Namibia

Dates	Months	Comments
1967	2	Preliminary visit to see if fieldwork could be conducted
1968–1969	18	Fieldwork for the Ph.D.
1970–1971	2	Fieldwork before and after teaching at Witwatersrand University in Johannesburg
1972–1973	2	Field visit before and after teaching at the University of Cape Town
1987	2	Sabbatical fieldwork after long absence caused by South Africa's refusal to issue a visa
1988–1990	9	HDL project in Katutura, Khomasdal, and Windhoek; SPSS workshop
1991–1993	24	First Katutura Survey of 369 households with data on 1,865 people. Topics included migration patterns and attitudes, household and individual demographics, and attitudes about urban life. Applied research projects at research institute of the University of Namibia, Katutura, included in some of these projects
1992 and 1994	6	Nationwide Namibian Broadcasting Corporation surveys for TV, radio, and marketing
1996–1998	36	Second Katutura Survey consisting of data on 524 households and 2,142 people; same topics as first survey. Teaching at the University of Namibia. Applied projects including the Namibian Migration Project and the Southern African Migration Project
2001	6	Working on the Southern African Migration Project
Total	107	

Katutura still bears some resemblance to the place I saw in 1967 when I first visited Namibia (then called South West Africa) as a young graduate student. At that time, the country was administered by the government of South Africa under a mandate from the League of Nations. The United Nations had been trying unsuccessfully to gain sovereignty over Namibia since 1948 when the United Nations was founded; at the core of the dispute was South Africa's illegal administration of the country and the implementation of apartheid policies. Only after a more than twenty-year-long war of liberation fought against South Africa by the South West African People's Organization (SWAPO) and internal resistance to apartheid policies by black (and some white) Namibians living in the country did Namibia became independent in March 1990.

The township of Katutura is located northwest of Windhoek, the capital of the country, about two and a half miles (4 km) from the center of town. The Windhoek municipality developed it in the 1950s as an apartheid township similar to other townships elsewhere in southern Africa. Only black Namibians could live there; a permit based on employment was necessary to obtain rental housing; housing was assigned on the basis of ethnicity; and blacks were viewed by the government and municipality as temporary urban residents who "ideally" would return to the rural/communal areas when they retired. Unemployed people had to leave Katutura and Windhoek if they were unable to find new work. During the apartheid years, urban migration was controlled by permits and passes needed to reside in Katutura. Since the 1980s, and especially after independence in 1990, people have been free to migrate to town, and many have done so.

Prior to the development of Katutura, black Namibians lived in a "location" west of Windhoek exclusively for "nonwhite" people, called the Windhoek Main Location. Separate residential areas called "locations," in which the indigenous African population lived apart from whites, have been part of the urban geography of Windhoek ever since the late nineteenth century. Some of the early Windhoek locations were occupational in character. During the German colonial period, *Truppenwerft* and the *Polizeiwerft* were for those employed by the *Schutztruppe* and the police, respectively, while others lived in huts throughout the town and its vicinity (Wagner 1951:89). *Werft* is the locally used German word for location, called *lokasie* in Afrikaans. The Nama word meaning "black people's place" is especially descriptive. After 1912 most black Namibians lived in the Windhoek Main Location. The government and the municipality informed people that the Windhoek Main Location was going to be closed, and they would have to move to Katutura. The Windhoek Main Location was called the Old Location after Katutura was built. People in the Old Location were opposed to moving to Katutura for many reasons: the requirement that they rent municipal houses and land which they were not allowed to own, the greater distance from Windhoek, the breakup of an established community that had been in existence for over fifty years, and general opposition to apartheid policies.

The very name, *Katutura*, which in Otjiherero means "we have no place to stay" or "a place where we do not stay," was suggested by local people as the name for the new township and was adopted by white authorities who did not understand the meaning. The name became a symbol of the opposition to the forced move. Opposition reached a peak on December 10, 1959, when a demonstration against the move turned into a confrontation with the police, who shot and killed 13 people and injured 42 (Jafta et al. 1995:39–40).[2] Subsequently, many people moved to Katutura because of fear and intimidation. The Old Location was closed in August 1968, and those people who had not moved were forced to leave. If apartheid urban planning had not been implemented in Windhoek, the modern-day urban geography of the area would be very different; most black Namibians would live close to the central business district and their places of employment.

The people of Katutura belong primarily to four major ethnic groups: Owambo, Herero, Damara, and Nama. They and others have been migrating to Windhoek from all over the country for over one hundred years. During the German colonial era, the Herero and Nama were forced to come to town to work after their devastating defeat by the German colonial army. Many Damara also came to town to escape the conflicts taking place around them. Herero, Nama, and Damara people have continued to migrate to Windhoek in recent years. The Owambo from the rural north first came on migrant labor contracts; and, later, when the contract labor system was abolished, they came on their own. Relatively few people have come from the Kavango and Caprivi areas to the east. In addition to the rural/communal areas, people have migrated to Katutura from the smaller towns, commercial farms, and other African countries.

Growth and Change of Katutura

Many changes have taken place in Katutura since 1968. The original Katutura was about one-fifth the size of the current township. It consisted of five ethnic areas, four for the major ethnic groups, and a mixed area for everybody else. About 20,000 people lived in the township in 1968, including about 4,000 Owambo men living in a migrant labor compound near the entrance to Katutura. By 1997, Katutura's population had surpassed 110,000 and was growing daily. The urban geography of Katutura had already started changing in the 1970s when "Soweto" was added to Katutura, the name being taken from the Soweto township in Johannesburg. Soweto housing was municipal rental housing much the same as in old Katutura. However, beginning in the 1980s, with the abolishment of apartheid legislation, the township began to expand dramatically. New areas of Katutura were opened where houses and land could be purchased. These new areas virtually surrounded old Katutura, which became known locally as the old location. To the east, Sjandumbala (which means "more and more houses") was added adjacent to the old Owambo area; to the north Golgotha was developed; and to the south Freedom Square, Grysblok ("grey area"), and Bloedrivier ("blood river") were constructed. The Grysblok/Bloedrivier area is also called Lubowski by some, after the assassination of Anton Lubowski, an important SWAPO member. To the west, Luxury Hill (also called Rykmansdorp—"rich person's town") was developed, where better-quality housing was built on larger land parcels. Luxury Hill was probably planned to attract more affluent members of the Katutura community who might have moved into Windhoek. When Luxury Hill was developed, the future status of South West Africa was still uncertain and, although apartheid had officially been abolished, the structure of apartheid was still in place. Possibly, the urban planners were trying to keep people in Katutura.

The compound for Owambo migrant workers was closed and demolished in 1987, and the compound residents found accommodation elsewhere in Katutura;[3] some moved to private "minicompounds" where they lived in rented rooms with other migrants and ate in a common area. The "single quarters" had become a large vibrant community by 1991 with a large open-air market; it was renovated during 1996–1997. By 1993, a few shanty areas had developed in Katutura, but by 1997 the shanty areas with informal housing occupied about 25 percent of the township.

At the same time that Luxury Hill was developed for the more affluent, an area northwest of old Katutura was developed primarily for men displaced from the old migrant labor compound; this area became known as Hakahana (Oshiwambo for "hurry up"), and many Owambo men moved there. The Hakahana area is characterized by many small houses with one or two rooms, a number of traditional huts which are built adjacent to the concrete block houses, and many "Cuca Shops" where food and drink may be purchased. Housing in old Katutura and Soweto could now be purchased from the municipality, and some people took advantage of these opportunities to own the land and houses they had been occupying. To the west of Luxury Hill and Soweto, another area was developed in the mid-1980s which became known as Wanaheda (an acronym for Wambo-Nama-Herero-Damara) and which is itself almost as large as the old Katutura. For a while, it was also called Samora Machel after the first president of Mozambique, but that name did not last. In the 1990s, the major areas to be developed were Okuryangava to the north, also almost as large as the old Katutura, and Gorengava to the west of Wanaheda.

Katutura's development has primarily been west and north. A buffer zone still exists between Katutura and Khomasdal (the former "colored township") that is a sort of no-man's land where no housing has been constructed. This buffer zone does not effectively stop the movement of people between these two areas. However, the "western bypass," constructed during the early 1980s, effectively guaranteed that Katutura would never become part of northwest Windhoek. The western bypass is a double-lane divided roadway, which was originally fenced, that divides the suburbs of northwest Windhoek (Windhoek west) from Katutura. Although the "fence came down" because so many people walked across the road between Katutura and Windhoek, this roadway is an effective physical barrier between the two. However, it has not prevented people from relocating from Khomasdal and Katutura to the various suburbs of Windhoek.

The older and more established areas of Katutura are called the Central Katutura area including Wanaheda, Golgotha, Soweto, Luxury Hill, and the other older parts of the township; the newer part on the perimeter of the township is the North-West area. The 1997 population of Central Katutura was about 70,000 people, with about 40,000 living in the North-West area. Many people still refer to the entire area as Katutura. It is the fastest growing area in Windhoek and accounts for more than 60 percent of the urban area's population.

Methodology and Fieldwork

The 1960s Perspective on Urban Anthropology

My 1960s research was conducted from the perspective of urban anthropology and situational analysis. I took the perspective that for research to be urban anthropology it had to show how the city influenced the lives of the people being studied (Gulick 1968). I tried to do this by using Mitchell's (1966:48–51) situational approach, organizing my data on urban social structure into Mitchell's external determinants: (1) political and administrative limitations, (2) economic differentiation,

(3) heterogeneity, (4) population movement, (5) demographic disproportion, and (6) population density. Data on social relationships were divided into three categories representing different types of social interaction: categorical, structural, and personal (Mitchell 1966:49–50, 1969:9–10). Barth (1969), Epstein (1958), Gluckman (1960), and Mitchell (1956) all influenced my understanding of ethnicity, "tribalism" ("detribalism"), and social categorization. I was much more influenced by the view from the "Copperbelt" of Central Africa, that is, the Rhodes-Livingstone/Manchester school of Africanists, than the view from "Chicago," that is, the Park, Redfield, Lewis legacy in American anthropology (Hannerz 1980). I tried to develop a model for the stratification of Katutura and Windhoek based on racial and ethnic social categories as well as caste and class. It was within the context of these theoretical ideas that I researched and wrote about the highly structured, racially stratified, apartheid society of Katutura, Windhoek, and Namibia. However, not all anthropologists shared this perspective about urban anthropology or even accepted the idea that urban anthropology was a legitimate field within anthropology. There was even more uncertainty about appropriate fieldwork methods and how to conceptualize the culture concept within a heterogeneous urban setting.

Doing Fieldwork in the 1960s

I was one of the first foreign students to have the opportunity to conduct research in Namibia while it was colonized and occupied by South Africa. The few anthropological studies conducted in Namibia were primarily by Afrikaans-speaking *Volkerkunde* students from South Africa who worked within the ideology of apartheid.[4] Doing fieldwork in Katutura in the 1960s was not easy. As a young, white, male foreign graduate student wandering around in Katutura, I was probably a strange sight. Most whites only came to Katutura to sell things or look for sex; I had nothing to sell and I was not looking for sex, although it was offered. I often found myself going to interviews that were canceled, trying to interview people who were reluctant to talk, and struggling to understand seven different languages. I had no base from which to work in Katutura; when an interview was over I had to leave. Initially, I had to obtain a permit to enter Katutura every time I wanted to go; later I got permits for several months at a time. Some black Namibians suspected I was a spy for the South African government, while whites suspected I was spying for the United Nations. Both extremes of suspicion reflected the prevailing political climate. The black population resented and was hostile toward the South African government and municipal authorities who enforced apartheid policies. In the late 1960s, the recommendations of the Odendaal Commission Report (Government of South Africa 1964) to formalize apartheid in Namibia were rigorously implemented, and the country was administered like a fifth province of South Africa.

My research was a wide-ranging study of urban social structure, urban migration, social relationships, and voluntary associations. Black Namibians were the major study population. At the beginning of the research, many people were suspicious of my motives. People declined to be interviewed and some even expressed open hostility. While I was going through municipal records, an angry Afrikaner clerk wanted to know why I did not study my own "Black problem" at home. Several times the security police contacted people I had interviewed. Until that sort of interference stopped, people were reluctant to be interviewed. I suspect it stopped because the police and special branch officers got bored waiting for me to do something provocative. After three or four months, people got used to seeing me, and my presence aroused less suspicion. There were other difficulties. The Old Location closed in 1968, and people were forced to move to Katutura under protest. Katutura had concrete block municipal housing, and rental costs were fifty times greater than in the Old Location. People were experiencing much hardship, and an inquiring white anthropologist was not always welcome. I recall going with a research assistant into a private home where beer was sold, sitting down and talking to a few people, and then watching as my assistant stopped a drunk customer from hitting me on the head with a beer bottle. People in some ethnic groups were harder to reach than others. Interviews with Herero residents were totally unsuccessful until I met with Chief Clemens Kapuuo, a leader of Old Location residents who refused to move to Katutura, who spread the word that it was all right to talk to me.

Several different types of data were collected during the 1960s research. One database was an opportunity sample of one hundred informants interviewed with the assistance of two black Namibian research assistants. It was not possible to survey the townships in any systematic or random manner because of the suspicion and even hostility with which interviews with strangers were met. Advance scheduling of interviews was necessary, and usually a friend or relative of the person being interviewed sponsored me. Limited participant observation was possible. I had opportunities to meet informally with key informants and to attend social activities in Katutura. An offer to take free wedding photographs brought many wedding invitations. It was never easy to move about Katutura and be inconspicuous. I relied heavily on my two research assistants, for without their help and goodwill, the research would not have been possible. They made introductions, explained people's behavior, arranged interviews, obtained invitations to parties, and explained my presence. In the 1960s, the presence of an anthropologist asking questions and seeking interviews with people was a strange and unusual event.

Perhaps because of the difficulties interviewing people, I made extensive use of public records. I conducted surveys of employment contracts, Katutura housing records and visitor's permits, travel pass records, magistrate and church marriage records, and municipal reports. All of my data analysis was done manually. It appears obvious now, but was not so clear then, that the extensive use of these records was a result of the difficulty of interacting with people. Katutura, Windhoek, and Namibia were rigidly stratified places where apartheid was enforced on everybody. I made many requests to be allowed to visit the rural communal areas in the north and in central Namibia; however, I was never allowed to visit these areas. My personal experience of Namibia was limited to Windhoek, the other towns, the commercial farming area, and my occasional drives through communal areas when I hoped not to be caught by the police. In spite of the fact that the fieldwork was not easy, I was reluctant even then to leave the field. I only left after Elizabeth Colson (my dissertation chairperson) wrote to me saying that my support would be terminated if I did not come back. She said it was time to return to Berkeley, write up my dissertation, and get a job.

The 1980s/1990s Perspective on Urban Anthropology

Unlike the 1960s, it is no longer necessary to justify urban anthropology as a legitimate field (cf. Kemper 1991). Urban anthropology has expanded greatly and, although its domain seems to defy precise definition (cf. Breitborde 1994:3–9; Sanjek 1990:154), in most places the use of both qualitative and quantitative research methods is accepted. However, when I presented a seminar on the Katutura project at the University of Cape Town in 1992, I was surprised that it was still necessary to defend quantitative methods and applied urban anthropology.[5]

Migration, social stratification, poverty, ethnicity, and social organization were the major topics of my Katutura research, and they are still major themes of urban anthropology (Kemper 1991:383). Kemper (1979) has suggested a model for urban migration research that has both macro and micro levels: macro in the sense that structural features shape the socio-cultural-historical context within which urban life exists, and micro in the sense that individual voices can be heard (cf. Mitchell 1969). I have used a macro/micro model for recent research and publication about Katutura as well as for the national migration studies that I recently directed at the Social Sciences Division of the Multi-Disciplinary Research Centre (MRC) at the University of Namibia: the Namibian Migration Project (NMP; Pendleton and Frayne 1998) and the Namibian component of the Southern African Migration Project (SAMP; Frayne and Pendleton 1998, 2000).

Doing Fieldwork in the 1980s and 1990s

During the 1980s, an interim government under South Africa's authority administered Namibia, most of the apartheid laws were abolished, and many changes took place. In 1987, after a thirteen-year absence, I returned to a changed Namibia and it took me a little time to adapt. For example, when I met Legio Skrywer, one of my research assistants from the 1960s, in Keetmanshoop (a town in the south), he told me to come over for a drink. I asked him how I should get to the location, and he informed me that he no longer lived in the location! When I met Namibian friends on Windhoek's main street (now called Independence Avenue instead of Kaiser Strasse), we shook hands and talked without being conspicuous.

I was able to have an office at BRICKS (a community development NGO) in Katutura and to recruit many fieldworkers for a citywide study, called the Health and Daily Living (HDL) Project, conducted during 1988–1989 (Pendleton and DuBois 1990). In addition to fieldworkers recruited with the assistance of BRICKS, I worked with Annelie Odendaal from the Sociology Department at the Academy (the forerunner of the University of Namibia), and we selected some sociology students who were trained to do data collection in Windhoek and Khomasdal. The University Centre for Studies in Namibia (TUCSIN) also offered me a base to work from at that time, and I spent many evenings using their computer to enter data. The Nyae Nyae Bushman Foundation was also based at TUCSIN, and I had the opportunity to visit with various people associated with the project, including Megan Biesele and John Marshall.[6]

When I returned to Namibia in 1987, I did so with new interests and experience in quantitative research methods and applied research. After two years as a visiting professor at the University of Hawaii (1979 through 1981) and with the experience of working on the Hawaii–Samoa Stress Study, I had developed an interest in quantitative methods and applied anthropology. I added an applied anthropology emphasis to the master's program at San Diego State University and included in the program a course that I developed on quantitative data analysis using SPSS. However, I found myself teaching applied courses with only limited experience in applied work. During the 1980s, I worked with Bruce Harris on a street people project and with Al Velasco on a development project in Barrio Logan, both in San Diego. I used to conduct my applied seminars in Barrio Logan during those years. Several of my students did applied master's theses on urban San Diego topics. However, my applied experience was soon to increase when I started going back to Namibia.

I was enthusiastic about the prospect of doing a follow-up study of Katutura, but I had no idea how far-reaching the influence of Namibia would be on my work and my life. The subsequent independence of Namibia in March 1990 marked the beginning of a new era for the country, with significant economic development and change. Independence also saw the founding of the University of Namibia, which has become my base in recent years.

The new research projects in Katutura were based on systematic, stratified sampling methods, trained fieldwork teams, and modern quantitative data analysis techniques. Qualitative methods such as participant observation and case studies were also used with much more success than in the past. It was easier to move about in Katutura, visit people, conduct interviews, and make use of research assistants and fieldworkers. It was also more fun to do the research. The hostility and suspicion of the past have given way to much more open and accessible opportunities for research. Like Namibians who gained their freedom in 1990, I also gained mine in the sense that I could now travel anywhere in the country and work on both basic and applied research projects on a variety of topics such as rural and urban development, national radio and television broadcasting, internal and cross-border migration, and poverty. Many of these projects were commissioned by the Namibian government and provided me with an opportunity to have input into official policy and planning.

Major Findings from the Katutura Research

Major findings reported in my 1974 book and in other publications (Pendleton 1970, 1975, 1976, 1978, 1979) were (1) how harsh, humiliating, and pervasive was the imposed apartheid system, (2) how the ethnic and racial categorization of people affected their view of who they were, (3) how the social structure influenced people's lives, (4) how people adapted to the system, (5) how the society was racially stratified with whites on the top and blacks on the bottom, with most people in Katutura poor with little economic differentiation, and (6) how apartheid was more rigorously implemented in Namibia than in South Africa. Mitchell's theoretical model of external determinants and types of social relationships provided the framework within which to describe these findings.

The HDL Project in 1988–1989 was the first citywide study in Namibia based on a representative sampling of the whole urban population (Pendleton and DuBois 1990). Although most apartheid legislation had been abolished by 1988, the HDL findings were that people and households in Katutura were significantly less well off than people and households in Khomasdal and Windhoek: (1) they earned far less money; (2) a larger percentage of people were unemployed; (3) smaller percentages of people were in professional and managerial professions; (4) larger percentages of people had less education; and (5) larger percentages were female-centered households, which had the least resources of all household types. Other results from the HDL scales showed that Katutura people were more at risk for negative life change events, drank more alcoholic beverages, reported more problems related to drinking, and had lifestyle patterns related to their poverty.

The Namibian Institute for Social and Economic Research (NISER) was founded in 1989,[7] and I was fortunate to be able to work on the first research projects that were undertaken: the 1991 Katutura Survey (Pendleton 1991) and a baseline socioeconomic study of the Oshakati/Ondangwa urban area in the north of the country (Pendleton, LeBeau, and Tapscott 1993). The 1991 Katutura Survey was part of a larger project on urbanization in postindependence Windhoek (Frayne 1992). The major topics of the 1991 Katutura Survey were urban migration, urban/rural linkages, individual and household demographics, social problems, housing, and attitudes about urban life. Results from the 1991 Katutura Survey, case studies, and participant observation in Katutura, as well as data from various other projects,[8] were all utilized for new books on Katutura (Pendleton 1994, 1996). The focus of the Katutura research had shifted from apartheid research to basic and applied urban anthropology and social science.

Major findings about Katutura reported in these publications fall into three broad categories: change, stratification, and urbanization. Many changes have taken place in postapartheid Katutura. People are free to travel, take up residence, and look for employment. Since over half the housing in Katutura is privately owned, many people can build on to their houses themselves, rent out rooms for additional income, sell their homes, or leave them to their children. Housing and business ownership do not depend on racial classification; they depend on the ability to pay. The ability to pay has, in fact, become a very important factor of life in postapartheid Katutura, and economic stratification has become a reality of life for people in Katutura households. About half the households are below the minimum household level of subsistence (HSL), and half are above it.[9] For those below the HSL, getting by on scarce resources is a way of life. Households in old Katutura are not as well off as those in new Katutura; households in Luxury Hill are substantially better off than those in old Katutura; female-centered households have a difficult time getting by on limited resources; and male-centered households in Wanaheda and Hakahana do better than female-centered households. Men in male-centered households have more mobility and substantially fewer dependent children to take care of, which in part explains their somewhat better situation. There are wealthy people in Katutura today and there is much more employment diversity, but there still are many poor and unemployed.

Looking for work is a way of life for many residents of Katutura. About 35 percent of the adult population who want to work cannot find employment, although some of these people have skills and work experience. High unemployment and the growth of the informal sector of the economy are both closely related to the rapid urbanization that Katutura is experiencing. However, the informal sector in Katutura is dominated primarily by trading and hawking, with little fabrication or recycling of products such as one sees in other African cities (Norval and Namoya 1992). The brewing and selling of beer from private homes is a major informal sector activity by women.

Rapid urbanization and unemployment have created social problems. Street children are a common sight in Windhoek. Crime in Katutura and Windhoek has never been higher. Many people have become desperate for money, and robberies and muggings occur almost daily. There are gangs that operate out of Katutura, and the *botsotsos* are feared by all. The high consumption of alcoholic beverages such as *!kharib, tombo,* and bottled beer is widespread, and those who have the least resources drink the most. Drinking has been a feature of township life from the first locations, but it has reached unprecedented levels today. Other important household problem areas are food, debts, money, housing, and unemployment (Pendleton 1997:21).

The strength of ethnic identity is less today than it was before, but stereotypes are still strong, as LeBeau (1993) found in her study of ethnicity. However, many social, economic, and ethnic boundaries no longer coincide as they did in the past, and this has reduced the significance of ethnic categories. For example, the ethnic endogamy percentage in Katutura today is much lower than it was before, and the areas of new Katutura are much more ethnically integrated than the old areas, where one still can see the door letters and numbers indicating the ethnic section in which the house is located; for example, D2/21 referring to Damara section 2, house 21. However, ethnic identity is still the strongest social identity for many who are poor. Those with professional and skilled employment are able to associate with people on the basis of occupational or recreational interests, but those who are poor and unemployed have few social identities other than ethnicity.

Katutura will remain a location for a long time yet. The reasons are many. The urban structure of the apartheid society is still in place. About 60 percent of the population of Windhoek lives in Katutura on about 20 percent of the urban area's land, and few have serious prospects of living elsewhere in Windhoek. The cost of land and housing will keep the poor in Katutura, and the poor are still primarily blacks. Those blacks who achieve upward mobility may choose to remain in Katutura, living in nicer homes on larger lots, perhaps in Katutura's Luxury Hill; or they may move to Luxury Hill in Windhoek or some other Windhoek suburb where they fit in socioeconomically. Many blacks live in Windhoek today, but they are middle- and upper-class people whose employment allows Windhoek residence. Some areas such as Hochland Park (the site of the Old Location) and Windhoek West are integrated, but others are not. Under the force of economic segregation, ethnic segregation will continue for the foreseeable future.

A Model for Rural–Urban Migration to Katutura

The chief town planner of Windhoek estimates that, if migration to Windhoek continues at its present rate, the population will double by about 2014 to 400,000; about 50 percent of the urban area's housing will be shanties; and Katutura will no longer be able to accommodate all the shanties and low-cost housing. Natural increase accounts for some of Katutura's growth, but a significant amount is due to urban migration. Why has migration to Katutura and Windhoek become so popular since independence? What kind of model can be used to understand the migration? The model I use looks at causes at both the macro and micro levels. The major macro factors are political history, poverty, population and environment, and culture. They define the context within which people make decisions about migration. The model is developed more fully in Pendleton and Frayne (2000) and Frayne and Pendleton (2001). Following is a brief description of each factor.

Political History

The colonial occupation, including wars with both the German and South African armies and the implementation of a capitalistic economy, established radical inequalities in development (regional inequalities) that still exist today in spite of modest rural development since independence. In addition, the rural communal areas lack income-producing activities, and crop/livestock production methods are at the basic subsistence level. For examples, see Yaron, Janssen, and Maamberua (1992) for the Kavango; and Directorate of Rural Development (1992), Iken et al. (1994), Couch and Pendleton (1998) for the eastern and southern communal areas. Regional inequalities and lack of income-producing activities influence rural–urban migration to Katutura.

Poverty

For a developing country, Namibia has a relatively high gross national income (GNI) of US$1,960 (1995; NEPRU 1998:54–55). However, this masks the reality that many households live in poverty.[10] The Lorenz curve for individual income, based on the 1993–1994 household income and expenditure study by the Central Statistics Office (1996:143–144), reports a Gini coefficient of 0.70, reflecting the highest skewed income distribution reported worldwide (UNDP 1997:9). Ten percent of households (about 5 percent of the population) account for about 44 percent of total private consumption, while the remaining 90 percent of households (about 95 percent of the population) account for the remaining 56 percent of total private consumption (Central Statistics Office 1996:15). Annual per capita income for the rural north is below US$200; for the rural central areas, about US$200; for the commercial farming areas, under US$300; and for the towns, estimated at US$1,275 (Central Statistics Office 1996:147, 274). Because of widespread rural poverty, people migrate to Windhoek and Katutura in the hope that their situation will improve.

Population and Environment

The Namibian population has an estimated doubling time of about twenty years (Arowolo 1994:103; Frayne 1993:202) and is not evenly distributed as a result of regional inequalities in both environmental conditions and political history. Due to poor rainfall and low carrying capacity, the rural central land is widely recognized as marginal. The location of the rural central communal areas on the west, east, and south of the commercial farming area reflects a history of much commercial farm area claimed as traditional land by the Herero, Damara, Nama, and Bushmen, but usurped by the German and South African colonial governments for occupation by white settler farmers (primarily Afrikaners and Germans). The Namibian constitution does not allow for ancestral land claims; however, such claims are a frequent agenda item at land conferences due to population pressure on existing communal land areas.

Drought is endemic to Namibia and is the primary environmental factor that impacts migration. Naeraa and associates (1993:433) report that the migration of household members to urban areas and the sending of children to other relatives in rural and urban areas are common coping responses at the household level to the influence of drought in Namibia. Population pressure and drought also are important factors in rural–urban migration (cf. Devereux et al. 1993).

Culture

The rural–urban migration experience is reflected in various terms and concepts found in Namibian languages. Among the Owambo, someone who has moved from a rural area and stays in town is referred to as *Ombwiti*. If you frequently visit your rural area, then you will not be called *Ombwiti*. People who do not visit have broken their ties and are *Ombwiti*; they have lost their roots. People who are born in town and stay there are called *Ondakwatwa*. The root *twa* is a common Bantu root for foreigner or stranger. Someone who goes to town for the first time is called *Kashuku*. Going to town to look for work is a little like an initiation ritual for young people. Coming to Windhoek or other towns in central Namibia to look for work is called *Uushimba* (Oshiwambo). However, the term does not apply to Ondangwa, Oshakati, Rundu, or Katima Mulilo, the urban communal towns of the north. These places are not seen as "foreign" towns; they are considered local towns and are different sorts of places. This may be to a large extent because the ethnic and sociocultural makeup of such places is both relatively familiar and homogeneous. Similar terms about the urban migration experience exist for people in the Kavango and Caprivi. However, the Herero, Damara, and Nama do not have terms like *Ombwiti*, which reflects their long experience with town life in the central part of Namibia.

The words and the meanings attached to the migration experience suggest conflicting attitudes about the experience of rural–urban migration and the phenomenon of urbanization. Towns are perceived to offer opportunities for alternative lifestyles that simply do not exist in the rural areas. From this perspective, towns appear desirable and people who have done well there are admired. However, the process of becoming urban also represents a threat to traditional values and to kinship relations, particularly in those urban areas where ethnic heterogeneity is the greatest. And this threat is greatest for those from the rural north. The connotations of the urban phenomenon are negative, and migrants are seen as people at risk of alienation. While all communities probably share this ambivalence toward change, material advancement, and modernity, ethnic groups that are predominantly urban tend to emphasize the positive aspects of the urbanization process, while more rural-based communities, such as those in the north, view town life and townspeople with greater skepticism.

The macro features create a context within which only some people decide to migrate; others do not. Micro data reveal the actual patterns of migration from migration history data collected as part of the 1996 Katutura Survey and the Namibian Migration Project (NMP). Case studies also provide more qualitative detail about migration strategies. Katutura is an important destination for the Owambo, Herero, Damara, and Nama. There are established communities of people from each of these groups in Katutura, and new migrants often stay with kin or friends prior to establishing their own independent household. This helps to explain why people from the Caprivi and the Kavango rarely migrate to Katutura even though the Kavango is about the same distance from Windhoek as the rural north home of the Owambo: there are no established communities of people from the Kavango and Caprivi in Katutura. However, this could soon change with paved roads and combi-taxis regularly traveling to Windhoek from these areas. Because the Owambo migrated to Windhoek on labor contracts during the apartheid years, and some Owambo people managed to remain in town in spite of the regulations against it, established Owambo communities have developed. Herero, Damara, and Nama people have been living in Windhoek throughout the colonial period, and they come to Katutura from the rural central communal areas and other towns. The three major reasons urban migrants give for coming to Katutura are economics (jobs and money), family issues (e.g., change of residence due to marriage or a death in the family, or simply to move in with relatives), and education. Other less important reasons are living conditions, environmental factors, and health care. Many migrants list multiple reasons for migration, reflecting the complex nature of their decisions to migrate. Men and women migrate for the same reasons, but the relative importance is different; economics is more important to men and family/living conditions are more important to women. Of the adult female migrants to Katutura, almost half have come in recent years, indicating a substantial increase in urban migration by women. Hansen (1997:45–46) also reports a substantial increase in women urban migrants to Lusaka, Zambia.

Case studies of migrants to Katutura show that some think that they will easily find good employment, and they are shocked when they realize it will not happen. Others know that jobs are hard to find, but they come anyway. It may be somewhat analogous to playing the lottery when you continue to play with the small hope that you may win. The case study of a thirty-two-year-old Owambo man from the rural north is a typical example of rural–urban migrants. He was influenced by relatives and friends in the rural area who had worked in Windhoek and had bicycles and nice clothes. He discussed migrating with his family members, who supported the idea because they expected him to send money to them in the rural north. He came to Katutura because he knew he would find people from his rural area, and he came to find work and earn money. Rural poverty was the major reason for migration. He has not found a regular job and earns money hawking (selling earrings and nail polish in Katutura). He wants a job in construction because he thinks it is the only work he is qualified to do. He says his time in Katutura and Windhoek has been difficult. He says he heard that jobs were easy to find in Windhoek and now he knows it was a lie. Some of the people he knows have left Katutura and returned to the rural north, but he thinks they will be back because "you can't stay there looking at your family starving." He thinks that more people from his village in the north will come to Windhoek and that some may be lucky and find employment.

Through my work at NISER, the Social Sciences Division of the Multi-Disciplinary Research Centre, and the Sociology Department at the University of Namibia, I have taught many Namibians about anthropology, sociology, and research methods. They have been trained in both qualitative and quantitative research methods; some of the skills have included data entry, data analysis, proposal writing, and report preparation. It began in 1988, when I conducted a workshop on data analysis using SPSS-PC for people at the Academy, the forerunner of the University of Namibia. Many of the people who now do data analysis with SPSS were my students in that workshop. The European Community funded subsequent workshops for NISER, and Namibians were trained on various NISER and SSD projects. A data-processing lab modeled on the one at San Diego State University was established at NISER. That lab continues at SSD, supervised by a Namibian whom I trained, where all SSD survey projects as well as many contract projects are processed. Three of my San Diego State University students have completed master's theses on Namibian topics, two of which included Katutura data (Black 1995; Couch 1996; and LeBeau 1991). Other European and Namibian students I assisted with their postgraduate research in Katutura include Amunyela (1998) and Sandberg (1998). I have also assisted colleagues at the University of Namibia with postgraduate degree research.

Impact on the People

Because my 1974 book was banned in Namibia, I assumed that people there were unaware of it. However, that was not the case. In 1990, I met Dr. Peter Katjavivi, now the vice-chancellor of the University of Namibia, and he told me how valuable my book on Katutura had been. He said it was one of the few non–South African sources of information about what was happening to black Namibians in the capital. He added that my book was widely read by Namibians in exile. During my visits to Namibia between 1987 and 1990, I also met people who opened desk drawers and pulled out copies of the 1974 book (sometimes photocopied) that they had obtained and kept hidden.

Some people had unpleasant experiences because of my 1960s research and the publication of my findings. Beatrice Sandelowsky (a Namibian educator, archaeologist, and founder of the University Centre for Studies in Namibia) only told me in 1994 how she had been called into the security police office in 1978, shown a copy of the book, and asked if she agreed with the findings. She said she did and was told to leave the country; but she did not leave. The security police also questioned Legio Skrywer, one of my research assistants, because of his contact with me.

Since 1987, my work in Namibia has had a different reception. My 1994 book was published in Windhoek, has been widely read and commented on locally, and is used in classes at the University of Namibia. The book launch was held at the National Gallery in Windhoek, and it was attended by over a hundred Namibians and reported in the local media. It was a very moving experience for me to launch a book about Katutura in the country where my first book had been banned. The Planning Department of the Windhoek municipality, ministries of the Namibian government, and nongovernmental organizations (NGOs) have used my research and writing on Katutura. The research in Katutura and elsewhere in Namibia has provided me with the opportunity to train many Namibians in fieldwork methods, data analysis, and report writing. Not only have I taught research methods to Namibians at the University of Namibia, I also have lectured to tour guides and interested members of the public about Katutura at the Namibian Academy for Tourism and Hospitality.

The Future

Now that I am planning to live in retirement (after 2002) in Namibia, I hope to conduct a survey of Katutura every five years and to continue participant observation and the collection of case studies on a regular basis. These surveys and other ongoing projects should ensure that information about Katutura will still be collected in the future. My influence in the SSD and in the Sociology Department at the University of Namibia has created an interest in continuing the Katutura research. The SSD data archive contains datasets, codebooks, and copies of research reports from all the SSD projects including the 1991 and 1996 Katutura surveys. Copies of the applied reports for SSD also have been placed in the applied anthropology documentation project at the University of Kentucky.

Katutura has also become a popular place to conduct research, and I have assisted other scholars with their projects. Research in Katutura has been conducted from various perspectives and includes cultural geography (Peyroux and Graefe 1995), anthropology (Gibson 1991), history (Lau 1993), politics (Pendleton et al. 1993), edited books with articles on various topics about Katutura (Melber 1988 and von Garnier 1986), training (Lewis and van Rooi 1991), health (Cogill and Kiugu 1990), ethnicity (Diener 1995). Current postgraduate research in progress focuses on healers (LeBeau) and national identity (Kristin Kjaeret).

I was reluctant to leave Namibia in the 1960s and I am even more reluctant to leave today. I have frequently said that I get more satisfaction from doing research and teaching in Namibia than in the United States. My short-term fieldwork has become a long-term commitment to research, teaching, and development work. It is about much more than Katutura.

How did this happen? I think the answer for me is that I found a niche where anthropology and social science had a purpose and use, and I did also. At first, it was about apartheid and the inequalities of the social system and how that had affected people. Now it is about change, development, and making use of anthropology and social science to train, teach, and work on development issues.

Notes

I would like to acknowledge the following people for their valuable comments and suggestions on previous drafts of this chapter: Bruce Frayne, Robert V. Kemper, Linda McPhee, Beatrice Sandelowsky, Hendrie Scheun, and Cheryl Simpson.

1. My use of ethnic group categories is informed by the extensive literature on "tribalism" and ethnicity in the global and African context (e.g., Hannerz 1980:119–162; Southall 1997:38–51). I have used *ethnic* rather than *tribal* because of the many valid criticisms in the literature for *tribe* and *tribal; ethnic group* also denotes a situation in which one group or subculture is in contact with other groups, which is the case in Namibia.

With the possible exception of some San and Himba groups living in remote areas of the country, all ethnic groups in Namibia are part of the larger social system (both urban and rural) involving other groups as well as the national economy. The major ethnic categories (and languages usually associated with the categories) mentioned in this chapter are Owambo (Oshiwambo; including the seven related ethnic groups Kuanyama, Ndonga, Kuambi, Ngondjera, Kualuthu, Mbalantu, and Ndolonkati-Eunda), Herero (including Himba-Otjiherero), Nama (Nama), Damara (Nama), Afrikaner (Afrikaans), German (German), and Coloured, which refers to people of both African and European ancestry (Afrikaans and English). Certain apartheid-era terms such as *Coloured* are still used widely in Namibia in spite of their obvious objectionable "racial" quality. The situation for the Kavango and Caprivi regions is more complicated. People from these areas are generally identified with the area from which they come (when they are outside these areas, elsewhere in Namibia) because of the complicated ethnic/language situations of these areas. For example, Kavango people usually speak Rukwamgali but may "ethnically" be Hambukushu, Gciriku, Sambu, Bunza, or Kwangali. Major ethnic groups of the Caprivi are the Mafwe and Basubia, who also speak Lozi. Thus, some ethnic terms used in this paper refer to specific subcultures such as the Damara, while others are geographical areas such as Kavango, and others are collective terms for several related subcultures such as Owambo. The terms used in this chapter are those in general use at the national/macro level; they are used by the people themselves and by others. Categorical ethnic stereotyping has been studied in Windhoek by LeBeau (1991) and Pendleton (1975) and in the Caprivi by Fosse (1996).

2. A recent film based on archive materials and interviews with older people who remember the confrontation has been made by Christian Scholz, a Namibian filmmaker (P.O. Box 11083, Windhoek, Namibia). The film captures very graphically the strong opposition to the move that existed and the brutality of the authorities in suppressing the demonstration. Many Namibians have referred to the December 10, 1959, events as the Namibian "Sharpeville." Also, a video made by the Namibian Broadcasting Corporation on Katutura highlights many of the findings in the Katutura books.

3. The contract labor system, in which men were employed on contracts of between twelve and eighteen months, paid very low wages, and required to return to their rural homes when the contract was finished, was officially abolished in 1975.

4. A major exception to this is Robert Gordon's work. Although born in Namibia and educated at Stellenbosch University in South Africa, he conducted fieldwork for his Ph.D. in anthropology on mine workers near Windhoek in the 1970s (Gordon 1977), and he has been an outspoken critic of the *Volkerkunde* anthropologists.

5. Cf. Scheper-Hughes (1995:415), who comments on the "business as usual" and "noninvolvement" of the Anthropology Department at the University of Cape Town.

6. Being associated with TUCSIN and UNAM gives me the opportunity to meet most visiting anthropologists, including Alan Barnard, Walter van Beek, Ingolf Diener, Bill Haviland and Rob Gordon (who got a tour of Katutura), Heidi Hendrickson, Richard Lee, Marshall Murphee, Ida Susser, Inge Tvedten, and Polly Wiessner.

7. In 1993, NISER was replaced by the Social Sciences Division (SSD) of the Multi-Disciplinary Research Centre.

8. The other projects included the Integration of Returned Exiles, Former Combatants and Other War Affected People (Preston et al. 1993), Household Health and Nutrition Survey (Cogill and Kiugu 1990), and surveys for the Namibian Broadcasting Corporation (Pendleton and LeBeau 1992; LeBeau and Pendleton 1994).

9. The household subsistence level data for Windhoek come from regular surveys of cost of living conducted by the Institute for Development Studies and Research at the University of Port Elizabeth (Potgieter 1996).

10. Various measures of poverty have been used to study the Namibian situation: the household consumption model, in which households below the median household income are considered poor (50 percent classified as poor; Central Statistics Office 1996); the food index model, in which percentage of household income used on food is calculated and those households for which the percentage is in excess of 60 percent are defined as poor (50 percent classified as poor or very poor; Central Statistics Office 1996); and the food basket model, which makes use of a poverty datum line (67 percent classified as poor; Devereux et al. 1995).

References Cited

Amunyela, Helvi-Mwahala
(1998) "Urban-Rural linkages: A case study of female migrants in Babilon Informal Settlement, Windhoek, Namibia." Unpublished M.S. thesis. Agricultural University of Norway.

Arowolo, O.
(1994) "The population situation in Namibia." Pp. 78–112 in *Population, Human Resources and Development Planning in Namibia*. Windhoek: National Planning Commission.

Barth, Fredrik
(1969) *Ethnic Groups and Boundaries*. Boston: Little, Brown.

Black, Patricia
(1995) "Knowledge, attitudes and practices about contraception of urban and rural Owambo women in Namibia." Unpublished M.A. thesis. San Diego State University.

Breitborde, Larry
(1994) "Urban anthropology in the 1990s: W(h)ither the city? An introduction." *City and Society Annual Review 1994*:3–10.

Central Statistics Office
(1996) *Living Conditions in Namibia*. Main Report. Windhoek: National Planning Commission.

Cogill, Bruce and Solomon Kiugu
(1990) *Household Heath and Nutrition in Katutura and Selected Northern Areas of Namibia*. Windhoek: UNICEF.

Couch, Denise
(1996) "Issues in rural development: A comparative study of communal areas in Eastern and Southern Namibia." Unpublished M.A. thesis. San Diego State University.

Couch, Denise and Wade Pendleton
(1998) *Issues in Rural Development: A Socio-Economic Comparison of Eastern and Southern Communal Areas*. Social Sciences Division, Multi-Disciplinary Research Centre, Research Report No. 32. Windhoek: University of Namibia.

Devereux, Stephen, Ben Fuller, Richard Moorsom, Colette Solomon, and Chris Tapscott
(1995) Namibia Poverty Profile. Social Sciences Division, Multidisciplinary Research Centre, SSD Research Report No. 21. Windhoek: University of Namibia.

Devereux, Stephen, Martin Rimmer, Debbie LeBeau, and Wade Pendleton
(1993) *The 1992/93 Drought in Namibia: An Evaluation of Its Socio-Economic Impact on Affected Households*. Social Sciences Division, Multi-Disciplinary Research Centre, Research Report No.7. Windhoek: University of Namibia.

Diener, Ingolf
(1995) "Deverrouillage ethnique dans l'espace urbain namibien: Le cas de Windhoek." *C.N.R.S.* 53.

Directorate of Rural Development
(1992) *Socio-Economic Survey Southern Communal Areas*. Windhoek: Directorate of Rural Development, Ministry of Agriculture, Water and Rural Development.

Epstein, A. L.
(1958) *Politics in an Urban African Community*. Manchester: Manchester University Press.

Fosse, Leif
(1996) "Negotiating the nation in local terms." Unpublished M.A. thesis. Department and Museum of Anthropology. Oslo: University of Oslo.

Frayne, Bruce
(1992) *Urbanisation in Post-Independence Windhoek*. Research Report No. 6. Windhoek: Namibian Institute for Social and Economic Research.
(1993) "The potential role of urbanization in achieving global sustainability: Towards establishing an urbanization transition model." Pp. 193–217 in S. Arlinghaus and W. Drake (editors), *The Dynamics of Transition: Population–Environment Interaction*. Ann Arbor: University of Michigan.

Frayne, Bruce and Wade Pendleton
(1998) *Report of the Findings of the 5th Nation Public Opinion Survey for Namibia*. Social Sciences Division, Multi-Disciplinary Research Centre, Research Report No. 34. Windhoek: University of Namibia.
(2000) "Namibia on South Africa: The attitudes of Namibians to international migration and immigration policy." Pp. 86–118 in J. Crush and D. McDonald (editors),

On Borders: Perspectives on Cross-Border Migration in Southern Africa, Cape Town: IDASA.
(2001) "Migration in Namibia: Combining macro and micro approaches to research design and analysis." *International Migration Review* 35(4): 1054–1085.

Gibson, Diane
(1991) "Changes in the position of matrilineal Oshiwambo-speaking women in Katutura, Namibia." Unpublished seminar paper. University of Cape Town, Social Anthropology Seminar.

Gluckman, Max
(1960) "Tribalism in modern British Central Africa." *Cahiers d'Etudes Africaines* 1:55–70.

Gordon, Robert
(1977) *Mines, Migrants and Masters.* Johannesburg: Ravan Press.

Government of South Africa
(1964) *The Commission of Inquiry into South West Africa Affairs 1962–63.* Pretoria: Government Printer.

Gulick, John
(1968) "The outlook, research strategy and relevance." Pp. 93–98 in Elizabeth Eddy (editor), *Urban Anthropology.* Athens: University of Georgia Press.

Hannerz, Ulf
(1980) *Exploring the City.* New York: Columbia University Press.

Hansen, Karen
(1997) *Keeping House in Lusaka.* New York: Columbia University Press.

Iken, Adelheid, Debbie LeBeau, Manfred Menjengua, and Wade Pendleton
(1994) *Socio-Economic Survey Eastern Communal Areas.* Windhoek: Directorate of Extension and Engineering Services, Ministry of Agriculture, Water and Rural Development.

Jafta, M., N. Kautja, M. Oliphant, D. Ridgway, K. Shipingana, U. Tjijends, and G. Veii
(1995) *An Investigation of the Shooting at the Old Location on 10 December.* Windhoek: Discourse/MSORP Publications.

Kemper, Robert V.
(1979) "Frontiers in migration: From culturalism to historical structuralism in the study of Mexico-U.S. migration." Pp. 9–21 in Fernando Camara and Robert V. Kemper (editors), *Migration Across Frontiers: Mexico and the United States.* Albany: SUNY Institute for Mesoamerican Studies.
(1991) "Urban anthropology in the 1990s: The state of its practice." *Urban Anthropology* 20 (2):211–223.

Lau, Brigitte
(1993) "The old location." Pp. 20–23 in A. Heywood and B. Lau (editors), *Three*

Views into the Past of Windhoek. History Conference, 1–3 June 1993. Windhoek.

LeBeau, Debbie

(1991) "Namibia: Ethnic stereotyping in a post-apartheid state." M.A. thesis. San Diego State University.

(1993) *Namibia: Ethnic Stereotyping in a Post-apartheid State*. Research Report No. 5. Windhoek: Namibian Institute for Social and Economic Research.

LeBeau, Debbie and Wade Pendleton

(1994) "All Media Survey in Namibia and the Namibia Product Usage Survey." Consultancy reports prepared for the Namibian Broadcasting Corporation through the Social Sciences Division, Multi-Disciplinary Research Centre. Windhoek: University of Namibia.

Lewis, Michael and Gert van Rooi

(1991) *A Study of the Prospects for Training of Young Unemployed Women in Katutura*. Research Report No. 8. Windhoek: Namibian Institute for Social and Economic Research.

Melber, Henning

(1988) *Katutura-Ghetto im Alltag*. Edition Südliches Afrika No. 24. Bonn: Informationsstelle Südliches Afrika e.V. (issa).

Mitchell, J. Clyde

(1956) *The Kalele Dance*. Rhodes-Livingstone Paper No. 27. Manchester: Manchester University Press.

(1966) "Theoretical orientations in African urban studies." Pp. 37–68 in Michael Banton (editor), *The Social Anthropology of Complex Societies*. London: Tavistock.

(1969) *Social Networks in Urban Situations*. Manchester: Manchester University Press.

Naeraa, Trini, Stephen Devereux, Bruce Frayne, and P. Harnett

(1993) *Coping with Drought in Namibia: Informal Social Security Systems in Caprivi and Erongo*. Cape Town: Clyson Printers.

NEPRU

(1998) "Poverty, inequality and policy in Namibia." Pp. 51–102 in *In Search of Research*. Windhoek: NEPRU.

Norval, D., and R. Namoya

(1992) *The Informal Sector within Greater Windhoek*. Windhoek: First National Development Corporation.

Pendleton, Wade

(1970) "Ethnic group identity among Africans in Windhoek, South West Africa." *African Urban Notes* 5:1–14.

(1974) *Katutura: A Place Where We Do Not Stay. The Social Structure and Social Relationships of People in an African Township in South West Africa*. San Diego: San Diego State University Press.

(1975) "Social categorization and language usage." Pp. 63–89 in Wade Pendleton and

Clive Kileff (editors), *Urban Man in Southern Africa*. Gwelo, Rhodesia: Mambo Press.
(1976) "Herero reactions: The pre-colonial period, the German colonial period and
the period of South African colonialism." Pp. 167–194 in David Chanaiwa (editor),
Profiles of Self Determination. Northridge: California State University Foundation.
(1978) "Urban ethnicity in Windhoek." Pp. 125–142 in Brian DuToit (editor), *Ethnicity in Modern Africa*. Boulder, CO: Westview.
(1979) "Urbanization and development in Namibia (South West Africa)." Pp.
293–302 in R. A. Obudho and Salah El Shakhs (editors), *African Urban Systems and
Urban Development: A Planning Perspective*. New York: Praeger.
(1991) *The 1991 Katutura Survey Report*. NISER Discussion Paper No. 9, Windhoek:
Namibia Institute of Social and Economic Research.
(1994) *Katutura: A Place Where We Stay. Life in a Post-Apartheid Township in Namibia:
Katutura Before and Now*. Windhoek: Gamsberg Macmillan.
(1996) *Katutura: A Place Where We Stay. Life in a Post-Apartheid Township in Namibia*.
Revised second edition. Monographs in International Studies, Africa Series, Number
65. Athens: Ohio University Press.
(1997) *Katutura: Migration and Change in the 1990s*. Social Sciences Division, Multi-
Disciplinary Research Centre, SSD Research Report No.16. Windhoek: University
of Namibia.

Pendleton, Wade and Barbara DuBois
(1990) *Health and Daily Living Survey of Windhoek, Namibia (1988–1989)*. NISER
Research Report 2. Windhoek: Namibia Institute of Social and Economic Research.

Pendleton, Wade and Bruce Frayne
(1998) *Report of the Results of the Namibian Migration Project*. Social Sciences Division, Multi-Disciplinary Research Centre, SSD Research Report No. 35. Windhoek:
University of Namibia.
(2000) "Migration as a population dynamic in Namibia." Pp. 273–295 in *Population,
Development and Environment Interactions: Evaluating Alternative Paths for Sustainable Development in Botswana, Mozambique and Namibia*. Vienna: Institute for Integrated Systems Analysis (IISA).

Pendleton, Wade and Debbie LeBeau
(1992) *Socio-Economic Analysis of Radio Listener Attitudes in Namibia*. A consultancy
report prepared for the Namibian Broadcasting Corporation. Windhoek: Namibian
Institute of Social and Economic Research.

Pendleton, Wade, Debbie LeBeau, and Chris Tapscott
(1993) *A Socio-Economic Assessment of the Oshakati/Ondangwa Nexus*. Research Report
No. 6. Windhoek: Namibian Institute of Social and Economic Research.

Pendleton, Wade, Toivo Shiimbi, Victor Tonchi, Winnie Wanzala, Gerhard Totemeyer,
and Cornelius Pontac
(1993) *A Study of Voting Behaviour in the 1992 Namibian Regional and Local Government Elections Plus Election Statistics*. Windhoek: University of Namibia (sponsored by

UNESCO and the Friedrich Ebert Stiftung).

Peyroux, Elizabeth and Olivier Graefe
(1995) "Precarious settlements at Windhoek's periphery." *CRIAA* 54(4). Windhoek.

Potgieter, J.
(1996) "The household subsistence level in the major urban centres of the Republic of South Africa." Institute for Development Studies and Research. Port Elizabeth: University of Port Elizabeth.

Preston, Rosemary, Sue Brown, Tove Dix, Colin Gleichmann, Dicks Kandando, Debbie LeBeau, Stella Makanya, Wade Pendleton, Colette Solomon, Kristof Tamas, and Pam Zinkin
(1993) *The Integration of Returned Exiles, Former Combatants and Other War Affected Namibians.* Final Report. Windhoek: Namibian Institute of Social and Economic Research.

Sandberg, Katharina
(1998) "How women and men get by: Hawking in Katutura, Namibia." Unpublished Sociology thesis. University of Oslo.

Sanjek, Roger
(1990) "Urban anthropology in the 1980s: A world view." *Annual Review of Anthropology* 19:151–186.

Scheper-Hughes, Nancy
(1995) "The primacy of ethical: Propositions for a militant anthropology." *Current Anthropology* 36(3):409–420.

Southall, Aidan W.
(1997) "The illusion of tribe." Pp. 38–51 in R. Grinker and C. Steiner (editors), *Perspectives on Africa.* Oxford: Blackwell Publishers.

UNDP
(1997) *Human Development Report.* Windhoek: UNDP with UNAIDS.

von Garnier, Christine
(1986) *Katutura Revisited.* Windhoek: Angelus Printing.

Wagner, Gunter
(1951) "Ethnographic survey of South West Africa." Unpublished manuscript. Windhoek: Department of Bantu Administration and Development, Ethnological Section.

Yaron, Gil, Gertie Janssen, and Usutuaije Maamberua
(1992) *Rural Development in the Okavango Region of Namibia.* Windhoek: Gamsberg Macmillan.

CHAPTER THREE
MYSORE VILLAGES REVISITED
T. Scarlett Epstein

Introduction

In the course of taking my first degree in economics as an adult student at the University of Manchester (England, 1950–1953), I was taught by W. Arthur Lewis. I suspect that this accounts for my becoming interested in the problem of the economic development of less-developed societies. However, unlike my eminent supervisor, who analyzed the development process from the heights of a macroeconomist, I was more interested in the social aspects of development. I soon began to appreciate that here I would have to turn for inspiration to social sciences other than economics. It was this search for enlightenment on the social dimensions of economic development that brought me into social anthropology.

Fortunately for me, there was at that time a team of outstanding social anthropologists gathered at Manchester including Max Gluckman, Elizabeth Colson, Victor Turner, and others. Their research in Central Africa and subsequent analysis of field material seemed to me to provide just the sort of insight into social processes that is necessary in trying to understand the full implications of the development of less-developed societies. Accordingly, as soon as I graduated in economics, I decided that I wanted to conduct a lengthy intensive study of a locality and, by means of participant observation, examine economic development at the micro level.

By way of fortunate coincidence, M. N. Srinivas happened to be visiting professor at Manchester just about the time I had to finalize my Ph.D. research outline. I discussed my research interests with him, and he suggested an area in south India where he himself had done research and which seemed to present the very problem I was particularly keen to study. The literature on Indian village life, supported by Srinivas's personal accounts, exerted a powerful influence on me, so much so that I decided to become a nonconformist of the Manchester School and do my fieldwork in India rather than in Africa. In doing so I followed in the footsteps of F. G. Bailey, another Manchester student, who had just completed his fieldwork in India when I was ready to start mine. I drew up a research proposal for a study entitled "Economic Development and Social Change in One South Indian Village." With Gluckman's support, I managed to get a Rockefeller Research grant that financed my study.

59

Sugarcane planting. Photo by T. Scarlett Epstein.

Microstudies

I began my fieldwork in south India in November 1954, when I settled in a village I subsequently named Wangala, which had a population of 985 individuals residing in 192 households. Wangala is situated in Mandya District of what was then Mysore State but which has since become Karnataka State. The village is multicaste with peasants as the "dominant" caste (Srinivas 1959). The villagers speak Kannada, a Dravidian language. Mandya District is part of the semiarid tropics. Farmers had depended on irregular and scarce rainfall for the necessary water to facilitate cultivation of subsistence crops. Two millets, ragi (*Sorghum vulgare*) and jowar (*Eleusine coracana*), had been grown as staple crops and provided the basic diet for most villagers. The advent of canal irrigation in Wangala prior to the outbreak of war in 1939 enabled farmers to venture into cash cropping. The specific reason for selecting Wangala as a research site was my interest in studying the impact of irrigation on village economic and social organization.

I was fortunate in being invited to live in a Brahmin home in Mysore City, where I spent three weeks prior to moving into Wangala. During this brief spell, I managed to learn the rudiments of Kannada. I also engaged Suri, my research assistant, a graduate in statistics from the University of Mysore. He came with me to Wangala and helped me throughout my two years of fieldwork. As a Brahmin and a vegetarian, he could find no place to live in the village, as there was not a single Brahmin household. Therefore, we shared a house and I kept a vegetarian kitchen.

Originally, I intended to study only one village. However, after I had been in the field for some time I began to appreciate the difficulty of studying changes that had occurred in the past. I wanted to be able to see what Wangala society had been like before village lands had become irrigated so as to be in a better position to gauge and understand the changes that had taken place. Accordingly, I tried to discover a village in the same culture area, reasonably near Wangala, but with only dry lands. I reasoned that a study of such a village would enable me to see what Wangala must have been like before irrigation. To put it briefly: I wanted to recreate Wangala in its preirrigation state. I did find a village, not too far away from Wangala, whose lands lie above canal irrigation level and therefore remain dry. The village, which I subsequently called Dalena, had a population of 701 individuals residing in 153 households. In my innocence, I expected Dalena to have continued fairly unchanged throughout the years that neighboring villages had come to enjoy the benefits from irrigation. It did not take me long to discover, after I had started fieldwork in Dalena, that no village remains static while surrounded by a changing environment. Irrigation in the area had aroused out of their almost-stagnant conditions not only villages like Wangala, which benefited directly from canal water; but also dry-land villages like Dalena, where men sought new opportunities outside the borders of their own village. Thereby Mandya, a small but rapidly growing town, became the center of an integrated regional economy.

In 1956, on completion of my two years of fieldwork in south India, I returned to Manchester, wrote my thesis, and published it in 1962 as a book. I hoped that someday I would be able to restudy Wangala and Dalena, but because of financial constraints I saw little chance of ever being able to do so. None of my village friends was literate in English, and only a few could write the vernacular. Thus, I could not correspond with any of them and lost touch altogether. Subsequently, I changed my regional interest to the Pacific and conducted research in New Guinea.

Quite unexpectedly, at the beginning of 1970 while I was at the Australian National University, I received an invitation to return to south India from a young German sociologist. He and an Indian student, both attached to the University of Nürnberg, had used my earlier publication as base data and conducted a follow-up study in Wangala and Dalena. They volunteered all possible help and even offered to make available to me their experienced research assistants. I immediately began to make arrangements to take advantage of this rare opportunity. I managed to return to "my" south Indian villages in July 1970—fourteen years after I had left. Before going on to evaluate my own experience of a restudy I want to discuss the advantages and disadvantages of different types of comparative research, of which long-term studies are only one.

Types of Comparative Microstudies

Social scientists outside the profession—economists, in particular—frequently criticize anthropological microstudies for their parochialism. By focusing on one small society, which is never randomly selected, a microstudy fails to produce data that lend themselves readily to large-scale generalizations. It may be very interesting to know the specific characteristics of one small-scale society, but what insight can be discerned from this for a better understanding of at least some aspects of society in general? Though anthropological research is essential to gain insight into social processes and culture patterns, the narrow horizon of microstudies is a serious drawback. Comparative microstudies provide one way to overcome this. There are different types of comparative microstudies. They are by no means mutually exclusive, but in fact would produce best results if one were conducted to reinforce the others. In what follows, I draw mainly on my own research experience as exemplary material. However, I suggest that many of the propositions I discuss lend themselves readily to generalizations over large numbers of anthropological microstudies.

Mesoregional Studies

My own earlier microstudies, like so many others of their type, were conducted in isolation from other ongoing fieldwork in India or anywhere else. Because of time and resource limitations I could focus on only a few aspects of the problems I had set out to study. For instance, I know now that it is impossible to analyze fully the impact on the socioeconomic system of villages in Mandya District without research in the town of Mandya itself. To study the development of an integrated regional economy necessitates an integrated regional approach. O. H. K. Spate (1973:xiv) rightly warns anthropologists of the dangers of regarding as microcosms the individual villages studied: "It is sometimes forgotten that any number of traverses do not add up to a triangulation. . . . Why is the useful concept of meso-regional analysis so often overlooked? . . . But for this too a firm basis of detailed local studies is necessary." Spate thus stresses the need for a number of complementary studies to be conducted in the same region. This is precisely what I now think ought to have been done when I began my fieldwork in south India. My own village studies would have been much more meaningful had they been set within the context of a broader research scheme focusing on economic development and social change in the Mandya region. The comprehensive data that are likely to emerge from such an exercise would provide a much sounder basis for restudy at a future date than is the case with my own isolated microstudies. Moreover, if in the first instance my own research had been conceived of as part of or leading to a mesoregional study, I would have viewed irrigation in its wider setting and would never have been so foolish as to believe it possible to find a village economy that had remained static while neighboring areas developed. I would have been better prepared than I was to study Dalena, the dry-land village, the development of which symbolizes the process of regional integration of villages in Mandya District. I have been advocating for some time now the advisability of studying Mandya town. So far, I have not been successful in getting this research off the ground, but I am still trying.

There are available some examples of mesoregional studies: the Rhodes-Livingstone Institute encouraged studies in Central Africa with such objectives in mind; Douglas Oliver had a team of students working in the Solomon Islands. Two such programs are covered elsewhere in this volume: the Ramah Project organized by Kluckhohn and described by Lamphere, and the Harvard Chiapas Project organized by Vogt. The considerable difficulties involved in organizing mesoregional studies readily account for their paucity to date. First of all, there is the serious problem of finance; then there are the difficulties that are part of all team efforts; and, possibly most important, is the danger of providing a straitjacket for researchers. Though these are serious considerations to bear in mind, I suggest that they do not represent insurmountable obstacles. Financial support can be found; personal animosities and/or differences among team members can be ironed out; and researchers can be expected to collect at least a minimum of required core data, over and above which each can and should be encouraged to follow his/her own particular interests in the course of fieldwork. The more different social facts are brought to light, the more comprehensive the overall analysis is likely to be. The object of mesoregional studies is to analyze the interrelationships among economic, political, and general social variables in a regional context. The emphasis here is on the region; and it is therefore not surprising that it is Spate, a geographer, who advocates such studies. Mesoregional studies are not necessarily appropriate for all or even most anthropological research. They are relevant, though, to topics like the one I undertook to study in 1954. I should have expected that a large canal irrigation scheme not only would affect the intravillage organization, but would also change the total environment of villages in the area. Alas, at the time I was oblivious to the importance of village externalities. Furthermore, I was not in a position to tackle a mesoregional study singlehandedly.

Cross-Cultural Comparative Microstudies

Cross-cultural comparative microstudies are another possibility for comparative research. Such studies, by their very nature, are problem rather than region oriented. With hindsight, I now think it would have been wiser had I focused my investigation on a topic such as, for instance, the process of monetization of rural economies, which had already been examined in Africa (e.g., Watson 1958) and other developing societies. This would have helped to consolidate our understanding of one particular aspect of socioeconomic change. Instead I ventured into a relatively new field of inquiry. However, since canal irrigation is a widespread phenomenon in less-developed countries, it should have been easy for microstudies similar to my own to be conducted in other cultural settings. Such exercises would have helped to test my hypotheses that (1) irrigation helps to perpetuate the traditional socioeconomic system and makes farmers more village-introverted (which characterizes developments in Wangala), and (2) diversification of economic roles and relationships increases the rate of social change (which is based on Dalena's experience). I am aware of only two attempts to test these hypotheses systematically: one was conducted by a team of German geographers attached to the University of Heidelberg who studied irrigation in Sri Lankan villages, and the other by Kaja Finkler in Mexico (verbal communication). Their findings support my hypotheses. Obviously, many more studies in different cultural contexts are needed before these hypotheses can be regarded as fully verified. What is likely to emerge is that they will need refining to fit different circumstances. What sort of refinements may be necessary remains to be known.

There have been many attempts at cross-cultural analysis of the findings produced by anthropologists who conducted their research in different cultural settings. Very rarely, though, do researchers start by trying to test the same hypothesis in different cultural settings or put to the test a hypothesis resulting from the study of one society by conducting fieldwork in a different part of the world altogether. In this context my ongoing cross-cultural study of population growth and rural poverty may represent an interesting exercise (see the following discussion).

Long-Term Microstudies

Such studies can be of different types: continuous research in the same small society over a number of years; periodic restudies at regular or irregular intervals; and/or returning after a lengthy interval of time has elapsed since the original research. My own restudy of Mysore villages falls into the third category, for, as mentioned already, I had lost touch with the villages after completing my first spell of fieldwork in 1956; and I returned only in 1970. On the basis of my own experience I find it difficult to speculate whether all situations lend themselves equally well for returning—my own certainly did.

Two considerations apply to all three types of long-term microstudies: research focus, and new versus returning researcher(s). If the restudy focuses on the same social phenomena as the earlier research and the emphasis is placed on examining change over time, there is every reason to believe that the project would encounter little difficulty. However, research interests, just like societies, rarely remain static, even for the same worker. A restudy is likely to emphasize the importance of variables not emphasized in the first inquiry. This may create difficulties insofar as the base findings do not provide data for comparison, but it may be possible to extract the necessary data from the earlier field notes or other unpublished material. Even if this should be utterly impossible, I suspect that it is far better to have at least some related data available for an earlier period than to come to a society as a complete novice.

One of the first questions that arises in the context of a restudy is whether to encourage the original worker to go back or to arrange for one or more younger investigators, well versed in the earlier findings, to take a new look at the "old" society. There are pros and cons for both these approaches. A different researcher brings new ideas and a new personality to the restudy, which may help to neutralize any personal bias in the findings. Moreover, a younger generation of workers may approach the restudy from a completely new angle and use different methods of investigation, resulting in an account so different from the earlier findings that it may appear to bear no relation to the original research. I do not mean to imply that earlier research results should never be tested by a younger generation of investigators. This is only possible, however, if there is continuity in approach and if the restudy starts from similar premises and uses methods of inquiry similar to those of the initial research. On the other hand, a new worker, even though knowing the society's history, yet faces the problem of having to establish rapport.

It is important in this context to remember the human concern involved in microstudies. The researcher who spends at least a full year living with a particular small group of people not only learns about their lives but also becomes an important individual in their eyes. Many informants establish a firm personal attachment to the first investigator they encounter who shares their lives for a period of time. They are not readily prepared to transfer their allegiances to another individual. The mutual trust and respect established between the initial researcher and informants provides a favorable climate for a restudy. Most social anthropologists experience an increasingly marginal rate of data collection for a considerable part of their studies, which means that a restudy conducted by the original investigator need not take nearly as long as it would if a new researcher were involved.

The preceding points can be readily illustrated by my own experience in restudying Mysore villages.

Returning to Mysore Villages

The overall focus of my own interests hardly changed over time: in my initial study I concentrated on examining the interdependencies between economic and social developments, and this continues to be my concern. Thus, when I returned to south India, I went equipped with copies of all the material I had collected during my first spell of fieldwork (sketch maps, census forms, field notes, genealogies, household budgets, photographs, etc.). Much as I would have liked to spend another two years in the villages, personal circumstances made a long spell of fieldwork impossible. I could spend no more than five weeks.

My German colleague, Mr. Schönherr, at whose invitation I ventured back to south India, had told the villagers of my impending return. They had been convinced all along that he was my son, and therefore were not too surprised to learn of my revisit. In fact, they superimposed their own custom of categorizing relationships in genealogical terms and regarded as my kin every researcher who visited their village after I left. It emerged that at least seven or eight people had come to ask them questions of one sort or another, but none had stayed as long as I did and none was accepted by them as I had been. The warmth of their reception was overwhelming and remains one of my most treasured experiences. I had no problem whatsoever in reestablishing rapport and began to collect data from the first moment of my return. As it so happened, my first day back in the Mysore villages coincided with the wedding in Dalena of the daughter of one of the headman's younger brothers. It struck me immediately that there had been a change in wedding practice among peasants: whereas previously the groom's people met all expenditures, now it was the bride's family that paid it all. Pursuing this line of inquiry led to a lot of other interesting material. Data were flowing in at such a pace that I often typed my field notes until the early hours of the morning and was up again at 5 A.M. ready to collect more information.

Like most other anthropological fieldworkers, I too had made a number of special friends in the villages I studied. They were my best and most trusted informants. Most of them were five or more years older than myself. By 1970, some of them had died; the rest of us had aged; some had become ill or otherwise disabled. On my return, my old contacts were quickly renewed. Now that I was older myself, I also had closer links with an older age group of informants than I had had during my first spell of fieldwork. I discuss the impact of my changed social role on our relations in what follows. Here it suffices to say that as a female fieldworker, who played down the fact of her sex—I never wore a sari in the villages either during 1954 to 1956 or in 1970, so as to differentiate myself ostentatiously from village women and so avoid being identified with them—I was readily accepted by male villagers and also obviously had no difficulty in securing access to female society.

I began my fieldwork in 1954 by collecting a 100 percent socioeconomic census of the village households, which provided the basis for the compilation of a stratified random sample. Each of the sample households was then subjected to intensive qualitative as well as quantitative inquiry. With the aid of my earlier residential sketch maps of the villages—an invaluable help to restudies—I was able to identify most of my original sample households. In 1970, my time back in Mysore was too brief to allow me to repeat the exercise of collecting a 100 percent socioeconomic census, and therefore I lacked the basis for compiling another stratified random sample of all the households. I could, of course, have randomly sampled the villages by selecting one household out of every fifth or tenth house in the village streets, but I decided that this would not be a satisfactory procedure. I considered it more meaningful to reexamine some of the households in the original study.

In the intervening years, the "case study method" had been developed (Van Velsen 1967). Thus, I decided to concentrate on case studies of individual households. I selected one from each of the different economic strata of the villages: for Dalena, I chose one peasant magnate, one peasant middle-farmer, and one of the poor Scheduled Castes; for Wangala, I did the same but added one migrant laboring household, a new phenomenon in the village, to cover the full range of economic differentiation. I tried to learn as much as possible about the changes that had occurred in these households and spent many days just sitting with informants asking questions, but mainly listening to what was being said and observing what went on.

These detailed case studies of a few carefully selected households enabled me to give quantitative accounts of the increasing economic differentiation that had taken place in these villages, as well as to indicate the processes by which the rich farmers had increased their wealth and the poor landless Scheduled Castes laborers had become poorer not only in relative but also in absolute terms. By viewing village society as a system, I managed to piece together the different items of information like a jigsaw puzzle and analyze the overall process of social change. I found evidence for continued village introversion in Wangala and village extroversion in Dalena. I collected enough material to write at least one more book on the restudy besides the one I have already published (Epstein 1973). Under ideal conditions of restudy, I would have liked to update my 100 percent village census, compile another stratified random sample, and examine social change in depth; as well as to collect case studies. Alas, this was impossible!

Schönherr was nearing the end of his investigation by the time I arrived in Mysore. He conducted his inquiries with the aid of four indigenous assistants and focused on political organization and change. He had not attempted to learn the vernacular, and he conducted his investigations through an interpreter by means of long structured interviews, during each of which he tried to complete a questionnaire of several pages. Therefore, not only were his research interests not the same as my own, but more important still, his method of collecting data was also entirely different. He made appointments with informants either for them to come and see him or for him to turn up at the time and place they specified. It did not surprise me to hear that villagers frequently failed to keep the arrangements they had made with him, which made him feel frustrated. A number of my village friends asked me in confidence why I had not tried to make "my son" follow in his mother's footsteps and join the village life instead of remaining aloof, as was his practice.

The data Schönherr collected were thus of a different type and quality than my own. Since he asked different questions in a different way, his data did not lend themselves to cross-checking with my own. All his material was contained in questionnaires that readily lent themselves to quantitative analysis. During my visit, I shared accommodations with Schönherr and his research assistants. Every evening after we returned from our investigations I settled down to typing my field notes. Schönherr regularly watched me doing so with a puzzled look on his face; after about a week he got up enough courage to ask how it was that I had so much correspondence to do, for this is what he assumed I was typing. He was amazed when I told him that I was recording my field notes. I was equally amazed to find out that after more than a year of fieldwork he had not collected a single field note. It had never dawned on him that it might be useful to view political organization and change as part of an overall social process. His training in sociology had convinced him that political behavior can be abstracted from other social relationships. Therefore, he was sure that he needed only the answers to his questionnaires and no other data. Accordingly, I was not surprised when he kindly sent me a copy of his thesis—which he had submitted to the University of Nürnberg and for which he was awarded his doctorate—to see that his analysis of political organization and change in Dalena and Wangala was very different from the analysis I presented in my follow-up study. Anyone reading the two accounts might not even suspect that they relate to the same places.

It is this experience that convinced me of the need for continuity in the conduct of a restudy. Thus, wherever possible, I suggest that it is desirable for the same researcher to return to the same field location. If this is impossible, it is essential that the new investigator should at least contact the "ancestor" before embarking on the restudy, so as to be initiated competently into the complexities of the particular society that may not emerge fully from the published material. Moreover, such contact may provide a personal reference and an acceptable introduction to informants. I am convinced that Schönherr's relations with villagers in Wangala and Dalena would have been closer, and thus his research more fruitful, had he managed to contact me before he started his fieldwork rather than when he had almost completed it.

Another restudy of Dalena and Wangala was conducted in the 1970s altogether without my knowledge. A. R. Rajapurohit and Mabel Koilpillai, two economists working with the Bangalore Institute for Social and Economic Change, decided to restudy Dalena and Wangala by remote control: they did not reside in the villages and instead relied heavily on official statistics. They made no attempt to contact me before starting their studies and therefore failed to benefit from relevant information with which I could have provided them. Though I consider that their publication (Rajapurohit and Koilpillai 1981) indicates these shortcomings, I realize that in certain aspects their purely economic focus adds another dimension to my earlier studies.

In contrast to these isolated restudies, I tried to ensure continuity: I managed to encourage Ms. Sudha V. Rao, whose doctoral research I supervised, to locate her studies in Dalena. I arranged for Suri, who had been my research assistant in Dalena since 1955 and still has excellent rapport with the villagers, to introduce Rao to the Dalena people. This greatly facilitated her acceptance by the villagers. She focused on the relationship between education and rural development, an aspect of socioeconomic change to which I had not paid much attention. Yet all the publications on the village, together with my unpublished materials, provided Rao with invaluable background information. In turn, her restudy of Dalena in 1978–1979 and her subsequent publication (Rao 1985) added new insight to the socioeconomic change process I had begun to study in 1955.

Similarly, I got one of my other Indian doctoral students to restudy a village near Lucknow which was first studied in the early 1920s by one of Professor R. Mukerjee's students (1929); he managed to track down the original researcher. This man was then in his eighties but still alert. This personal contact gave the student important additional insight into the village society before he started his fieldwork. Moreover, the old man's nephew, the present postmaster in the village, helped the student to gain ready entry to the society. Of course, it may not always be possible for a new worker to contact the original investigator. For instance, another of my Indian students restudied Rampur, the north Indian village that Oscar Lewis (1958) made famous. Oscar Lewis being dead, she tried to establish contact not only with his widow, but also with one or another of the Indian research assistants who helped in the 1953–1954 village study. Mrs. Lewis gave the student access to her husband's unpublished field notes and photographs, for which we are grateful. One of the Indian research assistants, I. P. Singh, who had in the meantime become professor of anthropology at the University of Delhi, readily agreed to introduce the student to the villagers and also gave her much unpublished information on the village.

Research Training for Students

At the start of my first fieldwork, I had little guidance in how to collect various types of socioeconomic data. I had to improvise as I went along. I assume that many colleagues of my own or older generations of anthropologists can recount similar experiences. *The Craft of Social Anthropology* (Epstein 1967) was a long overdue guidebook for anthropological fieldwork and appears to provide valuable aid to budding fieldworkers.

The great diversity of data collected by the many individual anthropologists who conducted the large number of microstudies now available makes it difficult—sometimes even impossible—to make any meaningful comparisons and/or draw valid conclusions. It is scientifically unsound to assume that a common denominator runs through the many studies conducted by individuals with different academic backgrounds and interests, each using different methods of data collection. This extreme heterogeneity in the studies makes not only cross-cultural comparisons but also comparisons over time a dubious proposition. There seems to be a need to standardize the collection of at least a minimum core of data to facilitate not only cross-cultural comparative studies but also studies over time. This is obviously not easy to do, for it involves encouraging researchers to use standardized procedures at least in the collection of the core data; but it seems certainly worth a trial.

My own research can be seen as such an experiment in the standardized collection and analysis of cross-cultural microdata. I directed eight doctoral students (three Indians, two Kenyans, one Nigerian, and two Sri Lankans) who conducted microresearch in their respective home countries as part of my "Cross-Cultural Study of Population Growth and Rural Poverty." They tested the same hypotheses by means of identical, or at least similar, methods. Wherever possible, they restudied societies for which there are earlier reports available. Thus, not only do these studies have a cross-cultural dimension, but four of them also represent comparative investigations over time. Subsequently, I used the same research model with our "Action-Oriented Study of the Role of Women in Rural Development," in which eleven Asian doctoral students participated. Moreover, my own recent experience of restudy motivated me to think in terms of longitudinal research and its implications for field methods. Accordingly, I am encouraging my students to regard their present research as the beginning of long-term studies.

Returning and Its Advantages

The advantages of return visits over individual once-and-for-all microstudies appear so obvious that it is hardly necessary to outline them in greater detail. Most anthropological studies seek historical depth for their successful exercise, but this is often hard to come by. Restudies provide this important historical dimension. Moreover, they also facilitate the analysis of continuity and change over time. For instance, if I had not been able to restudy the Mysore villages, I would never have been in a position to analyze successfully the persistence of the traditional systems of hereditary labor relationships between farmers and resident landless laborers in Wangala and their disappearance in Dalena. Only the time perspective could provide the necessary insight for me to explain the operation of these social processes.

The results of reexposures à la Firth (1959) and Mead (1956) speak for themselves: they offer historical dimensions and theoretical depth that could never be the outcome of a once-and-for-all period of fieldwork.

I do not know whether equally startling results can be claimed for, or expected from, the other two categories of long-term microstudies, the continuous or periodic restudies. I have never been in a position to indulge myself in such research activities. I have been able to revisit south India on several occasions since 1970 and have always made it a point to return to Wangala and Dalena, but my stays have been too brief to conduct any serious fieldwork. I am now planning in collaboration with Schönherr another restudy of Dalena and Wangala.

Impact on the People Studied

The study of particular societies inevitably gains them attention they would otherwise never have received. Shrewd informants are quick to grasp this and to try to manipulate the fieldworker to their own advantage. For instance, when I first moved into Wangala, two of the village magnates tried to get me to intervene on their behalf with the Mandya Sugar Factory so that each of them would be offered a contract for growing cane on four acres instead of two acres, which was the general factory practice. Some villagers requested that I help bring about the establishment of a health center in Dalena; others wanted me to induce the authorities to set up factories outside their village to provide employment for residents, and so on. A common theme seemed to be running through these varied requests: they all aimed at exploiting the advantage of having an outsider live in their midst so as to benefit from developments exogenous to their own society. Needless to say, I could not possibly meet all their requests. However, I tried to help in problems encompassing either the village as a whole (e.g., arranging for immunization at the outbreak of a typhoid epidemic in Wangala in 1955), or affecting large numbers of people (e.g., helping the Untouchable community in Wangala obtain funds to purchase materials for a well of its own so that people no longer had to fetch their drinking water from a polluted pond). My interests in Wangala and Dalena, therefore, seem to have helped broaden the horizon of the villagers and to have sharpened their awareness of the world surrounding their own society.

On the whole, I think I can claim that the villages have benefited at least to a limited extent from my connection with them. However, I am also fully aware of the fact that I unintentionally raised aspirations in a number of my informants, which I never managed to help them realize, and which therefore must have caused them considerable frustration. It is still not clear in my own mind what I could have done to avoid this.

It is difficult to generalize the extent to which a village population's self-image may have changed as a result of having been studied. A researcher invariably seems to have the most impact on the closest friends and best informants. The following example indicates the impact my research has had on one such informant in helping to increase his awareness of the social processes of which he is a part and of the acute social problems surrounding him. As mentioned earlier, during my first field study, no single villager in Wangala was literate in English and only a few could write the vernacular. By the time I returned in 1970, some of the young boys whom I had helped to learn English had become university graduates. One of them, to whom I refer by the pseudonym Rampa (Epstein 1973:224), had just been awarded a first-class master's degree in economics at the University of Bangalore and had been offered a lectureship at a college in Mandya. Rampa had already read my 1962 book by the time we met in 1970. He congratulated me on the way I had managed to describe and analyze rural south India and confessed that he regarded my account as his bible for understanding village life. It was he who first suggested that my book be translated into the vernacular—a task that has been completed by the University of Agricultural Sciences, Bangalore. Rampa's account of his own experience, to my mind, symbolized the widening gap between rural societies and the trained few resulting from an education that has little relevance to village life. In my 1973 book, I discussed Rampa's case to illustrate that, insofar as education is expected to help improve rural living conditions, these young village graduates are a sad disappointment: they turn their backs on the village and look to the towns for their future careers.

I had given my young friend a pseudonym, but anyone familiar with Wangala has no difficulty in identifying his real name. Knowing that Rampa would read my restudy of his village and discover himself discussed in it, I was frankly a bit nervous before I met him again in Bangalore in 1974. However, he soon put my worries to rest; in fact, he told me that after having read and carefully considered my analysis of his lifestyle, he began to appreciate how wrong it had been of him to try and cut his links with his fellow villagers and ignore their plight. As a result, he decided to resign his lectureship in Mandya and join the Karnataka State public service, where he has since made his career in the field of development and extension administration. "If my education has not directly helped my native village, at least it will enable me to be of service to rural societies in general" were his own words on the subject. I was greatly impressed with the way young Rampa had taken into serious consideration my discussion of his attitudes, and I was gratified to see the impact this had on changing the course of his life. This had been more than I had ever dared to hope.

In the meantime, Rampa has become a senior official in the Karnataka State Development Administration. He now ensures that his native Wangala benefits from all the advantages the government offers rural areas. Wangala now has pumped water and electricity. Whenever I happen to be in south India, Rampa takes me to Wangala and proudly shows off all the improvements that have taken place there. His cabled request: "Inauguration of hospital and school building arranged on 1/2/1990 in Mangala kindly attend" clearly indicates how much he has used his official position to help Wangala's development. Every village needs a Rampa! When I mentioned to him that I would like to present all the many pictures I have taken over the years in Wangala to the villagers, he suggested building a hut there for the display of all my photos. This is our next project, and one that I strongly recommend other anthropologists follow. To provide our village friends with a photographic record of their recent history is the least we can and should do to express gratitude to our informants and village friends for having shared their lives with us.

Rampa may represent the odd case of a "success story." Though this may be so, I am extremely pleased to find that a bright and educated young man, indigenous to the very village I had studied, not only agreed with my analysis of the processes of social change I had observed, but was encouraged by it to increase his own commitment to rural development. Until recently, only a few people in Dalena and Wangala have read my books; all of them are young men educated by the English media. But now that both south Indian village studies have been translated into the vernacular and are available in their Indian reincarnation, they will be exposed to a much wider indigenous audience whose comments and criticisms I am eagerly awaiting.

Researcher–Informant Relations

In the time span between my two studies in Mysore, I not only grew older; I also changed my social role: from being defined by the locals as an unmarried "girl," I became a married mother of two daughters. I found that this social transformation of my person greatly facilitated my restudy. During my first fieldwork, some of my village friends left me in no doubt that they disapproved of a woman of my "advanced" years being without a husband and children. By the time I returned, I could satisfy them that I had fulfilled my "natural" role. Therefore, many older men and women approved of me more readily than during my first fieldwork. At the same time, I came to be recognized by younger villagers in somewhat of a parental role. I feel certain that this was an important factor in the influence I exerted over Rampa. His own mother had died in the intervening years, and he now looks up to me as if I were his mother. Other young villagers displayed similar attitudes toward me. On the earlier occasion, villagers could not readily fit me into any of their familiar social categories: I was a woman but, according to their norms, too old to be unmarried and without offspring; and the young men of the village in particular did not quite know what to make of me. But when I returned and showed the villagers photographs of my husband and children, everyone seemed more at ease with me; they were able to categorize their relations with me according to their own social roles. I still did not fit in completely, because my village age mates were already grandparents while my own children were still far too young to be married, but at least they found it easier to fit me into their system of classification.

Though undoubtedly I feel a great debt to many villagers, I thought it advisable from the point of view of academic objectivity not to get too involved in the lives of individual informants. I have given presents whenever the occasion warranted it (e.g., when a villager has a marriage in the household); I now correspond regularly with Rampa and have renewed my contact with Suri, the research assistant who helped me during my first fieldwork and joined me again in the restudy; I try to meet them every time I travel to south India and also to revisit Dalena and Wangala on these occasions. But I have refrained from helping individual villagers educate their children or from meeting any of their many specific demands. I have done this because I thought it important for me not to become identified with individual households and thereby to leave myself open to charges of favoritism. Whenever a specific request was made to me, I tried to explain at great length the reasons for my refusal. The villagers soon learned to accept this and, from their continuing friendly behavior toward me, I think I am justified in assuming that they have come to respect me for my neutrality.

My return to Wangala and Dalena has had an important effect on me in several respects. First of all, it suggested to me the importance of trying to work out the policy implications of my findings and to translate them into action-oriented programs, in order to try to improve the levels of living of the poorest sections in the societies I studied. This accounts for my including a section entitled "Some Palliatives of Socioeconomic Developments" in my 1973 book on south India. Second, I began to appreciate the importance of prediction in studies of socioeconomic change. This is reflected again in the 1973 book where I discuss what the future holds for Dalena and Wangala and other villages of similar types. Only time can tell whether my predictions will be realized, but one thing seems certain: only by making predictions can we expose our analyses to rigorous testing.

Third, meeting again my village friends after a lapse of fifteen years has made me feel much more humble in relation to them and has made me change my personal values and sets of priorities. This lesson was dramatically brought home to me when, on my return to Wangala, I sought to meet again one of my closest village friends who in the intervening years had gone almost blind. When I approached him he fumbled with his hands reaching out to touch me; when I took his hands in mine, he said quietly and with great dignity: "Now that I know you are still alive and have come back to see me again I can die in peace," which made me feel very small indeed.

Predictions: Incorrect and Correct

On the basis of my 1970 restudy, I ventured to forecast by extrapolation of what had happened since 1955 how Wangala and Dalena would change through the end of the twentieth century. Now, I am able to evaluate my own earlier predictions in the light of what has actually taken place up to the present moment (for more details regarding the contemporary situation in these communities, see the 1998 book by Epstein, Suryana-Rayana, and Thinme-Gowda and also the film produced in 1999 through the Institut für den Wissenschaftlichen Film Göttingen).[1]

Incorrect Predictions

When I prepared my predictions in the early 1970s, I did not realize the important role that education, technological progress, and party politics would play in shaping rural transformation. I have now come to appreciate what I should, of course, have realized in 1970; namely, that it takes a long time for the impact of these change factors to be felt. Many Dalena parents already realized in 1955 that education would increase their sons' chances of securing public service jobs. They considered a school certificate a passport to success. However, they did not appear to realize that the adoption of formal schooling would inevitably change the whole societal ethos. By sending their sons to school, parents unknowingly triggered a radical long-term change in a traditional culture that had always stressed conformity and punished nonconformity. Schools, with their emphasis on grading students' performances, not only introduced competition but also rewarded nonconformity: the student who performs best gets the highest marks. The education of the young while their elders were still illiterate upset the conventional relationship of respect between sons and their parents. These were the early teething troubles when formal education was first introduced into illiterate village societies. During my earlier studies of Wangala and Dalena, many of my village friends and informants had complained bitterly about their unsatisfactory relationships with their school-going children. In particular, their sons failed to show them the customary respect to which they felt entitled. At the time, I discarded their worries as the usual parental discontent with growing children. In effect, I failed to recognize that their complaints signified the beginnings of significant attitudinal and behavioral changes in Wangala and Dalena.

Education

When I returned again to my south Indian village friends in 1996, I found to my surprise that many were regularly reading newspapers and even indulged in reading books. As part of an unforgettable farewell function that Wangala villagers organized before my departure, they asked me to lay the foundation stone for a library building they had decided to build in my name and stock with books, journals, and newspapers. They wanted to make sure that young and old would have access to a flow of reading matter. In recent years, I have been able to exchange correspondence in English with some of the young village men. Some students are writing poetry and essays; they have a great variety of interesting job ambitions, even desiring to become film scriptwriters, lawyers, and the like.

Education appears to affect most aspects of life. It has made young couples appreciate the need to have fewer children and to adopt the use of contraceptive devices; it has made farmers learn and adopt more productive agricultural technologies; it has encouraged a concern for health measures such as safe water supply and drainage; and so forth. All this throws into relief the important part education plays in broadening villagers' horizons and in promoting fundamental changes in village life.

Technological Progress

In Wangala the adoption of high-yielding seed varieties and the use of agricultural machinery such as tractors and combine harvesters not only has increased crop yields but also has extended the area of cultivable land. This means that Wangala's output can support its increasing population, though there is, of course, differential access to food depending on the household's economic status.

In Dalena, too, at least some farmers have taken advantage of new agricultural technologies. They use power pump sets to irrigate their lands with canal water, so that they can grow sugarcane and paddy. A large number of power cane crushers and flour mills are now present in Wangala and Dalena. Easy access to motorized transport also has changed the village lifestyle. Trucks, buses, and scooters facilitate villagers' mobility. They can now go to Mandya and other nearby places even on the spur of the moment. This has furthered the urban impact on rural societies and is reflected in many recently built urban-style houses, modern furniture, kitchen equipment, and so forth.

Party Politics

I was fortunate in being able to observe the official attempts to introduce democratically elected village councils into Wangala and Dalena when I first stayed there in the 1950s. Fifteen years later, I found that the convention of hereditary *panchayat* membership was still an important feature, but that elected authority had made some inroads into the practice of status ascription. This made me expect wrongly a slow process of political change. I failed to consider the growth and strength of political parties and how this would affect village politics. I now know that, in order to secure election to the state legislature, candidates have to rally support from rural areas where the majority of the population still resides. Aspiring politicians of the major national political parties have been quick to realize that existing intravillage factions can provide them with ready block votes. Since faction leaders are usually the elders of the major peasant lineages, each faction constitutes a vote bank. To secure a faction's political support, candidates have to promise its leaders access to some of the resources the government allocates for village development in the expectation that, once elected, they will be in a position to keep their pledges. This process inevitably accentuates opposition between village factions and, furthered by the ready availability of alcohol in the villages, it often erupts into violence.

All this I failed to include in my 1970 predictions.

Correct Predictions

To be honest, I must admit that I was pleased to find that at least some of what I had predicted did materialize.

Village Introversion and Village Extroversion

In my 1973 book, I described Wangala's development as being predominantly village introverted in contrast to Dalena, which displayed village extroversion. I related these different styles of development to the different village environments: Wangala had access to canal irrigation while Dalena's lands remained dry. This led me to predict that the two villages would continue along these different paths of development for at least the next thirty years. This appears to have been the case: Wangala has experienced internal diversification of economic activities; its residents take Mandya as their model and aspire for their village to become a growth center for the surrounding area. Wangala still attracts immigrants. Villagers present a united front vis-à-vis the outside world and resist interference in intravillage matters by the major political parties. This is reflected in a strengthened social identity and cohesion.

As in most other Indian rural areas, factional opposition, personal animosities, and disputes still exist in Wangala. But residents still show interest in their fellow villagers' welfare. All of them appreciate the various amenities their village now provides and seem committed to continue along their path of village introversion.

Dalena, on the other hand, has lost much of its social identity. Villagers have become self-centered and are concerned only with their own economic well-being; their social identity with Dalena has almost completely disappeared. The low productivity of their dry land forces increasing numbers to seek a livelihood outside their village; many commute while others have already emigrated and cut their ties with their native place. Since Dalena is situated near Mandya on the highway connecting Bangalore and Mysore, it has already become almost a suburb of Mandya. Altogether, Dalena has pursued the path of village extroversion, and, unless the economic environment of the village changes drastically, I expect it will continue to do so at least for the next ten or twenty years.

Population Growth

My demographic forecast for Wangala and Dalena predicted a somewhat higher rate of population growth than has actually materialized. I now realize that I went wrong because I based my calculations on what I saw in 1970: there was then still an almost complete lack of interest in family planning and an absence of awareness of the disadvantages that come with a large number of offspring. However, what I failed to take into account at the time was the important role education can play in changing behavior in general and fertility behavior in particular. Over the years, schooling has certainly increased the younger generation's awareness of the advantages of smaller families. Many village women have undergone tubal ligation, pleased to have found an escape from regular childbirth.

However, the existing demographic structure of Wangala and Dalena is still so heavily weighted in favor of the under-fifteen-year-olds that a considerable rate of population growth is likely to continue for at least another generation.

My forecast for Mandya's population growth has been fairly accurate. By 1991, it had already reached 120,000 and it is likely that it will have reached 150,000 by the year 2000, which is what I had expected. It is, of course, always easier to forecast demographic changes for a town like Mandya, which grows mainly by attracting immigrants from near and far, than it is to predict changes in fertility behavior for individual small communities.

Gender and Caste Discrimination

Liberal state legislation has no doubt reduced the degree of gender and caste discrimination that used to exist in Wangala and Dalena, but gender and caste are still important determinants of a villager's socioeconomic role and status.

Relationships between male and female villagers have remained far from equal. In fact, drinking and gambling among men has resulted in a deterioration of living conditions for women. Many village men these days get drunk and pledge their wives' jewelry in gambling, which often leads to abuse and violence against women. As of yet, there is no strong women's lobby in these villages to claim and protect their human and constitutional rights. This may emerge with the advent of increasing numbers of educated village women.

Caste has continued to be an important principle of socioeconomic organization. The constitutional privileges awarded to Scheduled Castes and "Backward Castes" have further reinforced caste identity. In 1955, the difference between the caste and Scheduled Caste residential areas was obvious: a gap separated the two areas and most of the caste households lived in larger tiled-roof houses, whereas Scheduled Castes had only small thatched-roof huts. By 1996, the difference was overshadowed by the large expansion of housing sites and the numerous new reinforced-concrete houses for Scheduled Castes, built with government subsidies.

The Wangala and Dalena Scheduled Caste settlement has now become sandwiched between the Peasant caste homes. This does not, however, mean that closer relations have evolved between Peasants and their Scheduled Caste neighbors. The stigma of "Untouchability" persists: village coffee shops still use special glasses to serve Scheduled Castes, and the poorest village strata are composed primarily of Scheduled Castes.

However, as I had expected, there are signs of differentiation along class lines. For instance, though the majority of households in the Wangala settlement for the landless are Scheduled Castes, they do live side by side with a number of Functionary households. They reside in the same village section not because of caste identity, which used to be the overriding determinant of the settlement pattern, but because of their landlessness. However, there seem to be only a few occasions when unity among them manifests itself.

Class Differentiation within Caste

I expected the beginnings of class to occur in the two villages. While class differentiation certainly exists by now, it has not evolved in the way I had expected. Rather than the economy (i.e., the relationship to the means of production) acting as the overall dividing force between the different socioeconomic strata, caste is still the basis for social identity. What has happened is a polarization between the economic strata within each individual caste. There have been increasing numbers of landless Peasants and a declining proportion of middle-class Peasants, while Peasant magnates have become considerably wealthier. A similar process has taken place even among Scheduled Castes: large proportions of Scheduled Castes are landless, some are middle farmers, and there are now some professional upper-class Scheduled Castes, though admittedly the latter are still very small in number. Such a Scheduled Caste class differentiation is already noticeable in Dalena. Those Scheduled Castes who have managed to get educated and have secured some of the public service positions reserved for them constitute the elite. They live in new, large, and well-furnished houses. Their lifestyle obviously differs considerably from other and less fortunate Dalena Scheduled Castes.

In south Indian villages, it is in the interest of the poorer strata of the different castes to identify with their caste rather than with similar class members of other castes. The Scheduled Caste upper-stratum households managed to reach the higher status because, by identifying themselves as Scheduled Castes, they were entitled to take advantage of the preferential treatment the government offers them. Similarly, landless Peasants perceive that their only chance of improving their lot is to stress their Peasant identity; this enables them to take advantage of the privileges offered to Backward Castes, of which the Peasants are one. It would not have helped them to follow the Marxist thrust of "workers of the world unite; you have nothing to lose but your chains!" They themselves well realize this. Dalena landless Scheduled Castes do not see themselves in a conflict relationship with their own Scheduled Caste elite, but are in fact proud of their achievement. Liberal State legislation has certainly achieved a decline in caste discrimination, but caste has remained the overriding principle of social organization in south Indian villages. It looks as if it will continue to be so at least for the next few decades.

I now realize that in my 1970 forecast I must have been too much influenced by the cultural continuity I found in Wangala and Dalena after the fifteen years of absence that followed my first visit in 1955. Therefore, I assumed that it would continue for another thirty years. This made me overlook the impact of change factors, such as education, that take at least one or two generations before showing results. In sum, anyone making forecasts for such microsocieties by extrapolating from base-line information must take into account the impact of existing as well as future change agents.

Note

1. Entitled *Village Voices: 40 Years of Rural Transformation in South India*, this sixty-minute color film offers a unique opportunity to view the different paths of development in the two communities studied by Epstein and her colleagues. According to the film's publicity release, "It is the only study in the whole of India in which the same researcher covers a period as long as 43 years. The film not only presents how the villagers themselves see the changes that have taken place, but also how one of them, T. Thinme-Gowda, now a senior administrative official, perceives the development and how the expatriate researcher analyzes it. The film poses a challenge not only to developers but also to a wide public concerned with rural development." A project of the Institut für den Wissenschaftlichen Film Göttingen, the film is directed by Beate Engelbrecht, who was first involved in long-term ethnographic studies in 1980, while doing dissertation fieldwork in Tzintzuntzan, Mexico.

References Cited

Epstein, A. L. [editor]
   (1967) *The Craft of Social Anthropology*. London: Tavistock.

Epstein, T. Scarlett
   (1962) *Economic Development and Social Change in South India*. Manchester: Manchester University Press.
   (1973) *South India, Yesterday, Today, and Tomorrow: Mysore Villages Revisited*. New York: Holmes and Meier.

T. SCARLETT EPSTEIN

Epstein, T. Scarlett, A. P. Suryana-Rayana, and T. Thinme-Gowda
(1998) *Village Voices—40 Years of Rural Transformation in South India*. New Delhi:
Sage Publications.

Firth, Raymond
(1959) *Social Change in Tikopia: Re-Study of a Polynesian Community after a Generation*. New York: Macmillan.

Lewis, Oscar
(1958) *Village Life in Northern India: Studies in a Delhi Village*. Urbana: University of
Illinois Press.

Mead, Margaret
(1956) *New Lives for Old: Cultural Transformation—Manus, 1928–1953*. New York:
William Morrow.

Mukerjee, R. [editor]
(1929) *Fields and Farmers in Oudh*. University of Lucknow Studies in Economics and
Sociology, No. 4. Calcutta: Longmans, Green.

Rajapurohit, A. R., and Mabel Koilpillai
(1981) *Irrigation and Its Socio-economic Consequences*. Bangalore: Shiny Publications.

Rao, Sudha V.
(1985) *Education and Rural Development*. New Delhi: Sage Publications.

Spate, O. H. K.
(1973) "Foreword." Pp. xiii–xv in T. Scarlett Epstein (editor), *South India, Yesterday,
Today, and Tomorrow: Mysore Villages Revisited*. New York: Holmes and Meier.

Srinivas, M. N.
(1959) "The dominant caste in Rampura." *American Anthropologist* 61:1–16.

Van Velsen, Jan
(1967) "The extended-case method and situational analysis." Pp. 129–149 in A. L.
Epstein (editor), *The Craft of Social Anthropology*. London: Tavistock.

Watson, Walter
(1958) *Tribal Cohesion in a Money Economy: A Study of the Mambwe People of Northern Rhodesia*. Manchester: Manchester University Press.

CHAPTER FOUR

COLLABORATIVE LONG-TERM ETHNOGRAPHY AND LONGITUDINAL SOCIAL ANALYSIS OF A NOMADIC CLAN IN SOUTHEASTERN TURKEY

Ulla C. Johansen and Douglas R. White

Introduction

This chapter describes Johansen's Turkish fieldwork and our collaborative longitudinal study of nomad social dynamics (White and Johansen n.d.) based on a forty-year span of field visits, extensive oral histories, and a two-hundred-year genealogical database. On the basis of this case study, we elaborate a paradigm for diachronic network research on social organization in the context of long-term field research (see Brudner and White 1997; White et al. forthcoming).

Long-term field studies are not synonymous with longitudinal research, which entails the capacity to track samples of cases through time. Long-term fieldworkers can easily keep track of individuals anecdotally or examine small samples of cases systematically, but computers are needed as the size of populations or complexity of problems outstrips the capabilities of researchers. As a supplement to qualitative "hands-on" research, the capacity to track samples with the aid of computers can be tremendously helpful; especially when the issue is one of comparability of data over time. In the Gwembe Tonga project, for example, years of work were needed to bring the computerization of the project up to a level suitable for longitudinal analysis (White, Scudder, and Colson 1998; Clark et al. 1995). A similar collaborative effort for the Tzintzuntzan project was begun in 1998 and is still in progress (see the Tzintzuntzan Web site, currently available at www.santafe.edu/tarasco/Mexican.html).

Through longitudinal analysis, long-term field sites become crucial laboratories for monitoring changes that may benefit local peoples (Cernea 1996). Longitudinal analysis also offers a better interface between theories, methods, and the richness and embeddedness of ethnographic data. Both qualitative and quantitative data are necessary to capture the rich and shifting quality of people's lives. Longitudinal analysis, in this context, vastly enriches our understanding of social processes.

The aim of this chapter and of our forthcoming book (White and Johansen n.d.) is to show how "classical" long-term ethnographic studies of social organization, using genealogical and oral histories among other methods, can be reformatted

ULLA C. JOHANSEN AND DOUGLAS R. WHITE

A meeting of family heads in the large black tent of the *Tanïdïk Kïsï*. Photo by Ulla Johansen.

and reanalyzed by computer in terms of network analysis. In our book, using the Turkish case as an example, we describe new methods designed to facilitate network analysis of data from genealogies and narratives and show how to identify emergent structures in kinship networks, such as cohesive groups, using concepts defined in graph theory.

The Turkish study is a case in which kinship networks are central to social organization. It has a number of characteristics that make it perfect for longitudinal network analysis of social organization using genealogical data. Its patrilocal residential groupings are determined by genealogical links, as are its patrilineal extended families and linkages. Kinship links provide network supports for leadership positions and cohesion with the larger clan. Here we discuss how an analysis of kinship networks contributes to understanding the dynamics of social organization in the Turkish case, leaving out the details that can be found in our book.

It is not easy to find the right voice for a pair of anthropologists who work collaboratively but from different perspectives. A formal division of our chapter into two parts—one by the ethnographer and the other by the analyst—would not be appropriate, as Johansen took a direct interest in the analysis, as did White in the ethnography. We decided to retain our unifying "we" and at times, where appropriate, to break our dialogue into specific "Johansen" and "White" responses within our common enterprise. By emphasizing multiple voices in the ethnographic enterprise, we also hope to provide multiple possibilities for those researchers or members of the Aydïnlï who will one day read this study and view the enterprise differently. Perhaps our dialogue will make transparent some of the differences and similarities in our orientations to research and analysis, especially for younger anthropologists considering long-term field research.

Long-Term Fieldwork among the Aydïnlï

The nomads of the Turkish Antitaurus are officially named Yürük or Yörük ("nomad"), which is what those in the west wing of the Taurus Mountains, the Taurus proper, call themselves. In contrast, the nomads of the east wing, the Antitaurus, call themselves Aydïnlï ("people from Aydin"), a town and its hinterland in southwest Anatolia. The Aydïnlï and Yürük were organized in tribes, large political units of several thousand people; some of which, such as the Karakoyunlu ("people with black sheep"), have been documented since the thirteenth century (Sümer 1967). The Aydïnlï clan that Johansen (1965, 1994) studied had no traditional name, since they formed a distinctive group in the nineteenth century. They introduced themselves to her as Karaevli ("people with black houses"), a name which refers to the black goat-wool tents they lived in and which is sometimes given by sedentary people to full-time nomads. After they knew each other better, they advised Johansen to look at them simply as a branch of the Karahacïlï tribe. This implies a form of cohesion somewhere between a clan identity and an established tribal name.

Johansen: My interest in peoples with Turkic languages began in 1951 when I worked on my Ph.D. thesis on the Yakuts in Siberia. Since systematic fieldwork in the Soviet Union was impossible at that time, I decided to investigate Turkish nomadism in Turkey. The Aydïnlï study was my first fieldwork training. After having taken courses not only in anthropology but also in Turkish and Islamic studies at Hamburg University, I studied one semester at Ankara University and became friends with both senior and junior Turkish colleagues. I also was taught how to behave properly in Turkish society.

In the autumn of 1956, I visited a number of families among the Aydïnlï nomads of southeastern Turkey to get a first impression of their culture and to choose the lineage to which I would try to gain access. Turkish archaeologists Halet Çambel and Bahadir Alkim helped to make contact with these groups. As they did excavations in the area of nomadic autumn and winter camps, they were able to introduce me to a farmer who had business contacts with the nomads. This farmer became my first guide and consultant. From April to September of 1957, I spent half a year observing the nomads' daily routine: their economy, material culture, patterns of interpersonal relations, and Islamic folk religion. Since no studies on these nomads existed at that time, with the sole exception of a Turkish Ph.D. thesis on their physical anthropology and a Turkish traveler's report, I wished to write an ethnography. As a twenty-nine-year-old young woman—no more than a "girl," from the Aydɪnlɪ perspective—I could not establish my own household in their society, but had to live as a member of an extended family in the tent of my adoptive family. This was a "loner" type of fieldwork (Foster et al. 1979:10). I revisited the Aydɪnlɪ for short periods in 1964, 1970, 1982, 1989, and 1995. Among other things, I studied the social organization of the lineage and the whole clan. The consequence of my involvement—which became a lifelong commitment to document the Aydɪnlɪ's history—was a very intensive form of studying a nomad society.

Over the years, I worked on many other projects, but always kept my Aydɪnlɪ connections open by letters. There might be a hundred or so letters in response in my files, dictated by the old people and, in the last decades, written by the young people themselves. My adoptive brother, who became a clan leader, learned to write as a teenager although he never visited a school. Sometimes I have had phone calls from richer members of the clan during winter, when they are in town and if they know I may visit the next summer. We gossip freely in both directions, and I ask for news about their families: Who has married whom? Who has had babies? What professions do young people have now? How do they organize their lives if they give up nomadism? What ties have they still with the clan? Who is most popular now among the leaders? Has anyone died?

My biggest regrets were not to have written down my first field report immediately after my return from the research in 1958 and to have been too self-conscious in asking who would pay my salary, and for what? I became involved in museum fellowships and Central Asia research positions. My fieldwork proved critical to my subsequent teaching career. Before field research, I was not interested in theories or methods. Only after I could evaluate a theory or method in the context of my field experience did these become exciting for me.

Although my field trips lasted no more than six months at a time, and mostly included summers, it was during summertime that nomadic lifeways were most in evidence. The Aydɪnlɪ winter camps are in the lowland of southeastern Turkey, the so-called Çukurova, only a few meters above sea level, where they live dispersed among other groups. In summer this lowland is very hot and humid, with temperatures rising to 47 degrees centigrade in the shade. Thus, the goats and sheep have to be driven to the mountains, which rise at the inland side of Çukurova to a height of nearly 4,000 meters. In winter it is snowy and the temperatures reach minus 20 degrees centigrade, so herds and their owners have to come down before it gets too cold.

In the first decades of the Turkish Republic, the nomad clans had an interest in registering as settlers of the newly founded villages in former Armenian lands, which meant charge-free access to the projected villages' pasture grounds. In this way, the Aydɪnlɪ obtained a common summer pasture, a valley of about 12 kilometers in length with surrounding mountain ridges at a height of about 1,500 meters above sea level. This common territory was an important social camp for

those groups, but every autumn the patriarchs of the lineages were forced to enter into long negotiations concerning their winter camps with farmers or nomadic
groups who had obtained territories in these lowlands. Since the 1980s, spring
and autumn pastures have had to be paid for as well, due to the need for a pause
of about two weeks on the way up or the way down the 100- to 200-kilometer
migration routes.

Migrations were the occasions at which all nomads, men and women, had
the most contact with the outside world—with other clans, even tribes or villagers. They were forced to cross the territories of other groups at least two times
every year, in spring and in autumn. These migrations revealed in a profound way
the cultural changes during the time of the long-term fieldwork. In 1956–1957
most of the clans still migrated in the traditional form: the lineage went together
wearing their best garb, with beautifully decorated camels. These animals were
festooned with tassels, felt-plates with beads, and *kauris* and smaller bells at the
heads to control acoustically the regularity of their movements, as well as with
large bells at their sides, announcing the coming of the group at a considerable
distance. Migrating with the Aydïnlï, I saw that they had little concern if their
herds were damaging the borders of growing cereal fields along the way, nor did
they ask the villagers before they interposed a spring pasture of two to three weeks
on their common lands. "Farmers are cowards, they negotiate. Our tongues are in
the barrels of our rifles," declared a young man, pointing proudly to the weapon
that he, like every male nomad over fourteen, wore at his shoulder.

This attitude had changed fundamentally by 1970, when I again took part in
a migration. The nomad women did not wear their fancy dresses any longer, but
tried to look like farmers' women. There was no expression of festivity, joy, or
pride left in connection with the first migration day. Joint families—no longer
whole lineages—went together. Tractors with racks, which a few of the clan
members owned, transported the tent and household utensils of many families.
By 1982, only a few nomads were still camel breeders. Their animals were used
for the steepest parts of the way and all camel decorations had already been sold
to tourist antique shops in the bazaars of Adana and Kayseri. In 1995, the herds
of some families were even transported by trucks to avoid the hostility of farmers
living along the migration route. The scarce common land of the villages was under tight control of farmers and policemen.

Turkey saw its population grow from about 25 million, when I first met the
nomads, to about 65 million in 1995. What such dry numbers mean to the self-
consciousness of people can really be understood only through the experience of
long-term fieldwork.

White and Johansen: These dramatic changes in the situation of the Aydïnlï
are reflected in the network analysis, which includes demography, migration, and
changes in social organization. Because we also have network data from the genealogical reconstructions, combined with oral histories, we have provided in our

book a longer-term perspective on demographic and social changes from the clan's establishment in its present territory in the mid-nineteenth century.

In the process of her forty years of mutual acquaintance with the Aydïnlï, Johansen changed in their eyes from being a young foreign "girl"—albeit conversant in Turkish—to an elder "auntie" of the clan members with whom she had stayed so many times. The long-term fieldwork not only made her an observer of becoming old together with the Aydïnlï, but she had also shared their feelings at many occasions. Thus, the young people increasingly took her for a witness of their tribal life in the "good old time," because enormous changes had taken place since her early visits. The people of her age and their children, for example, had no school training, but now all children—girls and boys—go to school for at least five years. Many of the nomads, who have obtained permanent houses in the lowlands, now watch TV for some months of the year and are increasingly connected to elements of the global system.

Johansen: It may be useful to give younger anthropologists a sense of the field methods I used in collecting the genealogical data. Younger men, when asked, said at once to ask their fathers or fathers' brothers. To get genealogical information from the Aydïnlï patriarchs proved to be an easy task. Even the most prominent among them would give his genealogy and have it drawn into my large book in the manner anthropologists do. They reacted eagerly to my request to tell their genealogies, because quite obviously this gave them the opportunity to make known once more the long history of their families and the influential position of their ancestors. They immediately understood the genealogical drawings and wished to correct them by having me review them. And as soon as the man just talking named relatives whom he had in common with other men present in the tent, the latter began to supplement or correct the information he had given. The family heads of the clan are shown in the photograph, following one of the meetings in the large black tent of the clan leader (see photo at the beginning of this chapter).

Women, even elderly ones, laughed in embarrassment when I put the same question to them, and they said they did not know anything of the older times, either of the families they had married into or the families of their descent, which they had usually left at a young age. But when asked the names of people of their own generation, and especially those of their children and their children's children, the elderly women were better informed than the men. They could tell the exact sequence of children, even for those who died as infants. In this way, they could even estimate the age of the children and young people by counting a regular distance of two years between each birth for a woman.

In later fieldwork, when I came into tents of the clan's summer pasture for the first time in the season, the host would announce in the presence of as many men as possible: "Go to it, draw out my root, let us see!" The recitation was for the host a question of reputation. Sometimes, when I did not want to waste too much time, I showed the already written genealogy to my host and asked him to correct the data. I then recited his full genealogy in a loud voice waiting for his corrections, and men always laughed in amazement that a woman knew their genealogy. As my data grew, I knew it even better than did some of them. By the constant repetitions I had good control of the data and could eliminate errors. In this way, I traced back ancestral lines of the informants to ten "roots" and their descendants (White and Johansen n.d.).

Over the years, the focus of my study of social organization has remained enigmatic. In 1982, I decided to integrate all of my genealogical field notes and diagrams into a single large scroll consisting of successive sheets of graph paper, taped together, organized lineage by lineage. This compilation of genealogical data provided me with a way of assessing my data, but it formed a scroll some 40 feet long! The scroll served my research purpose of being able to assess genealogical connections as I wrote about different aspects of nomad life, but it was not in a publishable format. While the males were neatly organized in lineages, females each appeared in *two* places: once as a daughter and elsewhere as a wife. Across the bottom of the scroll I had drawn parallel colored lines that connected upward to the positions in which each woman appears once as daughter and once as wife. Had I to do it over again, whatever the method of keeping the genealogies, I would from the beginning assign unique identification numbers to each individual and, in addition to genealogical drawings, keep a numerically ordered file on individuals that also showed at least their parents and spouses, if not also their children by each spouse and siblings by each parent.

In formulating the goals of our collaboration, we had to answer two interwoven questions. Mine, deriving from the fieldwork perspective, was, What happened to the nomads in the last two hundred years? White's was, *Why and by what processes* did it happen? What role did social networks play in the dynamics of changing social organization and adaptation?

With a network approach that fitted naturally to an ethnographer's concerns with social organization, we reconstructed the developments resulting from the social rules of Aydınlı society. The network analysis was able to make these developments visible in a set of graphs that formed the basis for our analysis of changes in social organization and leadership.

Data Issues

Johansen: The problem of "minimum core data" in social anthropology was raised by A. L. Epstein (1967), then by T. Scarlett Epstein (1979), and more recently by Emilio Moran (1995). It was not an idea I took to the field back in 1956, but like many anthropologists I improvised on the spot. Exact birth dates, for example, were impossible to obtain from archival records, but general time frames could be inferred from narratives. In some societies it is important to have accurate birth order even if birth dates are not available, so where possible in the genealogies I listed children in order of birth.

Because the data regarding genealogies were systematically collected, with updating of genealogies during each visit since 1964, they are accurate throughout a period of nearly forty years. Discrepancies in memories about earlier ancestries have been closely examined, and corrected where possible, for the full two-hundred-year period of their coverage.[1] The genealogical data provide a longitudinal framework for analysis of social organization that encompasses but also goes beyond the framework of my field visits.

White: Not every fieldworker has genealogical data complete enough over a long enough time period to support a network analysis of social organization. On my visits to Cologne throughout the 1990s, after first meeting Johansen, it became evident to me that her genealogical scroll for the Aydïnlï, which had become well known at Cologne's Institute of Ethnology, could support a richly documented diachronic network analysis. For several years, I asked if she would simply assign unique ID numbers to each of the individuals on her scroll, which would allow the genealogical network to be transferred to computer. Our joint research project on the network analysis of her genealogies was able to begin when she did so in 1997.

After the persons in the scroll were numbered, we followed established methods (White, Batagelj, and Mrvar 1999; see also White and Jorion 1992) to code and analyze their genealogical links and attributes by computer. There were 1,309 individuals, including 364 married males and 386 married females in 412 marriages. The earliest generation, going back to seven of the founders (or remembered roots) of informants' ancestries, dates back to 1785.

Schneider's (1984) critique of genealogical studies notes the strong bias of many kinship studies to assume that biological ancestry (an obsession of societies that emphasize legitimacy in rights to inherited private property) constitutes the core of human kinship. Too often, genealogical data collection has been tied to some master scheme for reconstructing social structure.[2] Frameworks for minimum data should be constructed so as not to force rigid or inappropriate taxonomies of residence types, descent groups, and the like. Coding social organization as a collection of individuals and groups with networks and attributes has enormous advantages in steering clear of the pitfalls of many kinds of analysis previously used in kinship studies.

Johansen: While network methods have seemed to most anthropologists to serve only for specialized synchronic studies in places like cities, our study aimed at using diachronic network methods to study organizational change within a "traditional" population. Moreover, we used some of the most traditional and widely available types of ethnographic data such as genealogies and oral histories supplemented by biographical and actor-oriented information.

White: The requirements for minimum core data for genealogical studies used in a longitudinal network framework are rather simple. One must (1) identify each male and each female uniquely so as not to confuse those with the same name or similar names, (2) create an inventory of all marriages and multiple marriages of individuals, and (3) identify all children, keeping careful track of their parents, and, where known, children who died prior to reaching adulthood or died without marrying or having children. Even where exact birth, marriage, and death dates are lacking, the network ordering of genealogical generations creates a longitudinal framework for the analysis of different time periods. The result is a "rough cut" for assigning historical periods to the levels in the network. In the present case, these levels are highly correlated with Johansen's estimates from narrative sources as to the generational levels of individuals in their historical cohorts. Looking back to the first volume on long-term research (Foster et al. 1979:333), it is surprising that "minimum core data" did not include the minimal kinship links (mother and father) needed to construct genealogical networks. How could such an important dimension of ethnographic data have been ignored? Our study shows that a traditional technique of anthropology—the genealogical census—is now feasible within a database for a population whereas in 1979 relational or network databases were still well beyond our capabilities. Another factor that made genealogy problematic as a basis of analyzing social organization in 1979 was the link between the "personal data" of names and identities and the possibility of "open data banks" that were considered a potential time bomb "whose explosive potentialities cannot be predicted" (Foster et al. 1979:336). What we have seen, however, is an "explosion" of Internet-based public domain genealogies and archival materials on over 50 million people, and still expanding. The creation of genealogical software now makes possible the exchange, merging, and analysis of genealogical data. Finally, network analysis software such as Pajek (Batagelj and Mrvar 1997) now allows new approaches to the analysis of social organization using large-scale network data.

Network Analysis

Johansen: Most anthropologists are convinced that network analysis is something exquisitely synchronic, but in our work, White has demonstrated that network analysis also could be used to discover diachronic processes—even over more than two hundred years, as in the case of the Aydïnlï.

White: We used the ethnographic context of successive marriage events to define both long-term and immediate impacts of marriage events and relationships. We also examined the impact of environmental factors in shaping family relationships, alliances, social groupings, political support networks for emergent leaders, likelihood of migration, transmission of cultural knowledge, and so forth. While such an approach may be complemented by the study of other events, it still is commensurate with an understanding that "the essence of culture is change . . . and there seems to be only one way to get necessary data for an adequate anthropological analysis: through long-term research" (Pospisil 1979:142). We have tried to provide a dynamic representation of events, and their impacts through time that, when coupled with a rich ethnographic database and the ethnographer's long-term experience of change, can contribute to the development of a dynamic theory of culture.

Thus, we were interested not only in demographic changes, but also in how genealogical linkages created network patterns relevant to social organization and social practices. The graph theoretical concept used to identify cohesive groups in the kinship networks was that of *bicomponents*, defined in graph theory as sets of nodes (here, marriages) in which each pair had two or more independent paths connecting them through ties of descent. Since the nodes are marriages, multiple paths of relationship trace out what is called in social anthropology either "marital relinking" between families, or blood marriages.

The graph in figure 4.1 shows the entire network of intermarried descent lines associated with relinked marriages, starting from marriages of clan founders at the top of the graph to those of the present day at the bottom. In this graph, marriages are represented by nodes (circles), distributed across eight historical

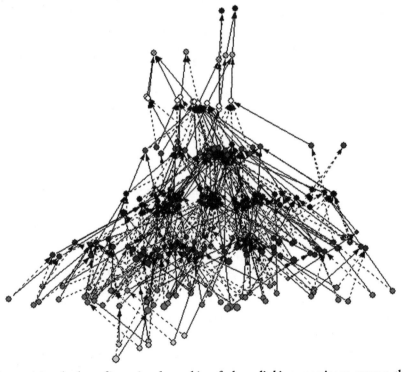

Figure 4.1. A three-dimensional graphic of the relinking marriages among the Aydīnlī.

network generations, while the dashed and solid lines, respectively, show lines of male versus female descent. Graphs such as these become the object of a network analysis of kinship and marriage.

Johansen: As an ethnographer, I found the term *structural endogamy* (White 1997; Brudner and White 1997) particularly apt for describing the pattern and boundaries of intragroup marriage among the nomads, as defined by relinking. Here was a way to describe what many ethnographers observe about the effects of marriage patterns on social cohesion, while making precise the delimitation of boundaries of cohesive groupings within the society. Detailed results can be found in White and Johansen (n.d.).

White: A network approach such as ours, focusing on the genealogical network and how other social processes connect to it, is still partial, and a full ethnography of the Aydïnlï nomads based on the existing field material would occupy many volumes. The problem of "longer" and "thicker" data generally is especially characteristic of long-term field studies. It is still true, as Hofer (1979) noted for Hungarian ethnography, that present forms of publication could hardly begin to make available all the basic data. For the Aydïnlï project, however, Johansen and I have begun to make a sample of her photographic collection available as an Internet publication, with each photo dated and annotated in time. We plan to post to the Web the complete genealogies—not for living persons, but for the ancestral generations of Aydïnlï—as a supplement to our book (http://eclectic.ss.uci.edu/~drwhite/turks/). In this way, we will overcome a much-neglected consideration in long-term studies: the creation of systematic data sets that can, eventually, become historical data in the public domain.

Johansen: In the photo book I kept for the Aydïnlï, I annotated the content of every one of about 2,500 photos according to the persons or groups and the place where the photo was made. Since 1982, I have used some additional tapes for long reports on the nomads. On a daily basis, I wrote field notes, partly in a sort of shorthand, with a list of the signs used in them so that others could later decipher them. Many of these notes were later copied out in full and made into a data catalogue, parts of which are now on computer.

White: Hence, we can expand the concept of network representation to include all kinds of data, including not only diachronic data but also links from individuals, groups, and nodes at other levels of organization, as expressed in both visual and textual data files. Thus, we have the beginnings of suitable computer-based methodologies for longitudinal analysis of field data.

Networks, Migration, Leadership, and Conflict

It is obvious that longitudinal analysis of a kinship and marriage network can yield important insights about marriage choices, marriage rules, and marriage systems

ULLA C. JOHANSEN AND DOUGLAS R. WHITE

(White 1999). Our work shows how the analysis of marital relinking is involved in many of the fundamental structures and processes of the formation, adaptation, and potential dissolution of any society. For the Aydïnlï of Turkey, our longitudinal network analysis demonstrates the following:

1. In the process of clan formation, the relinking of marriages by a limited set of ancestral families created the basis of the cohesion and solidarity of the clan, from the earliest generation to the present.

2. The formation of multiple networks—whose intersections and contending principles define both the multiplex and heterogeneous relationships among individuals—is dynamically involved in the continual emergence and shifting reemergence of patterns of social grouping and cohesion. New marital relinkings in each generation have the effect of altering or reconstituting groupings of relatives vis-à-vis others, thereby influencing patterns of migration and leadership coalitions.

3. Shifting network groupings provide an explanation for the Aydïnlï's use of loosely structured concepts such as *aile* (for families, extended families, minimal lineages, and larger joint families) and *kabile* (for tribes or larger lineages).

4. The potential dissolution of the clan is reflected by disentanglement, or increasing scarcity of intermarriage (relinking) within the group, involving not just an increase of marriages with other groups, but also a breakup of the structurally endogamous core of Aydïnlï society.

Presenting the empirical results that support our argument about the centrality of network dynamics to social change and adaptation among the Aydïnlï is beyond the scope of this chapter (see White and Johansen n.d.).

Analysis of Leadership and Conflict

Johansen: One of the advantages of long-term fieldwork was that I became witness to the passing of leadership across three generations, and the competition for leadership among four lineages. Among the Aydïnlï, leadership is neither hereditary nor formal; there are no formal offices of clan or lineage leaders, only leading *tanïdïk kïsï*—"known persons"—whose influential personalities provide informal leadership to the clan during succeeding generations. Nor is leadership restricted to any one lineage. The dispersion of successive leaders across different lineages is a source of divisiveness, and there are often rivals for leadership in other lineages.

White: One of my first structural observations from the marital relinking calculations was that every one of the *tanïdïk kïsï* over all generations had married so as to relink with the giant cohesive bicomponent of the clan (as in the graph in figure 4.1). This led me to investigate the means by which cohesive factions supported each leader and how these factions operated, within the overall bicomponent of the clan, in competing with one another for the passing of leadership from one generation to the next.

Johansen: Nomad leadership, as an activity, becomes visible in group discussion with those who voluntarily come to gather in the tent of a *tanīdīk kīsī*. It includes mediation of disputes, common problem solving, and coordination of activities. Because there is respect for age and experience, however, it is primarily the older men who discuss in the *tanīdīk kīsī's* tent, while the younger men listen. A great amount of time is spent in discussion over monies to be exchanged at marriage, thus showing the importance of marriage bonds among the nomads. The informal councils often discuss marriage decisions that add flexible adaptations of reciprocity rules in building social solidarity. For example, if two marriages are arranged simultaneously, such as the exchange of daughters, the payments of bride money are canceled, and interfamily reciprocity is direct rather than indirect.

White: Every marriage may act as a new relinking that creates or reinforces a locally cohesive subgroup. I developed the hypothesis that cohesive subgroups of the clan, and central positions of leadership within the clan, are established dynamically by denser kinship ties and marital relinking that provide the basis of their support. The bottom line for clan leadership is that a successful candidate for *tanīdīk kīsī* can have a small but intense following whose members span the clan, or a large and less-intense following; but in any case the members of the cohesive set must span the clan and cannot simply occupy a solidarity group with very close ties that excludes other subsets in the clan. Through successive generations, emergent loci of leadership slowly rotate around the clan center as different segments of the clan are articulated to the center. Given a clan with a relatively stable center, each successive leadership faction (after the settlement in eastern pastures circa 1875) is focused on a different lineage, but also links both to the center of the clan and reaches out to other subgroups. Rotating around a central axis of clan cohesion, shifts of leadership over time sweep through different segments or factions of the clan to augment overall political connectivity of each successive lineage group (and their closer allies) to both the clan center and its peripheries.

Johansen: Long-term fieldwork also enabled me to observe conflict, expressed through feuding, in relation to cohesion and leadership. I saw four episodes of shootings and ensuing blood revenge during each of my first three stays before 1964. Feuding had not altogether ceased in 1970, but there were no feuds by 1982. Our network analysis of changes in the kinship basis of political leadership found an unexpected correlation with the decline of feuding. Above all, the rules for feuding respect kinship distance, reckoned first of all by patrilineal connections. The closer the kin involved in potential disputes, the greater is the potential for disruption of local groups, the more serious are the consequences and the more feuding is avoided and mediation sought in the case of disputes. In contrast, the more distant the relation between the parties, the more severe the feuding and the larger the group mobilized (Boehm 1987). Feuds between two clans or a clan and a village were important up to about 1980 (cf. Johansen 1995), a time when leadership structure changed away from kinship cohesion and toward education and external political-economic ties as the basis of leadership.

White: In developing our ideas of how the nomads adapted to changing environmental pressures, we took into account elements such as feuding and solidarity within a general framework for understanding the coevolution of social behaviors and social rules that "let people forge new bonds, invent new institutions, and find better ways of doing things" (Postrel 1998:112). Our findings on political factions and social cohesion led me to hypothesize that solidarity cannot be so strong within lineages as to exacerbate rivalries into feuding. There are advantages to exchange, trust, and cooperative relationships between lineages established through marriage (e.g., bride-money payments) and the ensuing cooperation between siblings-in-law. The rule that every woman must be paid for by bride money does not give lineage members privileged status, but creates an egalitarian basis for creating cooperation and exchange through marriage.

A relinking marriage is a signal of commitment to stay within the nomad group. It equips subsequent children with two parents experienced in the nomad way of life, whose relatives have been members of the group, and thus with a variety of role models for cultural socialization. The cohesion of the nomad groups arises out of relinking, but the bicomponent created by relinking does not act like a magnet nor prevent the children of relinking marriages from leaving the clan. Such decisions are voluntary.

The various kinds of social groupings in nomad society—such as clans, lineages, and cohesive groupings of leaders and their followers—divide the loyalties of individuals and prevent the bonds of solidarity from becoming overly restrictive. In this context, we used Lindenberg's (1998) framing approach to social solidarity to help show how shifting groups and levels of cohesion operate dynamically within nomad society, with marital relinking as one of the important dynamic operators.

Impact and Benefits of Long-Term Research

White: One of the major implications of a long-term study is that other researchers or community members can use the data to ask new questions. Although Johansen characterizes her fieldwork as a typical "loner" study, it was the systematic character of the long-term data and genealogies that later attracted me to ask new questions about her materials on social organization, leadership, and the dynamics of adaptation in nomad lifeways. And once the data are in a computerized form, researchers from the next generation also can pose new questions or continue the fieldwork.

The use of genealogical methods in our monograph (White and Johansen n.d.), for example, provided us with the ability to trace not only the genesis of the nomad clan from its origins in the eighteenth century, but also the movement of clan and village peoples back and forth as the clan grew in size. Whether this process will lead to the dissolution of the clan as a nomadic society is an ongoing question for analysis.

Johansen: I am excited by the possibility of new questions and new research, although there are other motivations for continuing a long-term study. Like Scudder and Colson (1979:251), I didn't go back to the field only to check on various hypotheses, but also out of concern for the people who had been so generous to me in my studies and to know what was happening to them as their situations were changing. One of my family members, my adopted son Ralf, went with me on a summer visit and was heartily welcomed, especially in that he was half Turkish and had a Turkish second name by which he was called, "Yildiray." Ralf's presence changed my status as well: no one referred to me as "girl" after that, although for many younger people I was *hala* ("father's sister") because I was the sister of Dede and his brother Aliboz. Other younger people called me *teyze* ("mother's sister"), the familiar way to address elder women; older people used my first name, Turkicized, with the meaning of "the rosy." Over the years, as many members of the clan quit nomadic life and moved to different places, it became hard to visit old friends. And as many of my colleagues at Ankara University have died, my relations to Turkish colleagues have become more distant in recent years.

I am looked on as a fairly rich old "auntie" by the young people, especially since the Turkish *lire* is low in value and my salary seems astronomical for Turks—and of course I am a sort of relative at least for the Kirbasa and Koca bey lineages. Now, I am a member of the old generation and have to take care of the young generation in a patriarchal way. I have made contributions many times at weddings and funerals, have helped persons to avert little insolvencies, and even have assisted in buying a car for a crippled young man. But these people have helped me to have success in my life, and so I do whatever I can for them.

My presence and my help have had an impact on the Aydinli and, of course, on the value people place on the many benefits of nomadic life, although it is increasingly difficult these days. Perhaps some of the girls have been inspired to go further in school because of me, and people have been delighted when I bring photos or show them my published articles, especially with photographs and captions. Perhaps their greatest amusement came in 1982 when I brought about one hundred slides from my visits in 1956, 1957, and 1964, which I showed to members of the clan by means of a battery-operated projector. Ralf ran a tape recorder, and I wrote down the commentary on the pictures. A great many came to the tents in the evenings when I showed the pictures. Everybody wanted to see them again and again, and most discussions went on about identification of people in this way: "Look, there is Crazy Ahmet" (the use of nicknames is common). "No, this cannot be Crazy Ahmet. Crazy Ahmet never wore such a coat." "But it is Crazy Ahmet, only he was much younger then." And so on.

My general questions about the difference in life between then and now were disregarded in all the fun, because people were so delighted to see themselves or their late relatives in the pictures. My plans for this approach to studying culture change had to be abandoned. Who was I to impose, the friendly and dear old auntie, when the culture itself takes over?

White: Johansen's story illustrates beautifully that methods also have an experimental character and that well-laid plans can go awry. Serendipity often plays a beneficial role in research (Foster 1979:182), as with the creation of the genealogical scroll: who would have expected that it would give new results via network analysis? I would emphasize as well that, like all research results, ours are provisional. Nowhere is the provisional character of research more evident than in long-term research, where the passage of even a few years can lead to a change in perspective on what is and has been happening in people's lives (Meggitt 1979:116–122). On the one hand, Kemper (1979:206) has noted the benefits of long-term research: "Long after today's theoretical fads and methodological innovations have been tossed aside, the data collected carefully and patiently over several decades in key ethnographic settings will continue to provide a basis for testing new ideas." On the other hand, Lamphere (1979:42) has argued:

> Anthropology has been characterized by major shifts in theoretical interest from one decade to the next, so that despite increasingly sophisticated theory and concomitant methodology, data collected one decade may be of limited use to the next generation of researchers. . . . We need to avoid this and consider what kinds of data will be most useful 10 to 20 years after a project has been started.

With today's changing theoretical interests, changing technologies, and rapid turnover of ideas and methodologies, long-term research projects continue to invite new research strategies.

Notes

1. There is some selection bias here since it is the ancestors of those living in the 1950s who are remembered in this genealogy, and some ancestors who were members

of the early clan in its new location may not have left descendants. But since residence is strictly virilocal, and only females marry in, the memory of ancestry within the clan itself is likely to be highly accurate, especially since it is reconstructed from multiple sources.

2. The founder of "the genealogical method" in anthropology, W. H. R. Rivers (1910), moored his advocacy of genealogical studies in the idea that actual behaviors, such as those reflected in the events of marriage practices, would be consonant with symbolic forms in language, such as kinship terminology.

References Cited

Batagelj, Vladimir and Andrej Mrvar
(1997) *Networks / Pajek: Program for Large Networks Analysis.* University of Ljublana, Slovenia.

Boehm, Christopher
(1987) *Blood Revenge: The Enactment and Management of Conflict in Montenegro and Other Tribal Societies.* Second Edition. Philadelphia: University of Pennsylvania Press.

Brudner, L. A. and D. R. White
(1997) "Class, poverty, and structural endogamy: Visualizing networked histories." *Theory and Society* 26:161–208.

Cernea, Michael
(1996) "Social organization and development anthropology: The 1995 Malinowski award lecture." *Environmentally Sustainable Development Studies and Monographs Series,* No. 6. Washington, D.C.: World Bank.

Clark, Samuel, Elizabeth Colson, James Lee, and Thayer Scudder
(1995) "Ten thousand Tonga: A longitudinal anthropological study of southern Zambia: 1956–1991." *Population Studies* 49:91–109.

Epstein, A. L. [editor]
(1967) *The Craft of Social Anthropology.* London: Tavistock.

Epstein, T. Scarlett
(1979) "Mysore villages revisited." Pp. 209–226 in George M. Foster, Elizabeth Colson, Thayer Scudder, and Robert V. Kemper (editors), *Long-Term Field Research in Social Anthropology.* New York: Academic Press.

Foster, George M.
(1979) "Fieldwork in Tzintzuntzan: The first thirty years." Pp. 165–184 in George M. Foster, Thayer Scudder, Elizabeth Colson, and Robert V. Kemper (editors), *Long-Term Field Research in Social Anthropology.* New York: Academic Press.

Foster, George M., Thayer Scudder, Elizabeth Colson, and Robert V. Kemper [editors]
(1979) *Long-Term Field Research in Social Anthropology.* New York: Academic Press.

Hofer, Tamás
(1979) "Hungarian ethnographers in a Hungarian village." Pp. 85–102 in George M. Foster, Thayer Scudder, Elizabeth Colson, and Robert V. Kemper (editors), Long-Term Field Research in Social Anthropology. New York: Academic Press.

Johansen, Ulla
(1965) "Die Nomadenzelle Südost-Anatoliens." Bustan 2:33–37.
(1994) "Feldenfahrungen bei den Aydïnlï." Pp. 27–40 in Albert Kunze (editor), Yürük: Nomadenleben in der Türkei. Munich: Trickster Verlag.
(1995) "Regeln der Blutrache." Pp. 401–420 in D. Schorkowitz (editor), Ethnohistorische Wege und Lehrjahre eines Philosophen: Festschrift für Lawrence Krader zum 75. Geburtstag. Frankfurt am Main: Peter Lang.

Kemper, Robert V.
(1979) "Fieldwork among Tzintzuntzan migrants in Mexico City: Retrospect and prospect." Pp. 189–208 in George M. Foster, Thayer Scudder, Elizabeth Colson, and Robert V. Kemper (editors), Long-Term Field Research in Social Anthropology. New York: Academic Press.

Lamphere, Louise
(1979) "The long-term study among the Navajo." Pp. 19–44 in George M. Foster, Thayer Scudder, Elizabeth Colson, and Robert V. Kemper (editors), Long-Term Field Research in Social Anthropology. New York: Academic Press.

Lindenberg, Siegwart
(1998) "The microfoundations of solidarity: A framing approach." Pp. 61–112 in Patrick Doreian and Thomas Fararo (editors), The Problem of Solidarity: Theories and Models. Amsterdam: Gordon and Breach Publishers.

Meggitt, M. J.
(1979) "Reflections occasioned by continuing anthropological field research among the Enga of Papua New Guinea." Pp. 107–126 in George M. Foster, Thayer Scudder, Elizabeth Colson, and Robert V. Kemper (editors), Long-Term Field Research in Social Anthropology. New York: Academic Press.

Moran, Emilio F.
(1995) The Comparative Analysis of Human Societies: Towards Common Standards for Data Collecting and Reporting. Boulder, CO: Lynne Rienner.

Pospisil, Leopold
(1979) "The Tirolean peasants of Obernberg: A study in long-term research." Pp. 127–144 in George M. Foster, Thayer Scudder, Elizabeth Colson, and Robert V. Kemper (editors), Long-Term Field Research in Social Anthropology. New York: Academic Press.

Postrel, Virginia
(1998) The Future and Its Enemies: The Growing Conflict over Creativity, Enterprise, and Progress. Chicago: Free Press.

Rivers, W. H. R.
(1910) "The genealogical method of anthropological enquiry." *Sociological Review* 3:227–234.

Schneider, David M.
(1984) *Critique of the Study of Kinship.* Ann Arbor: University of Michigan.

Scudder, Thayer and Elizabeth Colson
(1979) "Long-term research in Gwembe Valley, Zambia." Pp. 227–254 in George M. Foster, Thayer Scudder, Elizabeth Colson, and Robert V. Kemper (editors), *Long-Term Field Research in Social Anthropology.* New York: Academic Press.

Sümer, Faruk
(1967) "Kara Koyunlular." *Türk Tarih Kurumu Yayinlarindan* VII, 49. Ankara.

White, Douglas R.
(1997) "Structural endogamy and the graphe de parenté." *Informatique, Mathématique et Sciences Humaines* 137:107–125.
(1999) "Controlled simulation of marriage systems." *Journal of Artificial Societies and Social Simulation* 2(3). <http://www.soc.surrey.ac.uk/JASSS/JASSS.html>

White, Douglas R., Vladimir Batagelj, and Andrej Mrvar
(1999) "Analyzing large kinship and marriage networks with Pgraph and Pajek." *Social Science Computer Review* 17(3):245–274.

White, Douglas R. and Ulla Johansen
(n.d.) *An Introduction to Network Analysis of Genealogy and Politics: Social Dynamics in a Nomadic Society.* Manuscript.

White, Douglas R. and Paul Jorion
(1992) "Representing and analyzing kinship: A new approach." *Current Anthropology* 33:454–462.

White, Douglas R., M. Schnegg, L. A. Brudner, and H. Nutini
(forthcoming) "Conectividad múltiple y sus fronteras de integración: Parentesco y compadrazgo en Tlaxcala rural," in Jorge Gil and Samuel Schmidt (editors) *Redes Sociales: Teoría y Aplicaciones.* México, D.F.: Universidad Nacional Autónoma de México.

White, Douglas R., Thayer Scudder, and Elizabeth Colson
(1998) NSF Proposal (funded): "Long term dynamic assessment of impacts of world-system, development and ecological processes on local socioeconomic change in Gwembe Valley, Zambia 1988–90."

Part II
LARGE-SCALE PROJECTS

Most anthropological fieldwork, whether long-term or short-term, is done by lone ethnographers. Occasionally, graduate students may be invited to join their mentor on a part-time basis, typically during summers when classes are not in session. Rarer are team projects in which a group of anthropologists (or other specialists) participate intentionally in a large-scale enterprise.

In the early years of professional fieldwork, when funds were limited and ethnologists were committed to "salvaging" as rapidly as possible as much information as possible from as many "cultures" as they could encounter during brief field trips, large-scale projects were few in number. The few exceptions, such as the Torres Straits Expedition of 1898–1899, led by Alfred Cort Haddon (1901, 1903), took a "natural history" approach to gathering data in the field that assumed that human communities could be studied in isolation. As Geertz (1988:115) has observed, anthropologists of that era shared a worldview that included the "image of primitive societies as 'natural laboratories,' anthropology's Galapagos."

In the 1930s, Alfred L. Kroeber (University of California, Berkeley) obtained sufficient funds to gather—through an "element list" approach—ethnographic and ecological information about every indigenous group from the Rocky Mountains to the Pacific Coast. According to one of the participants in the project, "An enormous amount of effort was put into the Element List Survey by a dozen or so persons working in the field. . . . Members of the project began comparing lists, vying with one another to think of elements not previously included" (Steward 1973:45). In addition to Kroeber himself, fieldworkers in the project included Burt W. Aginsky, Homer G. Barnett, C. D. Chretien, Harold E. Driver, Philip Drucker, Frank J. Essene, Edward W. Gifford, John P. Harrington, Isabel Kelly, Stanislaus Klimek, Verne F. Ray, Julian H. Steward, Omer C. Stewart, and Erminie W. Voegelin—virtually everyone who passed through the Berkeley Department of Anthropology in that period. The results of their labors appeared between 1935 and 1950 in some twenty-six separate monographs in the *University of California Publications in American Archaeology and Ethnology* and the *University of California Anthropological Records*.

In the same era, the Carnegie Institute of Washington was funding a large-scale Middle American Project, which involved archaeologists, ethnologists, physical anthropologists, and other specialists who participated in a multifaceted effort to understand the contemporary Maya of Yucatán in the light of their pre-Columbian and colonial experiences.

As one component of the Carnegie enterprise, Robert Redfield (University of Chicago) coordinated a study of four communities (Tusik, Chan Kom, Dzitas, and Mérida) chosen to illustrate four points along the "folk-urban continuum." Initiated in 1930, the Yucatán Project involved several fieldworkers (Alfonso Villa Rojas in Chan Kom and Tusik, Asael Hansen in Mérida, and Redfield and his wife Margaret in Chan Kom and Dzitas) who worked separately and together for several years during the early 1930s, as the first phase of what Villa Rojas (1979:54) has described as "Redfield's plan of long-term studies in the Mayan region."

At about the same time that Redfield was completing the Yucatán Project, Clyde Kluckhohn (Harvard University) was initiating a large-scale, long-term project among the Navajo in the American Southwest. He selected the off-reservation Navajo community of Ramah, New Mexico, as the site for multi-disciplinary student training. The initial field studies were carried out from 1936 through 1948 and involved continuous visits and revisits, mostly during summers, in loosely organized teams. As recounted by Lamphere in her chapter on "The Long-Term Study among the Navajo," the goals of the project were broadly ethnographic and in accord with Kluckhohn's notion that culture consisted of "designs for living" (Kluckhohn and Kelly 1945:97). Interested more in pattern than in process, Kluckhohn saw his role and that of his colleagues and students as being "interpreters," "brokers," and "intermediaries." He hoped that the project's publications would lead to more humane decisions on the part of those who actually made policy with regard to such important issues as health, education, and land use.

The Ramah Project was followed from 1949 to 1955 by another Harvard-based project, known as the "Comparative Study of Values in Five Cultures." Funded by the Rockefeller Foundation, the Values Project was directed by Kluckhohn and two Harvard colleagues, the archaeologist J. O. Brew and the sociologist Talcott Parsons, with John Roberts and Evon Vogt acting as field directors. During the Values Project, nearly forty researchers, from anthropology and related social sciences, worked in and around Ramah on diverse topics—some of which were only vaguely related to "culture and personality" concerns. The National Science Foundation funded additional field research related to the training of anthropology graduate students in the early 1960s and then again in the early 1970s.

In Lamphere's view, these large-scale projects at Ramah were limited by the prevailing theoretical frameworks within which Kluckhohn and his colleagues labored. By focusing on issues related to culture and personality, they neglected the external forces impinging on contemporary community life, instead treating the Navajo as if they were living in pristine isolation.

In contrast, the Lake Powell Research Project, funded from 1972 to 1977 by the Research Applied to National Needs (RANN) program of the National Science Foundation, involved ethnographers in interdisciplinary applied research not only with other social scientists but also with physical scientists. The anthropology subproject focused on the economic impact of strip-mining and power plant construction on three Navajo communities: Page, its nearby rural areas (Lechee), and nearby Black Mesa. The project focused on process, especially the long-range changes in the local economy and social organization and their relation to the broader American economy and political structure.

Although numerous anthropologists and other scholars continued to work with Navajo groups after the end of the Lake Powell Research Project, the next major large-scale enterprise did not come along until 1993, when Thomas J. Csordas received an initial five-year grant from the National Institute of Mental Health (NIMH) for "The Navajo Healing Project" and then another grant to continue the research through 2001. This project differs from earlier large-scale projects among the Navajo in its intentional efforts to combine outside anthropologists with Navajo researchers. As Lamphere points out, "Only this style of ethnography, combined with a long-term approach, can elucidate the complex and multilayered sets of experiences in the three healing traditions among the Navajo. . . . Thus, Csordas and his collaborators are able to achieve a level of analysis that was simply beyond the dreams of Kluckhohn, Vogt, and other anthropologists of an earlier era."

Only since the 1950s, when significant government and private foundation funds began to flow into "foreign area" research, did opportunities for large-scale, long-term projects come to anthropologists. One well-known example was the Vicos Project (formally called the Cornell-Perú Project), begun by Allan Holmberg in 1951 with the support of Carlos Monge, a Peruvian anthropologist and medical doctor. The project, designed as an applied anthropology intervention into the lives of the persons living in and around the Vicos hacienda in the highlands of Peru, was sustained with direct involvement by Cornell until 1964 and continued with Peruvian government support until 1974. More than a dozen American and Peruvian anthropologists participated in the project, but no synthesis of their work has appeared to date (Dobyns and Doughty 1971; Mangin 1979).

Coincidentally, while Kluckhohn was finishing up his career of long-term, multidisciplinary work among the Navajo, two other Harvard-related projects were being initiated.

First, Vogt took what he had learned as field director of the Values Study and—in coordination with Alfonso Villa Rojas and other Mexican anthropologists associated with the Instituto Nacional Indigenista (INI)—designed a large-scale, long-term enterprise known as the Harvard Chiapas Project. Initially intended to examine some thirty-seven Tzotzil and Tzeltal communities located in the hinterlands beyond the administrative center of San Cristóbal de las Casas, the fieldwork began in 1957 with a "small grant" from NIMH. The project shifted to large-scale operation when Vogt obtained a five-year grant from NIMH for the 1958 to 1962 period. In 1960, another component was added to the project when small numbers of undergraduates (from a university consortium of Harvard, Columbia, Cornell, and Illinois) were included in summer field research, through funding by the Carnegie Corporation of New York. The involvement of students in summer research received continued funding through NSF and then by the Harvard Summer School up to 1975.

In his chapter, "The Harvard Chiapas Project: 1957–2000," Vogt recalls that the project initially was concerned with analyzing the role of INI among the Tzotzil and Tzeltal populations in the Chiapas mountains and in assessing the determinants and processes of cultural change. However, by 1960, Vogt realized that he had overestimated the possibilities for the project and had miscalculated its aims. Therefore, he shifted the focus toward the gathering of basic linguistic and ethnographic information in one area (in and around Zinacantan, a ceremonial center with about eight thousand residents) rather than scattering the team's efforts over many topics and areas. During 1963–1964, the NIMH grant renewal included an expansion into the Tzeltal region in and around Chamula, with a population of thirty thousand living in a ceremonial center and nearly a hundred hamlets. In addition, a separate project on aerial photography (funded by NSF) involved anthropologists at Chicago and Stanford.

Vogt observes that, by 1980, a total of 142 project fieldworkers had engaged in research in Chiapas for a summer season or longer. Subsequently, after Vogt's retirement from Harvard, major responsibility for continuing the research enterprise in Zinacantan and in Chamula passed to his former students, now professionals in their own right, especially Frank Cancian (University of California, Irvine), George A. and Jane Collier (Stanford), Gary H. Gossen (SUNY, Albany), John B. Haviland (University of Vermont), and Robert M. Laughlin (Smithsonian). The productivity of these, and other, participants in the Harvard Chiapas Project is apparent in the more than forty books and monographs, more than two hundred articles, and the variety of other scholarly and literary works published so far.

The second large-scale, long-term project coming out of Harvard involved a hunting-gathering population now known as the Ju/'hoansi, but formerly called the !Kung Bushmen and later the San, who lived by foraging for game and wild vegetable foods in the hinterlands of what are now the independent nations of Namibia (then South West Africa) and Botswana (then Bechuanaland). As Richard Lee and Megan Biesele point out in their chapter, "Local Cultures and Global Systems: The Ju/'hoansi-!Kung and Their Ethnographers Fifty Years On," the modern history of ethnographic research among the Ju/'hoansi, led by Laurence and Lorna Marshall, began at Harvard but was largely self-financed by the Marshall family, themselves residents of Cambridge, Massachusetts. From 1951 through 1959, the Marshalls led a series of expeditions to the Nyae Nyae region of what was then South West Africa, involving not only family members but also a number of collaborators. The Marshalls did not return to the region until 1978, when John Marshall came back to make more films but also ended up helping to establish the Nyae Nyae Development Foundation of Namibia.

In 1963, another Harvard project, led by Irven DeVore and Richard Lee, began field studies in the Dobe area of Bechuanaland, focusing on ecological problems such as hunting and gathering techniques, land use, and group structure. In 1967, DeVore and Lee returned to the Dobe area, where they were joined over the next few years by other fieldworkers who collectively came to be identified as the Kalahari Research Group (KRG). In 1973, these investigators organized the Kalahari Peoples Fund as a way to funnel money and expertise to the people of Dobe. The KRG continued into the 1990s as a loosely knit but increasingly diverse group of some fifteen scholars who were developing in a number of different directions. In addition to the Marshalls and the KRG, other researchers from Germany and Japan carried out studies among the Ju/'hoansi.

As Lee and Biesele report, both the Ju/'hoansi and their ethnographers have changed in the past four decades. The lifeways of the people have been transformed so dramatically (and traumatically) that some of the researchers have shifted their stance so that they might document the impact of these changes. Some also have become actively involved in development projects in an effort to expand the dismal range of options otherwise made available by normal government agencies and through nongovernmental organizations (NGOs).

What are some lessons to be learned from large-scale, long-term projects, such as those carried out among the Navajo of the American Southwest, among the Tzotzil and Tzeltal in the highlands of Chiapas, and among the Ju/'hoansi in the far reaches of Namibia and Botswana? Clearly, one result of several decades of intensive and extensive field studies is that we know much more about these peoples than is known about other comparable groups anywhere in the world. Although not all of these projects were intended to be long-term projects or to develop into such large-scale enterprises, the success of the first phases of the research—from initial concept and funding through fieldwork, data analysis, and write-up—provided the foundation on which to build more complex collaborations.

Certainly, one of the major problems of such projects is the need to recruit and to nurture top-flight graduate students who will themselves make commitments to continue in the project. Each of these ethnographic cases created a considerable administrative burden for the directors, all of whom have had the support of large research institutions with experience in handling complex long-term enterprises. Perhaps it should be no surprise that each of these projects was, at least in part, affiliated with Harvard, one of the leading universities in the world, with one of the top departments of anthropology in the United States from the 1930s onward.

Once these projects were established and the variations in personnel and funding were being managed successfully, theoretical and methodological concerns still remained. The teams showed considerable diversity and openness in dealing with the division of research among team members, as well as in finding graduate students or other professionals to handle special research topics. Considering the stresses of fieldwork, the accounts of these projects suggest that interpersonal conflict and professional enmity have remained remarkably under control for long periods.

Finally, the trajectory of these projects suggests that large-scale, long-term ethnographic enterprises may have a distinctive life cycle, moving from an initial focus on purely "scientific" issues to an awareness of the broader political and economic forces that influence the circumstances of the peoples being studied and the perspectives of their ethnographers. The shift from the externally driven approach of the initial Navajo Ramah Project of the 1930s to the collaborative approach of the Navajo Healing Project of the present day reflects an awareness among anthropologists that new frameworks are needed to carry out successful research projects in today's world. The increasing involvement of the Kalahari Research Group (and the Marshalls' research team) in establishing NGOs to improve the lives of the Ju/'hoansi is a response to the changing conditions in which the people and ethnographers are embedded.

In the end, these projects offer fieldworkers the opportunity to go far beyond ethnography as a solitary slice of time in a specific place. Participation in a large-scale, long-term project means that new ethnographers enter a field in which the people already have gained an understanding about who anthropologists are (and are not) and what anthropologists do (and do not do). In the long term, if anthropologists are fortunate, the enterprise becomes a collaboration between ethnographers and people.

References Cited

Dobyns, Henry and Paul Doughty [editors]
(1971) *Peasants, Power, and Applied Social Change: Vicos as a Model*. Beverly Hills, CA: Sage Publications.

Geertz, Clifford
(1988) *Works and Lives: The Anthropologist as Author*. Stanford: Stanford University Press.

Haddon, Alfred Cort [editor]
(1901, 1903) *Reports of the Cambridge Anthropological Expedition to the Torres Straits*. Cambridge: Cambridge University Press.

Kluckhohn, Clyde and W. H. Kelly
(1945) "The concept of culture." Pp. 78–105 in Ralph Linton (editor), *The Science of Man in the World Crisis*. New York: Columbia University Press.

Mangin, William
(1979) "Thoughts on twenty-four years of work in Perú: The Vicos Project and me."
Pp. 65–84 in George M. Foster, Thayer Scudder, Elizabeth Colson, and Robert V.
Kemper (editors), *Long-Term Field Research in Social Anthropology*. New York: Academic Press.

Steward, Julian H.
(1973) *Alfred Kroeber*. (Leaders of Modern Anthropology Series.) New York: Columbia University Press.

Villa Rojas, Alfonso
(1979) "Fieldwork in the Mayan region of Mexico." Pp. 45–64 in George M. Foster,
Thayer Scudder, Elizabeth Colson, and Robert V. Kemper (editors), *Long-Term Field
Research in Social Anthropology*. New York: Academic Press.

CHAPTER FIVE

THE LONG-TERM STUDY AMONG THE NAVAJO
Louise Lamphere

The Navajo, with a population estimated at 270,000 in the year 2000, are the largest Native American group in the United States, and their 18-million-acre reservation is about the size of New England. Anthropological research on the Navajo dates back into the late nineteenth century. Thousands of publications touch every facet of their lives (Bahr 1999). This abundance of research gives us an opportunity to examine the special place of long-term research in comparison with shorter studies and to evaluate the contributions of long-term projects on the Navajo since the first one more than sixty years ago.

As anthropology has developed, the prevailing theories surrounding research on Navajo culture have been transformed, as have techniques of data collection and codification. In addition, the situation of the Navajo and other Native American groups has substantially changed. There is, I believe, a dialectical or interactive relationship between anthropological theory and method, on the one hand, and the economic, social, and cultural setting of the study population, on the other. The relationship that holds for one decade and determines the nature of research may not be relevant or useful fifty years later. Just as the data and results of a project begun in the 1930s might seem arcane and unhelpful given the needs of the present-day Navajo population or the interests of contemporary researchers, so might ongoing or future research seem out of place and irrelevant fifty years from now.

Research on the Navajo by anthropologists and other Anglo scholars has been extremely varied, in terms of both the topics chosen for investigation and the research design employed. Although much writing on the Navajo is intended to be about the Navajo Nation as a whole, most research has been carried out in the context of particular communities where Anglo researchers have lived and studied. Projects have been carried out by "lone" investigators, by teams of two, and by larger groups, either loosely or tightly organized.

The Navajo themselves have been actively engaged in research and publication since the mid-1970s, particularly through the Rough Rock Press (formerly the Navajo Curriculum Center). The roles of Navajo translators and collaborators have been recognized, and since the late 1980s more publications

Four generations of females in Navajo culture. Photo by Wesley Thomas.

have appeared jointly authored by Navajos and Anglos or published by Navajos alone. The founding of the Navajo Studies Conference in 1986, the appearance of *Diné Be'iina'* and *The Journal of Navajo Education*, two journals which specialized in Navajo research, and the emergence of the Navajo Studies Departments at both the Shiprock and Tsaile branches of Diné College (formerly Navajo Community College), provided new outlets for scholarship by both Anglos and Navajos in the 1980s and 1990s. This has centered some scholarly work on the reservation rather than at universities outside of the Navajo Nation.

Long-term research has ranged from restudies of the same community by the same investigator, to restudies by different investigators (sometimes students of the initial researcher), to continuous investigation by a number of investigators over a substantial period of time. In this chapter, I emphasize large-scale team research, beginning with the earliest and perhaps most famous long-term Navajo research enterprises: the Ramah Project and the Comparative Study of Values in Five Cultures Project, both directed by Clyde Kluckhohn and both focused on the Ramah Navajo. I touch only lightly on long-term research as it developed in the period following the Ramah research (1957–1972) and instead highlight the Lake Powell Research Project as an example of long-term research in the 1970s. For the period since 1985, the most significant long-term research has been the continuing work of Kunitz and

Levy (both of whom worked earlier on the Lake Powell Research Project) and the Navajo Healing Project directed by Thomas Csordas. In addition, other Anglo scholars continue to publish the results of short-term and long-term research, utilizing data from new reservation-wide, team-oriented projects as well as from a critical reassessment of older ethnographic sources, while Navajo investigators either publish as collaborators or pursue their own teaching or research interests.

In discussing long-term research, I also examine the way particular projects portray the Navajo as "objects," "subjects," or collaborators. Between 1938 and 1970, anthropological researchers tended to gather "hard" data, first to aid cross-cultural understanding and administrative policy, and later for scientific use in making cross-cultural generalizations. Anthropologists were the investigators; Navajo culture was the object of investigation. Beginning in the 1970s, Native American groups in the United States and Canada began to assert their legal rights and attempted to alter their relationship to the economy and supralocal political institutions. With the advent of tribal sovereignty and tribal control over many institutions on reservations (the Bureau of Indian Affairs [BIA], local schools, community colleges, health and community service programs, and growing tribal bureaucracies), research became first more policy oriented and then more collaborative and engaged in cultural preservation.

The Ramah Project: 1936–1945

Kluckhohn conceived of the Ramah Project after he had completed his Ph.D. and had begun his appointment at Harvard University. He had already spent considerable time (during 1923 and in the summers of 1926–1929) in the Ramah area, south of Gallup, New Mexico, and had written briefly about his experiences in his two chronicles of reservation travels, *To the Foot of the Rainbow* (1927) and *Beyond the Rainbow* (1933). The Ramah Navajo (population 400 in 1940) were pushed to the south of the town of Ramah when it was settled by Mormons in the 1880s and, at the time of Kluckhohn's initial study, lived in hogan clusters scattered over several townships. As off-reservation Navajos, their claims to land were tenuous. Mormon and Texas ranchers held some sections, interspersed with land allotted to Navajos during the early part of the twentieth century, land purchased by the Navajo tribe in the 1940s, or land still held by the Bureau of Land Management.

Kluckhohn's original plan had been to conduct a long-term study of the socialization of Navajo children, using the Ramah community as an ethnographic backdrop. However, he was soon dissatisfied with the ethnographic phase of the project, since his initial description showed that "we had not yet mastered the basic patterns, let alone the cultural dynamics" (Kluckhohn 1949:v). By 1939, Kluckhohn felt that a long-term study was necessary to overcome the "flat, one-dimensional quality" of most anthropological studies. He was impressed by the suggestion of Donald Scott, director emeritus of the Peabody Museum of Harvard University, that it would be useful to study a population over time, watching it change and grow.

The research gradually evolved into a multidisciplinary long-term project, since Kluckhohn felt that "multiple observations by different persons and multiple approaches by individuals who had received their training in various disciplines" (Kluckhohn 1949:v, vi) would enrich both ethnographic recording and the study of socialization. Alexander and Dorothea Leighton, both psychiatrists, were perhaps the most important contributors to the project during the 1939–1942 period. Fifteen graduate students in anthropology from Harvard and other institutions participated in summer fieldwork, and Kluckhohn lists several psychologists, physicians, and psychiatrists among his collaborators (Kluckhohn 1949:x). The loose integration of this team project seemed to complement its interdisciplinary character. Fieldworkers pursued topics of their own interest or investigated subjects (e.g., the family as a "small-group culture" or Navajo ceremonialism) that seemed appropriate to the field situation (e.g., living with a family or attending the frequently held curing ceremonies).

By 1949, when publications were beginning to appear, Kluckhohn wrote that the aim of the project was a series of reports devoted to special topics such as the history of the community, ceremonialism, social organization, and even basketry. Some studies would focus on theoretical topics, whereas others were to deal with the relationship of individuals to their culture; an overall report would integrate the various aspects of Ramah Navajo culture.

In other words, the goals of the project were broadly ethnographic. Kluckhohn was committed to a vision of ethnography that involved the accumulation of the minute details of everyday life, a commitment closely allied with his definition of culture. For Kluckhohn, culture consisted of "designs for living" (Kluckhohn and Kelly 1945:97) or "the set of habitual and traditional ways of thinking, feeling, and reacting that are characteristic of the ways a particular society meets its problems at a particular point in time" (Kluckhohn and Leighton 1946:xviii).

Following Benedict, Kluckhohn saw these structured ways of thinking and doing as "patterned." By *pattern*, Kluckhohn meant an overt, conscious aspect of culture, a discrete interrelated set of facts that produce structural regularities in the realm of ideas (ideal patterns) or consistencies in social relationships and action (behavioral patterns) (Kluckhohn 1941). In contrast, patterning at the covert level was characterized by the term *configuration*, a generalization from behavior that was largely unconscious or unverbalized by the participants in a culture.

The concepts of pattern and configuration helped Kluckhohn to deal with variation in Navajo life both in examining topics of general ethnographic interest (e.g., ceremonialism, social organization) and in studying socialization and personality. To ascertain overt patterns was to make sense out of the myriad details and to pull together conflicting statements about what should be done in a given

111

situation and what individuals actually do. This interaction between a definition of culture and Kluckhohn's commitment to detailed observation can be seen in his early work on Navajo religion (see bibliography in Kluckhohn 1962) and in his monograph on Navajo witchcraft (Kluckhohn 1944). In each publication, he dealt carefully with the number of informants consulted, the statements agreed on by most informants, and deviant statements. On some topics, his method was to gather "every (or virtually every) relevant datum" in the community being studied (Kluckhohn 1962:250). From this corpus of details on a particular topic Kluckhohn abstracted his patterns, often ethnographic generalizations (e.g., that ceremonial instruction is always paid for) or tabulations showing variation (e.g., the close biological relatives in the Ramah area from whom ceremonies were learned). Likewise, from detailed observations on a number of topics, Kluckhohn abstracted what he considered to be the important configurations or unconscious patterns of Navajo culture: "fear of malevolent intentions of other persons," "distrust of extremes," and "the spirit outlet" (that is, a break in a pottery or weaving design) (Kluckhohn 1941:125). Unfortunately, a summary of patterns was often very abstract and disembodied from the data, so that it is often unclear how a particular pattern is related to information or tabulations presented elsewhere in the publication.

These same theoretical and methodological concerns—the collection of ethnographic details and the abstraction of patterns and configurations—also oriented Kluckhohn's study of socialization. Even Kluckhohn's definition of culture as abstracted patterns led him to be interested in the relationship between culture (as a set of elements described by the analyst) and the individual (the personality who learns cultural patterns in the process of "culturalization"). To understand this process and the resulting variation in personalities, the Ramah Project focused on the socialization of forty-eight children (about one-third of the total number of children at Ramah), a group selected by Kluckhohn and the Leightons to represent children from various age groups, economic backgrounds, and family clusters. In making behavioral observations of children, the aim was to record everything seen and heard, checking observations against a list of important topics so that relevant information would not be missed (Kluckhohn 1962:251).

In addition, Dorothea Leighton and other fieldworkers administered a number of psychological tests (intelligence tests; projective tests, including the Thematic Apperception Test and Rorschach; and a battery of psychological tests) to Ramah children, and these supplemented the observations recorded in field notes and kept in the growing Ramah Files. Most of the forty-eight children were followed over a period of several years, and the results of the testing and case study material on individual children are reported in *Children of the People* (Leighton and Kluckhohn 1947) and in several articles. Like the work on ceremonialism and witchcraft, the study of Navajo personality was designed to give a precise indication of the patterns of Navajo personality as well as an indication of the variation in individual personality configurations.

The loose organization of this team project probably facilitated the possibility of interdisciplinary work, a relatively new approach in the late 1930s, and allowed the collection of ethnographic material to progress along with the parallel culture and personality study. Both kinds of data were geared to producing detailed descriptions of Navajo culture and individual adaptations, rather than to isolating natural or cultural cycles or testing of hypotheses.

From our vantage point today, it is easy to understand the limitations of the Ramah Project, in terms of both data collection and theory. Most of the fieldwork took place during the summer months, although the Leightons' field research extended over most of the year. Most of the students conducted their studies in either one or two field seasons, worked through interpreters, and learned very little, if any, of the Navajo language. The short exposure to Navajo culture and the lack of control of the language inhibited the kinds of topics that could be studied and the ways in which data could be collected and related to each other.

Information was kept on individuals and families in the community, and field notes were categorized under a set of topics devised by Kluckhohn, since the Human Relations Area Files (HRAF) system had not yet been developed and adopted. These were kept in the Ramah Files at Harvard. Much of the material was collected in terms of the anthropologists' categories, not those of the Navajo. This is true of the Peabody Museum Papers on ethnobotany, land use, sex practices and reproduction, and the material on Navajo personality (which was interpreted in terms of the psychological categories worked out by professional psychiatrists and psychologists). It is less true of the material on ceremonialism by Kluckhohn and Wyman, in which an elaborate system of translation of Navajo terms for ceremonies, parts of ceremonies, ritual paraphernalia, and plant medicine was worked out, and of the monograph on witchcraft in which Kluckhohn used Navajo categories to sort his data.

Researchers did pay attention to Navajo words and terminology, carefully noting and translating names for plants, for example. However, the overall structure of what we now call a "domain" was not worked out. In some cases, today's reader cannot ascertain the significant Navajo categories and in others, where categories are presented, we cannot determine how they are indexed (e.g., in a taxonomy, paradigm). Even with the data on Navajo ceremonialism, I feel that the order is partly imposed by Kluckhohn and Wyman rather than being a reflection of an informant's ordering of events or terms. More useful than the Ramah Project writings on Navajo ceremonialism are the Navajo texts (often with interlinear translations) collected between 1929 and 1934 by Father Berard, since these provide raw material for understanding the content of Navajo ritual as well as the context of important symbols and concepts.

In the 1960s, the cultural neutrality of projective tests and the usefulness of interpreting modal personality structure or personality configurations began to be questioned. Attention turned away from "culture and personality" studies and focused on studies of symbolic interaction, cognitive development, or conceptions of the self and ethnopsychology (the study of personality and emotion in terms of native categories). Life history material has remained popular, but none of the Ramah life histories is as lengthy or as interesting as *Son of Old Man Hat* (Dyk 1966) or *Sun Chief* (Simmons and Hine 1963).[1] In other words, most of the Ramah personality data do not fit into contemporary frameworks; nor are they relevant to recent interests in social structure, political economy, gender, ethnicity, or issues of tribal sovereignty and cultural preservation.

Even the short description of Ramah social organization written by Kluckhohn and published posthumously (Kluckhohn 1966) is disappointing. As David Aberle (1973:90–93) has pointed out, Kluckhohn's tabulations were precise, but they tended to be enumerations on one variable, not associations of two or more variables. Connections between one pattern and another are not made, so that differences are not brought into conjunction with each other. Most importantly, interpretation is often substituted for explanation. From the Ramah monograph one gets no sense of how Navajo life fits together as a system and how personality, social structure, and culture are related. I feel that this is directly connected to the use of culture as a major organizing concept and the particular definition of culture that Kluckhohn used. By concentrating on patterns and configurations, and by abstracting these one by one from informant statements and behavioral observations, one gets little sense of the relationships among patterns. Where a relationship is presented, it is often imposed by the investigator, and when a single pattern is explained, it is done through Western psychological theory or functionalism.

Finally, the focus on patterns meant that process was ignored. Kluckhohn had felt that he was working toward a more accurate description of the culture of a population in order to understand change, but, at least at that stage in the Ramah research, cultural cycles (such as that of domestic groups) were not studied nor were unidirectional changes analyzed (such as the importance of population growth for resource utilization, the increasing impact of neighboring groups, and the effect of institutions such as schools on Navajo culture). In the period 1936 to 1948, Kluckhohn appears still to have been under the profound influence of American anthropology as shaped by Franz Boas. Although Kluckhohn was never a student of Boas, he was committed to a view of culture as patterned elements without a clear framework for analyzing relationships among individuals, groups, and shared ideas except as abstract patterns.

Kluckhohn's theoretical framework and his commitment to precise ethnographic recording are also related to his position on the ethical responsibilities of the researcher. His views on the relationship between anthropologists and native communities were expressed both in his publications and in "behind the scenes" activities on behalf of the Ramah Navajo and the Navajo Nation as a whole (Adair 1973). Kluckhohn accepted, implicitly, the relationship between a nation-state and an ethnic minority like the Navajo. He felt that one of the major questions of the time was understanding how minority peoples could be dealt with so that they would not be a perpetual problem and so that human values embedded in their lifeways would not be lost to the rest of humanity (Kluckhohn and Leighton 1946:xvi).

Kluckhohn viewed the situation of the Navajo in the late 1930s and early 1940s as "the nation's foremost Indian problem." He saw their situation as one of adjusting to (perhaps inevitable) "technological change," yet felt that this process could be less disruptive if "human needs" and cultural differences were taken into account. The problem was one of inadequate communication between administrators and Navajos, and Kluckhohn sought to make government and private programs more effective through social science research and publication that communicated the native culture to members of the larger U.S. society. "The central aim of this book," Kluckhohn and Leighton (1946:xix) explain in discussing *The Navajo*, "is to supply the background needed by the administrator or teacher who is to deal effectively with the people in human terms."

Anthropologists are, therefore, "interpreters," "brokers," or "intermediaries"— those who translate native cultures to others, including those teachers, health personnel, government agents, and other administrators who have to "deal with" minority populations. Even though the categories of the ethnography were those of current anthropological theory or derived from Western categories, the emphasis was on presenting Navajo culture in its own terms as "baseline," in order to record later changes and responses to contact with other cultures. In this conception of the anthropologist's role, there is little analysis of power relationships, of inequality, and of poverty. Change is viewed as inevitable, the product of contact between two cultures (defined neutrally with regard to each other), but there is no analysis of the economic, political, educational, and religious institutions which impinge on life within minority populations and determine relationships between traders and customers, teachers and students, doctors and patients, and government agents and clientele.

In a personal way, however, Kluckhohn did his best to make the wishes of Navajos known to the appropriate authorities. For example, he took an active role in helping the Ramah Navajo become part of the United Pueblo Agency rather than under the jurisdiction of the more distant and unresponsive Window Rock Agency, and he was an important witness for the Navajo Tribe in their Land Claims Case. Kluckhohn, in these and other activities, took the informal role of "broker," mediating between the Navajo and non-Navajos, much the same role he filled in the more formal context of published anthropological scholarship.

Kluckhohn saw no contradiction between purely anthropological and scientific problems and the potential usefulness of this material for those involved with policy decisions relating to Navajo life. He felt that his study of Navajo culture and personality patterns would lead to more humane decisions on the part of those who actually made policy with regard to health, education, and land use. His writings were not directed toward specific policy decisions, but in his personal actions he worked to bring about the decisions he felt Navajos wanted.

The Comparative Study of Values
in Five Cultures: 1949–1955

In 1948, the study of the Ramah Navajo became part of a new team project. In the years following World War II, Kluckhohn's participation in the formation of the Department of Social Relations at Harvard and his growing interest in the social theories of his colleague Talcott Parsons turned him to the study of values. Kluckhohn's predisposition for interdisciplinary research was compatible with the philosophy of the department, and Parsonian structural-functionalism provided a more sophisticated formulation of the relationship between culture and personality. Parsons's analysis of the social system posited a series of analytic layers: the biological organism, the personality, the social system (with four functional subsystems), and culture. Social interaction in Parsons's "action frame of reference" was oriented by "pattern variables" or, in later formulations, by "value orientations." Kluckhohn had disagreements with Parsons's framework (for example, in positing social structure as autonomous from culture), but the term *value orientation* and sociological functionalism as an approach undoubtedly influenced his thinking about values (Edmonson 1973:176).

The Comparative Study of Values in Five Cultures Project was a six-year enterprise, funded for $100,000 by the Rockefeller Foundation and administered through the Laboratory of Social Relations under an advisory committee consisting of Kluckhohn, J. O. Brew, and Talcott Parsons. John M. Roberts and Evon Z. Vogt served as the field directors. Between 1949 and 1953, more than thirty-seven fieldworkers from a variety of social science disciplines conducted research on a number of specific topics.

The Values Project focused on an empirical study of values and their variation, using a comparison of five communities in the Ramah area: the Mormons, the Texan Homesteaders, the Spanish Americans, the Zuni, and the Navajo. Kluckhohn felt that the Ramah area was an ideal setting for comparison since the five communities were small in size, were subject to the same historical process, and yet contrasted in important ways (Kluckhohn 1951a:ix).

The goal of the project was to explore why cultural variations and differences persisted among these communities, given the similar environment and technology available within the region. In other words, the project was to work toward a more complex understanding of one aspect of culture (values) rather than to study process and change as such. In this context, the Ramah Navajo were treated as if they were not a subpopulation within the larger Navajo culture (where generalizations could be made that applied to the Navajo as a whole), but instead as a complete "society" to be compared with four other non-Navajo populations.

One of the immediate problems of the project was to define the concept of "values" and to provide a framework for studying them. In reaching an early definition, Kluckhohn utilized his previous writing on the concept of culture. He defined *values* in terms of "orientations toward experience which influence choice," a notion not too different from that of *pattern* or *configuration* (Edmonson 1973:168–69, 174). Later, Kluckhohn's (1951b:395) published definition included the notion of "the desirable" to distinguish values from culture in general. "A value is a conception, explicit or implicit, distinctive of an individual or characteristic of a group, of the desirable which influences the selection from available modes, means, and ends of action."

During the course of the Values Project three schemes for the study of values emerged: Ethel Albert's classification (Vogt and Albert 1966) adopted the categories of Western philosophy; Florence Kluckhohn's sociological value-orientation scheme postulated variations in value orientations along six universal dimensions (Kluckhohn and Strodtbeck 1961); and Clyde Kluckhohn's own framework for comparison of value-emphases depended on binary oppositions derived from structural linguistics and distinctive feature analysis (Vogt and Albert 1966:12). Kluckhohn did not fully explicate his scheme until the mid-1950s after most of the fieldwork for the Values Project had been completed. It reflected his increasing disenchantment with functional explanations and the influence of structuralism on his thinking (see Lamphere and Vogt 1973:98–100). That no single scheme was adopted by all researchers reflected not only the difficulty of constructing a framework for studying a topic as abstract as values, but also the loose integration and interdisciplinary composition of the project.

Like the Ramah Project, the Values Project emphasized a permissive policy that allowed fieldworkers considerable freedom in their choice of topic, methodology, and analysis. Not only were diverse definitions of values used, but some fieldworkers specialized in a single culture while others compared two or more of the five cultures. Some work focused on values, while other research concerned the relationship of values to an aspect of environment, personality, or culture (Vogt and Albert 1966:4). Taking all the projects together, it seems likely that, while investigators acknowledged the relationship between their studies and the general topic of values, they focused on topics of more immediate interest only peripherally related to values.

These studies of the Ramah Navajo did, however, build on the ethnographic and theoretical base already provided by Kluckhohn and his coworkers in the early 1940s. Some studies "filled in" data not previously collected, explicitly or implicitly using Kluckhohn's statements about Navajo cultural patterns and configurations in examining these "new" areas. Examples include the study of aesthetic and philosophical aspects of Navajo culture, such as David McAllester's study of *Enemy Way Music*, George Mill's book on *Navajo Art and Culture,* and John Ladd's monograph on Navajo ethics, *The Structure of a Moral Code* (all listed in the bibliography of Vogt and Albert 1966).

Of all these Ramah monographs, I have always been the most impressed by Ladd's book. Though based on only two months of fieldwork, it provides a "microlevel" analysis of Navajo "norms" and moral precepts that offers an extremely accurate picture of what Navajos are like.

Two other studies, Vogt's (1951) "Navajo Veterans" and Rapoport's (1954) monograph on missionary activities expanded the use of psychological tests and life history data begun by Kluckhohn and the Leightons and also dealt with change and acculturation. They illustrate both the type of culture and personality studies current in the early 1950s and the integration of anthropological, sociological, and psychological methods that was part of the Harvard Social Relations milieu. Both authors used Kluckhohn's list of implicit configurations as a "baseline" for determining Navajo values (Vogt 1951:35–38; Rapoport 1954:51–54). Both designed their own psychological tests in addition to using standard personality tests and collecting life histories. Furthermore, these studies entailed a research design more complex than anything attempted during the Ramah Project. Both investigators focused on subpopulations within the Ramah Navajo community and formulated specific hypotheses that could be tested with their data. Not only was hypothesis testing a more sophisticated approach than formulating questions, as Kluckhohn and his coworkers had done, but these hypotheses reflected, in each case, a model of the relationship between the individual personality, the social situation, and various aspects of culture such as values. While the Ramah Project remained descriptive, these studies looked for relationships among variables and viewed aspects of Navajo life as forming some sort of "system."

Other aspects of the Ramah Project were carried on into the Values Project. Fieldworkers continued to contribute their field notes to the growing Ramah Files. New file drawers were set aside, some for each of the five cultures, and notes (dittoed in multiple copies) were filed on five-by-eight-inch sheets under as many HRAF system categories as applied to the material. Like Kluckhohn's previous categories, the new system was imposed from the outside rather than based on Navajo concepts. Even the schemes for describing values were derived from external categories: this was necessary, perhaps, for cross-cultural comparison, but was not as faithful to Navajo distinctions as later approaches have been.[2]

An overall appraisal of the Values Project did not appear until 1966, several years after Kluckhohn's death (Vogt and Albert 1966). It contains comparisons among the five cultures on a series of topics rather than an overall synthesis of the study of values alone. By the time the book appeared, interest in values in anthropology had waned and other theoretical approaches and new methods had emerged.

The Values Project did not alter the anthropologists' relation to the native community, but did change their mission to nonanthropological audiences. Partly because of its cross-cultural nature, the Values Project aimed at a more abstract scientific understanding of values, instead of emphasizing the practical and policy-oriented ways in which cultural interpretation could affect the actions of teachers, administrators, and health personnel. The task was to understand "human behavior," the universal features of society and culture, rather than the workings of one culture or a particular community. This mirrors, I think, the turn away from "applied anthropology" or more action-oriented approaches in the late 1950s and 1960s in an attempt to build a more rigorous anthropology that could be more closely connected with cross-cultural generalizations and with the findings of other social sciences.

Just as the Ramah Project concentrated on the culture of the Navajo as more or less isolated from the social forces that impinged on it, the Values Project was, in its original conception, a study of five "cultures" or "societies" in isolation from the larger nation-state. It was perhaps naïve to see each of these five communities as being five "societies" or "cultures." Important historical connections between the larger "cultures" and the Ramah area communities were ignored, and the power relationships among these populations and with outside forces were largely unexplored. All cultures were assumed to share the same technology, rather than having differential access to an economic system controlled from outside the region, and the microenvironmental differences among their habitats were discounted. In discussing differences among the five "political systems," emphasis was on local decision-making patterns, while the implications of subordination to the wider society were not explicitly drawn.

Research on Ramah during the 1960s and 1970s

A third phase of research in the Ramah area was mainly characterized by the presence of summer field schools in ethnography (in 1962, 1963, 1964, and 1972) and some individual short-term research (Blanchard 1971). As a participant in the 1963 field school supported by the National Science Foundation (Lamphere 1964) and as someone interested in the study of land use, domestic group organization, and authority patterns (Reynolds, Lamphere, and Cook 1967), I was in a position to understand the difficulties of the use of long-term research data by a "new generation" of anthropologists. There are many problems in using previously collected material when no one with firsthand knowledge of that project is available and when changes in research methodology and theoretical orientation alter the usefulness of a given body of material. These issues are much more important in assessing the Ramah Project and the Values Project as examples of long-term research than are either their team composition or their loose organization.

As a well-studied community with already established contacts and a substantial data file (located at the Laboratory of Anthropology in Santa Fe since its transfer from Harvard in 1963), Ramah should have been an ideal location for continued training and research in ethnography and social anthropology. However, Kluckhohn's death in 1960 severed the personal ties between anthropologists and the Ramah Navajo. Many of Kluckhohn's students moved on to other research areas or began to work on other parts of the Navajo reservation. Links to individual families were lacking, as was someone with a thorough knowledge of the community who could have interpreted the masses of accumulated data. It was as if the "key" to the Ramah Files had died with Kluckhohn. Only hours of digging through "cut up" field notes revealed facts that might easily have come to light in a conversation with him.

Problems in using the files were related to the kinds of data collected and to the categories used in filing, which were in turn determined by the theoretical foci of the Ramah Project and the Values Project. Economic data were only to be found in "bits and pieces"; basic demographic and land-use data were incomplete. In general, it was difficult to gain an overall picture of the economic and social structure of the community, since Ramah research (intended as descriptive ethnography or studies of personality and values) had not focused on these types of data. For instance, in one search through the Ramah Files, I located the 1948 census but not a version updated through the 1950s. Particularly lacking was a classification of individuals into households and residence groups and the linking of these to a map indicating spatial location of kin groups and land use. Kluck-hohn's genealogy of the Ramah Navajo (obtained from Richard Kluckhohn), the 1963 Tribal Census for Ramah, and the Allotment Files (then located in the Gallup Area BIA Office) were much more useful for constructing an analysis of residence patterns and land use than anything I found in the Ramah files.

Long-Term Research in Other Navajo Communities

While research in Ramah had focused on general ethnography, on Navajo personality, and later on values, fieldwork carried out by Malcolm Carr Collier at Navajo Mountain in 1938–1939 and by William Y. Adams sixteen years later at Shonto indicated an interest in local social and economic organization, a trend which characterized much community research in the 1960s. Many projects began as individual, two-person or team projects on a short-term basis and later were continued either by the same researcher or by others with access to the original data. The two major projects involving more than two researchers were those sponsored by Cornell University at Fruitland and Many Farms. Both focused on culture change—the former on the ramifications of an irrigation project and the latter on the impact of a new health clinic—and both were very much in the mainstream of 1950s-style "applied anthropology."

In many ways, the research of the late 1950s and 1960s overcame the theoretical and methodological difficulties of the Ramah research. Fieldworkers did a much better job of collecting economic and social structural data on local communities (Shepardson and Hammond 1970; Lamphere 1977; Aberle 1981b). They went much further in understanding Navajo cultural categories. Better control of the language by several investigators made it possible to investigate problems such as social structure, health, and ceremonialism according to Navajo taxonomy and conceptualization (see Witherspoon 1975). A "thicker," more complex understanding of Navajo culture and social relationships has come about not only from new methodological approaches and better collection of demographic, economic, and social structural data, but also from the sum total of a large number of short-term and long-term studies in different areas of the reservation.

Over the decades, the Navajo Nation has changed considerably. The Ramah community exemplifies some of these changes. During the 1960s, the community became more completely integrated into Navajo tribal politics and programs. A new Chapter House was constructed, an FM radio station started, and a community-controlled high school founded when the Navajo community took over the Mormon school which was being closed due to declining enrollments. A new suburban housing complex was built on reservation land about five miles east of Ramah. In the 1970s, a new multi-million-dollar elementary and high school complex was built away from the Mormon town in the heart of the Navajo residential area. A health clinic owned by the Ramah Navajo School Board also serves this population.

These changes seem strangely unrelated and untouched by previous anthropological research. There was some resentment against anthropologists; for example, the 1972 field school had difficulty placing students with families and gaining cooperation from some Navajos (Blanchard 1977). On the other hand, a student quarterly published during the 1970s, *Tsa aszi'* (*The Yucca*), illustrates that young Ramah Navajos were doing their own ethnography. The journal included pictorial essays on cultural patterns (medicines, proverbs, traditional hair styles, and dress) and daily activities (how to shear sheep, butcher, weave a rug, prepare natural dyes, and make a silver bracelet). Drawings and poetry were also published. By the late 1970s, the community had gained a more definite sense of itself and more control over its political affairs. In the process, some community members came to question the validity of traditional anthropological research done by outsiders and its usefulness in terms of Ramah's own goals.

These changes were characteristic of those felt throughout the Navajo reservation in the 1960s and early 1970s and serve as a backdrop for understanding the Lake Powell Project, a very different kind of long-term research project. Throughout the Navajo reservation, the growth of county and Bureau of Indian Affairs (BIA) schools, Indian Health Service facilities, and new industries reflected the increasing impact of Anglo-dominated institutions. Government and tribal programs increased, ranging from the poverty programs of the 1960s to legal services and community-controlled schools in the 1970s. The Tribal Government faced complex disputes and negotiations regarding the Hopi–Navajo Joint Use Area, licensing of Anglo traders, industrial development, and natural resource utilization (including coal strip-mining and power plant construction). These developments indicated not only a new level of change for the Navajo Nation, but also the need for a new kind of anthropological research.

The Lake Powell Project: 1972–1977

The Lake Powell Research Project, "Collaborative Research on Assessment of Man's Activities in the Lake Powell Region," represented the involvement of anthropologists in interdisciplinary research with physical scientists and other social scientists. Through a large grant from the NSF RANN (Research Applied to National Needs) Program, geologists, biologists, geochemists, and other environmental scientists studied the impact of the Glen Canyon Dam and Lake Powell on the surrounding environment as well as on the development of coal-burning power stations surrounding the lake. Anthropologists collaborated not with psychologists, psychiatrists, and sociologists as in the Ramah Project, but with lawyers, political scientists, and medical personnel to study the impact of water and power development on human populations. The overall project was composed of several disciplinary and interdisciplinary subprojects, including three (anthropology, epidemiology, and law/political science) which dealt with the Navajo in relation to Lake Powell. Each of these subprojects centered on a narrow problem or set of topics. They employed a variety of techniques and team-research approaches (Henderson and Levy 1975).

The anthropology subproject, headed by Jerrold Levy (principal investigator) from the University of Arizona and Lynn Robbins (senior investigator) of the Huxley College of Environmental Studies, focused on the economic impact of strip-mining and power plant construction on Navajo families in three communities: Page, its adjacent rural area (Lechee), and nearby Black Mesa. Several families in the adjacent Kaibeto–Red Lake area studied between 1960 and 1969 by Levy and Stephen Kunitz were used as a control group. These Lake Powell microstudies were built on two kinds of previous research: short-term, reservation-wide, and community-specific studies on such topics as social organization, homicide, suicide, and drinking patterns; and long-term contact with families in the Kaibeto–Red Lake area, supplemented by recent fieldwork on kin-group adaptations since the 1920s.

The microstudies combined participant observation techniques with an extensive survey. A sample of seventy-five to a hundred households in each community was queried regarding household and residence group structure, income and economic resources, industrial work experience, cooperative patterns, health, and political behavior. These data were analyzed to document changes in the economy, social organization, and cooperative networks in the three communities. Other papers published by the project dealt with an analysis of Navajo voting patterns (Levy 1977), the impact of power production on Navajo development (Robbins 1975a), Navajo participation in labor unions (Robbins 1975b), and the impact of industrialization on Navajo households (Callaway, Levy, and Henderson 1976).

These anthropological microstudies involved a tighter program of team research than that conducted in Ramah, with the exception of Florence Kluckhohn and Strodtbeck's (1961) survey on value orientations. This tighter team organization was aimed at both the isolation of long-term trends and the testing of a series of specific hypotheses. The Lake Powell Research Project was well equipped to examine "process," especially long-range changes in the microeconomy and social organization of the Navajo and in the relationship of the Navajo Nation to the broader Anglo-American economy and political structure.

To complement these anthropological surveys, the law/political science sub-project took a "case study" approach to understanding the history of Navajo water rights and how they were affected by the legislation that permitted the construction of Lake Powell. In collaboration with the anthropology subproject, two lawyers investigated the history of the Navajo Generating Plant and the role of the Navajo Tribal decisions to develop the coal resources on Black Mesa. This focus on the relationship between state government, federal agencies, private industrial interests, and the Navajo Tribe had been missing in most previous ethnographic research (Mann, Weatherford, and Nichols 1974; Mann 1976).

Navajo Research since the 1980s: Toward the Navajo Healing Project

Even though the Lake Powell Project dealt with policy-related issues, it was still funded and carried out by non-Navajo investigators. With the increasing importance of cultural resource management and the growth of Diné College and community-controlled schools, research and publications by Navajo scholars and teachers began to appear in the 1970s.

Diné College, through its Navajo Studies Program and the Diné College Press, has published more than thirty books documenting important historical events, such as the Long Walk and Livestock Reduction (Roessel and Johnson 1973, 1974), as well as a history of Navajo education (Thompson 1975). The Navajo Curriculum Center (which is now the Rough Rock Press), operating out of the Rough Rock Demonstration Project and Community-Controlled School, published a version of the Navajo origin story (Yazzie 1971), a pictorial history of the Navajo (Roessel 1980), a collection of biographical sketches (Hoffman 1974), a book on the *Kinaalda* or girls' puberty ritual with text in both Navajo and English (Begay 1983), and a book on Navajo women (Roessel 1981). During the mid-1980s, it published a Navajo Oral Tradition series written in both Navajo and English by Alfred W. Yazzie, a Navajo *hataalii* from Fort Defiance (Yazzie 1984).

The same strip-mining and power line projects that inspired the Lake Powell Project also spawned a great deal of archaeological contract work as federal law necessitated a study of any land to be disturbed by roads, power lines, mines, or other projects. Most of this research is strictly archaeological and some of it has been based in the Navajo Nation Cultural Resource Management Program and the Navajo Nation Archaeology Department. However, some archaeological projects have utilized cultural anthropologists who have conducted ethnohistorical research on kinship and land-use patterns. Klara Kelly (1986) has published a fine study of the McKinley Mine area near Window Rock, and Fred York (1990) has studied Navajo settlement outside the eastern boundaries of the Navajo Reservation and in the Chaco Canyon area. In 1986, the Navajo Nation created a Historic Preservation Department, and, as employees of the department, Kelly and

Navajo researcher Harris Francis collaborated in a reservation-wide study of Navajo sacred places (Kelly and Francis 1993, 1994).

A number of Anglo scholars have continued to conduct research on the Navajo reservation. Much of this research was not located in a particular community, but treated the reservation as a whole; and several projects, although framed in terms of a scientific problem, had policy implications (for health issues, mining, and environmental issues, etc.).

Originally involved in the Lake Powell Research Project in the 1970s, Stephen Kunitz and Jerrold Levy have continued studies started during that project and also have expanded their horizons. They have examined issues of the Navajo life career, both in terms of aging (Kunitz and Levy 1991) and in terms of social/health issues such as drinking. Some twenty years after their initial publication (Levy and Kunitz 1974), they issued a follow-up study (Kunitz and Levy 1994). Recently, after more than thirty years of collaborative research with the same population, they have assembled a collection of papers focused on the origins, trajectory, and consequences of alcohol use among the Navajo (Kunitz and Levy 2000). In addition, Levy has ventured beyond his long-term work on health issues to ponder the myths and verities of Navajo origin stories (Levy 1998).

Other scholars have found their work taking on new significance because of changing legislation and legal issues involving the Navajo and other Native American populations. For example, Charlotte Frisbie (1987) continued her research on Navajo religion by focusing on Navajo ceremonial *jish*, or medicine bundles, and their disposition. Her book has become particularly relevant since the passage of the Native American Graves Protection and Repatriation Act (NAGPRA) in 1990. Federal agencies and museums must now repatriate human and cultural remains, including sacred objects, but the private art market (where many *jish* circulate) has remained unaffected (Frisbie 1993).

While David Aberle continued to publish on kinship (1981a, 1981b, 1985, 1989) based on his long-term research in Pinon, perhaps more significant has been his role as a member of the American Anthropological Association ad hoc panel on the Navajo–Hopi Land Dispute. During the height of the dispute, Aberle offered yearly updates on the progress of the conflict and the impact of relocation on Navajo families (e.g., Aberle 1993).

During the 1980s, a new generation of Anglo scholars, especially students (e.g., Mark Bauer and Mark Schoepfle) of Oswald Werner at Northwestern and students (e.g., Eric Henderson, Christine Conte, Ann Wright, Scott Russell, and Tracey Andrews) of Jerrold Levy at the University of Arizona, completed dissertations on the Navajo. Many of these young scholars subsequently collaborated with Navajo researchers and translators (often teachers at Diné College) on topics relevant to contemporary Navajo life. For example, Mark Schoepfle collaborated with several researchers including Navajo researcher Ken Begishe on a study of the Navajo–Hopi Land Dispute (Schoepfle et al. 1979) and worked with Navajos on a study of Navajo perception of energy development on the Navajo environment (Schoepfle et al. 1978). Mark Bauer and Frank Morgan (Navajo scholar at NCC Shiprock) published on Navajo conflict resolution (Bauer and Morgan 1987). More recently, Anne Wright and Mark Bauer, along with Navajo researchers Frank Morgan and Ken Begishe, conducted a study of Navajo beliefs and practices surrounding infant breast-feeding (Wright, Clark, and Bauer 1993; Wright et al. 1993).

Current issues of anthropological theory have been examined in the Navajo context. For instance, studies of the transformation of the informal economy among the Navajo from 1868 to 1995 (Francisconi 1998) and the question of gender identity and personhood among the Navajo (Schwarz 1997) not only provide valuable data, but also offer new perspectives on questions posed by earlier researchers among the Navajo.

Nor have earlier Navajo research projects been exempt from critical reflection and reanalysis. For example, Katherine Halpern and Susan McGreevy (1997) have reconsidered the cultural studies done by Washington Matthews between 1880 and 1894, while James Faris (1996) has provided a critical history of the photographic representations of the Navajo since the 1870s. In 1993, Willow Roberts [Powers], then a doctoral student at the University of New Mexico, interviewed a number of researchers, colleagues, and students of Kluckhohn for a dissertation on the Values Project. In setting the Values Project in its historical and theoretical contexts, her work helps us to discern to what extent the Ramah Research Files can provide useful data for further research in those five communities (Powers 2000).

In 1986, Charlotte Frisbie and Dave Brugge organized the first Navajo Studies Conference at the University of New Mexico for the purpose of collating and disseminating some of the research back to the Navajo people. Over two hundred persons heard some thirty papers on archaeology, history, religion, and social organization. Most of the presenters were Anglo scholars, but there were sessions on the issues of repatriation of sacred objects and the Navajo–Hopi land dispute, both of which involved presentations by Navajos. Over the years, the emphasis has shifted from scholarly sessions to a combination of scholarly papers and a variety of traditional activities (shoe games, Yeibichai dances), recognition banquets, tours of archaeological sites, and film showings. More Navajo scholars or Navajo Nation employees and teachers give presentations, as evidenced by an examination of the history of the conferences held through the year 2000 (cf. www.sjc.cc.nm.us/Campserv/NAP/conference/navstudy.html).

Diné Be'iina', published by Diné College, Shiprock, and the *Journal of Navajo Education*, published by editor Daniel McLaughlin, were important in the late 1980s and 1990s for scholarly work, poetry, and writing on educational issues. A great deal of interest has focused on issues of language maintenance and literacy in Navajo in a period when language loss is becoming more acute.

Several Navajo scholars are teaching at universities in the Southwest. Roseanne Willink is teaching Navajo language and linguistics courses at the

University of New Mexico; Mary Ann Willie is at the University of Arizona; Alice Neuendorf (1983), author of a Navajo/English bilingual children's dictionary, has been an assistant professor of bilingual education at Northern Arizona University; and Jennie R. Joe is the director of the Native American Research and Training Center at the University of Arizona. Joe's work on disabilities issues (1980; Joe and Miller 1987; Joe and Locust 1989; Joe and Young 1994), diabetes (Joe and Young 1993), drug issues (Joe and Young 1992), relocation (Scudder et al. 1982), and even firefighters (Joe and Miller 1993) have been important contributions in the area of applied medical anthropology.

The Navajo Healing Project

In 1993, Thomas J. Csordas began a five-year study of Navajo healing (comparing traditional, Native American Church, and Charismatic Christian forms). Although initiated and funded by non-Navajos, this project has been much more collaborative than long-term projects begun in early decades. Ethnographic interviews and observations have been gathered for ninety-five healers and eighty-four patients within the different healing traditions across the Navajo reservation. Several articles (see a special thematic issue of *Medical Anthropological Quarterly*, especially Csordas 2000 and Lamphere 2000) and two dissertations (John Garrity and Elizabeth Lewton) already have been completed. In 1999, the project received a three-year continuation from the National Institute of Mental Health (NIMH).

The Navajo Healing Project demonstrates the strengths of a methodology that is becoming more prevalent in anthropological research. Research teams combine anthropologists from outside the community with researchers from within the community itself or members of the same ethnic population. This collaborative team approach has meant that the Navajo Healing Project can examine a much broader range of healing traditions throughout the reservation than has been possible in the past. Only this style of ethnography, combined with a long-term approach, can elucidate the complex and multilayered sets of experiences in three healing traditions among the Navajo. Moreover, the inclusion of Navajo researchers has meant that frameworks more compatible with Navajo categories can evolve as the research continues. Thus, Csordas and his collaborators are able to achieve a level of analysis that was simply beyond the dreams of Kluckhohn, Vogt, and other anthropologists of an earlier era.

Conclusions

Research on the Navajo has gone through four phases since the 1930s. Large-scale, long-term research projects have been important in all of these phases. In the first phase, represented by the Ramah Project, Kluckhohn and his students researched specific ethnographic topics with careful attention to details and vari-

ation. Kluckhohn's theoretical interest in culture and in covert and overt patterning led him to generalized abstractions about Navajo culture phrased in anthropological categories, not those of the Navajo. The Ramah population was seen as
a laboratory for understanding Navajo culture in general; the focus was on the
community itself rather than on its place in the larger society. The policy orientation that underlay some of Kluckhohn's and Leighton's research seems almost
naively paternalistic by the standard of the twenty-first century, as some researchers (Adams 1993; Faris 1993) now acknowledge.

In the second phase, beginning with the Values Project in Ramah and continuing through the community research of the 1960s, culture was still an important analytic concept, but more attention was paid to a theoretical framework that
integrated various aspects of culture, personality, and social structure. More consideration was given to understanding Navajo social structure and culture in terms
of Navajo categories (Witherspoon 1975; Lamphere 1977), but few were able to
link changes in Navajo life to an analysis of the impact of American economic
and political forces upon the Navajo.

In the third phase, exemplified by the Lake Powell Research Project of the
1970s, Anglo anthropologists were able to combine careful collection of local-
level socioeconomic data with analyses of the Navajo Nation's relationship to
state, federal, and private industrial interests concerned with resource development. The Lake Powell Project was not concerned with describing Navajo culture
per se. Rather than treating local communities as isolates, the project explicitly
studied the links between the Navajo and the "outside" world and was policy oriented. However, in both the second and third phases, Anglo research interests and
a commitment to a scientific paradigm continued to determine both long-term
and short-term studies.

In the fourth phase, exemplified by the Navajo Healing Project, from 1993
through 2001, anthropological research has been conducted in a much different
setting than existed in earlier times. The Navajo Nation has established more
institutions interested in research and published materials (e.g., Diné College,
the Historic Preservation Department). In this context, research has become
more collaborative and more defined by Navajos who work in these institutions.
This reorientation also has characterized research with other Native American populations (Merrill, Ladd, and Ferguson 1993; Dongoske, Ferguson, and
Yeatts 1994).

Applied research connected with cultural resource management (CRM), historic preservation, repatriation, and policy-related issues such as aging, diabetes,
drinking, and relocation has become as important as traditional topics such as
Navajo cultural patterns, ceremonialism, values, kinship, and social structure.
With the need for more teaching materials in both English and Navajo, there is
renewed interest in biography (or life history) and Navajo history. Institutions
such as the Navajo Museum, Diné College, and the Navajo Nation Preservation
Department could become long-term repositories for research.

The extent to which Anglo researchers and universities will continue to contribute to long-term study of the Navajo depends, I think, on the willingness of non-Navajos to collaborate with Navajo scholars and to forge their research agenda in concert with local communities where research takes place and with other institutions on the reservation. The example of the Navajo Healing Project demonstrates that long-term studies *can* be transformed from Ramah-style enterprises designed, funded, and conducted by non-Navajos using external cognitive categories. I imagine a future in which collaborative long-term research efforts will continue to evolve. Conceived and directed by Navajo principal investigators, the next generation of long-term studies surely will demand new methods, new theories, and new forms of collaboration among Navajo and non-Navajo anthropologists.

Notes

I would like to thank Willow Roberts Powers for reading the first version of this chapter and for providing helpful comments concerning the field notes for the Ramah Project and Values Project.

1. In the late 1980s and early 1990s, interest in life histories resurfaced. Joyce Griffen has edited and annotated the previously unpublished life history of "Lucky" collected by Alexander and Dorothea Leighton (1992) and is working on another life history for publication. Various segments of the Navajo population are often interested in the publication of life histories for use in classrooms and as a part of preserving Navajo traditional life.

2. Willow Roberts Powers reminded me that the way in which data were classified often resulted in irrelevant material being placed in a category. For example, a description of a young Hispanic traveling to Grants to go drinking was categorized under "Non-Alcoholic Beverages" (which were not mentioned in the notes), "Alcoholic Beverages," and "Children's Games." Using the files can be frustrating since one may read through several inches of notes without finding much of interest; she has found the chronological notes filed under each fieldworker's name to be much more rewarding to use.

References Cited

Aberle, David F.
(1973) "Clyde Kluckhohn's contributions to Navaho studies." Pp. 83–93 in Walter W. Taylor, John L. Fischer, and Evon Z. Vogt (editors), *Culture and Life*. Carbondale and Edwardsville: Southern Illinois University Press.
(1981a) "A century of Navajo kinship change." *Canadian Journal of Anthropology* 1:21–36.
(1981b) "Navajo coresidential kin groups and lineages." *Journal of Anthropological Research* 37(1):1–7.
(1985) "Recent changes among Black Mountain Navajos." Paper presented at the Ad-

vanced Seminar on Temporal Change and Regional Variability in Navajo Culture, School of American Research, Santa Fe, NM.
(1989) "Education, work, gender, and residence: Black Mesa Navajos in the 1960s." *Journal of Anthropological Research* 45(4):405–430.
(1993) "The Navajo-Hopi land dispute and Navajo relocation." Pp. 153–200 in Michael M. Cernea and Scott E. Guggenheim (editors), *Anthropological Approaches to Resettlement.* Boulder, CO: Westview.

Adair, John
(1973) "Clyde Kluckhohn and Indian administration." Pp. 71–82 in Walter W. Taylor, John L. Fischer, and Evon Z. Vogt (editors), *Culture and Life.* Carbondale and Edwardsville: Southern Illinois University Press.

Adams, William
(1993) "Growing up in colonial Navajoland." Pp. 305–310 in June-el Piper (editor), *Papers from the Third, Fourth, and Sixth Navajo Studies Conferences.* Window Rock, AZ: Navajo Nation Historic Preservation Department.

Bahr, Howard M.
(1999) *Diné Bibliography to the 1990s: A Companion to the Navajo Bibliography of 1969.* Lanham, MD, and London: Scarecrow Press.

Bauer, Mark, and Frank Morgan
(1987) "Navajo conflict resolution." *Diné Be'iina': A Journal of Navajo Life* 1(1):149–160.

Begay, Shirley
(1983) *Kinaalda: A Navajo Puberty Ceremony.* Rough Rock, AZ: Navajo Curriculum Center.

Blanchard, Kendall
(1971) "Religious change and economic behavior among the Ramah Navajo." Ph.D. dissertation. Southern Methodist University, Dallas, Texas.
(1977) "The expanded responsibilities of long-term informant relationships." *Human Organization* 36(1):66–69.

Callaway, Donald, Jerrold Levy, and Eric B. Henderson
(1976) "The effects of power production and strip mining on local Navajo populations." *Lake Powell Research Program Bulletin* 22.

Csordas, Thomas J.
(2000) "The Navajo Healing Project." *Medical Anthropology Quarterly* 14(4):463–475.

Dongoske, Kurt E., T. J. Ferguson, and Michael Yeatts
(1994) "Ethics of field research for the Hopi Tribe." *Anthropology Newsletter* 35(1):56.

Dyk, Walter
(1966) *Son of Old Man Hat: A Navaho Autobiography.* Lincoln: University of Nebraska Press.

Edmonson, Munro S.
(1973) "The anthropology of values." Pp. 157–197 in Walter W. Taylor, John L. Fischer, and Evon Z. Vogt (editors), *Culture and Life*. Carbondale and Edwardsville: Southern Illinois University Press.

Faris, James C.
(1993) "Taking Navajo truths seriously: the consequences of the accretions of disbelief." Pp. 181–186 in June-el Piper (editor), *Papers from the Third, Fourth, and Sixth Navajo Studies Conferences*. Window Rock, AZ: Navajo Nation Historic Preservation Department.
(1996) *Navajo and Photography: A Critical History of the Representation of an American People*. Albuquerque: University of New Mexico Press.

Francisconi, Michael Joseph
(1998) *Kinship, Capitalism, Change: The Informal Economy of the Navajo, 1868–1995*. New York and London: Garland Publishing.

Frisbie, Charlotte
(1987) *Navajo Medicine Bundles or Jish: Acquisition, Transmission, and Disposition in the Past and Present*. Albuquerque: University of New Mexico Press.
(1993) "NAGPRA and the repatriation of jish." Pp. 119–127 in June-el Piper (editor), *Papers from the Third, Fourth, and Sixth Navajo Studies Conferences*. Window Rock, AZ: Navajo Nation Historic Preservation Department.

Halpern, Katherine Spencer and Susan Brown McGreevy [editors]
(1997) *Washington Matthews: Studies of Navajo Culture, 1880–1894*. Albuquerque: University of New Mexico Press.

Henderson, E. B. and Jerrold E. Levy
(1975) "Survey of Navajo community studies 1936–1974." *Lake Powell Research Project Bulletin* 6.

Hoffman, Virginia
(1974) *Navajo Biographies*, volume 1. Phoenix, AZ: Navajo Curriculum Center Press (available from Rough Rock Press).

Joe, Jennie R.
(1980) "Disabled children in Navajo society." Ph.D. dissertation. University of California, Berkeley.

Joe, Jennie R. and Carol Locust
(1989) *Government Policies and the Disabled in American Indian Communities*. Tucson: Native American Research and Training Center.

Joe, Jennie R. and Dorothy Lonewolf Miller
(1987) *American Indian Perspectives on Disability*. Tucson: Native American Research and Training Center.

(1993) *Firewarriors: Native American Wildland Firefighters.* Tucson: Native American Research and Training Center.

Joe, Jennie R. and Robert S. Young [editors]

(1992) *Indian Firefighters—Drug Free Workplace: Proceedings of a Conference Held in Tucson, AZ, March 27–28, 1991.* Tucson: Native American Research and Training Center.

(1993) *Diabetes as a Disease of Civilization: The Impact of Culture Change on Indigenous Peoples.* Berlin: Mouton de Gruyter Press.

(1994) *NIDDM and Indigenous Peoples: Proceedings of the Second International Conference on Diabetes and Native Peoples.* Tucson: Native American Research and Training Center.

Kelly, Klara B.

(1986) *Navajo Land Use: An Ethnoarchaeological Study.* Orlando, FL: Academic Press.

Kelly, Klara B. and Harris Francis

(1993) "Places important to Navajo people." *American Indian Quarterly* 17(2):151–170.

(1994) *Navajo Sacred Places.* Bloomington and Indianapolis: Indiana University Press.

Kluckhohn, Clyde

(1927) *To the Foot of the Rainbow.* New York: Century.

(1933) *Beyond the Rainbow.* Boston: Christopher.

(1941) "Patterning as exemplified in Navaho culture." Pp. 109–130 in Leslie Spier (editor), *Language, Culture and Personality.* Menasha, WI: Sapir Memorial Publication Fund.

(1944) "Navajo Witchcraft." *Papers of the Peabody Museum of Archaeology and Ethnology* 22(2). Cambridge, MA: Harvard University.

(1949) "Introduction: The Ramah project." Pp. v–x in Alexander H. Leighton and Dorothea Leighton, "Gregorio, the hand trembler." *Papers of the Peabody Museum of Archaeology and Ethnology* 40(1). Cambridge, MA: Harvard University.

(1951a) "Foreword: A comparative study of values in five cultures." Pp. vii–xii in Evon Z. Vogt, "Navajo veterans." *Papers of the Peabody Museum of Archaeology and Ethnology,* 41(1). Cambridge, MA: Harvard University.

(1951b) "Values and value-orientations in the theory of action." Pp. 388–433 in Talcott Parsons and Edward Shils (editors), *Towards a General Theory of Action.* Cambridge, MA: Harvard University Press.

(1962) "Studying the acquisition of culture." Pp. 244–254 in Richard Kluckhohn (editor), *Culture and Behavior: Collected Essays of Clyde Kluckhohn.* New York: Free Press of Glencoe.

(1966) "The Ramah Navaho." Bureau of American Ethnology, Bulletin 196, *Anthropological Papers,* No. 79.

Kluckhohn, Clyde and W. H. Kelly

(1945) "The concept of culture." Pp. 78–105 in Ralph Linton (editor), *The Science of Man in the World Crisis.* New York: Columbia University Press.

Kluckhohn, Clyde and Dorothea Leighton

(1946) *The Navaho.* Cambridge, MA: Harvard University Press.

Kluckhohn, Florence and Fred L. Strodtbeck
(1961) *Variations in Value Orientations: A Theory Tested in Five Cultures*. Evanston, IL: Row, Peterson.

Kunitz, Stephen J. and Jerrold E. Levy
(1991) *Navajo Aging: The Transition from Family to Institutional Support*. Tucson: University of Arizona Press.
(1994) *Drinking Careers: A Twenty-five-year Study of Three Navajo Populations*. New Haven and London: Yale University Press.
(2000) *Drinking, Conduct Disorder, and Social Change: Navajo Experiences*. New York: Oxford University Press.

Lamphere, Louise
(1964) "Loose-structuring as exhibited in a case study of Navajo religious learning." *El Palacio* 71(1):37–44.
(1977) *To Run After Them: The Social and Cultural Bases of Cooperation in a Navajo Community*. Tucson: University of Arizona Press.
(2000) "Comments on the Navajo Healing Project." *Medical Anthropology Quarterly* 14(4):598–602.

Lamphere, Louise and Evon Z. Vogt
(1973) "Clyde Kluckhohn as ethnographer and student of Navajo ceremonialism." Pp. 94–135 in Walter W. Taylor, John L. Fischer, and Evon Z. Vogt (editors), *Culture and Life*. Carbondale and Edwardsville: Southern Illinois University Press.

Leighton, Alexander H. and Dorothea Leighton
(1992) *Lucky, the Navajo Singer*. (Edited and annotated by Joyce J. Griffen.) Albuquerque: University of New Mexico Press.

Leighton, Dorothea and Clyde Kluckhohn
(1947) *Children of the People*. Cambridge, MA: Harvard University Press.

Levy, Jerrold
(1977) "Changing Navajo voting patterns." *Lake Powell Research Project Bulletin* 47.
(1998) *In the Beginning: The Navajo Genesis*. Berkeley: University of California Press.

Levy, Jerrold E. and Stephen J. Kunitz
(1974) *Indian Drinking: Navajo Practices and Anglo-American Theories*. New York: John Wiley and Sons.

Mann, Dean
(1976) "Water policy and decision-making in the Colorado River Basin." *Lake Powell Research Project Bulletin* 24.

Mann, Dean, Gary Weatherford, and Phillip Nichols
(1974) "Legal-political history of water resource development in the Upper Colorado River Basin." *Lake Powell Research Project Bulletin* 4.

Merrill, William L., Edmund J. Ladd, and T. J. Ferguson
(1993) "The return of the *Ahayu:da*: lessons for repatriation from Zuni Pueblo and the Smithsonian Institution." *Current Anthropology* 34(5):523–555.

Neuendorf, Alice
(1983) *A chíní bi naaltoostsoh, a Navajo/English Bilingual Dictionary.* Albuquerque: Native American Materials Development Center.

Powers, Willow Roberts
(2000) "The Harvard study of values: Mirror for postwar anthropology." *Journal of the History of the Behavioral Sciences* 36(1):15–29.

Rapoport, Robert N.
(1954) "Changing Navaho religious values: A study of Christian missions to the Rimrock Navajo." *Papers of the Peabody Museum of American Archaeology and Ethnology* 41(2). Cambridge, MA: Harvard University.

Reynolds, Terry, Louise Lamphere, and Cecil Cook
(1967) "Time, resources, and authority in a Navajo community." *American Anthropologist* 69(2):188–199.

Robbins, Lynn A.
(1975a) "The impact of power developments on the Navajo Nation." *Lake Powell Research Project Bulletin* 7.
(1975b) "Navajo participation in labor unions." *Lake Powell Research Project Bulletin* 15.

Roessel, Robert A. Jr.
(1980) *Pictorial History of the Navajo from 1860 to 1910.* Rough Rock, AZ: Navajo Curriculum Center, Rough Rock Demonstration School (Rough Rock Press).

Roessel, Ruth
(1981) *Women in Navajo Society.* Rough Rock, AZ: Navajo Resource Center, Rough Rock Demonstration School (Rough Rock Press).

Roessel, Ruth and Broderick Johnson
(1973) *Navajo Stories of the Long Walk Period.* Tsaile, AZ: Navajo Community College Press.
(1974) *Navajo Livestock Reduction: A National Disgrace.* Tsaile, AZ: Navajo Community College Press.

Schoepfle, Mark, K. Begishe, R. Morgan, A. Johnson, and P. Scott.
(1979) *The Human Impact of the Navajo-Hopi Land Dispute: Navajo Viewpoint.* Tsaile, AZ: Navajo Community College Press.

Schoepfle, Mark, et al.
(1978) "A study of Navajo perception of the impact of environmental changes relating to energy resource development." Third Quarterly Report. Shiprock, AZ: Navajo Community College.

Schwarz, Maureen Trudelle
(1997) *Molded in the Image of Changing Woman: Navajo Views on the Human Body and Personhood.* Tucson: University of Arizona Press.

Scudder, Thayer, Elizabeth Colson, David Aberle, B. Gilbert, Jennie R. Joe, et al.
(1982) *No Place to Go: Effects of Compulsory Relocation on Navajos.* Philadelphia: ISHI Press.

Shepardson, Mary and Blodwen Hammond
(1970) *The Navajo Mountain Community: Social Organization and Kinship.* Berkeley: University of California Press.

Simmons, Leo W. and Robert V. Hine
(1963) *Sun Chief: The Autobiography of a Hopi Indian.* New Haven: Yale University Press.

Thompson, Hildegard
(1975) *The Navajos' Long Walk for Education: A History of Navajo Education.* Tsaile, AZ: Navajo Community College Press.

Vogt, Evon Z.
(1951) "Navajo veterans: A study of changing values." *Papers of the Peabody Museum of American Archaeology and Ethnology* 41(1).

Vogt, Evon Z. and Ethel M. Albert [editors]
(1966) *People of Rimrock: A Study of Values in Five Cultures.* Cambridge, MA: Harvard University Press.

Witherspoon, Gary
(1975) *Navajo Kinship and Marriage.* Chicago: University of Chicago Press.

Wright, Anne L., Mark Bauer, Clarina Clark, Frank Morgan, and Kenneth Begishe
(1993) "Cultural interpretations and intracultural variability in Navajo beliefs about breastfeeding." *American Ethnologist* 20(4):781–796.

Wright, Anne L., Clarina Clark, and Mark Bauer
(1993) "Maternal employment and infant feeding practices among the Navajo." *Medical Anthropology Quarterly* 7(3):260–280.

Yazzie, Alfred W.
(1984) *Navajo Oral Tradition,* volumes I, II, III. Rough Rock, AZ: Navajo Resource Center (Rough Rock Press).

Yazzie, Ethalou
(1971) *Navajo History,* volume 1. Written under the direction of the Navajo Curriculum Center. Many Farms, AZ: Navajo Community College Press. (Available from Rough Rock Press.)

York, Fred
(1990) "Capitalist development and land in northeastern Navajo country, 1880s to 1980s." Ph.D. dissertation. State University of New York at Binghamton.

CHAPTER SIX

THE HARVARD CHIAPAS PROJECT: 1957–2000
Evon Z. Vogt

Introduction

The Harvard Chiapas Project was conceived in Mexico in the summer of 1955, designed during 1956–1957 at the Center for Advanced Study in the Behavioral Sciences at Stanford, and initiated in Chiapas the summer of 1957. It was in continuous operation from 1957 to 1980 with one or more field researchers in Chiapas each year and has continued more sporadically from 1981 to the present.

In the summer of 1955, I was invited by Dr. Alfonso Caso, then director of the Instituto Nacional Indigenista (hereafter, INI), to attend a meeting in Mexico City of INI field center directors and other personnel to discuss and evaluate INI programs in the Indian zones in which they were operating, principally the Tzotzil-Tzeltal area of the highlands of Chiapas, the Mazatec area of the lowlands of Veracruz and Oaxaca, and the Tarahumara region of the Western Sierra Madre. Following the meeting, I was invited to visit INI centers in Chiapas and Veracruz with Manuel Gamio, then director of the Interamerican Indian Institute, and Gonzalo Aguirre Beltrán, then deputy director of INI. We drove through Oaxaca to Tehuantepec and on to the highlands of Chiapas, where we stayed at INI headquarters in San Cristóbal Las Casas and made daily trips out to Indian villages to visit schools, clinics, and experimental farms.

Emotionally and intellectually, it was love at first sight for me. I found the cool, high (7,000–9,000 feet) mountain terrain covered with pine and oak forests, the rugged barrancas carved into the limestone, and the volcanic peaks all to be breathtakingly beautiful. I was impressed by the Mayan-speaking Indians I met, with the people of each *municipio* dressed uniformly in distinctive, colorful styles, and by the fact that these Tzotzil and Tzeltal communities appeared to present one of those rare opportunities for research in anthropology utilizing the method of controlled comparison (Eggan 1954; Vogt 1964c, 1994b, 1995). The historical frame for the comparison had been set by the fact that the people of all thirty-seven Tzotzil and Tzeltal communities were directly descended and differentiated from a small group of Proto-Tzeltalans

Juan de la Torre Lopez at age 25 using a typewriter to record Zinacanteco tales in Tzotzil for publication by the House of the Writers in San Cristóbal Las Casas. The Tzotzil writers have more recently shifted to computers. Photo by Evon Z. Vogt.

who occupied the Chiapas highlands about a millennium ago. The geographical frame for the comparison was set by the natural habitat—the highlands of Central Chiapas and their immediately flanking lowlands which the Tzotzil and Tzeltal had continued to occupy in nearly contiguous communities. The continuing uniformities observed derived from shared historical antecedents, from shared experiences with the Spanish Conquest, and subsequent political impacts. The variations derived from unique local cultural drifts as the population diversified, from differences in adaptations to micro-niches within the ecological setting, and from detailed differences in the impacts of the conquest and subsequent political developments. By controlled comparative analysis, I felt that it should eventually be possible to state with some precision the hierarchy of decisive factors that accounted for the present uniformities and variations.

During 1956–1957, while a Fellow at the Center for Advanced Study in the Behavioral Sciences, I had the opportunity to think through the project design and to apply for grants. Over the Christmas holidays, the Center funded a trip to Chiapas where I met with Alfonso Villa Rojas, then director of the INI Center for the Tzotzil-Tzeltal zone, and members of his staff, with whom I visited Indian communities to make additional arrangements for research.

The First Phase

Initial funding proved difficult but, finally, for the summer of 1957, I received a grant from the Small Grants Program of NIMH (National Institute of Mental Health) and my graduate student assistant, Frank C. Miller, was funded by the Doherty Foundation. So, the first phase of the project began very modestly—one graduate student and a Land Rover purchased in Tuxtla Gutiérrez, the capital city of Chiapas. Miller and I spent August 1957 making a reconnaissance of the Tzotzil-Tzeltal region, by Land Rover, by horseback, and on foot.

With the suggestion and assistance of Villa Rojas, Miller decided to study health care delivery in the *municipio* of Huistán during 1957–1958 and was installed in an INI clinic in the isolated hamlet of Yalcuc. I decided to work in the *municipio* of Zinacantan and began to make preliminary contacts in the ceremonial center itself and in the hamlet of Paste'. During 1957–1958, I received the welcome news that my major application to NIMH had been successful and that I would be funded for five years. In the summer of 1958, I returned to Chiapas, joined by Nick and Lore Colby, who succeeded Miller as graduate student assistants and spent the 1958–1959 academic year working in Zinacantan on problems of education, Indian-Ladino relations, and the study of the Tzotzil language (Colby 1966). They were joined by Pierre L. van den Berghe, who worked on Indian-Ladino relations.

In the summer of 1959, Robert M. Laughlin served as graduate assistant, working in Zinacantan during 1959–1960 on mythology and beginning his *The Great Tzotzil Dictionary of San Lorenzo Zinacantán* (Laughlin 1975). At the same time, Manuel T. Zabala Cubillos came from the National School of Anthropology and History in Mexico City to do a study for us on the salt industry of Zinacantan. In 1960–1961, Frank and Francesca Cancian replaced Laughlin as student assistants and initiated their researches on the cargo system and on the study of the Tzotzil family as a small group (Cancian 1965; Cancian 1975).

My own work during the summers of 1958 and 1959 was focused on trying to get a basic grasp of some of the ethnography of Zinacantan, notably the cargo system and the organization of shamans. In the summer of 1958, my wife and I and our four children lived in quarters provided by INI at the edge of San Cristóbal, and from there I traveled to Zinacantan Center and to the hamlet of Paste' to visit Indian schools and a few families that we knew. Rapport was especially difficult to establish at first—not only all the people, but also the dogs and the sheep, ran to hide in the cornfields as we drove into the hamlet in the Land Rover and stopped by the trail for a picnic lunch. But after a time, curious people reemerged from the tall corn and began to engage us in conversation—with their halting Spanish and my even more meager Tzotzil. Before long we were providing transport for people and for bags of maize and chickens to the market in San Cristóbal. Many of the Zinacantecos had never been in an automobile before; both men and women became dizzy at speeds over five miles per hour and the women sat, by preference, on the floor of the Land Rover since they had never sat on a chair or bench in their lives.

By the summer of 1959, INI had constructed a small field house for us next to the school in Paste', for which we paid construction costs. We spent most of the summer in the hamlet, learning a great deal about the school and its operation, but less than I would have liked about the rest of the community. I did become well acquainted with the secretary of the school committee, who later became one of my principal shaman informants, and with the Zinacanteco schoolteacher, who I learned later was the most important political boss in Zinacantan. More productive, however, in learning about the basic ethnography were long interviews with a Zinacanteco who had formerly worked in the INI puppet show and as an informant for Nick Colby. These interviews actually proved to be more fruitful when we worked in San Cristóbal—away from the noises and interruptions of hamlet life—so part of the summer was spent in an apartment we retained in town. In the spring term of 1960, I had a leave of absence from Harvard to engage in field research in Chiapas. Since our children were in school, I went alone. I lived in the field house in Paste' and took my meals with a neighboring Zinacanteco family. For the first time, I was observing and participating in the flow of everyday Zinacanteco life. By May, I was able to attend the all-night lineage and waterhole ceremonies performed by the shamans in this hamlet, which were crucial to our understanding of the structure and dynamics of Zinacanteco hamlet life. However, even after these six months in the hamlet, I was still unable to obtain permission to attend a curing ceremony. I knew they were taking place almost daily, for I would hear the chanting of the shamans and the blowing on the ritual gourds to summon the lost souls. But, it was not until the summer of 1961—four seasons after the project began—that I was finally invited to a curing ceremony, performed in that instance by the former secretary of the school committee whom I had first met over two years earlier.

The Second Phase

Meanwhile, beginning in the summer of 1960, the second phase of the Chiapas Project was initiated—the inclusion of small numbers of carefully selected undergraduates in the summer field research. This undergraduate fieldwork began as part of an interuniversity program funded by the Carnegie Corporation of New York. The Harvard Chiapas Project collaborated with Professors Charles Wagley and Marvin Harris at Columbia and Professor Allan Holmberg and his colleagues at Cornell to train and place undergraduates from the three universities at field stations in Mexico, Brazil, Peru, and Ecuador. We later added the University of Illinois, represented by Professor Joseph B. Casagrande, to the consortium. The program was so successful that it was extended for a number of years under the sponsorship of the National Science Foundation; in later years the Harvard Summer School sponsored the Harvard part of the program, which continued in Chiapas through 1975.

By the summer of 1960, there had been a shift in the field strategy of the project. My original objectives proved to be far too ambitious. Moreover, we were too closely associated with INI to get at the needed basic ethnography. I had originally proposed a five-year project that was tightly designed to describe the changes that were occurring in the cultures of the Tzotzil and Tzeltal as a result of the action program of INI and to utilize these data for an analysis of the determinants and processes of cultural change. I argued that the field setting provided an unprecedented opportunity for controlled research on several aspects of cultural change. Within a radius of 30 miles of San Cristóbal Las Casas, a Ladino town of some 25,000 inhabitants, the contemporary 200,000 Tzotzil and Tzeltal Indians lived in scattered communities in the mountains. These Mayan-speaking Indians were first brought into contact with Europeans in 1528 when the town of San Cristóbal was founded by the Spanish conquerors, the ancestors of the present Ladino population.

In the 1930s, the *municipio* of Oxchuc was studied by Alfonso Villa Rojas (1947), and in the 1940s four additional *municipios* were studied by Professor Sol Tax and a group of Mexican students. Tax (1943, 1944) and his students first worked mainly in Zinacantan for a period of six weeks. Later, three of the students undertook further fieldwork: Fernando Cámara Barbachano (1952) in Tenejapa, Calixta Guiteras-Holmes (1961) in Chenalhó, and Ricardo Pozas (1959) in Chamula. Ruth Bunzel (1940) also worked briefly in Chamula in the 1930s before she went on to Chichicastenango in Guatemala. These data provided a useful early baseline for the investigation of more recent cultural changes.

In 1950, INI established its operating center in San Cristóbal and launched an elaborate program of change that included health education and the establishment of clinics, more formal schooling, the establishment of Indian-controlled stores in each village, the construction of roads, and the improvement of crops and agricultural practices. With this program, INI became the most important event to affect the Indian cultures since the Spanish Conquest. I proposed to take advantage of this laboratory situation to describe the cultural changes that were currently occurring and could be observed firsthand. By using the baseline data from the 1930s and 1940s, by careful study of the new stimulus for change (i.e., the INI program), and by continuing observations over the years, I hoped to trace the sequence and directions of cultural change in detail.

The second aim of the project was to utilize the descriptive data for an analysis of the determinants and processes of cultural change. The crucial determinants of change fall into two major categories: (1) the properties of the two cultures that come into contact and (2) the types of interrelationships established between them (Vogt 1957). Among the properties of the culture that I proposed to study in accounting for the processes of change were the value system which appears extraordinarily persistent and exercises certain controlling effects on the rates and directions of change

(Vogt 1955), and the social structure which may (in rural Mexico) be tightly organized in a "closed" corporate community that is resistant to change, or more loosely organized in an "open" community that is more vulnerable to change (Wolf 1955). Preliminary data from Chiapas had suggested this contrast as a crucial variable in cultural change. An important factor in the types of relationships established between cultures appeared to be the extent to which the new program of change is "forced" or "permissive," the thesis being that changes backed by force or power are less likely to be accepted than are new patterns presented to an American Indian group under permissive conditions that allow for freedom to make choices and for a selective process of adaptation (Dozier 1955). Preliminary data from Chiapas had also suggested that this variable was highly significant in accounting for variations in the adoption of, or resistance to, new patterns.

Inasmuch as the Indian population was relatively large and their settlements numerous, the action programs of INI reached the Indian communities in variable degrees and with variable results, a fact of importance for my research design, which was to be based on a series of comparative studies:

1. The modernization program compared to those that have a record of marked "resistance" to change

2. "Open" communities compared with "closed" corporate communities

3. More "permissive" programs compared with more "forced" programs of change

By 1959 it had become clear that (1) we had underestimated the amount and complexity of ancient Maya social organization and culture that are still viable in these communities; and (2) by focusing on INI programs and the ways in which the Indians responded to these, we were obtaining only part of the data necessary for a penetrating study of the problems. We were, in a word, getting too much of an "outside" view and too little of an "inside" view. I now believe I miscalculated for two reasons. (1) The presence of Catholicism (including the dozens of cross shrines), the links of the communities with the Mexican government, the use of Mexican money, and the use of the Spanish language all led me to think that, in spite of the basic use of Tzotzil by the Indians, the people were essentially Mexican peasants, much like those described by Robert Redfield and Oscar Lewis in Tepoztlán. (2) My previous field research had been in the American Southwest where all Indian cultures had been under anthropological scrutiny for a hundred years before I began my work there. Even though this early anthropological work had been spotty and some of it superficial, it nevertheless had built up an enormous corpus of basic ethnographic data—a corpus lacking in the case of the highland Chiapas cultures.

Therefore, in 1959, I decided to concentrate on basic linguistic and ethnographic work in one *municipio* (Zinacantan), rather than scattering our efforts over many topics and areas. We obviously had to cover this ground before much could be achieved in the study of cultural change. Lore Colby, a trained linguist, completed a study of the basic elements of Tzotzil grammar and compiled a Tzotzil-Spanish dictionary, which she had started in the fall of 1958.

The change in strategy also involved (1) detaching ourselves more and more from the government program and its technicians, and (2) identifying ourselves more with the conservative segments of the Indian communities. Among other things, we started wearing items of Indian clothing, rather than dressing as Ladinos, and we started living in Indian houses. Both of these moves were complex procedures. We found, for example, that it was appropriate in the Indian view to dress as Indians only insofar as we learned to speak Tzotzil. We had to engage in very complicated negotiations to rent Indian houses or move in with Indian families. I mention these field procedures because, while living in Navajo hogans or Zuni houses in New Mexico had long been standard operating procedure for anthropologists there, living with Indian families had rarely, if ever, been done by anthropologists in Mexico or Guatemala.

In the *municipio* of Zinacantan, fewer than 1,000 Indians lived in the ceremonial center where the churches, the town hall, and a few stores are located. The other 7,000 lived in outlying hamlets, ranging in population from 50 to slightly over 1,000. The hamlets are subdivided into "waterhole" groups of one or more patrilineages living around communal waterholes. These patrilineages consist of a series of patrilocally extended families, each occupying a *sitio* (homestead) with two to four houses surrounded by their maize fields. Our students arranged to take up residence in one of the houses in a *sitio*. Our approach to placing students in houses was modeled on that used by the Zinacantecos themselves in asking favors of others. We would visit the male head of a household, present him with a liter of sugarcane liquor, and explain that we wanted the student with us to live in his house, learn the Tzotzil language and customs, and help with household work. If the student were a woman, she would assist with tortilla making and carrying wood and water; if the student were a man, he would assist with farming activities. We explained carefully that the student knew how to eat Zinacanteco food and that he or she would reimburse the family for meals, normally at five pesos a day. We added that the student knew how to sleep on a *petate* ("reed mat") and had brought a sleeping bag for warmth at night. If the family did not wish to have a student guest, the household head would politely refuse the liquor, and we would then go on to another house. If the household head accepted the liquor, it indicated he accepted the student. He ordered the liquor served to all, and by the time the ritual drinking was over, everyone was in a state of pleasant intoxication and the bargain had been sealed. The student remained from four days to two weeks at a time in the home of his Zinacanteco hosts, participating in the full flow of Tzotzil life as represented by this extended family and their neighbors. When the student tired of the diet of tortillas and beans three times a day or detected that his hosts needed a rest from his presence, he or she would return to

San Cristóbal to spend some days writing up field notes, conferring with the field director, and exchanging experiences with other members of the field party who happened to be in town at the same time. If the arrangement in the field went well, a student would return to the same household all season. If it did not, or if the nature of the research topic demanded more comparative data, the student moved to other hamlets and households during the field season.

We also shifted policy with respect to problem areas that were the focal points for study each year. We abandoned (until later) the effort to understand directly the influence of the government program on the Indian communities and moved to a study of a number of basic domains of the culture. By the end of 1960, the results had become exciting. We now knew we were dealing with Indian cultures that were fully as complex and intricate in religion and ceremonial organization, and to some extent in social organization, as southwestern pueblos such as the Zuni and Hopi.

The Third Phase

In 1963 and 1964, I initiated the third phase of the Harvard Chiapas Project. This involved renewal of the NIMH grant and expansion of our operations to include Chamula in our intensive field research. The inclusion of Chamula made our field research even more complex and difficult. Zinacantan had proven to be complex enough, having at that time a population of some 8,000 living in a ceremonial center and fifteen hamlets. But Chamula had a population of about 30,000 living in a ceremonial center and nearly a hundred hamlets. More importantly, I added another methodological phase to our operations: the aerial photography project, funded by the National Science Foundation and sponsored jointly with Professor Norman A. McQuown of Chicago and Professor A. Kimball Romney of Stanford. From 1963 to 1969, we accomplished the following objectives: the taking of aerial photographs of three types (cartographic, high-acuity panoramic, and low-level oblique) of the highlands of Chiapas with the aid of the Itek Corporation of Palo Alto, California, and the Companía Mexicana Aerofoto of Mexico City; the establishment of an aerial photo laboratory at Harvard with a Reader-Printer and a zoom stereoscope for viewing and working with the photographs; and the production of a basic file of photomosaics and maps for the study of settlement patterns, land use, population densities, and so on in the Chiapas highlands (Vogt 1974).

Fieldwork went well through the 1960s, and rapport with both Indians and Ladinos became better each year as we learned more fluent Tzotzil and extended our range of contacts. Each spring at Harvard we offered an informal course in Tzotzil, taught by the person who knew the most Tzotzil. Since I was not as fluent in the language as many of my gifted students, I never had the privilege of teaching this course. It was taught by a junior colleague or a graduate student, or at times by one or more undergraduates who proved to have superior control of the language, and I was one of the students. All students intending to go into the field the following summer took this course and my seminar in field methods. Some of the sessions in the methods seminar were devoted to field reports by students from the previous year; this served to communicate experience directly and keep members of the project in intellectual and personal touch with one another through the years.

During the 1960s, we also gradually developed a series of project traditions that helped to build and keep morale high among students. Most meetings between the field leader and students were on a one-to-one basis, similar to individual tutorials, held either at field headquarters or in the field situation, when the field leader visited the student in some remote hamlet or while traveling together on foot along the mountain trails. We held a midsummer conference and a final conference at which each student presented reports and received comments and criticisms. We also organized dances at field headquarters, either with marimba bands (to which our Indian and Ladino friends were invited and in which they participated) or with taped music for square dances. Furthermore, a student whose birthday occurred in the summer field season enjoyed a Mexican-style celebration with mariachis playing early morning *mañanitas* and with tamales, rum, and coffee for breakfast, or a gala midday luncheon with mariachis and always a *piñata*. These parties not only brought together all our students to honor the birthday person but also provided hospitality for our Indian and Ladino informants and friends, and they were often attended by fifty to a hundred people. Our more athletically inclined students also helped to provide a series of games that promoted morale at field headquarters. Volleyball, horseshoes, darts, and table tennis were played almost daily.

Research conducted in Chiapas during the 1960s included the following: John D. Early collected data on the ceremonies of the Zinacanteco cargoholders during the academic year 1962–1963 (Early 1965); the following year, 1963–1964, Daniel B. Silver undertook a systematic study of the rituals performed by the shamans in Zinacantan (Fabrega and Silver 1973). In 1965–1966, Victoria R. Bricker studied the patterns of ceremonial humor; and in 1966–1967 George and Jane Collier, who had already spent summers doing field research, returned for a full year to work on land use and inheritance and to collect law cases (Collier 1975; Collier 1973). They were joined by Frank and Francesca Cancian, returning for a second full year in the field (Cancian 1979), and by Elena Uribe Wood, who studied patterns of *compadrazgo* in Zinacantan and Chamula. During 1968–1969, Gary H. Gossen worked on Chamula oral narrative, while Victoria Bricker returned for a second field stint to study ritual humor in Chamula and Chenalhó (Bricker 1973). In 1968, Sarah Blaffer Hrdy also did field research for her senior thesis at Harvard (Hrdy 1972).

The Crisis

Then, in December 1969, an event occurred that nearly ended the project. Thieves, who have never been identified, broke into the Church of San Lorenzo in Zinacantan Center in the middle of the night and stole a silver cross from the wall and the golden chalice from the main altar. Zinacanteco officials saw the tracks of tennis shoes (which were often worn by anthropologists) outside the church, and within hours word spread throughout the *municipio* that the anthropologists must have stolen the sacred objects. Later, we found that two other churches had been broken into the same night (one in San Cristóbal and the other in San Felipe at the edge of San Cristóbal) and colonial art pieces removed. Fortunately, two very experienced and gifted fieldworkers, John Haviland and Francesco Pellizzi, were in Chiapas at the time, and they managed to ride out the political storm with the aid of Mexican government authorities, the bishop, and various priests, all of whom reassured the Zinacantecos that we were not the thieves. Since the thieves have never been apprehended nor the art objects recovered, we have concluded that some kind of internationally organized "ring" dealing in stolen art was probably involved and that the objects are now in New York, London, or Paris. What made the Zinacanteco reaction especially sharp was their belief that the silver cross had been found in a cave by an ancestral figure and that it had the power to "make money." It took at least five years for us to recover the rapport that we had had before this unfortunate event.

By the early 1970s, we finally had good control of the ethnographic data in Zinacantan and increasingly adequate control of the data in Chamula, especially from the work of Gary H. Gossen, Priscilla Rachun Linn, Thomas Crump, and Jeffrey C. Howry; as well as some data on the neighboring Indian *municipios* and the Ladino *municipio* of San Cristóbal Las Casas, which was particularly studied by Felisa M. Kazen in connection with her field study of a textile factory in the city. We began to engage in more controlled comparative studies and also returned to the basic questions I began with concerning the impact of Mexican government programs on the Indian cultures. Jan Rus III and Robert F. Wasserstrom specifically investigated these problems.

Most summer seasons I served as field leader as well as carrying on my own research. I also had a spring term (1960) and a fall term (1971) in Chiapas, so that I have been able to witness the full calendar round. My total time in the field from 1957 to 2000 has been ninety-six months. The seasons when I could not be in the field throughout the summer, I appointed experienced younger colleagues to serve as field leaders: Duane Metzger in 1960, Frank Cancian in 1962, George Collier in 1964 and 1966, John Haviland in 1971, Priscilla Rachun Linn in 1972, and Jan Rus in 1975. By the summer of 1980, a total of 142 project fieldworkers had engaged in research in Chiapas for a summer season or longer.

Colleagues often inquire how long I plan to continue the project. My answer is that I plan to continue in Chiapas for the rest of my life, although now that I am retired I tend to do less field research there and devote more time to writing and publishing. Meanwhile, it is a source of great satisfaction to me that the long-term anthropological research I initiated with the Harvard Chiapas Project continues in the fieldwork of the next generation, notably that of Victoria R. Bricker

(1973, 1981), Frank Cancian (1965, 1972, 1979, 1992), George A. Collier (1975), Gary H. Gossen (1974b, 1999), John B. Haviland (1977, 1981), and Robert M. Laughlin (1976, 1980, 1988, 1993, 1996), all of whom have ongoing research projects.

Methodology

The principal advantage of a continuous long-range project over a short-range one, or a series of revisits, is the depth, quality, and variety of understandings achieved—understandings of the basic ethnography and of the trends and processes of change. If the long-range project also involves a sizable team of students and younger colleagues who make one or more revisits and keep abreast of all the publications, then there is the added advantage of having a variety of fieldworkers with varied training and different theoretical biases who are forced to reconcile their findings and their analyses with one another.

From the start, the Chiapas Project has operated with the agreement that all fieldworkers deposit a copy of their field data in the central archives at Harvard and, in return, all fieldworkers have access to all data; further, each fieldworker normally circulates manuscripts to other members of the project for comment and criticism in advance of publication. While I sometimes find it maddening to have to rewrite an article or chapters of a book three or four times in response to sharp comments from my colleagues, I am convinced the final products are always better for it—both ethnographically and analytically. This procedure is a far cry from the long tradition in anthropology of one fieldworker who spends one or two years with a tribe and then returns to produce the monograph, which not only stands as God's Truth about the tribe but also is processed into the Human Relations Area Files (HRAF) and thereby becomes the basis for a case in cross-cultural studies. It may be that the ethnographic data were excellent and basically correct, but we have only the word of one anthropologist to depend on, and my guess is that the materials are sometimes superficial. I note with interest that whenever there has been a revisit by some other anthropologist there has followed, I believe without exception, a celebrated controversy in the journals about who was right and who was wrong.

A second important advantage to a long-range project is the development of rapport with the communities under observation. There is something about constantly returning each season—in our case, with the rains—that seems to reassure most people and to engender feelings of mutual trust. This situation makes it possible to be doing significant fieldwork upon arrival, and the fieldworker does not have to go through the motions of coping with the local bureaucracy each season. On the Chiapas Project, this long-range rapport has led to significant results in three areas: the study of native theories of the universe; the design and execution of specialized experimental studies; and deeper understanding of the trends of cultural change.

Native Theories

We have achieved a degree of understanding of native Tzotzil theory and belief that could not be attained in a project of shorter duration. Field studies of native cognitive structures have often suffered from either a lack of the intimate insights supplied by a thorough knowledge of the native language, or a tendency to portray belief as monolithic or unchanging across the social universe. Although the first years of our fieldwork were hampered by our lack of fluency in Tzotzil, one of our fieldworkers, Dr. Robert M. Laughlin (1975), over some thirteen years elicited more than 35,000 entries for his Tzotzil dictionary; while another, Professor John B. Haviland (1981), developed grammatical descriptions which now allow new fieldworkers to achieve fluency in Tzotzil in six months of solid study.

At the same time, our varied training has extended our understanding of the native conceptual system in important ways. Frank Cancian (1965), for instance, has described the ritual cargo system of the Chiapas highlands as an economic system of social prestige ranking. Others of us have incorporated Cancian's insights into an analysis of how, in native theory, the cargo system represents a complex system of gifts and offerings between humans and the gods. Gary Gossen, working in Chamula on oral narrative and cosmology, discovered in the mythical order that lies behind the system of ritual cargos and curing ceremonies a correlation between mythical time and social space, social chaos and disorder being associated with times and places deep in the past and as distant and barbarous as Guatemala, Mexico City, and the United States, while social order is symbolized by current ritual behavior of the officials in the modern ceremonial centers (Gossen 1974b). Further, Gossen discovered that conservative Chamulas not only maintain the ancient Tzotzil solar calendar of eighteen months of twenty days each with a five-day unlucky period at the end, but also that flower-changing ceremonies for the saints are still performed on the basis of this twenty-day month (Gossen 1974a). In addition, there are still carefully calculated cycles of time—the agricultural cycle, the weather cycle, the fiesta cycle, the phases of the moon—which permit two Chamulas conversing together to specify the exact day of the year by the ancient calendar (Gossen 1974a).

Gossen also discovered puns, riddles, and children's games that are far more subtle and complex than we previously believed to exist. The games have proven to offer models for Chamula social structure, models which are extraordinarily interesting. For example, there is one game in which five small children arrange themselves from the most senior in age to the most junior in age—reflecting the kinship system—and take the respective roles of an older, middle, and younger brother, a chicken, and a weasel. The three older children join hands and place the chicken (domesticated) in the center. Then the weasel (wild) attempts to break into the protective circle to capture and kill the chicken. The game appears to represent not only one of the basic principles of Tzotzil social structure (i.e., age grading) but also to be a metaphorical comment on the relationship between wild and domestic animals, as well as aiding socialization in teaching children to care for domestic animals.

Our understanding of these domains of Tzotzil culture has been built up, step by step, only by intimate knowledge of the Tzotzil language, of bodies of data from both Chamula (Gossen 1986, 1999) and Zinacantan for controlled comparative study, and by utilizing a variety of theoretical approaches. A long-range project is imperative for these kinds of cumulative, cross-checked results.

Special Studies

Our long-range project also has had tremendous potential for the successful execution of specialized, experimental studies. Our heavy investment in developing rapport over the years has made it possible to experiment with hundreds of subjects, rather than just a handful of them, and to draw representative, and even total, samples of the universes being studied. Richard Shweder, for example, was able to perform a variety of carefully controlled procedures matching fifty shamans with fifty nonshamans (Shweder 1972). Drs. T. Berry Brazelton, John S. Robey, and George A. Collier (1969), in two summers of study, were able to examine and give tests of psychosocial development to nearly one hundred Zinacanteco infants. Frank Cancian was able to study economic motivation in two communities of nearly 1,700 people by training key informants to recruit every household head and administer to him a lengthy questionnaire in the Tzotzil language (Cancian 1972). George Collier, utilizing aerial photographs, completed an exhaustive study of land tenure practices in one community where, several years ago, questions of land ownership would have been too delicate to broach (Collier 1975). George Collier and John Haviland worked together on a "Who's Who in Zinacantan" in which a panel of informants from each of the major hamlets would converse freely around a tape recorder about the important people in each hamlet—political leaders, shamans, wealthy corn farmers, and so forth. The panel discussions not only generated penetrating data for Collier, who was studying the determinants of political power, but also for Haviland, who was studying gossip and utilizing it to understand the dynamics of social structure (Haviland 1977).

In each of these instances, fieldwork prior to the execution of the study allowed the researchers to formulate theoretically meaningful and, at the same time, practical, experimental designs.

Cultural Change

A third advantage of our long-term project is the opportunity it has provided to study firsthand the trends of cultural change. In order to systematize these observations on change from year to year, we attempted to take a reading each season on a number of indices of change. Our observations during the early years of the project revealed that these indices are both crucial and measurable markers of change. Some of these mark the degree of "modernization" that is taking place in the Indian villages; others are measures of nativistic trends in traditional Indian life. Examples of these indices follow:

1. *Incidence of bilingualism.* During the decades 1940 to 1960 there was a net increase in monolingualism in Tzotzil in the highlands of Chiapas. But now, the scales have been tipped in the direction of increasing control of Spanish on the part of the Indians.

2. *Housing styles.* The trend is from the traditional thatched roof, with wattle-and-daub walls, to tile roofs with adobe walls.

3. *Clothing styles.* The shift is from the traditional (Colonial Period) Indian dress to styles of clothing worn by Mexican peasants. This change is fast for men, very slow for women. It is noteworthy, however, that traditional men's *chamarras* (jackets) and women's *rebozos* (shawls) with increasingly exuberant embroidered floral designs are retained as symbols of "Indianness."

4. *Household equipment.* This includes the addition of corn mills, tortilla presses, metal pots and pans.

5. *Roads and modes of transport.* More and better roads have led to a shift from foot travel to more bus and truck travel.

6. *Surnames.* The shift is from the traditional Tzotzil system to the Mexican system.

7. *Participation of Indians in Ladino institutions.* For example, arranging loans with governmental agencies, joining labor unions, using Ladino courts—all of which are on the increase on the part of the Indians.

8. *Numbers of practicing shamans.* These numbers are on the increase; an index of "nativism."

9. *Shifts in drinking customs.* Surprisingly, there has been a marked change compared to thirty years ago. The Chamulas and Zinacantecos, for reasons we do not yet thoroughly understand, are consuming far less liquor. I suspect one of the basic reasons is the increased morale of Indian communities that was an unanticipated consequence of the arrival of INI, the first official agency in 450 years to pronounce they had arrived to champion the rights and customs of the indigenous population (Vogt 1994c).

10. *Adoption of public utilities: water lines and electricity.* Acceptance is proceeding apace.

11. *Population growth.* It is explosive and a real problem.

Have we found disadvantages to our long-term research, and especially that involving teams of fieldworkers? I perceive two disadvantages. One is that sometimes it has been impossible to recruit top-flight students who may prefer, instead, to undertake field research in still unstudied areas of places like New Guinea or Brazil. When the Harvard Chiapas Project started, this was not a problem since it was an unstudied ethnographic area with all the usual exotic challenges. But now, as we sit in seminar rooms at Harvard and describe how tough it was in the beginning, we sometimes find we have inspired the students to look elsewhere for "wild and hairy" field sites instead of coming to work in what they perceive to be the already heavily studied highlands of Chiapas. When I point out that there are still dozens of Tzotzil and Tzeltal *municipios* that have scarcely been touched, I do not always succeed in convincing them.

The other disadvantage is the amount of administrative time it takes to run a long-term project. My administrative burden was not so heavy as it might have been, for I deliberately kept the number of graduate students small and selective—not more than one or two a year for most of the time. The undergraduates have posed more problems since there were many applications each year, not only from Harvard and Radcliffe, but from other schools as well, and it was difficult to keep the numbers at about six each summer, especially when former students wished to return. Since some of the best graduate students have been recruited from undergraduate field programs, I was always reluctant to limit the numbers. But perhaps the most vexing administrative problem occurred when members of the project did not get on well with one another—for various and complicated reasons—and I will not pretend that we have not had a few celebrated intraproject conflicts. In the long run, most of these have been resolved to the point where the "combatants" have participated together in symposia at anthropology meetings. Generalizing about the sources of these conflicts is difficult, but one thing seems clear. They have, surprisingly, *not* arisen over possessive feelings about field data or ideas, but rather more because of differences in research style and field methods and in intellectual and political presuppositions.

If I could start over, would I do things differently? In retrospect, it would seem that I might have been able to get at more penetrating ethnographic data in the first phase of the project than I did. But, given the enormous difficulties of establishing rapport with closed and highly suspicious Indian communities, there was probably no real alternative to the different strategies we used. We were first sponsored by, and closely associated ourselves with, INI, which, as a champion of Indian interests, had developed closer rapport than that enjoyed by most of the local Ladino population. Through INI, we met and employed our first informants and established our field house in Paste'. Still later, when I discovered that living next door to Indian families was much less productive than living with them, we donated the field house to the schoolteachers and established a field headquarters in rented buildings at the edge of San Cristóbal. With this headquarters as a base, we could move out to the hamlets to live with Indian families for periods of days or weeks, then return to base to write up data and, even more important, to reciprocate hospitality when our Indian friends came to see us. This pattern of alternation was crucial for our research operations because, unlike the Mexicans, the Indians of Zinacantan and Chamula have no patterns of visiting each other unless there is some explicit purpose such as borrowing an axe, buying a chicken, or asking for a loan of money. Furthermore, the data that can be gathered by informal interviewing and observation while living on a day and night basis in a one-room thatched house with an Indian family so exceeds the data that can be gathered from a short stay during the day that there is no comparison. On the other hand, the periods of relative calm at field headquarters are ideal for thinking, writing up data, and for formal interviewing of informants away from the distractions of hamlet life.

Research Results

Our research results to date are found in some 40 books and monographs, 180 articles, 2 novels (Wilson 1966, 1972), 2 ethnographic films (Krebs 1967), 21 Ph.D. dissertations, and 32 senior theses listed in the Harvard Chiapas Project Bibliography (Vogt 1978); and in Vogt, *Field Work Among the Maya: Reflections on the Harvard Chiapas Project* (1994c). It is apparent that we have worked on many ethnographic fronts and have tilled different patches of theoretical turf. Over the years, I have deliberately encouraged my students and junior colleagues to develop their own ideas and work out their own methods of undertaking research. This policy was based on my experience with the previous Values Study Project in the Southwest (see Vogt and Albert 1966). I sometimes have wished that we had tried to establish a publication series with one press so that the results of the Chiapas Project would be less scattered. But presses have different interests, so we have utilized a variety of them, including especially the university presses at Chicago, Harvard, New Mexico, Oklahoma, Stanford, and Texas.

Reviewing my own published results, I have edited an INI volume which is a collection of reprinted articles in Spanish (1966), published a major monograph (1969), and a small paperback (1970b, second edition 1990, Spanish edition 1973). These volumes all emphasize descriptive ethnography rather than theoretical analysis.

With Alberto Ruz L., I have also edited *Desarrollo Cultural de los Mayas* (1964), based on the 1962 Burg Wartenstein Symposium, "The Cultural Development of the Maya," which contains a goodly amount of Chiapas material. I also edited *Aerial Photography in Anthropological Field Research* (1974), which contains five articles on various aspects of our aerial photo work in the highlands of Chiapas. These two volumes contain ethnographic data, but the emphasis is more methodological and theoretical. More recently published is my *Tortillas for the Gods: A Symbolic Analysis of Zinacanteco Rituals* (1976, 1993), which attempts a theoretical interpretation of ceremonial life.

In addition, I have published a number of articles, some of which were largely ethnographic in content, but several of which (e.g., 1961, 1964a, 1964b, 1964c, 1964d) have had a theoretical and methodological impact. In fact, these triggered a controversy with certain Mayan archaeologists that has reverberated through the journals and monographs for the last forty years. My basic argument is that it should be fruitful to examine the social and political structure and cosmology of the contemporary Mayan peoples in areas like the highlands of Chiapas for hints about the Classic Maya, rather than utilizing what are essentially Old World models of kinship, priesthoods, and so forth to make inferences. In particular, I hypothesize a conceptual (and perhaps historical) connection between the steep-sided mountains (that are homes of ancestral gods in Chiapas) and the pyramids in Classic sites (which it turns out are often tombs for prominent ancient Maya; see Vogt 1997a). At the least, since we find a close relationship between sacred shrines devoted to ancestors and various levels of social structure in highland Chiapas, it would seem worthwhile to explore the idea that the multiple pyramids in archaeological sites may symbolize differentiated sociopolitical units in Classic Maya society. The argument continues in two subsequent papers (1983, 1994b).

One of the most exciting developments concerning the relationship of sacred mountains to pyramids was the discovery by David Stuart of a glyph for "wits" (mountain) on the side of a pyramid at Copan, demonstrating that the Classic Maya considered their pyramids to be mountains created by humans (Stuart 1997).

Another paper which generated considerable interest, and which is pertinent in ongoing research (Vogt 1965), demonstrated how certain key structural and conceptual patterns are replicated in many domains and at various levels of the culture, ranging from child care to the supernatural world.

In my later years, I have turned more to an attempt to decode the rich ceremonial life of Zinacantan. Two preliminary papers (1970a, Vogt and Vogt 1970) led to my book (1976), *Tortillas for the Gods*. In these efforts I have used ideas stemming from Lévi-Strauss, Leach, Turner, Geertz, Douglas, and others to develop a structural analysis of the Zinacanteco ritual symbolism (see also Vogt 1997a, 1998a, 1998b; Vogt and Bricker 1996). I have also explored the Zinacanteco views of astronomy (Vogt 1997c).

Clearly, I have spent rather more time analyzing continuities than changes in Tzotzil culture (for exceptions, see 1967, 1968, 1990, 1992). For the most part, I have left the more sustained analysis of trends and processes of change to my students and colleagues (see, for example, Cancian 1992; Collier 1999). There are two reasons for this: the cultural continuities have continued to impress me and I often feel rather like A. L. Kroeber, who found that acculturation studies were "dreary." Nothing about the various trends we track and describe seems very astonishing. Tribal peoples are, in effect, becoming more like peasants, and peasants have a kind of dreary sameness all over the world.

Perhaps the most dramatic change affecting the Tzotzil-Tzeltal region of Highland Chiapas has been the Zapatista Rebellion that began January 1, 1994, with the Zapatistas taking over the town hall of San Cristóbal Las Casas as well as several other towns in Eastern Chiapas. These events have been studied in depth by George Collier (1999) and have been commented on by many former members of the Harvard Chiapas Project. I have attempted to provide some of the flavor of the unfolding events in three Op-Ed pieces in the *Boston Globe* (1994a, 1997b, 1999).

Meanwhile, my former students (now professionals in their own right) have been very productive in publishing their research results. In addition to their books cited here, an interesting selection of some of their recent articles appears in Bricker and Gossen (1989).

Impact of Our Research on the People in Chiapas

Our impact on the Indian cultures we study in highland Chiapas makes itself felt on two levels: (1) the immediate day-to-day relationships with the Indian families and communities, and (2) the more indirect effects stemming from our publications.

It is easy to exaggerate our day-to-day influence on the Indian cultures. For, although we have been doing fieldwork involving a large number of different researchers over the years, the Indian communities we study are relatively large. Even with a field party of as many as fifteen students, we are not so conspicuous in what is now a total Zinacanteco population of over 20,000 or the Chamula population of 100,000 as a single anthropologist is in a tribe of 200 people in the interior of Brazil. Further, we have never had more than two fieldworkers in a given hamlet with a population ranging between 500 and 1,500. We have had an impact on selected Indian families that we have employed as informants over the years. Not only have we employed members of these families fairly steadily for months at a time, but five young men (four Zinacantecos and one Chamula) have been brought to Harvard for as long as two months to assist in teaching Tzotzil to new students. While at Harvard, these men have lived either with my family or with younger colleagues or graduate students. Further, two of the Zinacanteco men have spent longer periods in Santa Fe, New Mexico, and at the Smithsonian Institution in Washington, D.C., assisting Robert Laughlin with his work on the Tzotzil dictionary. The same two attended the American Anthropological Association meetings in San Francisco in 1963 and had the frightening experience of seeing Oswald shot down on the TV screen following the Kennedy assassination. Needless to say, they wanted to return immediately to the safety of the highlands of southern Mexico.

All five of these men were literate in Spanish, but we taught them to read and write in Tzotzil; three of the five even learned to touch-type quite competently and are now comfortable using computers. For four of the five, I believe our major impact, in terms of both the salaries we paid them and the cross-cultural experiences we provided, served mainly to speed up the processes of economic advancement and modernization in their lives that might have occurred anyway. The steady salaries we paid and the skills we taught them permitted these men to get married sooner and/or to advance in the cargo system more quickly and to acquire better jobs with government agencies than would otherwise have been the case. Two of them recently served as mayors of their communities: one as the mayor of Zinacantan and one as mayor of Chamula.

The major negative impact occurred in the case of the Zinacanteco we first employed and who came to be highly dependent on us. His was a very special case. His mother is a Chamula who came to Zinacantan Center to weave for a Zinacanteco family and later married a Zinacanteco man. The father abandoned the mother; hence, our informant was brought up without the father's guidance and did not learn the proper techniques and usual corn-farming skills. He probably would have drifted away from the traditional way of life even had we not appeared—in fact, he was working as a puppeteer for INI when we first hired him. He was the only one who was really dependent on members of the project for economic support to get through his cargos and support his wife and five children, because his corn-farming efforts were always failures and he did not have steady employment elsewhere. He also suffered from cirrhosis of the liver from excessive drinking that usually began in connection with his ceremonial duties and was then prolonged by his psychological problems. This disease finally resulted in his premature death, and his widow died soon afterward. His children are now mostly grown and are fortunately in better shape. The eldest son, who is now responsible for his younger siblings, carries on the work of his father by working for the Chiapas Writers' Cooperative, a long-term project (founded by Robert M. Laughlin) that employs Tzotzil Maya to write and publish booklets on their myths and customs in their own language and has, over the years, taught more than a thousand Tzotzil-speaking Maya to read and write; this group is now also writing and producing successful plays based on Tzotzil mythology and oral narrative (Breslin 1992).

On another level, our publications have had some effects on the communities, although they are difficult to specify. We have made it a practice to give copies of our publications (especially those that appear in Spanish and/or have many photographs) to our Indian friends. They spend hours poring over the photographs and read selectively in the texts. Some of the books are proudly kept in boxes on household altars and brought out to show visitors. I suppose there is some small Hawthorne effect in this, insofar as it makes the Indians aware that they and their culture are important enough to be studied and written about. Robert Laughlin has reported (personal communication, April 25, 1993) that a group of Zinacantecos has constructed a museum in Zinacantan Center to show both their children and visiting tourists something of the traditional life and customs. The museum is housed in a large thatch-roofed house and will ultimately contain *manos* and *metates* on which they grind maize for tortillas, the type of pottery formerly in use, back-strap looms for weaving, and so forth. This group has conferred with Laughlin and with our books for details on the nature of life in Zinacantan thirty years ago.

The other impact stems from the reading of our books by government officials. We know that the governors of Chiapas and the president of the republic have had copies of my monograph on Zinacantan. When I gave a copy to the governor some years ago, he promptly gave it to the president and wrote me for another copy. The president probably looked at the photographs, but I do not know whether he read the monograph. We know that the governor, who was a well-educated neurosurgeon, did read our books and tried to learn from them. Whether any particular item of government policy toward the Indians has been altered by what he read, except the governor's insistence that government publications using Tzotzil follow the orthography we use, is not clear to me, except for one major development. This was the establishment of a government radio station in San Cristóbal that broadcasts in Tzotzil. This station would eventually have been established, but I am certain that it was put into operation years earlier than it might have been as a consequence of the governor's reading and acting on one of the predictions in the final chapter of my monograph.

Four former members of the Harvard Chiapas Project—George and Jane Collier, John Haviland, and Robert Laughlin—have built or purchased houses in San Cristóbal Las Casas and spend part of every year continuing their field projects in Chiapas. Their personal commitments augur well for the work of the project continuing into the twenty-first century.

References Cited

Brazelton, T. Berry, John S. Robey, and George A. Collier
  (1969) "Infant development in the Zinacanteco Indians of Southern Mexico." *Pediatrics* 44(2):274–293.

Breslin, Patrick
  (1992) "Coping with change, the Maya discover the play's the thing." *Smithsonian* 23(5):78–87.

Bricker, Victoria R.
  (1973) *Ritual Humor in Highland Chiapas*. Austin: University of Texas Press.
  (1981) *The Indian Christ, the Indian King: The Historical Substrate of Maya Myth and Ritual.* Austin: University of Texas Press.

Bricker, Victoria R. and Gary H. Gossen [editors]
  (1989) *Ethnographic Encounters in Southern Mesoamerica: Essays in Honor of Evon Z. Vogt, Jr.* Austin: University of Texas Press.

Bunzel, Ruth
  (1940) "The role of alcoholism in two Central American cultures." *Psychiatry* 3:361–387.

Cámara Barbachano, Fernando
(1952) "Organización religiosa y política de Tenejapa." *Anales del Instituto Nacional de Antropología e Historia* 4:263–277.

Cancian, Francesca M.
(1975) *What Are Norms? A Study of Belief and Action in a Maya Community.* Cambridge: Cambridge University Press.

Cancian, Frank
(1965) *Economics and Prestige in a Maya Community: A Study of the Religious Cargo System in Zinacantan, Chiapas, Mexico.* Stanford: Stanford University Press.
(1972) *Change and Uncertainty in a Peasant Economy: The Maya Corn Farmers of Zinacantan.* Stanford: Stanford University Press.
(1979) *The Innovator's Situation: Upper-Middle-Class Conservatism in Agricultural Communities.* Stanford: Stanford University Press.
(1992) *The Decline of Community in Zinacantan: The Economy, Public Life, and Social Stratification, 1950 to 1987.* Stanford: Stanford University Press.

Colby, B. N.
(1966) *Ethnic Relations in the Chiapas Highlands.* Santa Fe: Museum of New Mexico Press.

Collier, George A.
(1975) *Fields of the Tzotzil: The Ecological Bases of Tradition in Highland Chiapas.* Austin: University of Texas Press.
(1999) [with Elizabeth Lowery Quaratiello] *Basta! Land and the Zapatista Rebellion in Chiapas.* Revised edition. Oakland, CA: Food First Books.

Collier, Jane F.
(1973) *Law and Social Change in Zinacantan.* Stanford: Stanford University Press.

Dozier, Edward P.
(1955) "Forced and permissive acculturation." *American Indian* 7:38–44.

Early, John D.
(1965) "The Sons of San Lorenzo in Zinacantan." Ph.D. dissertation. Harvard University.

Eggan, Fred
(1954) "Social anthropology and the method of controlled comparison." *American Anthropologist* 56:743–763.

Fabrega, Horacio, Jr. and Daniel B. Silver
(1973) *Illness and Shamanism in Zinacantan: An Ethnomedical Analysis.* Stanford: Stanford University Press.

Gossen, Gary H.
(1974a) "A Chamula calendar board from Chiapas, Mexico." Pp. 217–254 in Norman

Hammond (editor), *Meso-American Archaeology: New Approaches*. Austin: University of Texas Press.

(1974b) *Chamulas in the World of the Sun: Time and Space in a Maya Oral Tradition*. Cambridge, MA: Harvard University Press.

(1986) [editor] *Symbol and Meaning Beyond the Closed Community: Essays in Mesoamerican Ideas*. Albany: Institute for Mesoamerican Studies, State University of New York at Albany.

(1999) *Telling Maya Tales: Tzotzil Identities in Modern Mexico*. New York: Routledge.

Guiteras-Holmes, Calixta
(1961) *Perils of the Soul: The World View of a Tzotzil Indian*. Glencoe, IL: Free Press.

Haviland, John B.
(1977) *Gossip, Reputation, and Knowledge in Zinacantan*. Chicago: University of Chicago Press.

(1981) *Sk'op Tzotz'leb: El Tzotzil de San Lorenzo Zinacantan*. México, D.F.: Centro de Estudios Mayas, Universidad Nacional Autónoma de México.

Hrdy, Sarah C. Blaffer
(1972) *The Black-Man of Zinacantan: A Central American Legend*. Austin: University of Texas Press.

Krebs, Stephanie L.
(1967) *Shunka's Story: A Woman's Life in Zinacantan*. (20 min., 16-mm color film).

Laughlin, Robert M.
(1975) *The Great Tzotzil Dictionary of San Lorenzo Zinacantán*. (Smithsonian Contributions to Anthropology, No. 19.) Washington, D.C.: Smithsonian Institution Press.

(1976) *Of Wonders Wild and New: Dreams from Zinacantán*. (Smithsonian Contributions to Anthropology, No. 22) Washington, D.C.: Smithsonian Institution Press.

(1977) *Of Cabbages and Kings: Tales from Zinacantán*. (Smithsonian Contributions to Anthropology, No. 23) Washington, D.C.: Smithsonian Institution Press.

(1980) *Of Shoes and Ships and Sealing Wax: Sundries from Zinacantán*. (Smithsonian Contributions to Anthropology, No. 25) Washington, D.C.: Smithsonian Institution Press.

(1988) *The Great Tzotzil Dictionary of Santo Domingo Zinacantán*. (Smithsonian Contributions to Anthropology, No. 31) Washington, D.C.: Smithsonian Institution Press.

(1993) [with Dennis E. Breedlove] *The Flowering of Man: A Tzotzil Botany of Zinacantán*. (Smithsonian Contributions to Anthropology, No. 35) Washington, D.C.: Smithsonian Institution Press.

(1996) *Mayan Tales from Zinacantán: Dreams and Stories from the People of the Bat*. Washington, D.C.: Smithsonian Institution Press.

Pozas, Ricardo
(1959) "Chamula, un pueblo indio de los altos de Chiapas." *Memorias del Instituto Nacional Indigenista*, No. 8. México, D.F.: Instituto Nacional Indigenista.

Shweder, Richard A.
(1972) "Aspects of cognition in Zinacanteco shamans: Experimental results." Pp. 407–412 in W. A. Lessa and E. Z. Vogt (editors), *Reader in Comparative Religion: An Anthropological Approach.* New York: Harper and Row.

Stuart, David
(1997) "The hills are alive: Sacred mountains in the Maya cosmos." *Symbols* (Spring):13–17. Peabody Museum, Harvard University.

Tax, Sol
(1943) *Notas sobre Zinacantan, Chiapas.* University of Chicago Library, Microfilm Collection of Manuscripts on Middle American Cultural Anthropology, No. 20.
(1944) "Information about the municipio of Zinacantan, Chiapas." *Revista Mexicana de Estudios Antropológicos* 6:181–195.

Villa Rojas, Alfonso
(1947) "Kinship and nagualism in a Tzeltal community, Southeastern Mexico." *American Anthropologist* 49:578–588.

Vogt, Evon Z.
(1955) *Modern Homesteaders: The Life of a Twentieth-Century Frontier Community.* Cambridge, MA: Belknap Press of Harvard University Press.
(1957) "The acculturation of the American Indians." *Annals of American Academy of Political and Social Science* 311:137–146.
(1961) "Some aspects of Zinacantan settlement patterns and ceremonial organization." *Estudios de Cultura Maya* 1:131–146.
(1964a) "Ancient Maya concepts in contemporary Zinacantan religion." *VIᵉ Congrès International des Sciences Anthropologiques et Ethnologiques* 2:497–502. Paris.
(1964b) "Ancient Maya and contemporary Tzotzil cosmology: A comment on some methodological problems." *American Antiquity* 30:192–195.
(1964c) "The genetic model and Maya cultural development." Pp. 9–48 in E. Z. Vogt and Alberto Ruz L. (editors), *Desarrollo Cultural de los Mayas.* México, D.F.: Universidad Nacional Autónoma de México.
(1964d) "Some implications of Zinacantan social structure for the study of the ancient Maya." *Actas y Memorias del XXXV Congreso Internacional de Americanistas* 1:307–319. México, D. F.
(1965) "Structural and conceptual replication in Zinacantan culture." *American Anthropologist* 67:342–353.
(1966) [editor] *Los Zinacantecos: Un Pueblo Tzotzil de los Altos de Chiapas.* Colección de Antropología Social, Vol. 7. México, D. F.: Instituto Nacional Indigenista.
(1967) "Tendencias de cambio en las tierras altas de Chiapas." *América Indígena* 27:199–222.
(1968) "Recurrent and directional processes in Zinacantan." *Actas y Memorias del XXXVII Congreso Internacional de Americanistas* 1:441–447. Buenos Aires.
(1969) *Zinacantan: A Maya Community in the Highlands of Chiapas.* Cambridge, MA:

Belknap Press of Harvard University Press.

(1970a) "Human souls and animal spirits in Zinacantan." Pp. 1148–1167 in Jean Pouillon and Pierre Maranda (editors), *Echanges et Communications: Mélanges offerts à Claude Lévi-Strauss à l'occasion de son 60ème anniversaire.* The Hague: Mouton.

(1970b) *The Zinacantecos of Mexico: A Modern Maya Way of Life.* New York: Holt, Rinehart and Winston.

(1973) *Los Zinacantecos: Un Grupo Maya en el Siglo XX.* Mexico, D.F.: SepSetentas 69.

(1974) [editor] *Aerial Photography in Anthropological Field Research.* Cambridge, MA: Harvard University Press.

(1976) *Tortillas for the Gods: A Symbolic Analysis of Zinacanteco Rituals.* Cambridge, MA: Harvard University Press.

(1978) *Bibliography of the Harvard Chiapas Project.* Cambridge, MA: Peabody Museum, Harvard University.

(1983) "Ancient and contemporary Maya settlement patterns: A new look from the Chiapas highlands." Pp. 89–114 in Evon Z. Vogt and Richard M. Leventhal (editors), *Prehistoric Settlement Patterns: Essays in Honor of Gordon R. Willey.* Albuquerque: University of New Mexico Press.

(1990) *The Zinacantecos of Mexico: A Modern Maya Way of Life.* Second Edition. Fort Worth: Holt, Rinehart and Winston.

(1992) "Cruces indias y bastones de mando en Mesoamerica." Pp. 249–294 in Manuel Gutierrez Estevez, Miguel Leon-Portilla, Gary H. Gossen, and J. Jorge Klor de Alva (editors), *De Palabra y Obra en el Nuevo Mundo 2: Encuentros Interétnicas.* Madrid y México, D.F.: Siglo XXI.

(1993) *Tortillas for the Gods: A Symbolic Analysis of Zinacanteco Rituals.* Paperback edition. Norman: University of Oklahoma Press.

(1994a) "Chiapas: Rebellion, ritual and the supernatural." OpEd, *Boston Globe,* May 31, 1994.

(1994b) "On the application of the phylogenetic model to the Maya." Pp. 377–414 in Raymond J. DeMallie and Alfonso Ortiz (editors), *North American Indian Anthropology: Essays on Society and Culture.* Norman: University of Oklahoma Press.

(1994c) *Fieldwork Among the Maya: Reflections on the Harvard Chiapas Project.* Albuquerque: University of New Mexico Press.

(1995) "Paradigmas teóricos y methodologías de campo para el estudio de larga duración de la continuidad y el cambio de la cultura Maya Tzotzil." Pp. 471–506 in J. Jorge Klor de Alva, Gary H. Gossen, Miguel Leon-Portilla, and Manuel Gutierrez Estevez (editors), *De Palabra y Obra en el Nuevo Mundo 4.* Madrid: Siglo XXI.

(1997a) "Maya ritual and cosmology in contemporary Zinacantan." *Symbols* (Spring):9–13, 38–39. Peabody Museum, Harvard University.

(1997b) "Three years after the rebellion, Chiapas is a thriving tourist spot." OpEd, *Boston Globe,* April 12, 1997.

(1997c) "Zinacanteco astronomy." *Mexicon* 19(6):110–117.

(1998a) "Some reflections on long-term field research in anthropology: Lecture in honor of George M. Foster," 13 November 1995. <http://www.sunsite.berkeley.edu/ Anthro/foster>

(1998b) "Zinacanteco dedication and termination rituals." Pp. 21–30 in Shirley Mock (editor), *The Sowing and the Dawning: Termination and Dedication Processes in the Archaeological and Ethnographic Record of Mesoamerica.* Albuquerque: University of New Mexico Press.

(1999) "Changes in Chiapas: Using the Internet and tourism, Zapatistas create a new image." OpEd, *Boston Globe,* May 1, 1999.

Vogt, Evon Z. and Ethel M. Albert [editors]

(1966) *People of Rimrock: A Study of Values in Five Cultures.* Cambridge, MA: Harvard University Press.

Vogt, Evon Z. and Victoria A. Bricker

(1996) "The Zinacanteco fiesta of San Sebastian: An essay in ethnographic interpretation." *Res* 29/30:203–222.

Vogt, Evon Z. and Alberto Ruz L. [editors]

(1964) *Desarrollo cultural de los Mayas.* México, D.F.: Seminario de Cultura Maya, Universidad Nacional Autónoma de México. 2nd edition, 1971.

Vogt, Evon Z. and Catherine C. Vogt

(1970) "Lévi-Strauss among the Maya." *Man* 5:379–392.

Wilson, Carter

(1966) *Crazy February.* Philadelphia: J. B. Lippincott.

(1972) *A Green Tree and a Dry Tree.* New York: Macmillan.

Wolf, Eric

(1955) "Types of Latin American peasantry." *American Anthropologist* 57:452–471.

CHAPTER SEVEN

LOCAL CULTURES AND GLOBAL SYSTEMS: THE JU/'HOANSI-!KUNG AND THEIR ETHNOGRAPHERS FIFTY YEARS ON

Richard B. Lee and Megan Biesele

The initiators of Ju/'hoansi[1] research in the Kalahari—the Marshall family in the early 1950s and then Lee and DeVore a decade later—never imagined that, over the course of the next half century, the research would become part of the ethnographic canon and a major industry for generations of anthropologists and students. Now also the darlings of the mass media, the Ju/'hoansi San have come to occupy a special place in both scholarly and popular imaginations.[2]

Known to millions as leather-clad hunter-gatherers wresting a living from the desert, it is sometimes forgotten that the Ju/'hoansi—like other foragers—have become increasingly drawn into the world system. Their remoteness and desert location, once effective barriers to colonization, no longer protect them. The cash nexus, poverty, class formation, bureaucratic control, and media manipulation—not to mention militarization, anomie, and alienation—became part of the daily lives of the Ju/'hoansi in the 1980s and 1990s. How long-term anthropological research has attempted to comprehend these changes and respond to the political and ethical issues raised by them is our subject in this chapter.

To orient the reader, we offer three images that register the scope and magnitude of social change among the Ju/'hoansi since the early days of fieldwork. During Richard Lee's 1963 research, the Dobe area's remoteness was measured by the fact that it received only one motor vehicle visit from the outside world every four to six weeks; perhaps a dozen vehicles a year. During his 1987 fieldwork, Lee counted a motor vehicle every four to six hours, over 1,400 per year, a one-hundred-fold increase! These vehicles brought a constant stream of government officials, health workers, drought relief shipments, and traders to the Dobe area, in striking contrast to the situation a generation before. By 2000, the situation had evolved further: several vehicles were present in the village of Dobe and a dozen others were scattered throughout the district.

Perhaps even more telling is a comparison that gives a sense of the changes in Ju/'hoansi worldview. At Dobe in 1963, Lee had the only radio in a fifty-mile radius; he was possibly the last North American to learn of the assassination of John F. Kennedy, tuning into the Voice of America by chance five days after Dallas. But when he tried to explain the tragic event to the Ju/'hoansi, no one had the slightest

The Honourable Kgau Royal /O/oo (standing at left), Ju/'hoan Member of Namibian Parliament and his family, with R. B. Lee, August 2001. Photo by David H. Lee.

idea who Kennedy was, and few of them had even a vague concept of America. Now fast-forward to the 1990s. In August 1991, during the attempted overthrow of Mikhail Gorbachev, the residents of Dobe were following the events in Moscow on their own transistor radios, dozens of them, and holding animated discussions as developments unfolded.

By April 2001, even more startling changes in communication had come into the lives of the Ju/'hoansi at Tjum!kui, just across the Namibian border from Dobe. Namibian president Sam Nujoma inaugurated the recently completed telecommunications infrastructure for Tjum!kui in a ceremony at which leaders of the Ju/'hoan community phoned the United States and spoke to an office at the United Nations. This plan was seen as a way to let other Namibians know that "the San are enabled to acquire information on their own from as far away as the USA."

These images offer a window on the epochal changes in the lives and circumstances of the Ju/'hoansi. The magnitude of these transformations has had something to do, we believe, with the curious schism that has emerged in scholarly and popular perceptions of the Ju/'hoansi and other indigenous peoples.

Some scholars prefer to see the Ju/'hoansi's current predicament as something that has always existed. Ignoring or discounting what was observed thirty years before, these "revisionists" regard today's poverty and close links to the wider world as not new, since in their view Ju/'hoansi people have been dominated by outsiders for centuries. The recent foraging ways of the Ju/'hoansi are thus seen as a "culture of poverty" and can bear no or little resemblance to the ancestral hunting and gathering cultures of southern Africa.

Then there are the more traditionally inclined outside observers, who see the dire circumstances of today's Ju/'hoansi, but frankly preferred them "the way they were," when they dressed in skins and foraged for a living. Refusing to acknowledge the passing of the old ways, such observers perpetuate the romantic image of the "noble savage" even in the face of contradictory evidence. The 1980s hit film *The Gods Must Be Crazy* (parts I and II) is a prime example, but some scholarship has not escaped this distortion.

Both perceptions fail to do justice to the Ju/'hoansi reality. The traditionalists ignore the fact that the Ju/'hoansi did not stop being "a people" when the last hunters laid down their bows and picked up their transistor radios. History moves on and the Ju/'hoansi have moved with it. The revisionists, by contrast, need to be made aware that the poverty, despair, and anomie of the present do not constitute the sum total of Ju/'hoansi history or even of the current reality. The Ju/'hoansi persist as a people, embattled and struggling, but a people nonetheless with a clear sense of themselves, rooted in what they themselves articulate as their history of autonomous hunting and gathering (Solway and Lee 1990; Lee and Hitchcock 2001).

One of the great virtues of long-term fieldwork in social anthropology is that it has the potential to bring together the two halves of these shattered perceptions and thereby to restore coherence and unity to the lives of the Ju/'hoansi, so severely shaken by the traumatic events of the last thirty years.

As the Ju/'hoansi people have come to political consciousness, there is an emerging determination to take hold of their own destiny, to fight against stereotyping, both positive and negative, to assert their political rights, and to revitalize their communities. In this respect, the Ju/'hoansi are following paths charted by aboriginal peoples in Canada, the United States, Australia, and elsewhere. One way they are doing this is in the rectification of names. The Ju/'hoansi have always called themselves "Ju/'hoansi"—meaning "real or genuine people"—and would like others to do the same. To acknowledge this new sense of empowerment, anthropologists and development agencies since 1990, particularly in Namibia, have adopted this term of self-appellation. This process of identity replacement will not happen overnight, and older terms such as "Bushman" and "San" along with the newer "Ju/'hoansi" (Ju/wasi) still will be encountered for some years to come.

Ethnographic Research among the Ju/'hoansi

As reported in a now-classic series of studies, in the 1950s and 1960s the Ju/'hoansi-!Kung were largely hunter-gatherers who foraged for game and wild vegetable foods with no domestic animals except dogs (and some groups lacked even these). About 900 lived in the Nyae Nyae area of South West Africa (now Namibia) and about 500 in the Dobe area of Bechuanaland (now Botswana). In the Dobe area, the Ju/'hoansi shared their large territory with some 300 recently arrived Herero pastoralists and their several thousand cattle.[3] South West Africa, a former German colony, had been administered by South Africa since 1919, whereas the British administered Bechuanaland. In neither area was there any direct governmental presence until about 1960.

The modern history of ethnographic research among the Ju/'hoansi begins with the Marshall family of Cambridge, Massachusetts.[4] Laurence and Lorna, their son John, and daughter Elizabeth began ethnographic research and filming in Nyae Nyae in December 1951 and continued there for a decade. Across the border, the Harvard project led by Irven DeVore and Richard Lee started work in Bechuanaland with the Dobe Ju/'hoansi in 1963. Ju/'hoansi perceptions of the two parallel research projects are worth noting. Throughout the 1960s, Dobe Ju/'hoansi would regale Lee and DeVore with stories of Marsharon!an!a ("Big big Marshall") and his legendary generosity, of giant giveaways of blankets and pots without number, in pointed contrast to the more modest offerings of a pinch of tobacco or an occasional head scarf of the Harvard group. Since the size of Laurence's handouts increased with each retelling, we became convinced that a Laurence Marshall cargo cult was on the verge of breaking out in the Nyae Nyae–Dobe area. (In actuality, the Marshall handouts were much more modest.)

Perhaps it was these invidious comparisons that spurred us on occasion to try to generate some cargo-like behavior of our own. In 1968, Lee had the noble if misguided notion to slaughter a Christmas ox and distribute the meat to the Ju/'hoansi at /Xai/xai. Their somber and grumbling reactions to the attempted largesse provided an effective object lesson on humility and leveling devices and ultimately led to insights into Ju core values, as chronicled in Lee's (1969a) oft-reprinted "Eating Christmas in the Kalahari."

Despite our perceived stinginess and bad manners, the Dobe Ju/'hoansi decided after a while that DeVore and Lee were not so bad after all. They let us stick around the Dobe area and even tolerated the bringing in of students and collaborators.

After initial contact with the Dobe Ju/'hoansi in October 1963, Lee spent fifteen months and DeVore two months living in the area in 1963–1964, focusing mainly on ecology; that is, hunting and gathering techniques, land use, and group structure. Soon after, at the suggestion of Sol Tax, DeVore and Lee organized the symposium on "Man the Hunter," held in Chicago in April 1966, bringing together students of hunter-gatherers from many countries and helping to stimulate new research directions (Lee and DeVore 1968).

The Kalahari Research Group

The symposium on "Man the Hunter" showed that, before studies of hunter-gatherers could be of real usefulness for general theory, a great deal more had to be known about the ethnography, ecological adaptations, worldview, and acculturative status of contemporary peoples. Second, it became clear that the range of specialized information required was too broad for any single investigator to collect.

In 1967, DeVore and Lee returned to the Dobe area, and the Kalahari Research Group (KRG) crystallized as students and specialists in a range of related fields joined the project. In late 1967, Nancy Howell began research on San demography, including reproductive histories and kinship and acquaintance networks. In early 1968, Patricia Draper, Henry Harpending, and John Yellen arrived at Dobe. Draper did an eighteen-month study of child rearing and subsistence of both nomadic and settled Ju/'hoansi. Harpending's work in genetic demography took him to camps all over northwestern Botswana where he interviewed and collected blood samples from nearly 2,000 San. Yellen, in collaboration with DeVore, did ethnoarchaeological studies of hunting behavior and settlement patterns, including the plotting of the floor plans of recently occupied campsites. Yellen and later Alison Brooks also excavated Stone Age sites in the area.

During 1967–1968, Stewart Truswell and John Hansen, both medical doctors, made two trips to Dobe to examine Ju adults and children. Truswell made a third trip in 1969 to work on heart disease. Drs. Trefor Jenkins and Jack Metz also carried out medical research. In September 1968, Richard Katz, a Harvard psychologist, came out for several months to study the Ju/'hoansi healing dance in collaboration with Richard Lee.

In mid-1969, the third wave of KRG fieldwork got underway. Mel Konner and Marjorie Shostak joined Harpending, Draper, and Yellen at Dobe, where Konner focused his work on the ethology of early infant development. Later, Nicholas Blurton Jones worked with Konner on several projects, including Ju/'hoan knowledge of animal behavior (Blurton Jones and Konner 1976). Shostak made studies of beadwork and musical instruments but devoted her major efforts to a collection of in-depth life history materials from a number of San women. One of these life histories was published as the now-classic *Nisa* (Shostak 1983).

Jiro Tanaka of Kyoto University, who had worked with the /Gwi during 1967–1968, returned in 1971 to the Central Kalahari Reserve to continue his ecological studies in parallel with Lee's ecological work in the Dobe area, 400 kilometers to the north. Mathias Guenther, though not formally a member of the KRG, was working at that time with the Farm Bushmen at D'Kar in the Ghanzi District.

In late 1970, Megan Biesele, a folklorist and ethnographer, arrived in the Dobe area to study Ju/'hoan oral literature, myth, and ritual. Most of her work was done at Kauri, about 150 kilometers southeast of Dobe. In addition to her ethnographic work, Biesele focused on the problems of social and economic change among the San. Her findings showed that drastic changes were in the offing for the remaining San groups.

A fourth stage in the Kalahari Research Project, roughly from 1971 to 1976, involved stocktaking and addressing the ethical issues raised by the San research. With the return of most of the fieldworkers, DeVore and Lee organized the

"Symposium on Bushmen Studies" held at the annual meetings of the American Anthropological Association in New York in November 1971. This led eventually to the book *Kalahari Hunter-Gatherers* (Lee and DeVore 1976).

A sense of the accelerating pace of change emerged clearly at this symposium. Pushed within the group primarily by Biesele, Lee, Konner, and Shostak, with support from Lorna and John Marshall, the group began to explore how it could fulfill its ethical and political commitments to the San. These discussions resulted in the formation, in January 1973, of the Kalahari Peoples Fund, designed to funnel money and expertise to Botswana San. This was the start of a long series of ventures in development anthropology.

In sum, some fifteen investigators associated with the project have carried out major studies of the San (see table 7.1). Most of the collaborators went on to develop distinguished careers of their own, both with Ju/'hoansi research and beyond it. And most have maintained links with the Ju/'hoansi into the 1980s and 1990s.

Table 7.1. The Kalahari Research Group (KRG)

Name	Current Affiliation	Research Interests
Megan Biesele	Texas A&M University	Folklore, ecology, development
Nicholas Blurton Jones	UCLA	Ethology, evolutionary ecology
Alison Brooks	George Washington University	Prehistory, anthropological theory
Irven DeVore	Harvard University	Ecology, evolutionary theory
Nancy DeVore	Harvard University, Anthrophoto	Photography
Patricia Draper	University of Nebraska	Child behavior, aging, evolutionary ecology
John Hansen	Medical University of South Africa, Johannesburg	Pediatrics
Henry Harpending	University of Utah	Demography, genetics, physical anthropology, Ju, Herero
Nancy Howell	University of Toronto	Demography, evolutionary ecology
Richard Katz	Saskatchewan Federated Indian Colleges	Ritual, healing, change
Melvin Konner	Emory University	Infancy, medical anthropology, evolutionary theory
Richard Lee	University of Toronto	Ecology, social organization, history, development
Marjorie Shostak (1945–1996)	(Emory University)	Life history, gender studies
Stewart Truswell	Sydney University, Australia	Medicine, health, and nutrition
John Yellen	National Science Foundation, Washington, D.C.	Ethnoarchaeology, prehistory

From 1976 until the 1990s, the KRG remained a loosely knit but increasingly diverse group of scholars who were developing in a number of different directions. The present diversity of theoretical positions and ethical stances within the KRG has come to mirror the diversity within the North American discipline at large. Some members, for example, embraced sociobiology in the mid-1970s, while others moved increasingly toward political economy and Marxism (for example, compare the works of Konner [1983] and Harpending, Rogers, and Draper [1987] with those of Lee [1988, 1990]). Some members of the research group became committed to San studies as essentially an "anthropology of development," while others remained steadfast in their adherence to a vision of "pure science" (cf. Kolata 1981).

None, however, has remained totally unaffected by the sea change undergone by the discipline of anthropology in the last two decades (Lee 1999). All KRG members have become more sensitive to issues of reflexivity, especially how gender, race, age, and authorial positioning have shaped anthropological perceptions. Even those scholars most committed to "science" have become more responsive to issues of context. Henry Harpending, to take just one example, in his late 1980s demographic work with the Herero, translated his preliminary reports into Otjiherero and distributed them widely within the now-literate Herero community.

The Marshall Studies

The Marshall-led research, begun at Harvard University but largely self-financed, had a rather different, but equally prolific, history of research and writing from that of the Kalahari Research Group. From 1951 to 1959, Laurence and Lorna led a series of expeditions, involving not only their family but also a number of collaborators, including Robert Dyson (archaeology), Robert Story (ethnobotany), and Nicholas England (ethnomusicology). The major results of the fieldwork appeared in several forms: first, a series of important papers by Lorna Marshall from 1957 to 1968, later assembled into two major volumes (1976, 1999); and second, a series of distinguished film studies made by John Marshall, including longer films such as *Bitter Melons* and *The Hunters*, as well as sixteen shorter films, such as *An Argument about a Marriage*, *N/um Tchai*, and *A Joking Relationship*. Elizabeth Marshall Thomas wrote a sensitive and nuanced account of the family's fieldwork in the now-classic *The Harmless People* (1959), which made the lives of the Nyae Nyae !Kung accessible to millions of readers.

For almost twenty years the Marshalls did not return to do fieldwork with the Ju/'hoansi. Then, in 1978, John came back to Namibia to make the film *N!ai: The Story of a !Kung Woman* (1980). This trip led to a major undertaking on John's part to stabilize a rapidly deteriorating social situation among the Namibian Ju/'hoansi, a situation characterized by social dislocation, alcohol problems, land loss, and militarization. To help the Ju/'hoansi organize to meet these threats to

Table 7.2.   The Marshall Group

Name	Affiliation, Location	Research Interests, Ethnic Groups
Laurence Marshall (1890–1980)	(Cambridge, Massachusetts)	General anthropology, Ju/'hoansi
Lorna Marshall	Cambridge, Massachusetts Peterborough, New Hampshire	Ethnography, religion, Ju/'hoansi, /Gwi
John Marshall	Documentary Educational Resources, Watertown, Massachusetts	Film, anthropology of development, Ju/'hoansi, /Gwi
Elizabeth Marshall Thomas	Peterborough, New Hampshire	Ethnography, literature, Ju/'hoansi, /Gwi
Patrick Dickens (1953–1992)	(Nyae Nyae Development Foundation of Namibia)	Linguistics, education
Robert Dyson	University of Pennsylvania	Archaeology
Nicholas England	California Academy of the Arts, Los Angeles	Ethnomusicology
Claire Ritchie	United Kingdom	Anthropology of development, film
Robert Story	University of the Witwatersrand, Johannesburg	Ethnobotany

their present and future viability, Marshall, along with Claire Ritchie, and later Megan Biesele and others, organized the Nyae Nyae Development Foundation of Namibia (discussed later). A partial list of the Marshall group's personnel is given in table 7.2, while table 7.3 provides information about other contemporary scholars who have conducted research in the Kalahari among the Ju/'hoansi or on related issues.

A Basic Bookshelf on the Ju/'hoansi from the Marshall and Kalahari Research Groups

It would be difficult if not impossible to try to summarize the full range of studies of Namibian and Botswana Ju/'hoansi since 1951. Twelve broad areas of research can be discerned, and each has spawned a critical literature ranging from dozens to many hundreds of citations. The following citations do not claim to be comprehensive, but are intended to indicate the range of studies and a few of the more frequently cited works.

1. *Social organization.* A series of classic papers by Lorna Marshall on social organization and social life, including kinship (1957), marriage (1959), band organization (1960), and talking, sharing, and giving (1961), are collected in Marshall (1976).

Table 7.3. Other Scholars

Name	Affiliation	Research Interests, Ethnic Groups
Hiroyuki Akiyama	Kyoto University	Social anthropology, ecology, /Gwi-//Gana
Alan Barnard	Edinburgh University	Kinship, ethnography, ecology, Nharo
Elizabeth Cashdan	University of Utah	History, behavioral ecology, /Gwi-//Gana
James Denbow	University of Texas	Iron Age archaeology, Botswana, Zaire
James Ebert*	Ebert Associates, Albuquerque, New Mexico	Archaeology, ecology, remote sensing, Botswana
I. Eibl-Eibesfeldt	Max Planck Institute, Seeweisen, Germany	Ethology, !Xo
Robert Gordon	University of Vermont	Political economy, history, media
Mathias Guenther*	Laurier University, Waterloo, Ontario	Social anthropology, change, folklore, religion, art, Nharo
H. J. Heinz (1917–2000)	(Maun, Botswana)	Anthropology, parasitology, change, !Xo
Robert Hitchcock*	University of Nebraska, Lincoln	Development anthropology, ecology, archaeology, history, Eastern Basarwa, Botswana, Namibia, and so forth
Trefor Jenkins*	South African Institute for Medical Research, Johannesburg	Genetics, medical research, nutrition, ethics, Botswana, Namibia, Zimbabwe, South Africa
Susan Kent	Old Dominion University of Norfolk, Virginia	Ecology, archaeology, nutrition, settlement patterns, theory, !Xo, /Gwi
Emmanuelle Olivier	CNRS, Paris	Ju
Harriet Rosenberg*	York University, Toronto	Aging, social reproduction, changing marriage patterns, Ju
George Silberbauer	Monash University, Melbourne, Australia	Social anthropology, ecology, /Gwi
Andrew Smith*	University of Cape Town	San archaeology, South Africa, Namibia, Ju
Jacqueline Solway*	Trent University, Ontario	Anthropology, development anthropology, kinship, gender, Bakgalagadi, Botswana
Sonia Speeter	Marburg University, Germany	History of the Marshall research, Ju
Kazuyoshi Sugawara	Kyoto University	Anthropology, /Gwi-//Gana
Ida Susser*	Hunter College, CUNY	AIDS, Ju/'hoansi
James Suzman	University of Namibia	Farm Bushmen, development, Ju

Renee Sylvain*	Dalhousie University, Nova Scotia, Canada	Farm San, political economy, gender and development, Namibia
Akira Takada	Kyoto University	Ethnography, politics, Heikum, !Kung
Jiro Tanaka	Kyoto University	Ecology, ethnography, change, /Gwi
Helga Vierich*	University of Alberta, Nova Scotia, Canada	Ecology, social change, development anthropology, Eastern /Twa
Thomas Widlok	Max Planck Institute, Halle, Germany	Language, politics, identity, Heikum
Pauline Wiessner*	University of Utah	Archaeology, ethnoarchaeology, exchange systems, Ju/'hoansi
Edwin Wilmsen	University of Texas	Archaeology, political economy, nutrition, history, theory, Ju/'hoansi, Herero

* Denotes scholars who have been involved in collaboration with members of the original KRG.

2. *Ecology.* A series of articles on ecology, diet, subsistence, and spatial organization by Richard Lee (e.g., 1968, 1969b; Lee and DeVore 1976) are collected in Lee (1979). See also Story (1958), Wehmeyer, Lee, and Whiting (1969), Vierich (1982), and Eaton, Shostak, and Konner (1988).

3. *Demography, genetics, and medical research.* See Nancy Howell (1979, 2000) and Henry Harpending (1976); Truswell and Hansen (1976); Truswell et al. (1972); Hansen et al. (1994). For model building in paleodemography, see Howell (1976). The second edition of Howell's *Demography of the Dobe !Kung* appeared in late 2000. Since 1996, Richard Lee and Ida Susser have been concentrating on AIDS in southern Africa, including its impact on the Ju/'hoansi (Susser 2000).

4. *Ethnoarchaeology.* See John Yellen (1976, 1977, 1990).

5. *Archaeology.* See Yellen and Brooks (1988) and Brooks and Yellen (1992).

6. *Child rearing and infant development.* See Patricia Draper (1975, 1976), Draper and Cashdan (1988), and Melvin Konner (1976, 1983).

7. *Aging and caregiving.* See Megan Biesele and Nancy Howell (1981) and Harriet Rosenberg (1990) for studies of aging among the Ju/'hoansi in the 1980s.

8. *Rituals, beliefs, music, and dance.* See Lorna Marshall (1962, 1969, 1999), Megan Biesele (1976, 1993b), and Richard Katz (1982). See also John Marshall (1971), Nicholas England (1992), Emmanuelle Olivier (1997), and Richard Lee (1993a). Richard Katz, Megan Biesele, and Verna St. Dennis (1997) recently published a lively update on the healing dance entitled *Healing Makes Our Hearts Happy*. For an excellent overview of San religion see Guenther (2000).

9. *Exchange networks.* Though not a member of the original research group, Polly Wiessner (1977, 1982) has done careful studies of *hxaro* exchange.

10. *History, social change, and contemporary problems.* See Solway and Lee (1990), Lee and Guenther (1991, 1993), Smith and Lee (1997), Biesele and Weinberg (1990), Biesele (1993a), Marshall and Ritchie (1984), and Ritchie (1989). See also Guenther (1986), Hitchcock and Holm (1993), Hitchcock (1982, 1993, 1996), and Volkman (1983).

11. *Film studies.* The films about the Ju/'hoansi are synonymous with the name of John Marshall. His films include *The Hunters* and *Bitter Melons*, from the 1950s, and *N!ai, Pull Ourselves Up or Die*, and *A Kalahari Family* from the 1980s and 1990s. He has worked closely with Claire Ritchie. Other films on the Ju/'hoansi include segments of the series "Childhood," for which Mel Konner was consultant and host; Richard Leakey's 1980 film *A Human Way of Life* from his BBC series "The Making of Mankind," and Yo-Yo Ma's 1994 film on Ju/'hoan music, *Distant Echoes*; both of the latter involved Richard Lee.

12. *Communicating knowledge to a wider public.* John Marshall's films as well as the writings of Elizabeth Marshall Thomas (1959) have been important here, as has an exhibit at the Peabody Museum, Harvard, on the "Ju/'hoansi, Then and Now," curated by Irven DeVore (Lord 1991). Biesele and Kgau Royal /O/oo (1997), a Ju/'hoan leader who has worked closely with anthropologists, have coauthored a book for young people in the Rosen Series, Heritage Library of African Peoples, entitled *San*. But when it comes to conveying a sense of the humanity of the Ju/'hoansi, Marjorie Shostak's *Nisa* (1983) has been, in the view of many, the most effective statement. Shostak died in 1996, but her follow-up book *Return to Nisa* was published in late 2000 by Harvard University Press.

Monographs and edited works with a variety of studies from several perspectives are included in Biesele (1986), Biesele et al. (1989), Kapfer, Petermann, and Thoms (1991), Leacock and Lee (1982), Lee (1979, 1993a), Lee and DeVore

(1976), Lee, Biesele, and Hitchcock (1997), and Marshall (1976). Other recent general works on the San include Barnard (1992a) and Gordon (1992).

Works specifically critical of the body of ethnographic research discussed here may be found in Schrire (1984), Wilmsen (1989), and Wilmsen and Denbow (1990). (For a bibliographic review of the "Kalahari Debate," see Barnard 1992b.)

Such an inventory of a body of scholarship, though useful, does little to convey the shifting terrain on which the studies were conducted. Even as the main studies were in full swing in the 1950s, 1960s, and 1970s, the pace of change was accelerating—earlier in Nyae Nyae, later in Dobe. We describe some of these transformations, dealing first with the Dobe area and second, the Nyae Nyae. We conclude with some observations on changing anthropological practice.

The Dobe Area: A Hunter-Gatherer Stronghold or *Coin Perdu*?

In 1963, perhaps three-quarters of the Dobe Ju/'hoansi were living in camps based primarily on hunting and gathering, while the rest were attached to Black cattle posts. It was the hunting and gathering camps that were the subject of sustained anthropological investigation in the 1960s (Lee and DeVore 1976). After Botswana's independence was declared in September 1966, the pace of change accelerated and has continued to accelerate up to the present.

In the Dobe area of 1964, there had been no trading stores, no schools, no clinics, no government feeding programs, no boreholes, and no resident civil servants (apart from the tribally appointed headman, his clerk, and constable). By 2000, all of these institutions were in place and the Dobe people had completed three decades of rapid social change. They had been transformed in a generation from a society of foragers—some of whom herded and worked for others—to a society of smallholders who eked out a living by herding, farming, and craft production, along with some hunting and gathering. The Dobe Ju/'hoansi today sit around their fires and smoke their pipes as before, but they also listen to their transistor radios, cook their store-bought mealie meal, brew home brew . . . and worry about the future.

Ju villages today look like other Botswana villages. The beehive-shaped grass huts are gone, replaced by semipermanent, mud-walled houses behind makeshift stockades to keep out cattle. Villages have ceased to be circular and tight-knit. Twenty-five people who used to live in a space twenty by twenty meters now spread themselves out in a line village several hundred meters long. Instead of looking across the central open space at each other, the houses face the kraal where cattle and goats are kept, inscribing in their living arrangements a symbolic shift from reliance on each other to reliance on property in the form of herds (Yellen 1990).

Hunting and gathering, which provided Dobe Ju with over 85 percent of their calories as recently as 1964, now supplies perhaps 30 percent of their food.

The rest is made up of milk and meat from domestic stock, store-bought mealie meal, and vast quantities of heavily sugared tea whitened with powdered milk. Foraged foods and occasional produce from gardens make up the rest of the vegetable diet. For most of the 1980s, government and foreign drought relief provided a steady but monotonous diet. At some waterholes there was so much available that surplus was often fed to the dogs.

When the government cut off general food distributions, the Dobe people at first were shocked and angry; but they quickly responded in creative ways. Mid-1987 saw a revival of hunting; men who hadn't hunted for years took it up again, and younger men who had never become skilled with bow and arrow hunted from horseback with spears. In a single week in July 1987, five eland were killed, more than had been taken in the entire previous year. The possession of horses was the key to hunting success. One old couple sold six of their cows to buy one horse and then sent young men on horseback out to hunt on their behalf.[5]

From as early as 1900 some Ju had been involved in boarding cattle for wealthy Tswana, in a loan cattle arrangement called *mafisa*, widespread in Botswana (Lee 1965; Hitchcock 1977). By 1973, about 20 percent of Ju families had some involvement as mafisa herders. The number grew through the 1970s, but in the 1980s people had become bitter about mafisa. They complained that cattle promised in payment for services rendered—usually one female calf per year—were not being paid and that without these beasts it was difficult to start one's own herd. Coupled with the withdrawal of government rations, the lack of mafisa soured some Dobe Ju/'hoansi about their prospects in Botswana.

The people saw what was happening in Namibia where the Nyae Nyae Development Foundation for Namibia (NNDFN) was helping Ju/'hoansi to drill boreholes and obtain cattle (see the following section). Dobe-area Ju wanted their own boreholes, and an overseas agency (Norwegian NORAD) was favorably disposed to financing the project. The Botswana government stonewalled an international proposal for five to eight boreholes. This showed that the government's once-liberal policies toward the San (known as Remote Area Dwellers, or Basarwa) were assuming an increasingly regressive character. In 1987, some Dobe people started a movement to leave Botswana and cross the fence to their relatives in Namibia, and by 1994 some had actually made the move.

Some compensating developments have brightened this generally gloomy picture. From 1986 on, a small parastatal agency, the !Kung San Works, purchased increasing volumes of Dobe-area crafts, primarily from Ju/'hoansi but also from Herero. This has had the effect of pumping considerable cash into the Ju economy, from a level of 400–500 pula per month (US$200–$250) before the marketing scheme to P5,000–7,000 (US$2,500–$3,000) per month at the peak of the scheme.

Unfortunately, opportunities were few for productive investment of the proceeds in infrastructure such as plows, bicycles, cattle, or horses. While some large stock were purchased, a distressing amount of cash was absorbed in buying beer, brandy, home brew materials, bags of candies, and the ubiquitous sugar, tea, and Nespray powdered milk.

Schooling and the problems of youth are another area of concern. When the first school opened at !Kangwa in 1973, some Ju parents responded quickly, registering their children and scraping together the money for fees and the obligatory school uniforms. Most Ju, however, ignored the school or withdrew their children when the latter objected to being forbidden to speak their own language on the school grounds or to the (mild) corporal punishment common in the Botswana school system. Despite the efforts of parents, teachers, and the school board to encourage attendance, absenteeism at the !Kangwa school remained in the 40 to 60 percent range into the 1990s.

In spite of these obstacles, at least four of the Dobe-area students did go on to secondary school in the 1980s. But even for these students—the first to get this far in the educational system—the road has not been easy. For the large majority of Ju/'hoansi with no (or little) formal schooling, job prospects are poor. As a result, a life of odd jobs combined with heavy drinking was not uncommon. It was a bitter irony of underdevelopment that, in the mid-1980s, some Botswana youths were attracted to Namibia where jobs as soldiers in the South African army were the only ones available.

Far more successful was the second and smaller of the two schools, at /Xai/xai, where a progressive headmaster wisely incorporated many elements of Ju/'hoansi culture into the curriculum. His initiatives were rewarded with strong parental and community support for the school and a correspondingly low absentee rate. The /Gwihaba Dancers, a troupe of /Xai/xai schoolchildren, not only won regional and national cultural competitions but even performed at Botswana's twentieth anniversary of independence celebrations in 1986 (Lee 1993a:177–181).

In the long run, Dobe-area Ju/'hoansi face serious difficulties. Since 1975, whenever wealthy Tswana have wanted to expand cattle production, they have formed borehole syndicates to stake out ranches in remote areas. With ninety-nine-year leases, which can be bought and sold, ownership is tantamount to private tenure. By the late 1980s, borehole drilling was approaching the Dobe area. If the Dobe Ju do not form borehole syndicates soon, with overseas help, their traditional foraging areas may be permanently cut off from them by commercial ranching.

Nyae Nyae: A Struggle for Survival

While the Dobe people had to meet the challenges of declining foraging, sedentarization, and the cold bath of immersion in the market economy, the Ju/'hoansi of adjacent Nyae Nyae had to deal with even more: massive resettlement, the imposition of apartheid, the loss of most of their land base, militarization, and finally the triumph and trauma of independence and postindependence Namibia.

Shortly after the Marshall expeditions of 1951 to 1959 had been completed, a South African civil servant arrived in Nyae Nyae to "civilize" the "wild" Bushman. Lured by promises of wage work, agricultural training, and medical care, the great majority of the foragers were assembled in the town of Tjum!kui (Tsumkhwe) in 1960. The settlement had been mandated only after the South African administration of the territory had ceded 70 percent of the traditional foraging areas of the Nyae Nyae Ju/'hoansi to other ethnic groups: 30,000 square kilometers of southern Nyae Nyae to Hereroland and 13,000 square kilometers of the north to Kavango and to the Kaudum Game Reserve.

For two decades, nine hundred to a thousand Ju/'hoansi were herded together under the watchful eye of South African authorities and missionaries. Weekly shipments of government rations supported the settlement, supplemented by some wage work and occasional trips out for bush foods. The enforced idleness and unaccustomed crowding took a heavy toll. Social problems, family violence, and home brew parties became a regular feature of life at Tjum!kui. Ironically, it was after decades of forced settlement, rising alcohol consumption, and government paternalism that South African filmmaker Jamie Uys came to Tjum!kui to film *The Gods Must Be Crazy*, which portrays the Ju/'hoansi as pristine hunter-gatherers so "untouched" that the mere appearance of a Coke bottle upsets the equilibrium of the society (Davis 1996).

John Marshall's (1980) excellent film *N!ai: The Story of a !Kung Woman* is a useful antidote to *The Gods Must Be Crazy*. It documents the militarization, anomie, and Saturday-night brawling that characterized Ju/'hoansi life at Tjum!kui at that time. It even contains a sequence of the filming of *The Gods Must Be Crazy*.

In 1978, the South African army began to recruit Nyae Nyae men into the South African Defense Forces (SADF) to fight the South West Africa People's Organization (SWAPO). Ultimately, 201 Battalion had about seven hundred Ju/'hoan soldiers, making the Ju/'hoansi one of the most heavily militarized peoples in Africa. The SADF recruitment campaign brought contradictory responses: the men were happy to have "work" and good pay; but the people were sharply divided on the morality of the war and which side to support (many !Kung quietly supported SWAPO, and some soldiers even tried to warn SWAPO units of impending attacks).[6]

Since engagements with the "enemy" were infrequent,[7] far more destructive was the presence of sudden wealth in the hands of so many young men away from their families. Alcohol consumption increased further, and drunken fights became more deadly. In a two-year period (1978 to 1980), John Marshall recorded six homicides, compared to an estimated four cases for the previous decade.

Even while the war, with all its dislocations, was going on, a new threat was emerging: the Department of Nature Conservation within the South West African administration was pushing strongly to have the Nyae Nyae area declared a game reserve from which all development, including livestock, was to be excluded. For their role in this scheme, a few Ju/'hoansi were to dress up in traditional clothes, do traditional dances, and sell curios to well-heeled tourists. The Ju/'hoansi were appalled by this scheme and opposed it vehemently. The people were well aware that their traditional way of life had been seriously compromised. They knew that their future lay not in being props in what John Marshall aptly labeled a "Plastic Stone Age," but in building up their herds and fields to establish themselves as smallholders with a mixed economy of foraging, farming, and wage labor. Happily, after years of protests, the scheme was dropped.

The Ju/'hoansi won this victory in part because by 1988 the tide in Namibia was turning against South Africa. The SADF had suffered a military defeat in Angola at Cuito-Carnevale, and the momentum was gathering for a UN-sponsored plan for Namibian independence. In the September 1989 elections, SWAPO won a clear majority, and the independent nation of Namibia came into being in March 1990.[8]

Despite the rejoicing at the end of seventy-five years of South African rule, independence for the Ju/'hoansi was not an unmixed blessing. To all intents, the new nation was broke, without developed energy sources, its minerals systematically extracted, and its former patron, South Africa, disappearing over the horizon. The hasty retreat was thrown into relief by the hundreds of demobilized Ju/'hoan soldiers, their livelihood vanished, lounging around their home communities with a great deal of time on their hands. At the same time, neighboring ethnic groups began to cast their gaze in the direction of the pristine grasslands of Bushmanland as a place to graze their vast herds of cattle.

With all these forces arrayed against them, the Nyae Nyae Ju/'hoansi have had a major ally in the form of the Windhoek-based Nyae Nyae Development Foundation of Namibia (NNDFN). Founded by John Marshall and Claire Ritchie in 1981, the foundation has lobbied hard in Namibia and internationally to preserve Ju/'hoansi land rights and community organization.

The foundation arose in response to moves by some Ju/'hoansi to cut loose from the squalor of welfare capitalism created for them at Tjum!kui. In the early 1980s, tiring of the incessant squabbling, hunger, and uncertainty, small groups of Ju/'hoansi had begun to move away to reestablish themselves on their traditional lands—called *n!ores*. By 1986, eight such groups had formed; by 1991, thirty of these "outstations" had established themselves; and by 1997 the number had stabilized at thirty-seven. Drawing on private donations and later international agencies, the NNDFN was able to provide funds to the newly formed Ju/wa Farmers Union (now known as the Nyae Nyae Farmers Cooperative) to drill boreholes and purchase small herds of cattle for these reassembled *n!ore* groups.

Even with the foundation's aid, the road to a semblance of self-reliance for the Nyae Nyae Ju/'hoansi has not been easy. First, the Farmers Cooperative had to fight interference from the South African bureaucracy that still controlled Namibia. Their small boreholes and cattle posts existed in the middle of what the administration still regarded as a vast game reserve. Between 1983 and 1986, lions decimated the herds of cattle; and elephants, seeking water, broke down several borehole pumps. At one village, the elephants were so destructive that the community had to erect an electrified fence to keep them away from the wind pump and dam. The atmosphere of struggle and uncertainty is conveyed forcefully in John Marshall's film N!ai, *Pull Ourselves Up or Die* (1986) and Biesele and Weinberg's book *Shaken Roots* (1990).

By the 1990s, despite the uncertainties, the Ju people have made several steps forward. The Farmers Cooperative developed into an effective representative of Ju/'hoan interests, standardizing the language with the help of a linguist, the late Patrick Dickens (Dickens and the Ju/'hoan Peoples Literacy Committee 1990), and drawing up a constitution and bylaws in Ju/'hoan (Nyae Nyae Farmers Cooperative 1989). These positive developments were facilitated during Megan Biesele's tenure as Foundation research director. It was during this period that the Ju/'hoansi were able to find ways of making their "voices" heard and becoming actors in their own right on the national stage and at international forums.

The future of the Nyae Nyae people and their land rights took a significant step forward with the convening of the National Land Conference in Windhoek in June and July 1991. The Farmers Co-op (NNFC) and the NNFDN came to the conference armed with legal opinions, maps, and surveys of the two hundred traditional *n!ores* (territories) into which the Nyae Nyae was divided, a complete set of bylaws and constitution for the NNFC in Ju/'hoansi and English, position papers, and other documents. The delegation was accompanied by lawyers, interpreters, and a press kit, as well as two television documentaries about the Nyae Nyae people and the challenges they were facing. One of the most effective components of the NNFC presentation was a detailed discussion of the traditional *n!ore* tenure system and how it was being adapted creatively to the tasks of economic development. It urged that any land law that came into force should acknowledge these forms of tenure and their legitimacy. In the end, the conference adopted most of the recommendations put forward by the NNFC. This was a major victory for the Ju/'hoansi, strengthened by the subsequent visit to Bushmanland of Sam Nujoma, the president of Namibia, who instructed local authorities to respect Ju/'hoansi land rights. This backing enabled the NNFC peacefully to remove neighboring pastoralists whose large herds of cattle had illegally occupied southern Bushmanland in the euphoria and confusion following independence.

The Nyae Nyae San are struggling against long odds to establish themselves as herder-foragers and as citizens in a modernizing state. But the legacy of decades of colonialism and forced acculturation is a bitter one: chronic drinking bouts and anomie are manifest. The thirty-seven outstation communities vary widely in their economic well-being and sense of identity, from bustling villages of one hundred to rural slums on the edge of hunger. It is too early to tell whether the battle for self-reliance will be won by the Ju/'hoansi of Nyae Nyae. If empowerment is the key to survival, then the land conference and its aftermath do offer a modest basis for optimism.

Ju/'hoansi at the Millennium: Progress and Poverty

Botswana

On visits to Dobe village in 1999, Lee and Biesele noted some major changes. First, the long and twisting ninety-mile road to the village had been vastly improved, with travel time cut from six or seven hours to two and a half hours. At Dobe waterhole, the 150 residents were living in eight small villages centered around a new borehole, engine, and water tank. The pride of the village, though, was a soccer field, where teams of local and outside youths played daily pickup games. Nearby, a preschool had been set up to give students two years of preparation before attending, as boarders, the main primary school located twenty kilometers away in !Kangwa. A dozen outsiders were resident in Dobe, including veterinary officials, teachers, construction workers, and border guards who patrolled the frontier two kilometers to the west.

On the downside, home brew sellers, formerly confined to !Kangwa, had arrived at Dobe, bringing daily drinking parties and social dysfunction. Dobe's most traumatic experience, however, had taken place in 1996, when a districtwide outbreak of bovine pleuro-pneumonia had necessitated destruction of the entire cattle population of the Northwest District. Some 140,000 head were slaughtered, including several thousand in the Dobe area, and their carcasses buried by bulldozers. Ju/'hoansi, who had been slowly building up their herds since the 1970s, lost everything. Although herd owners were compensated, the process of rebuilding herds has been slow.

Ecologists, however, were heartened at the welcome relief of pressure on the fragile ecosystem by the sudden withdrawal of bovine biomass. The new situation refocused attention on a prime preexisting "asset" of the Dobe area: the still abundant game populations. The creation of wildlife conservancies under the Community-Based Natural Resource Management Program (CBNRM) is an effort to combine environmental conservation with economic development. Small-scale wildlife conservancies have sprung up throughout Africa, with twenty-eight projects in Botswana alone. At /Xai/xai, near Dobe, the Thlabololo Development Trust (TDT) has created a wildlife management area controlled by the Ju/'hoansi, with Dutch overseas assistance. The trust caters to tourists who want to experience Ju/'hoan life and see game, while limited subsistence hunting and gathering by Ju themselves are allowed.

The Ju of Dobe are in the process of setting up a similar trust under the guidance of the Kuru Development Trust, a successful Botswana-based NGO with funding from Germany, Scandinavia, and the European Union. In preparation for the conservancy to be established at Dobe, the most thorough study of local ecology since the intensive research of the 1960s was carried out. The Land Use Study has demonstrated the feasibility of the Kalahari Peoples Fund initiative of the 1980s to drill a series of boreholes on Dobe's outer margins. Now revived, the plan will resettle Ju families and secure their land against the threat of land encroachment by Tswana cattle syndicates. The careful groundwork of Robert Hitchcock has been a key to implementation. As of April 2001, two successful boreholes had been drilled with several others in planning, funded in part by a grant from the Kalahari Peoples Fund based in Austin, Texas (see Kalahari Peoples Fund 2001 and its Web site www.kalaharipeoples.org).

Namibia

The Ju/'hoansi of Nyae Nyae traveled a similarly rocky road of triumphs and failures during the 1990s. After the independence of Namibia and the successful National Land Conference, there was much discussion of development options for the people of Nyae Nyae. After feasibility studies sponsored by the Nyae Nyae Development Foundation, the Nyae Nyae Wildlife Conservancy was set up in 1998. It was the result of a bold initiative, the Living in a Finite Environment (LIFE) Project, funded by USAID, which sought to combine conservation, game management, tourism, and rural economic development.

In 1996, the Tsumkwe Lodge opened, offering accommodations and tours to selected Ju/'hoan villages. The Nyae Nyae Farmers Cooperative launched its own ecocultural tourism program around the same time.

The early 1990s had been a stormy period for the NNFC and its funding source, the Nyae Nyae Development Foundation. Infighting among foundation personnel over conflicting philosophies of change and management styles mirrored in some ways the dissension within the Cooperative itself. In a dramatic move, the Ju/'hoansi asked foundation personnel in 1996 to withdraw to Windhoek and leave the running of the Co-op to the Ju themselves. After a general shake-up of both organizations, non-Ju staff were cut back and Ju took over almost all management positions. The results have been mixed, and adjustments to the balance are ongoing. Despite the efforts of the LIFE project and the NNDFN, the thirty-seven Nyae Nyae villages continue to vary widely in viability. In a recent study, Polly Wiessner (1998) evaluated the subsistence levels of a sample of villages and found that over a third were experiencing a serious shortfall in food supply. This is due, in part, to the absence of adequate transport; for example, at the Co-op's Baraka headquarters, some vehicles have been rolled and thus rendered undriveable.

The Village Schools Project has been one of the bright spots in Nyae Nyae. The project offers three years of preschool training in the local language and in English for six- to eight-year-olds to prepare them for the government primary school at Tsumkwe. Initiated by Biesele and colleagues in consultation with the Nyae Nyae communities in 1990, the project has assisted hundreds of Ju children in making the transition from village life to cope with the culture shock of life in an African residential school.

Regional Developments

The 1990s saw tumultuous changes in the political landscape of southern Africa: the independence of Namibia, followed closely by the release of Nelson

Mandela from prison in 1990 and his coming to power in South Africa's first democratic elections in 1994. The Ju/'hoansi speak of the recent era as the time of "//xabe" or "opening up," as new political and cultural spaces opened for San peoples. The founding of the Working Group for Indigenous Minorities of Southern Africa (WIMSA) as an umbrella group based in Windhoek has created a forum at which leaders from Dobe, Tsumkwe, Baraka, and many other communities can come together to get a sense of their common problems and together lobby for change. WIMSA delegations have traveled to Geneva, London, Stockholm, and New York and have received very sympathetic hearings from governments and NGOs. Wildlife conservancies and school programs are just two of the kinds of grassroots programs receiving international support.

Small Victories

To give some life to this account of broad trends, let us look at the lives of several individuals. Chu!ko N//au, a lively young woman from Bate, had been the first female student from the Dobe area to reach secondary school. Graduating from a junior secondary school in 1989, Chu!ko was hired as a clerk-interpreter in the !Kung San Works craft-buying operation in Maun and completed several years in that post before going to nursing school to train as a family-planning educator. Now in her early thirties, with two children (though no husband), Chu!ko has taken the post of family-planning educator attached to the !Kangwa clinic. She dispenses birth control advice and holds workshops to explain to rural women their choices, the first Dobe-area woman to hold such a high-status position.

The film *The Gods Must Be Crazy* was filmed on location in the Nyae Nyae area by South African director Jamie Uys in 1978. Along with its sequel, it became the highest grossing non-U.S. film up to that time. The role of "the Bushman" was played by N!Xau, a thirty–year-old Ju man from Tsumkwe. Portrayed in the press kit as a leather-clad hunter-gatherer, N!Xau in fact had never hunted and, when Uys "discovered" him, was employed in the Tsumkwe primary school as a cook (Davis 1996:90–91)! Despite the films' grossing over US$100 million, Uys paid N!Xau only the equivalent of US$2,000. The arts and film community of South Africa protested this scandalous underpayment, and before his death, Uys gave N!Xau US$20,000 plus a monthly stipend. With the money, N!Xau built a Western-style house on the main street of Tsumkwe where backpacking tourists can still see him on the porch drinking tea with his family.

The roller-coaster life of Kgau Royal /O/oo mirrors the ups and downs of the Ju/'hoansi from the 1960s to the 1990s. Born in 1964 (Lee was present at his birth), Kgau grew up in a close-knit, though unconventional, family. His father had been a good hunter while his mother and older sisters had participated in the new *shebeen* and home brew economy at !Kangwa. Displaying a keen intelligence as a child, Kgau was among the very first Ju/'hoan children to attend !Kangwa school after it opened in 1973. By 1985, the youthful-looking Kgau had made it into Maun Junior Secondary School, the first Ju from the Dobe area to do so. After graduation, his excellent English got him many jobs working as an interpreter with government offices, visiting anthropologists, and filmmakers. His personal life was stormy, however, with periods in prison (convicted for acts that could be viewed as "crimes of conscience") and a succession of girlfriends. After Namibia's independence in 1989, Kgau crossed the fence to answer the demand for educated English speakers in the new SWAPO-led democratic country. There, he made his mark in the Nyae Nyae Farmers Co-op as the presenter for the Nyae Nyae position paper at the famous National Land Conference, as a spokesperson at international conferences, and as President Sam Nujoma's interpreter when he toured Bushmanland. His language skills were the key to his role as coauthor of the book *San* (Biesele and /O/oo 1997).

Despite these successes and his considerable charisma, personal demons continued to destabilize his personal life. In 1997, Kgau /O/oo made a dramatic and positive personal turnaround. Elected to the post of Traditional Tribal Authority, he stopped drinking and devoted himself to the welfare of his constituents. His third wife, Paula, from an Angolan !Kung family displaced by the war, was a major influence in settling him down. News of his good work spread, and in 1999 President Sam Nujoma himself summoned Kgau to Windhoek. The Namibian constitution permits the president to appoint members of parliament from underrepresented and marginalized minorities. Nujoma offered Kgau one such seat, and he accepted. Now Kgau /O/oo sits in the national parliament, shouldering heavy responsibilities and staying in touch with his constituents in Tsumkwe by fax and cell phone.

Effects on Anthropological Practice

The Ju/'hoansi have changed and so have we. How has the anthropological community responded to the dramatic changes in Ju life and in the lives of other indigenous peoples? The responses have varied widely: from business as usual among the "traditionalists" to the dark postmodern visions of the "revisionists." Happily, the members of the Marshall and the Kalahari Research groups have avoided both these extremes.

First, most of the original researchers have continued to remain active in San research and advocacy into the 1980s and 1990s. In 1978, John Marshall returned, after an enforced absence of many years, to film *N!ai* and to co-found the NNDFN. Then, at one hundred years of age, Lorna Marshall (1999) completed her second monograph, *Nyae Nyae !Kung Beliefs and Rites*.

Many of the KRG Harvard group have continued research in the Dobe area well into the 1980s and 1990s. Biesele, Blurton Jones, Brooks, Draper, Harpending, Howell, Katz, Lee, Shostak, and Yellen all have made trips since the mid-1980s, as well as students and former students such as Bob Hitchcock, James Ebert, Elizabeth Cashdan, Renee Pennington, Helga Vierich, Jackie Solway, and Renee

Sylvain. In one way or another, their studies have attempted to document the pace of change and its impacts.

For some anthropologists, however, the magnitude of the trauma experienced by the Ju/'hoansi over the last thirty years has made it morally impossible to continue as before. Some researchers have become actively involved in shaping the future of the San, in expanding the narrow (and dismal) range of options open to them back in the 1960s and 1970s. The formation of the NNDFN has brought anthropologists into a very different relationship with the San: to provide strategic support to a peoples' movement, the Nyae Nyae Farmers Cooperative. The anthropologists concerned have made available to development workers, government bodies, and the people themselves all the social and cultural ecological understanding built up by research since the time of the Marshall and DeVore–Lee expeditions. The Austin, Texas–based Kalahari Peoples Fund carries on similar programs for San communities in Botswana and elsewhere.

The point at which science and reflexivity meet is perhaps the most compelling current feature of this rather striking example of advocacy anthropology. Becoming an "advocate" or "intervener" clearly alters the work of anthropologists; but given the stakes, what was the option? To the anticipated charge of conventional science that such intervention creates epistemological distortion, we would argue that knowledge produced in a situation where people are fully involved may be different, but is no less important. If anything, it is clearer and more vital.

The Ju/'hoansi and the Crisis in Hunter-Gatherer Studies

In closing, we would like to offer some brief reflections on the changes in anthropology at large, based on our observations over several decades of field research among the Ju/'hoansi. It is commonplace to note that the world has been living through a period of unprecedented and accelerating change. Only a half century ago, most people in the "West" regarded indigenous peoples with a mixture of condescension, fear, and contempt. In recent years, a more sympathetic view has emerged. A newly aware public has watched with growing dismay as the world's so-called primitive societies have been "disappeared" with the speed of light. Group after group has been settled, censused, inoculated, administered, and put to work in the fields, farms, sweatshops, and factories of the New World Order (cf. Marshall 1984).

However, in some anthropological quarters, the reactions to what many regard as a tragedy, or at least an injustice, have been curious, to say the least. To some colleagues, the very idea that as recently as the 1950s or 1960s, ethnographers could have spent their time with people who dressed in skin clothing and hunted and gathered for a living seems to have become a source of embarrassment. Far better to reconstitute indigenous peoples as long-term serfs or dependents of neighboring power holders than to acknowledge evidence of their authenticity and recent autonomy (cf. Lee and Daly 1999; Schweitzer, Biesele, and Hitchcock 2000).

For other anthropologists, ourselves included, it is a source of astonished delight that any people could have resisted the steamroller of modernity for so long. It is these latter anthropologists who have taken to heart Lévi-Strauss's injunction, given at the original "Man the Hunter" conference in 1966, that the mandate of anthropology, its "calling," if you will, is "to bear testimony to future generations of the ingeniousness, diversity, and imagination of our species—qualities of which evidence would soon be lost forever" (Lévi-Strauss 1968:349).

It is these divergent views, we believe, that underlie the schism in perceptions of the Ju/'hoansi we mentioned at the outset, what one of us has called "the crisis in hunter-gatherer studies" (Lee 1992, 1993b, 1999). For some partisans in these often-heated debates, there seem to be only two alternatives; either the Ju/'hoansi are totally pristine or, if not, they must be totally dominated. But, we ask, "Why does living in the present mean that a people must be totally divorced from their past?" Modernity and the market are powerful and pervasive; they are *not* all-powerful or totally pervasive. The Ju/'hoansi are enduring but not unchanging; they are adapting to the world system as fast as they can. Their newfound political and technical skills augment a formidable array of knowledge and practices inherited from their foremothers and forefathers: language, kinship and naming systems, rituals and mythology, subsistence practices, and above all their ironic sensibilities are the firm bases on which they are constructing their future.

Fortunately, in the wider world there are signs of convergence between the Ju/'hoansi agenda and changing perspectives among development agencies, aid workers, and scholars. The recent growth of interest in the notions of "tribal wisdom," biodiversity, and theories of common property management is demonstrated on the cover of *Time* magazine, in the pages of *Cultural Survival Quarterly* (cf. Miller/Cultural Survival 1993), through the *Millennium* television series (Maybury-Lewis 1992), in the United Nations' 1993 "Declaration of the Decade of Indigenous Peoples (1993–2003)," and in "green" politics everywhere.

These and similar happenings offer some indication that the wheel may be turning in favor of the preservation of "small peoples." Current views no longer regard contemporary foragers as museum specimens, and though the recognition of these peoples' rights to land is important, it is not their only claim to legitimacy. What is emerging is a broader recognition that they are repositories of invaluable knowledge regarding plants, animals, and localities. Most importantly, these peoples are coming to be seen as living embodiments of alternative modes of life that deserve to exist even in this hard-bitten, postmodern age. All of these emerging discourses challenge the current banalities of the New World Order and also offer hope that ecological and cultural diversity still has a place on this planet.

Notes

1. The following phonetic conventions will be used in this chapter: the "=" sign is the alveolar click usually represented by a forward slash and an equal sign overstrike; the apos-

trophe " ' " is the glottal stop, usually represented by the question mark without the dot or by the vertical stroke (superior); the exclamation mark "!" is the alveopalatal click; the single vertical slash " / " and the double vertical slash " // " represent two different clicks, the alveolar and the lateral, respectively.

2. The exhibit on the Ju/'hoansi at the Peabody Museum, Harvard, that opened in December 1991, still running in 2001, is an excellent example of how to express the genius of the ethnographic culture without romanticizing the past or denying the trauma of the present (Lord 1991).

3. Cattle were a relatively recent arrival in the Dobe area, dating from the turn of the century and occurring in significant numbers only from the 1950s. Black cattle posts also existed in the Nyae Nyae until 1956–1957, when the South African police expelled them back to Bechuanaland.

4. In the 1990s, two *Festschriften* appeared, both honoring John Marshall's contributions to ethnographic film (Kapfer et al. 1991; Ruby 1993).

5. The revival of hunting was encouraged by the government. After years of strict enforcement of game laws, the powerful Wildlife Department conducted an aerial survey and decided that the Dobe area had plenty of game and issued liberal licenses to all Ju who wanted them. Both women and men were issued licenses, with the result that men were able to hunt their wives' quotas as well as their own.

6. Also of interest were the reactions of anthropologists to the militarization of the Ju/'hoansi. Some saw it as a terrible injustice, a manipulation of a politically unsophisticated group to serve the ends of apartheid (e.g., Lee and Hurlich 1982). Others (e.g., Kolata 1981) saw the recruitment as a perfectly acceptable way of bringing the Ju/'hoansi into the "modern world," with the army providing good pay, technical training, and even specially downsized uniforms for the diminutive Ju.

7. But they did occur; see Biesele and Weinberg (1990:3–4) for a firsthand account.

8. Of the several thousand San soldiers in the SADF from all over Namibia and from Angola, hundreds accompanied the departing South African units to permanent bases in South Africa proper, while hundreds more were resettled in the barren and hitherto unoccupied Western Bushmanland. The several hundred Nyae Nyae Ju/'hoan veterans at least had communities to come home to.

References Cited

Barnard, Alan
   (1992a) *Hunters and Herders of Southern Africa.* Cambridge: Cambridge University Press.
   (1992b) "The Kalahari debate: A bibliographic essay." Occasional Papers, No. 35. Edinburgh: Edinburgh University: Centre for African Studies.

Biesele, Megan
   (1976) "Aspects of !Kung folklore." Pp. 302–324 in Richard Lee and Irven DeVore (editors), *Kalahari Hunter-Gatherers: Studies of the !Kung San and Their Neighbors.* Cambridge, MA: Harvard University Press.

RICHARD B. LEE AND MEGAN BIESELE

(1986) *The Past and Future of !Kung Ethnography: Critical Reflections and Symbolic Perspectives* (Festschrift in honor of Lorna Marshall). Hamburg: Helmut Buske Verlag.
(1993a) "The Ju/'hoan Bushmen: Indigenous rights in a new country." Pp. 33–39 in Marc S. Miller/Cultural Survival (editors), *The State of the Peoples: A Global Human Rights Report on Societies in Danger*. Boston: Beacon Press.
(1993b) *Women Like Meat: The Folklore and Foraging Ideology of the Kalahari Ju/'hoan*. Bloomington and Johannesburg: Indiana University Press and Witwatersrand University Press.

Biesele, Megan, Mathias Guenther, Robert Hitchcock, Richard Lee, and Jean MacGregor
(1989) "Hunters, clients and squatters: The contemporary socioeconomic status of Botswana Basarwa." *Kyoto African Studies Monographs* 9(3):109–151.

Biesele, Megan and Nancy Howell
(1981) "The old people give you life: Aging among !Kung hunter-gatherers." Pp. 77–98 in Patricia Amoss and Stevan Harrell (editors), *Other Ways of Growing Old*. Stanford: Stanford University Press.

Biesele, Megan and Kgau Royal /O/oo
(1997) *San*. New York: Rosen Publishing Group.

Biesele, Megan and Paul Weinberg
(1990) *Shaken Roots: The Bushmen of Namibia*. Johannesburg: EDA Publications.

Blurton Jones, Nicholas and Melvin Konner
(1976) "!Kung knowledge of animal behavior, or: The proper study of mankind is animals." Pp. 325–348 in Richard Lee and Irven DeVore (editors), *Kalahari Hunter-Gatherers: Studies of the !Kung San and Their Neighbors*. Cambridge, MA: Harvard University Press.

Brooks, Alison and John Yellen
(1992) "Decoding the Ju/wasi past." *Symbols* (September):24–31.

Davis, Peter
(1996) *In Darkest Hollywood: Exploring the Jungles of Cinema's South Africa*. Randburg and Athens: Ravan Press and Ohio University Press.

Dickens, Patrick and the Ju/'hoan Peoples Literacy Committee
(1990) *Ju/'hoan–English Dictionary*. Windhoek: Nyae Nyae Development Foundation of Namibia.

Draper, Patricia
(1975) "!Kung women: Contrasts in sexual egalitarianism in the foraging and sedentary contexts." Pp. 77–109 in Rayna Reiter (editor), *Toward an Anthropology of Women*. New York: Monthly Review Press.
(1976) "The learning environment for aggression and anti-social behavior among the !Kung." Pp. 31–53 in Ashley Montagu (editor), *Teaching Non-Aggression*. New York: Oxford University Press.

Draper, Patricia and Elizabeth Cashdan
(1988) "Technological change and child behavior among the !Kung." *Ethnology* 27(4):339–365.

Eaton, Boyd, Marjorie Shostak, and Melvin Konner
(1988) *The Paleolithic Prescription.* New York: Harper and Row.

England, Nicholas
(1992) *Music among the Ju/'hoansi and Related Peoples of Namibia, Botswana, and Angola.* New York: Garland Publishing.

Gordon, Robert
(1992) *The Bushman Myth: The Making of a Namibian Underclass.* Boulder, CO: Westview.

Guenther, Mathias
(1979) *The Farm Bushmen of the Ghanzi District, Botswana.* Stuttgart: Hochschul Verlag.
(1986) *The Nharo Bushmen of Botswana: Tradition and Change.* Hamburg: Helmut Buske Verlag.
(2000) *Tricksters and Trancers: Bushman Religion and Society.* Bloomington: Indiana University Press.

Hansen, J., D. Dunn, R. B. Lee, P. Becker, and T. Jenkins
(1994) "Hunter-gatherer to pastoral way of life: Effects of the transition on health, growth, and nutritional status." *South African Journal of Science* 89:559–564.

Harpending, Henry
(1976) "Regional variations in !Kung populations." Pp. 152–165 in Richard Lee and Irven DeVore (editors), *Kalahari Hunter-Gatherers: Studies of the !Kung San and Their Neighbors.* Cambridge, MA: Harvard University Press.

Harpending, Henry, Alan Rogers, and Patricia Draper
(1987) "Human sociobiology." *American Journal of Physical Anthropology.* Supp. 8:127–150.

Hitchcock, Robert
(1977) *Kalahari Cattle Posts.* Gaborone: Government of Botswana.
(1982) "Patterns of sedentism among the Basarwa of eastern Botswana." Pp. 223–267 in Eleanor Leacock and Richard Lee (editors), *Politics and History in Band Societies.* Cambridge: Cambridge University Press.
(1993) "Sub-Saharan Africa: Environment, politics and development." Pp. 160–178 in Marc S. Miller/Cultural Survival (editors), *The State of the Peoples: A Global Human Rights Report on Societies in Danger.* Boston: Beacon Press.
(1996) *Kalahari Communities: Bushmen and the Politics of the Environment in Southern Africa.* Copenhagen: International Work Group for Indigenous Affairs.

Hitchcock, Robert and John D. Holm
(1993) "Bureaucratic domination of hunter-gatherer societies: A study of the San in Botswana." *Development and Change* 24:305–338.

RICHARD B. LEE AND MEGAN BIESELE

Howell, Nancy
(1976) "Toward a uniformitarian theory of human paleodemography." *Human Evolution* 5:25–40.
(1979) *The Demography of the Dobe !Kung.* New York: Academic Press.
(2000) *The Demography of the Dobe !Kung.* Second Edition. Hawthorne, NY: Aldine de Gruyter.

Kalahari Peoples Fund
(2001) *Newsletter of the Kalahari Peoples Fund, Benefitting the Peoples of the African Kalahari and Other Arid Lands.* (P.O. Box 7855, University Station, Austin TX 78713). Volume 1, Number 1.

Kapfer, R., W. Petermann, and R. Thoms [editors]
(1991) *Jäger und Gejagte: John Marshall und seine Filme.* Munich: Trickster Verlag.

Katz, Richard
(1982) *Boiling Energy: Community Healing among the !Kung.* Cambridge, MA: Harvard University Press.

Katz, Richard, Megan Biesele, and Verna St. Dennis
(1997) *Healing Makes Our Hearts Happy: Spirituality and Cultural Transformation among the Kalahari Ju/'hoansi.* Rochester, VT: Inner Traditions.

Kolata, Gina Bari
(1981) "!Kung Bushmen join the South African army." *Science* 211:562–564.

Konner, Melvin
(1976) "Maternal care, infant behavior and development among the !Kung." Pp. 218–245 in Richard Lee and Irven DeVore (editors), *Kalahari Hunter-Gatherers: Studies of the !Kung San and Their Neighbors.* Cambridge, MA: Harvard University Press.
(1983) *The Tangled Wing.* New York: Harper.

Leacock, Eleanor and Richard Lee [editors]
(1982) *Politics and History in Band Societies.* Cambridge: Cambridge University Press.

Lee, Richard B.
(1965) "Subsistence ecology of !Kung Bushmen." Ph.D. dissertation. University of California, Berkeley.
(1968) "What hunters do for a living, or, how to make out on scarce resources." Pp. 30–48 in Richard Lee and Irven DeVore (editors), *Man the Hunter.* Chicago: Aldine.
(1969a) "Eating Christmas in the Kalahari." *Natural History* (Dec.):60–64.
(1969b) "!Kung Bushman subsistence: An input-output analysis." Pp. 47–79 in A. P. Vayda (editor), *Environment and Cultural Behavior.* New York: Natural History Press.
(1979) *The !Kung San: Men, Women and Work in a Foraging Society.* Cambridge: Cambridge University Press.
(1988) "Reflections on primitive communism." Pp. 252–268 in Tim Ingold, David Riches, and James Woodburn (editors), *Hunters and Gatherers, Vol. 1: Ecology, Evolution and Social Change.* London: Berg Publishers.

(1990) "Primitive communism and the origins of social inequality." Pp. 225–246 in Steadman Upham (editor), *The Evolution of Political Systems: Sociopolitics in Small-Scale Sedentary Societies*. Cambridge: Cambridge University Press.
(1992) "Art, science or politics? The crisis in hunter-gatherer studies." *American Anthropologist* 90(1):14–34.
(1993a) *The Dobe Ju/'hoansi*. (Second edition of *The Dobe !Kung*). New York: HBJ-Holt.
(1993b) "The primitive as problematic." *Anthropology Today* (Dec.):1–3.
(1999) "Hunter-gatherer studies at the millennium: A look forward (and back)." *Bulletin of the National Museum of Ethnology, Osaka* 25(4):814–841.

Lee, Richard, Megan Biesele, and Robert Hitchcock
(1997) "Three decades of ethnographic research among the Ju/'hoansi of northwestern Botswana." *Botswana Notes and Records* 25:96–115.

Lee, Richard and Richard Daly [editors]
(1999) *The Cambridge Encyclopedia of Hunters and Gatherers*. Cambridge: Cambridge University Press.

Lee, Richard and Irven DeVore [editors]
(1968) *Man the Hunter*. Chicago: Aldine.
(1976) *Kalahari Hunter-Gatherers: Studies of the !Kung San and Their Neighbors*. Cambridge, MA: Harvard University Press.

Lee, Richard and Mathias Guenther
(1991) "Oxen or onions: The search for trade (and truth) in the Kalahari." *Current Anthropology* 32(5):592–601.
(1993) "Problems in Kalahari historical ethnography and the tolerance of error." *History in Africa* 20:185–235.

Lee, Richard and Robert Hitchcock
(2001) "African hunter-gatherers: Survival, history, and the politics of identity." Pp. 257–280 in Mitsuo Ichikawa and Jiro Tanaka (editors), *African Hunter-Gatherers: Proceedings of the Eighth Conference on Hunting and Gathering Societies*. Kyoto: African Studies Monograph Series.

Lee, Richard and Susan Hurlich
(1982) "From foragers to fighters: The militarization of the !Kung San." Pp. 327–345 in Eleanor Leacock and Richard Lee (editors), *Politics and History in Band Societies*. Cambridge: Cambridge University Press.

Lévi-Strauss, Claude
(1968) "The concept of primitiveness." Pp. 349–354 in Richard Lee and Irven DeVore (editors), *Man the Hunter*. Chicago: Aldine.

Lord, Deane
(1991) "Life in the Kalahari Desert." *Harvard Gazette* (Dec. 13).

RICHARD B. LEE AND MEGAN BIESELE

Marshall, John
(1971) *N/um Chai* (film). Watertown: Documentary Educational Resources.
(1980) *N!ai: The Story of a !Kung Woman* (film). Watertown: Documentary Educational Resources.
(1984) "Death blow to the Bushmen." *Cultural Survival Quarterly* 8(3):13–16.

Marshall, John and Claire Ritchie
(1984) *Where Are the Bushmen of Nyae Nyae? Changes in a Bushman Society, 1958–1981.* Communications No. 9. Cape Town: Center for African Studies.

Marshall, Lorna
(1957) "The kin terminology system of the !Kung Bushmen." *Africa* 27:1–25.
(1959) "Marriage among !Kung Bushmen." *Africa* 29:335–365.
(1960) "!Kung Bushman bands." *Africa* 30:325–355.
(1961) "Talking, sharing and giving: Relief of social tensions among the !Kung Bushmen." *Africa* 31:231–249.
(1962) "!Kung Bushman religious beliefs." *Africa* 32:221–245.
(1969) "The medicine dance of the !Kung Bushmen." *Africa* 39:347–381.
(1976) *The !Kung of Nyae Nyae.* Cambridge, MA: Harvard University Press.
(1999) *Nyae Nyae !Kung Beliefs and Rites.* Cambridge, MA: Peabody Museum Press.

Maybury-Lewis, David
(1992) *Millennium: Tribal Wisdom in the Modern World.* Boston: Beacon Press.

Miller, Mark S./Cultural Survival [editors]
(1993) *The State of the Peoples: A Global Human Rights Report on Societies in Danger.* Boston: Beacon Press.

Nyae Nyae Farmers Cooperative
(1989) "=′Hanu a N!an!a′an: N//oaq!′ae Farmaskxoasi //Koa//Kae" ["Statutes of the Nyae Nyae Farmers Cooperative"]. /Aotcha, Namibia.

Olivier, Emmanuelle
(1997) "Namibie: Chants des Bushmen Ju'hoansi" (recording). Paris: Ocora/Radio France.

Ritchie, Claire
(1989) "The political economy of resource tenure in the Kalahari." M.A. thesis. Boston University.

Rosenberg, Harriet G.
(1990) "Complaint discourse, aging, and caregiving among the !Kung San of Botswana." Pp. 19–41 in Jay Sokolovsky (editor), *The Cultural Context of Aging.* New York: Bergin and Garvey.

Ruby, Jay [editor]
(1993) *The Cinema of John Marshall.* Chur, Switzerland: Harwood Academic Publishers.

Schrire, Carmel [editor]
(1984) *Past and Present in Hunter-Gatherer Studies*. Orlando, FL: Academic Press.

Schweitzer, Peter, Megan Biesele, and Robert Hitchcock [editors]
(2000) *Hunter-Gatherers in the Modern World: Conflict, Resistance and Self-Determination*. New York: Berghahn Publishers.

Shostak, Marjorie
(1983) *Nisa: The Life and Words of a !Kung Woman*. New York: Vintage Books.
(2000) *Return to Nisa*. Cambridge, MA: Harvard University Press.

Smith, Andrew and Richard Lee
(1997) "Cho/ana: Archaeological and ethnohistorical evidence for recent hunter-gatherer/agro-pastoralist contact in northern Bushmanland." *South African Archaeological Bulletin* 52:52–58.

Solway, Jacqueline and Richard Lee
(1990) "Foragers, genuine or spurious: Situating the Kalahari San in history." *Current Anthropology* 31:109–146.

Story, Robert
(1958) *Some Plants Used by the Bushmen in Obtaining Food and Water*. Botanical Survey of South Africa, Memoir No. 30. Pretoria: Government Printer.

Susser, Ida
(2000) "Culture, sexuality and women's agency in the prevention of HIV/AIDS in southern Africa." *American Journal of Public Health* 90(7):1042–1048.

Thomas, Elizabeth Marshall
(1959) *The Harmless People*. New York: Knopf.

Truswell, A. Stewart and J. D. H. L. Hansen
(1976) "Medical research among the !Kung." Pp. 166–194 in Richard B. Lee and Irven DeVore (editors), *Kalahari Hunter-Gatherers: Studies of the !Kung San and Their Neighbors*. Cambridge, MA: Harvard University Press.

Truswell, A. S., B. M. Kennelly, J. D. L. Hansen, and R. B. Lee
(1972) "Blood pressures of !Kung Bushmen in northern Botswana." *American Heart Journal* 84:5–12.

Vierich, Helga
(1982) "Adaptive flexibility in a multi-ethnic setting." Pp. 213–222 in Eleanor Leacock and Richard Lee (editors), *Politics and History in Band Societies*. Cambridge: Cambridge University Press.

Volkman, Toby Alice
(1983) *The San in Transition: Volume 1, A Guide to "N!ai: The Story of a !Kung Woman."* Cambridge, MA: Documentary Educational Resources and Cultural Survival.

Wehmeyer, A. S., R. Lee, and M. Whiting
(1969) "The nutrient composition and dietary importance of some vegetable foods eaten by the !Kung Bushmen." *South African Medical Journal* 43:1529–1532.

Wiessner, Polly
(1977) "Hxaro: A regional system of reducing risk among the !Kung San." Ph.D. dissertation. University of Michigan, Ann Arbor.
(1982) "Risk, reciprocity and social influences on !Kung San economics." Pp. 61–84 in Eleanor Leacock and Richard Lee (editors), *Politics and History in Band Society.* Cambridge: Cambridge University Press.
(1998) "Report to the LIFE Project on the situation in the villages of the Nyae Nyae Conservancy area." Unpublished. On file at Kalahari Peoples Fund.

Wilmsen, Edwin
(1989) *Land Filled with Flies: A Political Economy of the Kalahari.* Chicago: University of Chicago Press.

Wilmsen, Edwin and James Denbow
(1990) "Paradigmatic history of San-speaking peoples and current attempts at revision." *Current Anthropology* 31(5):489–524.

Yellen, John
(1976) "Settlement patterns of the !Kung: An archaeological perspective." Pp. 47–72 in Richard Lee and Irven DeVore (editors), *Kalahari Hunter-Gatherers: Studies of the !Kung San and Their Neighbors.* Cambridge. MA: Harvard University Press.
(1977) *Archaeological Approaches to the Present.* New York: Academic Press.
(1990) "The transformation of the Kalahari !Kung." *Scientific American* 262(4):96–105.

Yellen, J. and A. Brooks
(1988) "The Late Stone Age archaeology of the !Kangwa and /Xai/xai valleys." *Botswana Notes and Records* 20:5–27.

Part III
PASSING THE MANTLE: MULTIGENERATIONAL STUDIES

Among ethnographers, perhaps the best-known multigenerational field site is Chan Kom, a Mayan village in Yucatán, Mexico, first studied by Robert Redfield and Alfonso Villa Rojas (1934), then revisited two decades later by Redfield (1955). While Redfield certainly recognized the value of doing a restudy—and knew all too well the controversy that might arise from a new ethnographer coming to town (cf. Lewis 1951)—he did not search for someone to follow his own work in Chan Kom. Of course, Redfield did "discover" a young schoolteacher named Alfonso Villa Rojas, who eventually pursued graduate training in anthropology at the University of Chicago and then had a successful career as a Mayan scholar and anthropological administrator (Villa Rojas 1979). Through her connection with Villa Rojas, Mary Elmendorf (1976) became interested in studying women's issues in Chan Kom, as part of a large applied project (funded through USAID) in which both were involved. Subsequently, the Spanish anthropologist Alicia ReCruz (1996) did fieldwork among the people of Chan Kom, emphasizing the interplay of their traditions and the transformations wrought by migratory wage labor and tourism. Thus, although we are fortunate to have ethnographies describing Chan Kom in the 1930s, 1950s, 1970s, and 1990s, this is best seen as long-term ethnographic serendipity.

In contrast, there are a few noteworthy examples of *intentional* multigenerational projects, in which the senior ethnographers pass the mantle, as it were, to new researchers who then take responsibility to sustain the project into the future. To conclude this volume, we present here two well-known longitudinal studies—Tzintzuntzan and Gwembe—both of which involve some fifty years of continuing field research. The two projects differ in the original impetus and in the nature of the collaboration. The Tzintzuntzan project began as an opportunity to train students systematically in a supervised regional context. The Gwembe project came into being because Henry Fosbrooke, then director of the Rhodes-Livingstone Institute, was eager to document the long-term consequences to the Gwembe Tonga of the building of the Kariba Dam. The participants in the Tzintzuntzan project have, with the exception of the decennial ethnographic census, done independent research. The Gwembe project is now managed as a team with sharing of data, common research projects, and often joint publication.

George Foster began research in Tzintzuntzan in 1945 on a short-term basis. The original impetus for starting fieldwork in Michoacán was to train students enrolled in the graduate program at the National School of Anthropology and History (Mexico City); since Foster's return in 1958, more than a dozen graduate students from Berkeley and other universities have worked with Foster in the Lake Pátzcuaro region or in Tzintzuntzan itself. Among these students, Stanley Brandes and Robert V. Kemper, both of whom first came to Tzintzuntzan in 1967, have continued to work with its people and migrants. A third anthropological generation is represented by Scott Anderson, who did his dissertation research in the mid-1990s on issues related to growing old in Tzintzuntzan (Anderson 1998) and by Peter Cahn, who recently studied Protestantism in Tzintzuntzan and the adjacent lakeside communities for his dissertation (Cahn 2001). Foster has given all the anthropologists who have worked in and around Tzintzuntzan complete freedom to choose their own projects. Except for Anderson (whose time in the field fell at mid-decade), all have participated in one or more of the six decennial ethnographic censuses, although to Kemper has fallen the primary responsibility for maintaining this continuing source of "minimum core data." In addition, Foster's wife Mary (1969) has carried out linguistic research on Tarascan grammar in the nearby hamlet of Ichupio and also has done some ethnographic research in Tzintzuntzan itself.

Elizabeth Colson first went to the Gwembe Valley in 1949. She returned in 1956, accompanied by Thayer Scudder, to engage in a "before-and-after" study of the effects of the Kariba Dam development project on the Gwembe Tonga people. The research subsequently expanded to include social issues far beyond what was envisioned in the original study. As early as the 1960s, Colson and Scudder recognized the difficulty of maintaining a project of such scope with only two anthropologists and so made efforts to recruit others. Periodically, other investigators responded to the invitation and were involved in short-term projects within the larger scheme. Finally, in 1992, Colson and Scudder recruited three junior colleagues—Sam Clark, Lisa Cliggett, and Rhonda Gillett-Netting—who now share increasingly in the management of the project. They have been joined by Bennett Siamwiza, the first Gwembe Tonga member of the project team. The project is both multigenerational and multidisciplinary. This calls for careful socialization by gathering together as a team, as they did in 1999 in Chicago, where they spent many hours in conference about the Gwembe project during the annual meeting of the American Anthropological Association.

The great benefits of *intentional* long-term projects such as these are continuity and the ability to map out lines of research while still allowing for the possibility of what Foster has called "serendipity." Colson and Scudder make the crucial point that a long-term study develops its own dynamics. Change comes about through the changing interests of the participants, the changing contexts of the Gwembe people, *and* the dynamic of the process itself. The Gwembe research has been enriched by including new perspectives and new experts. Colson has observed that bringing in others served to startle her out of the ruts into which long-term ethnographers may fall, while Foster has written that, for the single researcher, the passage of time not only brings familiarity but also may diminish the frequency of serendipitous occurrences that prompt new questions.

The commitment by members of these two projects to collect "minimum core data" ensures that a basic profile of these communities is maintained over time. This is a rich source of data not only for these specific communities but potentially for comparative purposes. The data are of special value because they are embedded in decades of on-the-ground ethnographic experience. The participants in these projects are all aware of the manifold problems associated with gathering, coding, analyzing, storing, and retrieving what have become, over the decades, enormous data sets. Anyone contemplating similar studies will need to consider these problems and the resolutions suggested here.

The original project directors—Colson, Scudder, and Foster—acknowledge the importance of fresh ways of asking questions about situations observed so many times that they become comfortably familiar and no longer noteworthy. Those who have joined these ongoing projects most recently, Cliggett and Cahn, write of the benefits of joining their respective projects. They comment that settling into the field happens much more quickly because they have come into a setting where the senior ethnographers have already established friendships and trust. They add that, even as newcomers, they can begin work almost immediately with the data that come with being part of the team and that their observations can be checked against years of accumulated material. Cahn describes it this way: "I joined an ongoing dialogue that included my informants as well as those of my predecessors."

There are, of course, difficulties built into multigenerational projects. Paradoxically, one difficulty for newer members stems from one of the benefits—that of having a network already in place. It means that new researchers start their fieldwork with certain "inherited" obligations, some of which may not facilitate the research they came to do. Because they are perceived by the local people as extensions of the senior investigators, the newcomers have much less freedom to define themselves in their own right. For instance, on more than one occasion, Kemper has been asked by Tzintzuntzeños if he is Foster's son! Newcomers must worry about inadvertently injecting a note of dissonance into a harmonious field setting. Just as in any fieldwork, however, over time they develop their own personalities, make their own friends, and have their research acknowledged by the local communities.

For the senior anthropologists of a multigenerational project, disadvantages include having too many data to analyze and publish on a reasonable schedule, having to make notes and data available to other team members with enough context so that the newcomers can make sense of the data, and simply having to accommodate others in the field setting. In addition, the passage of time means that some friends may fall into economic hard times, and, inevitably, many will grow old and die. Scudder and Colson put it eloquently: "We have lived too long with the realities that the Gwembe people face daily not to be concerned about what happens to them. It is impossible to go away and forget that their lives go on." Professional advancement brings with it an increasingly busy life, quite apart from the self-imposed continuing responsibility to get back into the field yet another time. For Scudder and Colson, the success of their "Relocation Theory" has meant that they have been in great demand as consultants on applied projects involving the impact of large-scale dams or as experts on refugee issues.

One of the serious questions that any multigenerational project—indeed, any long-term project—must face is that of its continued existence. Many factors potentially affect decisions about this kind of long-term, even lifelong, commitment. First, the field of anthropology shifts in terms of theories and paradigms. The discipline is unlikely ever to return to synchronic, slice-of-time studies that assume contained and continuous cultures as objects of study, but it is difficult to predict the impact of current emphases on transnationalism, globalization, diasporas, borderlands, and so forth on long-term, place-specific research.

Many disciplinary shifts have to do with the changing global context—wholesale migration of labor from underdeveloped to developed countries; the creation of untold numbers of refugees as a result of genocidal conflicts, natural disasters, and the redrawing of political boundaries; a global economy and communication system in which no corner of the world is unconnected; and an increasing realization that the world's environment is being laid waste. Anthropologists have much to offer toward the understanding and resolution of these conditions. Cliggett argues that we ought to be at the core, not brought in to provide a kind of cultural color, because we *do* have real data to offer that, when integrated with materials from other disciplines, can generate powerful answers with significant policy implications for governments and for their peoples.

Patterns of employment for anthropologists also have changed. A generation ago, 85 percent of American anthropologists with a Ph.D. degree were on the faculties of colleges and universities. That proportion has dropped significantly, as more and more academically trained scholars find positions with governmental agencies, NGOs, corporations, international organizations, and research institutes. This, in itself, does not imply that those so employed cannot make commitments to long-term field research, but, at the very least, their participation will be different. The academy offers more sustained periods of time away from the institution and puts less pressure on its members to produce quick, action-oriented analyses. However, the academy has its own demands, which sometimes are incompatible with long-term, collaborative research. Publications must be original contributions and must be turned out on a regular schedule. Coauthored articles frequently are devalued, especially in social and cultural anthropology where monographs and single-authored articles have been the standard. Similarly, grants submitted by a team raise questions with university administrators about how "overhead" and "indirect costs" will be calculated and allocated among the participating institutions. Add to these institutional constraints the psychological lure of "new" field sites not yet explored by other anthropologists, as well as the implicit "hierarchy of purity" of field sites (Gupta and Ferguson 1997:13), and it is difficult to make a compelling argument for signing on to a multigenerational field project where the newcomer's voice is neither first nor senior.

Cliggett's chapter offers a thoughtful commentary on how she has dealt with all of these problems, ultimately making the decision that being part of the Gwembe team has made her and the others better scholars: "We have better data, better analysis, better interpretations, and better answers for important questions about the human condition than if we worked within the traditional solitary framework of most anthropologists."

Individuals make choices more easily than do institutions. Anthropology as a discipline, academic institutions, corporations, and even development agencies change directions slowly and with great effort, like turning the course of a great ship. After half a century, much of the success of these two multigenerational projects has been due to individual choice and commitment. From the pioneers who originated and have sustained these projects[1] those who have followed in this calling have learned the importance—even the necessity—of chronicling cultures across time and space. We trust that, in reading the stories in this volume, our colleagues in the social sciences, in academic institutions, and in funding agencies will be moved to provide a more dependable context for these unique ways of documenting and analyzing the long-term changes and continuities in the human condition.

Note

1. George Foster (in 1982), Elizabeth Colson (in 1985), and Thayer Scudder (in 1999) have been honored by the Society for Applied Anthropology with the Bronislaw Malinowski Award, presented annually "to an outstanding social scientist in recognition of efforts to understand and serve the needs of the world's societies and who has actively pursued the goal of solving human problems using the concepts and tools of social science."

References Cited

Anderson, Scott T.
   (1998) "Growing old in Tzintzuntzan." Ph.D. dissertation. University of California, San Francisco.

Cahn, Peter S.
   (2001) "When conversion is convergence: Evangelicals and Catholics in Tzintzuntzan, Mexico." Ph.D. dissertation. University of California, Berkeley.

PART III

Elmendorf, Mary L.
(1976) *Nine Mayan Women: A Village Faces Change.* New York: Schenkman Publishing.

Foster, Mary L.
(1969) "The Tarascan language." *University of California Publications in Linguistics,* Vol. 56. Berkeley: University of California Press.

Gupta, Akhil and James Ferguson [editors]
(1997) *Anthropological Locations: Boundaries and Grounds of a Field Science.* Berkeley: University of California Press.

Lewis, Oscar
(1951) *Life in a Mexican Village: Tepoztlán Restudied.* Urbana: University of Illinois Press.

ReCruz, Alicia
(1996) *The Two Milpas of Chan Kom: A Study of Socioeconomic and Political Transformations in a Maya Community.* Albany: State University of New York Press.

Redfield, Robert
(1955) *A Village That Chose Progress.* Chicago: University of Chicago Press.

Redfield, Robert and Alfonso Villa Rojas
(1934) *Chan Kom: A Maya Village.* Washington, D.C.: Carnegie Institution of Washington Publication No. 448.

Villa Rojas, Alfonso
(1979) "Fieldwork in the Mayan region of Mexico." Pp. 45–64 in George M. Foster, Thayer Scudder, Elizabeth Colson, and Robert V. Kemper (editors), *Long-Term Field Research in Social Anthropology.* New York: Academic Press.

CHAPTER EIGHT
LONG-TERM RESEARCH IN GWEMBE VALLEY, ZAMBIA
Thayer Scudder and Elizabeth Colson

Introduction

We began our study of the Gwembe or Valley Tonga of Zambia in 1956 when Zambia was the British Colonial Territory of Northern Rhodesia and Gwembe Valley was still a relatively isolated region served by few roads, schools, or shops. Within a decade it had been transformed; and since then each decade, sometimes each year, has brought new challenges.

Gwembe Valley occupies the Zambezi River valley between Victoria Falls and the confluences of the Zambezi and Kafue Rivers (figure 8.1). The valley floor lies at about 1,300 feet above sea level, flanked by 3,000- to 5,000-foot plateaus. In 1956 the larger part of the population lived on the north bank of the Zambezi in Northern Rhodesia, separated by a permeable international boundary from kin living on the south bank in Southern Rhodesia (now Zimbabwe). It is with the fortunes of the Zambian inhabitants of Gwembe that we are primarily concerned. Between 1946 and 1991 they were under a single administrative district, Gwembe District, which evolved into three subdistricts: Gwembe North, Gwembe Central, and Gwembe South. In 1991 these became formalized as separate districts: Siavonga, Gwembe, and Sinazongwe. To maintain continuity with earlier publications, we here retain the old designations and use *Gwembe* to refer to the former district and its subdivisions.

The experience of the Gwembe people since 1956 epitomizes what has been happening throughout much of the Third World, where the building of dams and other massive projects transforms physical environments, populations become more vulnerable to centralized power, and transnational economic forces transform the political and social environment. The Gwembe people have experienced both boom and bust, have found their countryside an arena for guerrilla warfare, have been forced to contend with environmental degradation, have suffered from new diseases (especially AIDS and cholera), have had to compete with incomers intent on exploiting local resources, and have been exposed to the planning strategies of international organizations as well as those of their own government. They have learned to think internationally of donors, foreign exchange, markets, passports, and visas.

Ted Scudder and Sam Clark (right) with Mazulu village children, 1995. Photo by Lisa Cliggett.

Beginning in 1956, one or the other (or both) of us visited Gwembe, at least briefly, on twenty-six different occasions, with the most recent being Colson's visit in 2001. Colson's earlier visit to Gwembe Central in June 1949 was incidental to research among the neighboring Plateau Tonga. Mary E. D. Scudder joined us in 1962–1963, 1972, and 1981–1982, while Roger Noll collaborated with us in 1972. Others associated with the study have been Jonathan Habarad, who spent fifteen months in Gwembe during 1987–1988; Sarah Madrid and Carlos Madrid, briefly in the summer of 1991; Sam Clark, some months in 1991, 1995, 1996, 1997–1998; Rhonda Gillett-Netting, in 1993 and 1997; Lisa Cliggett, eighteen months in 1994–1995, and in 1996, 1998, and 2001; and Ben Clark, in 1998, 1999, and 2000. Ute Luig and Ulrich Luig, who have worked in Gwembe South intermittently since 1987, are good colleagues with whom we have exchanged field data, although they are not part of the longitudinal study group.

The Gwembe Study through Time

Initiation of the Study

A longitudinal study was not part of the original research design conceived in 1955 by Henry Fosbrooke, then director of the Rhodes-Livingstone Institute (later the Institute for African Studies of the University of Zambia, and now the Institute for Economic and Social Research). When he heard that a hydroelec-

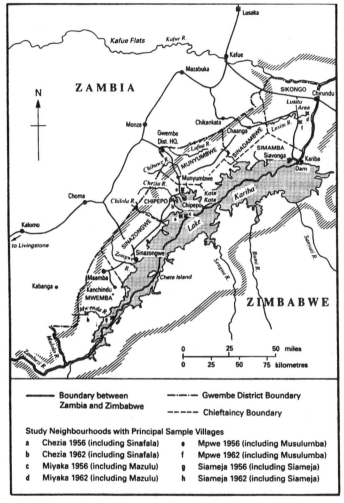

Figure 8.1. Gwembe District and Kariba Lake Basin, Zambia.

tric dam was to be built at Kariba Gorge on the Zambezi River (Soils Inc. in association with Chalo Environmental 2000), Fosbrooke recognized that the creation of Kariba Lake would challenge the Gwembe Tonga to adapt to new environments, and he planned for anthropologists to observe the process. The study was to include an initial period in 1956–1957 prior to resettlement and a return visit some years after the move to examine adaptation. The emphasis was to be on the long-term consequences of living in a new region rather than on the transition period associated with the disruption of resettlement. That period was assumed to be aberrant (Colson 1971b). We no longer accept this perspective since it assumes the following causal sequence: (1) a stable adaptation within a stable ecological context, (2) a disruption, and (3) the emergence of a new equilibrium within a social and physical environment also marked by stability.

Fosbrooke was inclined to opt for a ten-year interval between visits to give the people a chance to change from permanent and semipermanent cultivation of alluvial soils to shifting cultivation and lake fishing, but for logistical reasons he settled on a five-year interval. He recommended a third visit after another five years but sought financing (20,000 pounds, or $56,000) for only the first two phases of the study. We were then recruited to carry out the study. Colson had learned a dialect of Tonga and visited Gwembe during earlier research among the neighboring Plateau Tonga (1946–1947, 1948–1950). Scudder, with a background in biology and geography as well as anthropology, was recruited to work on Gwembe ecology.

It was not until 1962–1963 that we began to comprehend the long-term possibilities involved in a study of continuity and change among a people who, having been forcibly resettled in connection with a major dam, were soon to be incorporated within the independent nation of Zambia as colonial rule gave way to a new political formation. Since then, the Gwembe people have had to contend with further changes. Concomitantly, we have had to modify research plans and methods.

The article prepared for the 1975 Wenner-Gren Conference reported on the first twenty years of the study and was imbued with the optimism associated with the first ten years of Zambian independence when Gwembe District and its people fared relatively well (Scudder and Colson 1979). Since the mid-1970s, they have suffered, along with the majority of Zambians, from the plummeting of the Zambian economy. During the latter half of the 1970s, Gwembe residents also experienced disruptions associated with the war for Zimbabwean independence. Gwembe District borders Zimbabwe and, in consequence, became a war zone. Land mines and commando raids led to the death of at least one person in each of our study villages (Colson 1995). Zimbabwe's independence in 1980 was not followed by improvement in either the local or the Zambian national economy. Unfavorable government policies and adverse international terms of trade for Zambia's major exports and imports led first to a continued economic decline, and then to calamitous urban and rural poverty when structural adjustment programs urged on Zambia by its creditors brought the inevitable consequences of unemployment, disruption of basic services, and general malaise.

Gwembe has always been drought prone, but drought years increased in the 1980s and 1990s, making people dependent on imported food in 1981–1984, 1987–1988, 1991–1994, 1996, and 1998. In the mid-1980s, AIDS became a serious health problem. Zambia today has one of the highest AIDS mortality rates in the world. The impact on Gwembe, though grim, has been instrumental in bringing about changes in sexual practices. As health services have declined nationally, other diseases have acquired new significance. In 1991, cholera spread into Gwembe from cities where the infrastructure was breaking down. Drug-resistant strains of malaria and tuberculosis are also now common. Mortality rates have risen (Clark et al. 1995; Clark 2001).

Periodization

We have found it useful to break the twentieth-century history of Gwembe into four time periods, defined primarily by economic markers (Scudder 1985). The first (1901–1931) began with the establishment of administrative stations in the district by the British South Africa Company and ended eight years after the company transferred control over Northern Rhodesia to the British Colonial Office. During that period, the primary task of the administrators was to impose "law and order," collect taxes (which forced men to leave the district as labor migrants), and provide famine relief during the periodic years of hunger that have plagued Gwembe to the present. The second period (1932–1954) was characterized by a more active administration that attempted, in various ways, to alleviate hunger and to strengthen such recently established institutions as a district council and treasury and a local court system, as well as to encourage legislation against such practices as childhood betrothal. Both periods were prior to our involvement with Gwembe. Our field research documents the third and fourth periods.

The third period (1955–1974) was characterized by relatively rapid economic and political change triggered by the building of roads and other infrastructure associated with the Kariba resettlement and the fisheries in the newly formed Kariba Lake, by resistance to European domination symbolized by the formation of the Central African Federation, and then by the expansion of employment opportunities and governmental services during the first decade of independence. Living standards, as assessed by both the people and ourselves, rose for the majority during these years.

The fourth period, starting in the mid-1970s, has been characterized by economic downturn, exacerbated by political discontent which first focused on the single-party system initiated in 1972. The coming of a multiparty system in 1991 and the installation of a new government with different economic priorities and greater openness to criticism were associated with a brief euphoria when people believed that Zambia and Gwembe were entering a new period. Political disaffection then reemerged as inflation soared, corruption became increasingly apparent, intolerance of opposition increased, and the national economy contracted. During this period government has largely ceded its role in the provision of services to a multitude of donor agencies.

Kariba Dam and Its Impact

Since 1958, Gwembe landscape has been dominated by Kariba Lake, impounded behind the 400-foot-high dam which was begun in 1955 and sealed in late 1958. When the waters reached the reservoir margin in 1963, Kariba, then the largest human-made lake in the world, reached a length of over 170 miles and had a surface area of approximately 2,000 square miles. As the lake filled, it flooded land occupied by 57,000 people (on both sides of the Zambezi). Although those displaced were largely relocated within the lake basin, the majority were no longer "people of the Zambezi," as they had boasted for generations. They were moved back onto less fertile soils located toward the base of the Middle Zambezi escarpments. Later, during the 1980s and 1990s, more arable land became available when Kariba Lake shrank as a result of the years of drought, but the extent of the drawdown area was greatly reduced when the reservoir returned to full storage level in 2000.

For all their negative impacts, big dams do serve to incorporate local populations into a wider regional and often national system. In the Gwembe case, new roads were built to the dam site prior to the commencement of construction, and feeder roads were extended to relocation areas. Thousands of laborers responded to job opportunities at the dam site or in operations such as bush clearance around the perimeter of the future lake. Within a matter of months, isolation vanished. The new reservoir created a temporarily lucrative fishing industry, initially reserved for Gwembe fishermen. When it was thrown open in 1964 after independence, fishermen from as far away as Malawi, Mozambique, and Tanzania settled in Gwembe and married Gwembe women.

Any economic gains associated with Kariba Dam, however, must be evaluated in light of the reality that opportunities did not necessarily accrue to those who suffered losses. Many benefits, such as those relating to capital-intensive commercial fishing and to tourism, accrued to outsiders. Gwembe women lost rights in land, which undercut their position in subsequent years (Colson 1999). Many seniors who lost land and stock were unable to regain their old degree of affluence. Senior men lost status vis-à-vis younger men who had the strength to clear land, who were able to face the risks of fishing on Kariba Lake, or who were young enough to take advantage of new opportunities for education.

Zambian Independence

The Gwembe study spans the end of colonial rule and the creation of an independent Zambia. During 1956–1957, Northern Rhodesia was a colonial territory and a member of the short-lived Federation of the Rhodesias and Nyasaland (1953–1962), although the British Colonial Office retained responsibility for African affairs in Northern Rhodesia. Gwembe Tonga in Southern Rhodesia fell directly under the control of its settler government, which had very different policies for its African population. In Northern Rhodesia, settler political power was broken in 1962, followed by independence in 1964. Thereafter, deteriorating relationships with settler-dominated Rhodesia closed that country to Zambian labor migrants, including those from Gwembe District. Gwembe migrants then sought work in Zambia, and many took wives and children with them. This, and the new policies of the Zambian government (including universal primary school education and much-improved access to secondary and tertiary education), accelerated the incorporation of Gwembe people into a wider national polity of which they were scarcely aware in 1956.

Gwembe society, basically egalitarian in 1956, became increasingly stratified (Scudder and Colson 1980). In 1956 few were literate in any language; by 1972, probably every village in the district could boast of someone who had been to secondary school. At the start of the twenty-first century, Gwembe men and women in increasing numbers hold university degrees, earned both in Zambia and overseas. They are employed in professional jobs in Zambia and increasingly they also work elsewhere in Africa, Europe, and the United States. Many have graduated from teacher training or technical schools. Those assigned back in Gwembe form a new elite with local businesspeople, a few wealthy farmers, and other government employees. By the late 1990s, they were being joined by a few retired professional people who have returned home to start businesses and take part in local affairs. The Gwembe region also now has a substantial immigrant population, including fishermen and employees in its tourist industry and other enterprises.

In 1956, residence was in small villages. After the 1950s, Gwembe acquired four townships: three grew up around administrative centers; two (including one of the administrative centers) are industrial centers. Zambia's only coal mines opened in Gwembe South in 1965. Gwembe North has a power installation from which Kariba power flows to Zambian copper mines and other industries and to towns and farms along the railway line, but only at the end of the century was there talk of using that power to the direct benefit of Gwembe enterprises. All four townships have recruited diversified workforces, only some of whom originated in Gwembe.

During the "good years" immediately following independence, increased agricultural and veterinary services and the provision of credit encouraged a diversification of the village economy. In the early 1970s, cash cropping (of cotton in particular) and the sale of livestock replaced commercial fishing as the major source of local cash income. Profits were used to educate children and to purchase more productive equipment, with a successful minority also investing in village stores, tea houses, and bars. Carpenters, masons, and other craftspeople also then found a local clientele.

New opportunities at home were complemented by new job opportunities elsewhere in Zambia. These jobs were primarily for men, who were frequently accompanied by their wives and children. By the early 1970s, Gwembe families were to be found in all the towns along the railway in Southern Province (to which Gwembe District belongs), although the largest concentration was in Lusaka. Women used the opportunity to become marketeers to supplement family incomes and sometimes to maintain themselves as single women. Most migrants continued to maintain links with home areas; people, messages, cash, and other goods flowed back and forth between town and country, encouraged by the new availability of roads and transportation, while Radio Lusaka served both urban and rural areas.

Economic Downturn

In the mid-1970s, both rural and urban opportunities deteriorated for low-income people. A drop in the price of copper—which had provided approximately 80 percent of Zambia's foreign exchange—combined with rising oil prices to produce catastrophic economic consequences for most Zambians. Adverse international terms of trade were exacerbated further by the war for neighboring Zimbabwe's independence, which necessitated the expensive rerouting of exports and imports after the border was closed. Scarce funds went to support freedom fighters from much of southern Africa. Zambia's policies toward the rural areas were also major factors in the economic downturn (ILO 1981; Seidman 1979).

In Gwembe, the economic downturn and increased danger from Rhodesian land mines led to a cutback in all services in the late 1970s. Tsetse control ceased for a time, and a resurgence of bovine trypanosomiasis reduced cattle herds. Extension officers stopped their visits due to lack of fuel and fear of land mines. Health services and schools deteriorated as supervision slackened and supplies failed to arrive. Village stores and other businesses closed because they could not restock basic commodities or, in some areas, because they could not compete with government parastatals which sold commercial beer, bread, and sewn clothing (Colson and Scudder 1988).

At the very time opportunities in Gwembe were decreasing, worsening urban unemployment and inflation forced many urban migrants to return home. There they had to contend with land shortages, due to the original loss of land to Kariba Lake and to rapid population increase (Clark et al. 1995). By 1982, land pressure was at a point at which many newly married couples could not find land to clear for fields, nor could they count on obtaining sufficient land from kin even to raise subsistence crops, much less to engage in cash cropping. Many established farmers who felt the land pinch in the early 1980s began to leave Gwembe to pioneer land in western Southern Province, a hundred miles from home; later, others drawn by land hunger and better rainfall ventured further north into Lusaka and Central Provinces.

Continuity and Change in the Gwembe Study

Over the years the study has changed significantly, partly in response to the changing circumstances of the Gwembe people and partly due to our own changing interests, but also because a long-term study develops its own dynamics.

As we have attempted to understand continuities and change, the timing and sequencing of events have become more crucial. We have come to see current practices as devices applied to particular situations rather than as stable adaptations that will continue to be invoked. In turn, what is happening at the time of any one visit has the potential for a variety of futures. We find ourselves paying more attention to the interplay between national resources and policies and conditions in Gwembe. During 1956–1957, although decisions made in Salisbury,

Lusaka, London, and elsewhere were bringing upheaval to Gwembe, we took this as a given and looked primarily at how Gwembe people ordered their lives and how they viewed the future. During the 1960s and early 1970s, people became increasingly mobile, both geographically and socially, and it was clear that they used different frames of reference as they moved from situation to situation. During these years they saw the world as opening up to them, and they looked outward to the towns as sources of new ideas, styles, and luxuries. By the 1980s, they felt themselves newly constrained by forces beyond their control and understanding. Like other Zambians, they were concerned with the impact of international politics and talked much about "Forex" (foreign exchange), so desirable and so difficult to acquire. They also began to engage with international donor agencies—which help support schools and health services, provide wells and small dams as well as agricultural inputs and extension work, administer food-for-work programs in drought years, and employ some local people.

In response to this changing field situation, we have attempted to develop research designs and methods flexible enough to cope with the fluidity of people who move geographically, seize or reject new opportunities (or try to cope with the nonavailability of opportunities), use and avoid new national and international agencies, rethink and cling to old ideologies, and are becoming something else while trying to remain themselves (Colson and Kottak 1996).

Research Plans in 1956

Plans for the initial study were built on Colson's 1949 visit to Chipepo Chieftaincy in Gwembe Central and her experience with Gwembe migrants settled in Plateau villages. Most of those she encountered were from Chipepo Chieftaincy. We decided to begin work in two Zambezi neighborhoods in Chipepo. Nevertheless, we knew from published sources and talks with district officers that those living both upstream and downstream from Chipepo differed in dialect, subsistence systems, social organization, ritual, and general outlook. Hill residents also differed from those living along the Zambezi. On the other hand, neighborhoods on opposite banks of the Zambezi, although under different national regimes, freely exchanged populations and were similar in most respects. To write about Gwembe we would have to supplement work in Chipepo with other studies and also rely on information in the district files.

In the second phase, we wanted to compare responses to resettlement by Zambezi neighborhoods with different initial resources. We also wanted to examine the effect on host populations who had to share space and other resources with those resettled. Initially, we also wanted to compare the impact of the different resettlement policies of the regimes on either side of the Zambezi. Ideally, intensive studies should have been carried out in some ten neighborhoods and these supplemented with a general survey. This was too much for two people given a one-year time schedule, even if we had not also needed to look at local government, the local court system, and the roles of the district administration and various Christian missions. The government of Rhodesia/Zimbabwe simplified our choice by moving its people before we could settle in any Zimbabwe village. The study, therefore, became confined essentially to Gwembe District in Zambia. Short visits to villages in Zimbabwe during 1956–1957 and 1962–1963, and again after Zimbabwe achieved independence in 1980, have not been sufficient to permit us to follow developments in that country. Fortunately, in the 1980s, fieldworkers, some from the University of Zimbabwe, began research among Tonga speakers in Zimbabwe (see especially Bourdillon, Cheater, and Murphree 1985; Reynolds 1991; Reynolds and Cousins 1989; Schuthof and Boerenkamp 1991; Dzingirai and Bourdillon 1997; Wunder 1998; and, for an earlier study, see Weinrich 1977).

Given information available in September 1956, we planned intensive studies of river and upland neighborhoods in Chipepo and Mwemba Chieftaincies, in Gwembe Central and Gwembe South, respectively, to be followed by a quick survey of neighborhoods throughout Gwembe. We minimized work in the other five chieftaincies for the following reasons: Sinazongwe, another Gwembe Central chieftaincy, seemed much like Chipepo; Munyumbwe and Sinadambwe, both upland chieftaincies, would not be immediately affected by resettlement; Simamba and Sigongo, the two chieftaincies of Gwembe North, had small populations and in 1956 were slated to lose little land to Kariba Lake and to receive few persons resettled from elsewhere.

Only in mid-1957 did it become definite that a substantial number of villages from Gwembe Central, including two of the villages we had selected for intensive study, would be resettled below the dam in the Lusitu area in Gwembe North. One was our host upland village in Gwembe Central. This is only one instance of how unexpected events bedevil the planning of long-term research. We have encountered others and have learned that a rigid research design becomes a handicap over time.

For strategic reasons, we began work in adjacent neighborhoods in Gwembe Central. This permitted us to hold ecological variables constant, or at least to know where they differed, and we could join forces for such purposes as survey trips and obtaining supplies. Working in different neighborhoods gave us the maximum of independence and minimized the personal tensions that are bound to plague teamwork. We also became dependent on Tonga neighbors for companionship, an essential feature in good anthropological fieldwork. That we are still colleagues after forty-five years speaks to the wisdom of arranging team field research, whether short term or long term, so that each person has a large degree of independence as well as an investment in the advancement of the general study.

The subordination of our individual interests to the general project was handled by an agreement that each would provide the other with a copy of all field notes and that each had the right to publish independently using the total body of information. This agreement still stands and has worked well. Over the years we have shared ideas as we read field notes, talked, and pooled experience. Today, we frequently cannot remember who first had some productive insight or suggested the collection of new kinds of data. Although initially each was responsible for a particular aspect of the study, and this still holds true to some extent, we agreed to make notes on subjects which fell into the other's sphere; for example, Colson asked about daily diets and field types, while Scudder took note of disputes, rituals, and political meetings.

With the second phase of research in mind, we collected as much quantitative information as possible to permit us to measure the impact of resettlement using economic, demographic, and social variables. Each carried out a detailed census of one or more villages and collected the associated genealogies. The census form was adapted from one used earlier by Colson in Plateau Tonga villages (Colson 1954), and that census, in turn, was influenced (though at a good remove) by the form Clyde Kluckhohn developed in the 1930s for his long-term study of the Ramah Navajo. The census included the "core data" a social anthropologist needs even for a one-time study, but at the same time it provided a way of comparing the attributes of individuals and villages over time. The form included questions on birthplace, date of birth, clan, parents, marital history, children and siblings (including current residence), migration and work history, ownership of fields and stock, sale of farm produce (including stock), occupation, schooling, bridewealth payments, church affiliation, participation in cults, observation of food taboos, and other status attributes.

The first six months were largely devoted to work in the two Gwembe Central neighborhoods on the Zambezi River and examination of district records. Our plans for moving on after four months were thwarted by that year's high floods, which made movement up and down the Zambezi impossible. During the next six months, Scudder surveyed neighborhoods on both sides of the Zambezi to collect information on geographical features, agricultural systems, other subsistence techniques, neighborhood history, and the form of neighborhood rituals. He combined this with a continuing study of local fishing techniques as well as the colonial administration's program to train people in techniques suitable to lake fishing. Colson, while continuing work on political and legal institutions at the chieftaincy and district levels, undertook several additional intensive village studies. She first settled in the upland neighborhood of Gwembe Central originally slated to become host to one or the other of the two Zambezi neighborhoods, but subsequently relocated to the Lusitu area. Thereafter, she spent three months in two Zambezi neighborhoods in Mwemba Chieftaincy, Gwembe South. Time ran out before she could move to an upland neighborhood in Mwemba. Throughout the year, we also spent many hours at the district headquarters, copying annual reports and other files and talking with administrative and technical officers about resettlement and development plans.

By September 1957 much remained undone, but we had enough data to write descriptive accounts of Gwembe life prior to resettlement (Colson 1960, 1962, 1963; Scudder 1962) and data that would make it possible to examine how resettlement had affected economic resources, kinship arrangements, and various other essential features.

Second and Subsequent Stages

Subsequent research builds on the work of 1956–1957, but has expanded to tackle new questions as these emerged. Colson's visit in 1960, about fifteen months after the final move—when people were still short of food and fearful of the regions into which they had been thrust—was not in the original plan but came about as a response to a request for help in finding an explanation for a large number of deaths that occurred in 1959 among those resettled in Lusitu. We both went back as planned during 1962–1963, financed by the original grant. Thereafter, we have returned when we could, financing visits through other assignments, personal and university funds, and grants from the African Committee of the Social Science Research Council/American Council of Learned Societies (SSRC/ACLS), the National Science Foundation, and the John Simon Guggenheim Memorial Foundation.

Each return visit takes us back to neighborhoods studied during 1956–1957, but, given rapid population increases and population mobility, it has proven impossible to maintain census data on all seven villages in which censuses were carried out during 1956–1957. Even maintaining censuses for the remaining four villages has become increasingly onerous. On these four villages (Mazulu, Musulumba, Sinafala, and a section of Siameja), each located in a different neighborhood, we maintain time series data on demographic, economic, and social variables. Their combined resident population in 1956–1957 was 866 men, women, and children. In 1972–1973, it had risen to 1,528. Thereafter, increase slowed due to out-migration, with approximately 2,000 recorded in 1996 (Sam Clark, personal communication).

The total number of those followed reached approximately eight thousand by 1996, because demographic and some economic information is also collected on such former residents as we are able to trace (Clark et al. 1995). So far, we have been able to obtain information on the great majority of the "ever-resident" population. We therefore can contrast migrants with residents, and village with village, and even follow villages as units through time. As the work has proceeded, we have found it advisable to devise for each village a checklist showing all who have lived within it, with enough detail for easy identification. These checklists have proved invaluable. Most people love them and feel it important that they be in "the book." Checklists are also less bulky to carry than census printouts and enable us to collect information on births, deaths, marriages, divorces, changes in residence, and present whereabouts even during a short visit—since we can run through the lists with a few knowledgeable informants from each village.

Though the checklists continue to be useful for some analytical purposes, since 1995 Sam Clark has improved computer access to existing data and designed a relational database able to deal with genealogical relationships and life history material. Currently, information is coded for sex, births, deaths, marriage, divorce, education, residence during census years, and ethnicity of spouse. The old division of work between the two of us persists. Scudder is primarily concerned with ecology (1971, 1972, 1976) and economy (1983, 1984b, 1985, 1993) and the updating of one village in Gwembe North, for which he has detailed economic information and rather precise dating for births, and so forth. Colson continues to work on political, legal, and ritual matters (1964a, 1964b, 1966, 1969, 1970a, 1970b, 1971a, 1976, 1977, 1980, 1995, 1996, 1997) and does the updates of three villages in Gwembe North, Gwembe Central, and Gwembe South, on which economic information is less detailed. This is a conscious choice. We considered the advisability of following only two villages, on which we could maintain equally rigorous information, but decided that the overall variations among the four villages are of such interest that we should try to follow all four. Whoever makes a short visit to Gwembe checks as many villages as can be reached, while detailed censuses have been carried out during longer visits.

In the 1980s, local assistants began to keep journals in which they were to record births and deaths and various incidents that interest them, from concern over rainfall to village meetings, family tensions, the holding of rituals, cases of theft, and much else. Though their journals are no substitute for systematic updating through the checklists and new questionnaires, the records tend to be accurate and so help to establish other dates and also provide a corpus of Gwembe explication of what is happening. Without such diaries, it would have been increasingly difficult to maintain the demographic records. Jonathan Habarad updated all four village censuses during 1987–1988, but the task was exhausting and constrained him from branching out into research of his own choosing. In 1995, Clark undertook to train and supervise village assistants to maintain the censuses and also to use an event-specific questionnaire that includes information on marriage payments, economic status and activity, migration, and quarterly price lists. The supervision and payment of the field assistants during study group absences creates its own problems, as does arranging to receive records. The postal service is unreliable, given frequent theft, and village people do not have bank accounts given their distance from banks. Courier service is difficult for research assistants to access.

Incorporating New Phenomena in the Study

In the mid-1960s, our interest shifted from the Gwembe's responses to relocation to their responses to citizenship in a newly independent African nation whose policies had the stated intention of upgrading the lives of its citizens. Gwembe had been involved with the outside world prior to independence in 1964, but, during the following decade with its accelerated pace of development, Gwembe residents increasingly identified themselves as citizens of Zambia and tried to adopt urban standards accepted as appropriate to "modern" Zambians. They had some success in this respect due to their increasing access to cash incomes.

Production for urban markets became feasible with the improvement in transport. Construction in the Zambian capital and along the line of rail opened up many jobs for unskilled laborers, while the increasing number of people flocking to urban centers encouraged innovators to hustle a wide range of services. The educated found white-collar jobs. Gwembe people still attempted to exploit the resources of a region, but the region had become the whole of Zambia.

During 1962–1963, Scudder made a conscious effort to track down labor migrants from Mazulu Village. It was then commonplace in anthropology to assess the impact of labor migration on home communities, but few fieldworkers at that time attempted to look at what happened to migrants and residents as their lives intertwined. Methodologically, the task is feasible if one has the time and patience to track people down. Both of us initiated work among migrants from all four villages in Lusaka and along the line of rail during 1972–1973, and Scudder has followed migrants from Mazulu even further afield.

Government expenditures on rural areas during the first years of independence diversified the Gwembe economy. In the mid-1950s, both men and women worked almost exclusively as subsistence farmers when residing in Gwembe, while men worked as unskilled migrant laborers elsewhere. By 1973, occupational specialization had expanded vastly. The Kariba Lake fishery, which had been disrupted in the 1970s by Rhodesian raids, recovered slowly in the 1980s and since then has become the Gwembe's largest single source of employment, aside from village agriculture. Today the fishery includes two major components. One is the artisanal inshore gillnet fishery exploited by over two thousand licensed fishermen during the latter half of the 1980s. The other is the capital-intensive offshore fishery based on the Kariba Lake sardine (*Limnothrissa miodon*) in which hundreds of villagers work on the fishing rigs and in the lakeside processing camps, almost all of which are in the hands of expatriates.

The coal mines in Gwembe South, first opened as a government enterprise in 1964, employed a labor force of just under nine hundred by 1973, but then numbers steadily declined as production fell until the mines became largely inactive in 1996. Many men from Gwembe South are employed in privately operated amethyst mines located just over the district line, while hundreds of men and women from Gwembe North found seasonal employment during the 1990s—growing marigolds for food coloring—with an international agribusiness firm located lower down the Zambezi. Crocodile farms in Gwembe North and Gwembe South, also operating under expatriate ownership, offer other job opportunities. The Ministry of Education, the Ministry of Rural Development, and the Gwembe Rural Council also employ hundreds of full-time personnel. The large wheat/cotton farm of the multinational Gwembe Valley Development Company, which in 1985 had dispossessed people in nine villages from much of their land, employed seasonal laborers, some landless, until it went bankrupt in the late 1990s.

Although men and women from all four Gwembe villages found employment in fisheries, mines, commercial farms, and government agencies, such developments cannot be studied adequately using *village*-based samples. Therefore, we constructed special samples to examine this kind of diversity.

In 1962, Scudder began a study of the artisanal fishery (the Zambian sardine fishery emerged after 1980), which generated a separate sample of fishermen from villages throughout the district. By 1962, it also had become apparent that an increasing number of people were employed locally. So we then devised a questionnaire circulated in various district departments to collect data on those employed in Gwembe at jobs that required some degree of literacy. Shopkeepers formed another emergent category, and we collected information on the background and ambitions of shopkeepers and their sources of funding.

As educational opportunities increased for the Gwembe, we decided to investigate what education meant in the regional and national context. In 1965, 1967, and 1970, we circulated questionnaires to students in secondary schools serving Gwembe. Our purpose was to identify individuals for future study and to discover their backgrounds, financing, and ambitions. In 1973 we began a systematic study of Gwembe secondary school leavers—defined as those who, by December 1972, had attended at least one term of secondary school. They had attended some twenty schools located in both Southern and Central Provinces. By 1976, we had a list of 518 students, whom we called "the first 500." Using a pretested schedule, we interviewed 138 of the 518 in 1973 and another 29 in 1976 and 1978 (Scudder and Colson 1980). Starting in 1997 the large majority of those still living were reinterviewed by Cliggett and Zambian assistants.

Sampling was not sophisticated. Before branching out to a wider number of schools, we first constructed a list of those who had attended the one secondary school in Gwembe District (founded on the plateau in 1962 and shifted to Gwembe Central in 1964) on the assumption that it had educated the largest number of Gwembe students. We then traced as many on the list as possible. During each interview we asked respondents to name other Gwembe secondary school leavers working in the same locale and interviewed these in turn, thus building a snowball sample. Through this means we interviewed the majority of all Gwembe secondary school leavers working in Lusaka and in Livingstone (the major city in Southern Province) and in most towns lying between them, as well as most of those currently living in Gwembe itself. We believe the sample to be representative except in two respects: it overemphasized those residing in the southern half of Zambia and also overrepresented those employed as primary school teachers, especially if they worked in Gwembe District.

Since the mid-1970s, we ourselves have not created additional samples. Work with existing samples keeps us in touch with what is happening in the district when combined with other interviews and use of available records. During October 1990, for example, through interviewing individuals in the village or the fishery samples, Scudder was able to follow up on the development of the artisanal and *kapenta* fisheries, migration from inland areas and the Lusitu to the Kariba Lake foreshore, and participation in new development projects. In the

1990s, the three newcomers to the study (Clark, Cliggett, and Gillett-Netting) created samples of their own for studies they are undertaking on nutritional status, demography, migration, and the elderly.

The extension of the Gwembe study to urban migrants, to secondary school leavers, and to other elites who do not base themselves in villages, helped us to visualize the Gwembe population as belonging to a national and even international system. As a result, we do not find useful such concepts as "encapsulation," "compartmentalization," "rural-urban continuum," and "lagging emulation." As we have written elsewhere, villagers are no less "modern" (or "postmodern") than their urban kin or, for that matter, any other urban residents (Colson and Scudder 1975).

People move between town and country. In the early 1960s, fishermen on Kariba Lake sold their fish fresh at the lakeside, a practice favored by a number of factors including pricing and location of markets. By the 1970s, the comparative economic advantage lay with those fishermen who sold dried fish in the towns. The smarter fishermen soon realized this and transported and sold their catch to urban markets. Similarly, cotton farmers travel to the line of rail to cash their checks and make purchases, while the most profitable way to sell Gwembe tobacco is to hawk it as snuff in urban centers. When transport was readily available between 1964 and the mid-1970s, cotton farmers in Gwembe North realized that they could save on transport and service costs by shipping privately to the central ginnery in Lusaka rather than by selling through the government marketing system. They booked for the return trip the otherwise empty vehicles of wholesalers bringing goods to Gwembe stores—a mutually beneficial arrangement for everyone.

Small traders and business operators vary their efforts between rural and urban contexts. Men and women traders transport fish, chickens, and vegetables to markets on the railway line, and they readily shift their investments to where they hope to realize the most lucrative return. For example, one Gwembe businessman first worked as a fisherman and then used his savings to pioneer the hamburger business in Lusaka. From its profits, he built a fourteen-room house in a low-income suburb in Lusaka and then rented out most of its rooms. With further profits, he opened two shops in Gwembe North, leaving his Lusaka ventures in the hands of trusted kin. When the profits from his shops dwindled after the mid-1970s, he switched to commercial farming of cotton and hybrid maize.

Families explore the varied possibilities of town and country. Young married women often spend the dry season with husbands in town and cultivate village lands during the rains. They may give birth in town hospitals or, if in the village, in local health centers. Children are exchanged between town and country, often to obtain school places. Older men and women settled in the village may visit the towns several times a year, and some plan to move to live with urban-based children. They consult African doctors and diviners in urban areas and are treated in urban hospitals. Those residing in the rural area do not differ from urban kin in their general awareness of national politics, their consumption preferences, their willingness to utilize both Western and African medicines, their association with Christian churches, their explanations of misfortune, or their attachment to soccer. They listen to the same radio programs (and in 1994 three residents of one village purchased television sets, a harbinger of things to come). All this is evidence that we are looking at a single universe and that the choices being made, and the events that flow from them, relate to that totality.

By the mid-1980s, the Gwembe universe expanded through personal explorations and became increasingly international: at least one person from each of the four neighborhoods within which the sample villages are sited had lived for a time in Europe, North America, Asia, or Australia. The merging of Gwembe people into the wider national and international community is probably irreversible, though the terms on which this happens are anything but fixed. In the 1990s, economic conditions discouraged urban migration. At the same time, those who had been able to move up into the national elite during the period of postindependence expansion have become more remote from their rural backgrounds. Their children are even more remote. Entry into secondary and tertiary education is becoming more difficult for village children, as places are monopolized by children from elite families and from urban schools with more resources. We saw this as likely to happen, even though we were impressed in the early 1970s by the openness of Gwembe and Zambian society. We were cautious enough to write, "conditions can change again. Mobility may become restricted, both geographically and socially, by a shrinking economy and the consolidation of an elite class. Children born and reared in town in time may differ from their rural cousins" (Scudder and Colson 1980:240). Conditions did indeed change even as we were writing with the onset of economic decline in the mid-1970s.

The expansion of the Gwembe universe has been a research challenge (Colson and Kottak 1996). It has led to a reallocation of field time to cover many more bases, which means reduced time for informal contacts and participant observation. With independence, the Zambian government dismantled the old system of administration that channeled technical and administrative information through district offices. Though administrative and technical activities subsequently were centralized again at the district level, district offices do not yet produce a comprehensive annual report containing statistics (however dubious) on population, livestock, stock and crop sales, trading licenses, schools and attendance, health, court hearings, rainfall, and a general comment on the state of the district. Obtaining such information since 1964 involves time-consuming visits to various ministries in Lusaka or their local branches situated in several towns in Southern Province, and now also to three district headquarters rather than one. The national census is a new resource, but the information it provides is limited.

Since 1973, Gwembe has become a target area for various international donors, each with its own particular program and administrative locale, which may or may not publish studies prepared for it (e.g., Bakewell 1993; Brandt et al.

1973; Copestake 1990; Crowley 1985; Gsanger et al. 1986; Kamwanga 1997; Kasimona and Musiwa 1997; Klausen 1987; Milimo 1988; Mudenda 1990; Mwanza 1997; Njobu, Kasuta, and Siamwiza 1997; Simweemba 1989; Wood and Nachengwa 1985; Zambezi River Authority 1997). The great gain is that research by both Zambian and other scholars now complements our own (e.g., Banda 1985; Bredt 1980; Haantobolo 1990; Jarman 1968; Kasonde 1991; Ulrich Luig 1992, 1997; Ute Luig 1992, 1993a, 1993b, 1995a, 1995b, 1996, 1999; Matthews 1976, 1978, 1981, 1988; Reynolds 1968; Mukwena 1998; Price 1998; Siamwiza 1993; Tremmel and the River Tonga People 1994; Zaucha 1998). We do not have to try to do everything.

Some Theoretical Results of the Gwembe Study

Theoretical Considerations

Many revisits to Gwembe have taught us that anthropology, while more complicated than we once thought, is also more exciting. Its subject matter—and here we state our theoretical bias—is people making decisions through time in contexts which change both because of their own actions and because external conditions change in ways which neither they nor we are able to anticipate. Much of anthropology is still tied to system concepts derived from biology and the physical sciences, even though we chaff against them and criticize them. A major reason for this problem is that the most common type of fieldwork still centers on a single slice of time. This predisposes the use of terms and concepts that emphasize static as opposed to dynamic relationships and stresses integration as opposed to flux.

Gwembe Tonga are involved in dynamic sets of interrelationships that are situationally responsive. A major finding of our research has been the frequency with which people experiment, assess gains and losses, and decide whether to continue. People weigh their options and make choices, and then justify them if need be. While at any one time only a small number of households may be involved in innovation, many innovate over the long term. Between 1956 and 1994, a majority of the households in the sample innovated on one or more occasions.

On the other hand, Gwembe conceptual frames are resilient, perhaps because actual behavior can always be explained as due to special circumstances. However much exposed to education, church indoctrination, and urban influences, Gwembe people continue to emphasize the importance of matrilineal kin and to invoke witchcraft to explain most ills. In the mid-1970s, when a decline in living standards led to an increase in malnutrition and illness and to general unhappiness, the majority opted to blame the witchcraft of kin and neighbors rather than government policies. Witchcraft has been a possible explanation for misfortune throughout the research period, but in the early years open accusations were relatively infrequent, probably because accusers could be reported to colonial authorities and punished under the "witchcraft ordinance" (Colson 1966).

Beliefs about witchcraft are based on an entrenched view that humans, especially senior men, are strongly motivated by ambition, envy, and malice; and that, in their search for advantage, they are willing to sacrifice others, even close kin. Hardships associated with increasing economic differentiation at the village level activate suspicions. By the early 1980s, witchcraft had become the principal explanation for misfortunes, whether it be sickness of people or livestock, poor crop yields, or other adverse outcomes. In the early 1980s, every neighborhood in Gwembe summoned at least one "witch-finder," and in most neighborhoods almost every senior man was accused of being a witch and was forced to pay to be cleansed (Colson 2000).

In the 1980s and 1990s, witch finding became endemic in Gwembe, as elsewhere in Zambia. Witchcraft beliefs, however, have changed over the decades to accommodate the wider world within which Gwembe people operate. In 1956, witches could only affect those near at hand; by 1973, they were accused of traveling hundreds of miles in a second on magic horses and airplanes. In the early decades of our study, witches were kin, neighbors, or fellow workmates, all persons intimately involved with their victims. By the 1970s, they might be strangers out to drain the life force from victims to the benefit of powerful contenders for economic and political power. By the 1990s, stories circulated that gangs operating under a European or Indian boss were extracting organs for export to Europe and America to meet the demand for organ transplants, a practice labeled as witchcraft. Thus, Gwembe people now see both their life force (verbalized as the ability to work) and their bodies as being exploited by powerful national and international others who—like local magnates—are seen as eager to benefit from the misery of others.

To protect themselves against witchcraft or simply to empower themselves, Gwembe men continue to purchase medicines, usually from town-based practitioners. Women, who have less cash and less access to such medicines, are more likely to strengthen themselves through membership in healing cults. Such cults teach people how to deal with alien spirits who seize control of one's body and how to cope with the demons now said to be inherent in their own nature. These cults have continued to proliferate through the decades of the study, though the nature of the alien spirits usually reflects the particular fears of the moment (Ute Luig 1995b, 1999). Some of the cults draw on the teaching of Pentecostal churches. Fear of witchcraft and the envy associated with it—along with the increased consumption of alcoholic beverages and associated violence and a high incidence of theft, especially in hunger years—contributes to village disorganization and to the breakup of villages, whose coherence is already made difficult by a lack of land for expansion and by the expansion of their populations beyond traditional organizational frameworks. It also shifts much of the hostility engendered by failed government policies back into the home community and away from those officials responsible for making and carrying out policy.

Still, it would be a mistake to assume that social malaise will continue to evoke the same explanations and solutions to perceived problems. By the mid-1980s,

Gwembe Tonga had begun to revive old crafts to replace the factory-made goods no longer available or affordable. They experimented with a reordering of local government, using the village development committees instituted by government as a model (Habarad 1988), and elected committees to organize various activities they now deem necessary. The search for new spiritual support and the prominence of new churches are two other manifestations of the desire for change (Ulrich Luig 1997). In 1965, less than 5 percent of the population of Gwembe District identified itself as Christian; by 1988 over half of those living along Kariba Lake in Gwembe North did so (Copestake 1990). During the 1990s, people in the sample villages turned increasingly to Christianity and refused to participate in rituals and ceremonies they called "heathen." Conceptual frameworks may be resistant to change, but they are cultural constructs and so by definition are changeable.

The Formulation of Relocation Theory

The Gwembe study played a major role in developing a better theoretical understanding of the implications of compulsory resettlement, a development with which Scudder has been particularly concerned (Scudder 1966, 1973a, 1973b, 1975, 1997a, 1997b; Scudder and Colson 1982; Colson 1971b). His participation, during 1961–1962, in the study of the Nubian people of Egypt who were soon to be displaced by the Aswan High Dam scheme provided one basis for comparison with what happened in Gwembe. In the middle 1960s, he visited the Volta and Kainji Dam Projects in Ghana and Nigeria, which together displaced over 125,000 people. By then he had come to the conclusion that rural communities undergoing compulsory resettlement respond in the same general fashion irrespective of their sociocultural backgrounds and the policies of resettlement authorities, a conclusion later validated by a large number of studies. This led to the formulation of what he has called Relocation Theory.

Initially, because of the paucity of longitudinal studies, Relocation Theory dealt only with the years immediately preceding relocation, the process of physical removal, and the difficult period following removal, when people respond to the extreme stress associated with resettlement. In coping with this stress, the majority behave *as if* they saw sociocultural systems as closed systems. They cling to familiar people and familiar institutions, changing during the initial years following resettlement no more than necessary to come to terms with the new habitat and its inhabitants. Presumably because the level of stress is close to a critical threshold, radical changes from within (revitalization movements, for example) and from without (including attempts at social engineering by development planners) are rejected.

Records of Gwembe Tonga responses at different periods provided the empirical basis for initial theory formulation. In 1956–1957, we did not pay enough attention to indications that the threatened resettlement was already having an impact, nor did we arrange to observe what happened during the move. At that time, people did not seem particularly preoccupied by the threat of removal; many proceeded on the assumption that it would not occur. Even headmen who had been taken to the dam site built new homesteads at the old site in 1957, though they had been told that the move would take place within the year. We now recognize that they were adopting a strategy of denial, a common response to threat.

Our observations and Tonga comments during 1962–1963 made it clear that relocation involved multidimensional stress which began to diminish only in 1963, approximately four to five years after the move (Colson 1971b). By then, most people were economically on their feet; indeed, for many, material standards had improved. Full funeral ceremonials, greatly curtailed immediately after resettlement, reappeared. Personal and lineage shrines were rebuilt or newly initiated. Prophets were again active. The continued absence of communal rituals associated with a sense of belonging to a locale, however, pointed to a continued uncertainty about their future in the new areas. Despite this, the good harvest of 1963 reconciled many people to the new sites. Scudder hypothesized that at this stage (indicated by renewed self-sufficiency and familiarity with new habitat and hosts), people should begin to experiment with new possibilities that might lead to a period of rapid socioeconomic change. In fact, the rate of innovation is probably higher than before the move (cf. Barnett 1953). This would be due partly to increased confidence arising from the knowledge that they had survived the trauma of resettlement, partly to recognition of new opportunities, and partly due to a loosening of previous cultural constraints on innovation. Gwembe resistance to innovation during the early years of resettlement, however, represented at least in part a subversive protest against those who had displaced and humiliated them. The willingness to innovate evident during 1962–1963 was affected by the triumphant sense of empowerment shared by Africans throughout the country when the 1962 election spelled the demise of European control and the installment of an African-dominated government.

The relocation process, if it is to provide long-term benefits, involves four stages: the recruitment stage, the adjustment or the coping stage, the stage of potential socioeconomic development, and the final handing over/incorporation stage—with the entire process taking at least two generations (Scudder and Colson 1982). The same sequence of stages has been observed both in sponsored land settlement schemes of voluntary settlers and in spontaneous land settlement areas (Scudder 1984a, 1991).

Relocation Theory obviously has policy implications. As a consultant for the Bandama River Authority in the Ivory Coast in the late 1960s, Scudder made a number of policy recommendations based on the theory. More recently, it has been incorporated into the World Bank's guidelines for bank-financed projects that involve dislocation of populations (World Bank 1980; Cernea 1988), while the study of phenomena associated with involuntary resettlement has become a subfield of social science (DeWet 1993; Cernea and Guggenheim 1993; Cernea 1999; Cernea and McDowell 2000).

Contribution of the Study to the People of Gwembe

Some Gwembe people involved in the study have come to see our function in life to be the maintenance of their demographic histories. They even ask who will undertake that task when we are too old to carry on. Some have seen our publications and are pleased that they are known in Europe and America. Three books and one monograph were published through the Institute for African Studies (now the Institute for Economic and Social Research) to ensure that they were available within Zambia. Unfortunately, the Institute has lacked funds to keep them in print although all royalties were given to the University of Zambia and the Institute to further research in Zambia. Financial restraints on publication in Zambia have forced us to publish our last two books elsewhere and the only copies in Zambia are those we have sent to various agencies, to colleagues, and to some chiefs, headmen, and villagers. We have made a point of sending reprints of articles published in journals and books to the University of Zambia, as well as to interested persons in Gwembe and elsewhere.

It is difficult to point to more specific contributions to the welfare of Gwembe. Like many other anthropologists, we have made gifts in cash and kind, including assistance with school costs; or provided various services while in residence, such as obtaining information, dispensing medical supplies, or providing transportation. We do not know how to assess the impact of various consultancies we have undertaken in Gwembe: Scudder for FAO in 1967; Colson, M. E. D. Scudder, and T. Scudder for the Gossner Service Team in 1982; Habarad for the Gossner Service Team in 1988; Scudder for Harvest Help/Zambia in 1990; and Scudder for the World Bank in 1995 and 1996. Nor do we know how to assess the impact of Scudder's (1986) critique of the multinational Gwembe Valley Development Company.

Although Fosbrooke hoped the findings from 1956–1957 would influence the planning of resettlement, we were not asked to provide a written report or give formal advice. Informally, district officers and technical officers probed for what might be useful to them, but at the time neither they nor we thought us to be experts on resettlement. We could make predictions about the probable outcomes of certain proposed actions, based on the first year of study and anthropological precepts. Fortunately, it was accepted that we talk in general terms. Neither then nor later has either of us been expected to discuss the actions of individuals, nor would we do so if asked.

We could tell officials that their plan to move social units rather than individuals was in accord with anthropological theory, but that in Gwembe the significant social units were neighborhoods rather than villages. We urged that neighborhoods be moved as units and emphasized the recurrent plea of villagers that, if they must move, they be allowed to move inland along the tributaries about whose deltas they clustered. Old ties of kinship and friendship with those living along the tributary would ease their adjustment to a new region. We pointed out that fear of resettlement was exacerbated when people were asked to move to an unfamiliar area. With reference to the future lake fishery, we assured district personnel that Gwembe men were good fishermen given existing conditions and could be expected to adopt techniques for successful lake fishing, though they would need training and capitalization (Scudder 1960). We doubted, however, that they would operate any enterprise requiring the cooperation of a large number of men over time, given the individualistic nature of Gwembe work organization. We also questioned official optimism that expected the fishing industry to compensate people for the loss of arable soils. We predicted that a future crisis would occur when the first round of shifting cultivation had exhausted soils and new fields were not available. We queried the method of computing compensation for destruction of homesteads that placed a value only on the dwellings.

We had no hesitation in querying official plans to allocate land in resettlement areas on a per capita basis to males on the tax rolls. We stressed that both men *and women* owned land. We had no evidence that chiefs were regarded as custodians of the lands of a people who, for the most part, regarded chiefs as government officials rather than hereditary rulers. It seemed unlikely that people would take kindly to any allocation of land by chiefs or district officers; in fact, they refused to do so.

Finally, we were skeptical of the officials' belief that neighborhood shrines could be transferred to resettlement areas. Our observations had shown that these shrines represented not the communities that were moving but rather the relationship of these communities to particular known physical environments—thus, the shrines were the media through which communities tried to influence natural forces impinging on their particular locality. We not only expected that shrine custodians would lose their office, but also thought that both ritual and political leaders would be undermined by their failure to counter the government's demand that people move.

For the most part, officials disregarded our comments, either because they were helpless to change plans formulated at higher levels or because they thought us misinformed. Three of the five neighborhoods in our original study suffered disruption. We did not make a follow-up study of one neighborhood which moved as a unit; the other seemed the most contented by the mid-1960s of the four neighborhoods we continued to follow. Those that were moved inland along their own tributary found initial adjustment easier than those moved to unfamiliar terrain. People resented not being compensated for granaries and other homestead structures, as we had predicted, but we had not realized in 1957 how much strain the method of compensation would place on family relationships (Colson 1971b).

Scudder's work on fishing seems to have been influential in the decision to restrict commercial fishing on the Zambian side of Kariba Lake to Gwembe Tonga initially, and the early success of the fisheries is evidence of the rightness of the prediction that they would take to lake fishing. Furthermore, as we had predicted, the government was unsuccessful in trying to introduce larger units than the traditional workgroup composed of a single fisherman joined by a few relatives and hired hands (Scudder and Habarad 1991).

Our predictions with respect to land allocation were also borne out. People disregarded attempts to parcel out new fields on a per capita basis, so the attempt was abandoned. Following resettlement, we were struck by the continuity in the formal rules of land tenure even though resettlement for the moment revolutionized land holdings and the rights of cultivators to dispose of their holdings have varied greatly over the years. Immediately after resettlement, when everyone was cultivating newly cleared land, individual freedom to dispose of land was at a maximum. Thereafter, as the original cultivators died and their rights were inherited, land again became subject to lineage claims that compromised the freedom of the holder. Major fluctuations in actual rights can therefore take place without anyone raising questions about the advisability of reformulating rules of tenure (Colson 1967). People query particular claims rather than the system itself. In the 1990s, however, they were faced with a radical change in the Zambian law of inheritance, which provides for inheritance of a portion of an estate by spouses and children as opposed to matrilineal kin who, however, still try to demand the lion's share. At the beginning of a new century, they are facing an even more radical change as government policy now privileges the privatizing of land through survey and the issuance of formal title. With land increasingly being treated as a commodity, we fear that many will lose their holdings.

We predicted that resettlement would change the informal power structure of neighborhoods when the land base was destroyed. During 1956–1957, power was diffuse but linked to land ownership. Men with the biggest holdings of inherited alluvial soils were usually well off in food and livestock, which gave them influence over others. They could afford to marry a number of wives who not only did much of the agricultural work but also prepared food for guests. More wives meant more children and, since much of a girl's bridewealth was taken by her father, more wealth. When people were moved, the old land base which supported wealth differentials was eliminated, at least for the time being, for everyone had an equal chance to claim land in the new region. We thought it likely that younger men able to undertake the physical labor of land clearance would emerge as the dominant members of the community, while older men, deprived of their principal asset, would be reduced in status. The experience of many seniors bore this out, but we had not counted sufficiently on the importance of personal ability. Middle-aged men who had influence in 1956–1957 usually succeeded in reestablishing themselves by mobilizing a variety of assets to ensure that they obtained large fields of the best soils available. Young men, in fact, did improve their situation vis-à-vis their elders in the 1960s and early 1970s on account of the abundance of wage labor and the availability of land. One result was that they married earlier and the polygyny rate temporarily went up; another was that they established themselves in a position to become the dominant elders of the 1980s and 1990s. As conditions deteriorated during the latter part of the 1970s and the 1980s, still younger men were not able to follow their example. Polygyny rates fell, although that small percentage of elders who had the capital and energy to develop as cash-crop farmers on a substantial scale increased their labor force by marrying more wives.

We predicted that local shrines could not be moved. The district officers tried anyway; poles from the shrines were attached to the lorries that transported people to new sites in 1958 to leave a drag trail for the spirits to follow. But it was ten years later, after people had become familiar with their new habitats, that the first shrines were reestablished. Even twenty years later, many were skeptical of their authenticity, and, if they addressed themselves to any shrine, they preferred shrines associated with their hosts in the relocation area. Then the spread of Christian sects further undermined belief in the efficacy of such shrines.

A further prediction, borne out during 1962–1963, concerned the demise of the ritual office of shrine custodian who officiated over rituals associated with the annual cycle. We argued that since the office—like the shrine—was tied to a locality, it would be discredited when the spirits associated with the office failed to protect their people against forcible removal. Shrine custodians, or their heirs, became ritually active again only ten years later when shrines were rebuilt, but have never regained the status they held back in 1956. We also expected resettlement to discredit the political order created by the colonial administration and co-opted by the administration as an agent for resettlement. By 1957 it was already regarded as an enemy. Antagonism to chiefs, headmen, and officers of the Rural Council persisted through the 1960s. Indeed, by the 1960s, the majority of Gwembe people opposed the whole colonial hierarchy and gave their loyalty to the political party (ANC) that had protested the building of Kariba Dam and their removal. Resettlement gave people a vital interest in national politics but also left them highly suspicious of government's intentions. The majority appear to have accepted the replacement of the traditional system of local governance, based on chiefs and headmen, by the party system imposed under the single-party regime of the 1970s and 1980s, though after the 1991 demise of the one-party state and the party as an organ of local governance they accommodated the reemergence of the old hierarchy of chiefs and headmen.

Gwembe people ask what is the point of our research when they see no improvement in their own lives. After Zambian independence, the new regime was even less likely to be interested in our findings than were colonial officials. The formulation of Relocation Theory has *not* helped Gwembe or its people. Furthermore, we have yet to see a case where World Bank guidelines for dealing with forced relocation, and plans derived from those guidelines, have actually been implemented with favorable results for the majority (Scudder 1993). Therefore, let us state the case bluntly: involuntary community resettlement is never an appropriate development strategy. Furthermore, we remain skeptical that governments have either the financial ability or the political will to provide the extended, multiyear funding required for a successful resettlement program or for ameliorating the long-term problems associated with resettlements already in place.

A much belated test of this will be the ability of the Zambian government to move forward with the World Bank and the Development Bank of Southern Africa (DBSA) on a program for the rehabilitation of Gwembe to ensure that, at last, they benefit from Kariba Dam and its electricity. Beginning in 1995, Scudder was closely involved in interesting World Bank personnel in the need for such a project and in urging the bank to recognize its obligations, as one of the original financial backers of the dam, to carry out this project. He was also involved in setting up the Zambian study group that made specific recommendations for rehabilitation (Kamwanga and Njobvu 1997) and has advised on technical matters associated with the project and its implementation. Finally, the project was inaugurated in December 1998, with the Zambian Electricity Supply Corporation as the implementing agency. Progress has been slow for a variety of reasons, including a land mine explosion that killed a project consultant and funding delays from DBSA. Major goals include renovating the road system that linked Gwembe North to Gwembe South during the resettlement years, bringing electricity for schools and for irrigated agriculture, improving flood recession agriculture and grazing along the lakeshore, upgrading the village water supply, and meeting other special needs both within Gwembe and in the plateau area where so many have been driven by land hunger back home in Gwembe.

The Future of the Study

In 2001, the study is in its forty-fifth year. Its continuation depends on how satisfactorily we—and our new colleagues—can handle a number of increasingly serious problems.

Given the turmoil that besets so much of the world, maintaining a long-term study is always problematic: virtually any area of fieldwork may be placed out of bounds or the people dispersed in flight. Gwembe has been less seriously affected by such turmoil than many study areas, although, in 1978, at the height of the Rhodesian war, Colson could not visit any of the four villages, all of which were in the war zone. Fortunately, it was possible to interview migrants who had settled elsewhere. In the 1980s, as a result of the war, guns became readily available and armed robbery increased greatly. During 1987–1988, Habarad had to take precautions in one of the villages against being robbed. Gwembe was not as safe in the 1980s and 1990s as it was in 1956–1957 when the project began. So far, however, this has minimally affected the way in which we work.

Nor have we found it difficult to get permission to return, although some countries recurrently place barriers in the way of outside social scientists. We have suffered only the usual delays in receiving research permits. We do not have to spend time establishing our bona fides with district authorities and chiefs. In Zambia, we are known as scholars who have a commitment to the country and its people. The Institute of Economic and Social Research, the major center for social science research in Zambia, always provides us with both a home base and a warm welcome.

Funding has not been a problem, perhaps because a long-term study is relatively economical. Equipment can be stored in situ, and the time needed to obtain significant results on each visit is reduced. Over forty-five years, external funding of fieldwork for both of us (including travel, salaries, vehicles, field assistants, and supplies) has amounted to about $600,000; however, this has been possible because on occasion we accepted field salaries well below our regular salaries. Other times we have taken no salaries at all, and sometimes have paid other expenses, including for field assistants. Costs associated with write-up, including that for research assistance, have been supported partially by our universities, but also by grants from NSF, NIH, and the John Simon Guggenheim Memorial Foundation, and by our own funds. We have been prepared to help finance the study because we are interested in what we are learning. We also recognize that research must be published in some form or it is useless.

The problems we have encountered are primarily associated with the burden of maintaining the quantitative database and the difficulties of synthesizing an enormous body of material. We also continue to be concerned with how to recruit and incorporate colleagues who will be able to continue the study (see Cliggett, in this volume).

Data Collection and Analysis

As a long-term study progresses, fieldwork becomes easier because one is familiar with the area and the people and can plunge immediately into the situation. Familiarity, however, also makes for difficulties.

After several return visits, the initial excitement of discovery wanes. Recording much the same kind of information to maintain the quantitative base becomes drudge work. Most discovery occurs while analyzing trends back in the study rather than in the field. Nevertheless, fieldwork also continues to be rewarding as former mysteries are cleared up or a stray comment opens up whole new fields for exploration. There are also new things to observe, though we admit that we find soccer matches less enthralling than the old Drum Team competitions even though women continue to sing comparably scurrilous songs against opposing teams.

Tunnel vision is also a risk when so much time is devoted to one area. We try to avoid this by working in other regions and by reading widely. Other professional commitments sometimes conflict with the optimum timing of return visits. Where accurate dating is essential to determine sequencing, visits at short intervals are advisable. Ideally, one or the other of us should have visited Gwembe at least every two years since 1956–1957, but such a schedule allows little time for that essential element in research called write-up. It is the process of writing that generates new ideas which we then test back in Gwembe. It also allows us to share results with colleagues, and no research is valuable until it is shared.

Maintaining the village censuses has been especially onerous, due both to the geographical mobility of the population and to the increasing heterogeneity of Gwembe life. If it is not to dominate completely the study, we need to delimit a smaller sample for continued intensive study or rely more on local assistants for recording census data.

Collecting data is one thing; analysis is quite another. Whether we deal with quantitative or qualitative information, the size of the database is a challenge in itself. For quantitative material, through 1965 we were able to rely upon hand sorting. Much of what we collected in those years was tabulated and published (Colson 1960, 1966, 1971b; Scudder 1962; Scudder and Colson 1971). Thereafter, coding of the time series demographic data preempted a good deal of our time before Ben Clark could undertake his analysis. Handling data on field size and use as well as on the nature of environmental degradation has lagged until recently. Though Scudder measured the fields cultivated by Mazulu people in the 1950s, 1960s, 1970s, and 1980s, the increasing time requirement stopped further measurement until 2000 when Clark was able to remeasure all fields and, using computerized equipment, place them in an overall mosaic. Scudder also obtained several sets of aerial photographs that show changes in area cultivated in all four of the neighborhoods that include our most-studied villages. Since 1995, we have begun working with Eric Lambin and Carine Petit at the Catholic University of Louvain who have acquired remote-sensing images from 1986, 1992, and 1997 for the Lusitu area, where two of our four sample villages were relocated. Complemented by our time series of aerial photographs dating back to 1948, the data are available to show the relationship between land use and environmental degradation (Petit, Scudder, and Lambin 2001).

For an analysis of Gwembe economic behavior, we need an index of goods and services purchased by Gwembe Tonga. Bridewealth payments, for instance, have increased dramatically over the past forty years and are good indicators of how village elders perceive, react to, and create inflationary pressures. We are uncertain how to proceed with the index, however, given changes through time in Tonga preferences, on the one hand, and the frequent changes in the value of the national currency on the other. An indication of the inflation since the early 1960s is apparent from these figures: in 1964, US$1.00 exchanged for 0.50 Zambian kwacha; in 1986, for 2.20 kwacha; in 1987, at the time of the fiscal crisis, for 21 kwacha; in 1993 for 411 kwacha; in 1996, for 987 kwacha; and during Colson's most recent visit (June 2001), for more than 3,000 kwacha.

Deciding what to code and how to code it still leaves someone to deal with the mechanics of the job. Coding and cleaning data take an enormous amount of time. Hiring students as coders has not worked. They are unfamiliar with the material, have no knowledge of the region to make the work interesting, and make too many mistakes. Finally, working initially with Jonathan Habarad and more recently with Sam Clark, we recorded and cleaned all demographic data collected through 1996, a task which drastically reduced time available for other work.

An initial attempt to rely on computer analysis failed because of the limitations of a new experimental software system. So we decided to start again, this time using conventional computer software. In 1987, Douglas White (University of California, Irvine) brought his considerable expertise in computer programs to the Gwembe data. This collaboration both renewed our enthusiasm and enhanced the data processing. We were also able to enlist the interest of James Lee, a historical demographer at the California Institute of Technology, who worked with Sam Clark in the first analysis of the demographic data (Clark et al. 1995), while we continued to code the information they required and provided them with background historical and ethnographic information. We are also working with White in adding selected categories of socioeconomic data to the demographic time series database, and are supplying him with background genealogical information that can be used for purposes of kinship analysis. The intention is that eventually all coded information will be available, via an electronic journal or at least in electronic form, to other scholars.

Writing has its own problems endemic to publication through time. Readers of a new article cannot be assumed to be familiar with the project or the region, yet it is tedious for us to supply each time the same background information before turning to the current focus of interest. Writing is also difficult because no filing system copes with the changing interest of fieldworkers or their need to examine complex sets of data; relevant information is scattered through the voluminous field notes accumulated over time. Information has to be assembled and then somehow processed through one brain. Computers can retrieve, compare, and compute, but they are no substitute for a thinking anthropologist.

Protection of those whose lives are described concerns any ethnographer. This concern is compounded when one is writing about those followed through time, since one learns much about them that they might prefer to forget. There is also the risk of exposing them to retaliation by those in authority. Gwembe survival techniques include much that may be defined by government authorities as illegal. Therefore, we have written very little about such activities as poaching, smuggling, growth and sale of cannabis, and involvement in the trade in illicit gemstones, although this gives a lopsided view of Gwembe economy. We have also had to think carefully about how local critiques and subversive tactics against the larger system should be handled. We usually allow for a considerable time lag before publishing on such matters. We are also concerned about open access to our field notes and village diaries; inevitably, these are filled with what we call "unexpurgated gossip," which needs to be handled with care if people are to be protected.

We have tried to publish research results regularly, though this is now less easy. It was easy to envisage the first year's work as complete in itself. We were to describe what we found in 1956–1957 and did so in books on the social organization and ecology of the Gwembe Tonga (Colson 1960; Scudder 1962). Subsequent research through 1965 could be envisioned as dealing with uprooting and resettlement (Colson 1971b). Since then we have had to deal with a lengthening time span as we look at the continuing responses of Gwembe people to economic and political changes reflecting the dominance of international institutions. Two major studies deal with the impact of educational policies in the development of a new elite (Scudder and Colson 1980) and the increasing dominance of Gwembe life by drinking patterns associated with the commodification of beer (Colson and Scudder 1988). Articles, or chapters in books, have dealt with such topics as Gwembe economic history, the Kariba Lake fishery, relationships between Gwembe and the line of rail, land tenure, changes in adjudication patterns, the growth of ethnic politics, the resilience of matriliny, gendered responses to change, aging, the adaptive role of possession cults as people encounter new threats to their sense of identity, witchcraft, and more. We plan two further major full-length studies. One will deal with how Tonga religious concepts and ritual practices changed throughout the twentieth century as society diversified and old certainties were undermined. The other will deal with the socioeconomic history of the Gwembe Tonga from 1900 to 2000. While Colson will be the principal author of the first study and Scudder of the second, both monographs will be collaborative efforts.

Integrating New Colleagues

It is difficult to maintain a longitudinal study of this scope with a team of only two anthropologists, a fact we recognized long ago.

Since the 1960s, we have tried to enlist others in the study. Chet S. Lancaster was persuaded to work among the Goba, a Gwembe North chieftaincy that we had been unable to study (Lancaster 1966, 1971, 1974a, 1974b, 1977, 1981, 1987). In 1969, we solicited social scientists at the University of Zambia to use our core database in their own research and, during 1972–1973, included funds for Zambian consultants in our NSF grant. While Zambian colleagues were too involved in other commitments to take up the challenge, during the 1980s a number of them used some of our material in doctoral dissertations (Banda 1985; Mukwena 1998); and John Milimo, director of the Rural Development Studies Bureau in the University of Zambia, consulted with us in writing several reports on Gwembe (Milimo 1988).

During 1987–1988 Jonathan Habarad, a recent Berkeley Ph.D., spent fifteen months in Gwembe with NSF funding. Later, for personal reasons, partially stemming from the difficulties of taking over an ongoing study as complex as the Gwembe study in an area where living conditions were difficult, he decided not to return to Gwembe. In 1991 Michael Bollig of the University of Cologne, Carlos and Sarah Madrid (then students at Johns Hopkins), and Sam Clark (a student at the California Institute of Technology) visited Gwembe, but only Clark was able to make a commitment to the area and the study. He, Lisa Cliggett, and Rhonda Gillett-Netting were associated with us in what we saw as a "gradual handing over of field work" grant—a three-year NSF grant ending in July 1998. Clark recently completed a Ph.D. in demography at the University of Pennsylvania (2001) based on his own research within Gwembe (forthcoming) and the demographic data we have been able to supply him. Gillett-Netting, now on the faculty at the University of Arizona, was in Gwembe in 1993 for Ph.D. dissertation research in biological anthropology, on nutrition and growth (Gillett 1995b), for Indiana University. She included two of the Gwembe villages in her study and has revisited Gwembe for further work (Gillett 1995a, 1995b, 1996, 1997, 1998; Gillett and Tobias, in press). Cliggett's 1994–1995 research on changing family support systems for the elderly, based on one of our four sample villages, led to her dissertation (Cliggett 1997b) and several articles on their way to being published (2002, n.d.-a, n.d.-b, n.d.-c). Currently a member of the anthropology department at the University of Kentucky, she too has revisited Gwembe and is now concentrating on migrants and their continued relationship to Gwembe (1997a, 2000). All three have access to our field notes. We are experimenting with computer scanning of field notes so that they will be more easily accessible. This, however, is a mammoth task. Although we all still need to work out how to handle collaboration over time, it may well be that the problem of continuity is at last solved.

We are also exploring the archiving of field notes and associated materials in the Bancroft Library at the University of California, Berkeley, and at the California Institute of Technology. We also continue hoping to integrate Zambian colleagues into the study (Scudder and Colson 1968), with a serious possibility being Bennett Siamwiza, himself a member of a relocated Gwembe family and now a lecturer in history at the University of Zambia with a Ph.D. in history from Cambridge University.

Some Meanings to the Anthropologist of Long-Term Involvement

Long-term research has personal costs. We have already mentioned the possibility of developing tunnel vision.

Again, while much of the Middle Zambezi Valley is beautiful, living conditions for an anthropologist are arduous, especially since the mid-1970s and especially in the densely settled Lusitu where the carrying capacity of the land under existing systems of land use was exceeded as soon as it received six thousand relocated Gwembe Central people in 1958. Today, much of Lusitu, where two of the sample villages are located, is a dust bowl during the dry season, with cattle dying in low rainfall years. Many families are now desperately poor by our standards and, increasingly, their own. The 1990s were hard, with the gap between aspiration and achievement widening, especially for the majority of primary and secondary school leavers. This hurts: these are long-term friends who suffer and we can do little or nothing to prevent it. We are also watching the aging of old friends who are passing from vigorous maturity into old age and sometimes senility. As we too are growing older, our new age status offers new information and new insights, while closing off other avenues. We will never have the same friendships with the young now moving into positions of authority that we did with those they replace. There are costs in all this to anthropologists that should not be minimized.

On the other hand, we have gained new respect for Gwembe men and women because we have watched them contend over many years with good times and bad. Children have grown to maturity, flirted through early love affairs, married, and accepted responsibility. Some have faced the tragedies of barrenness, the death of children, the desertion or death of a spouse. Some friendly, outgoing young men have become grasping homestead heads and the focus of witchcraft suspicions. On the other hand, harassed young wives, beset by many children and with none old enough to be efficient helpers, have later emerged as happy middle-aged women, finally in charge of their world.

Predictably, a long-term study is likely to diminish the roseate hues in which so much of ethnographic description is couched. At the same time, the people who are the focus of the study become more the product of their own history and less the exemplars of universal cultural patterns. We have lived too long with the realities that the Gwembe people face daily not to be concerned about what happens to them. It is impossible to go away and forget that their lives go on.

It is this that pulls us back. We want to know what happens next and this means much more than just checking on various hypotheses. We also think that we are of some importance to those we have followed through the years. Even those who do not like us still see us as known entities—as people with whom they have shared past experiences, both pleasant and unpleasant. We are a continuity in their lives in a world of increasing discontinuities, as they are a continuity and help give meaning to ours.

Note

Over the years our debts of gratitude have steadily increased, to the Institute for Economic and Social Research and its many directors including Mubanga Kashoki and Oliver Saasa, and its affiliation officer, Ilse Mwansa; the Gossner Service Team who provided us with accommodations in Lusaka and at Nkandabwe in Gwembe and Harvest Help/Zambia for accommodation at Munyama; the Savory family of the Moorings, Monze, who have given hospitality, stored equipment, and provided much other assistance; to the administrative and technical officers who answered our questions and made records available; and to the chiefs, headmen, and village people who have been our hosts and instructors. We owe special gratitude to field assistants, including the late Benjamin Shipopa and Adam Chinga, Edward

Chifulwe, Chibilika Sinafala, Kashente Chifumpu, Paul Syanemba, Jelina Chasombwa, Mary Siamakabo, Denison Hastings Simalabali, Benard Simalabali, Christopher Kiwani, Stannard Sialenga, Bernard Siakanomba, Emmy Munsanje, Jailos Mazambani, Senete Adam Sikagoma, Rhoda Chipepo, Willy Drivus Chikuni, Shadreck Syajebu, Chester Ditwa, and Ward Syakapalu.

References Cited

Bakewell, O.
(1993) "Harvest Help Zambia 1993 census report." Unpublished manuscript. School of Social Sciences, University of Bath, UK.

Banda, Moses N. M.
(1985) "The Gwembe Valley: A study of local resource mobilization in Zambia." Ph.D. dissertation. Edinburgh University.

Barnett, Homer
(1953) *Innovation: The Basis of Cultural Change.* New York: McGraw-Hill.

Bourdillon, M. F. C., A. Cheater, and M. Murphree
(1985) *Studies of Fishing on Lake Kariba.* Gweru: Mambo Press.

Brandt, H., et al.
(1973) *Report on the Development Possibilities of Gwembe South Region (Zambia).* Berlin: German Development Institute.

Bredt, Rolf Friedrich
(1980) *Förderung des Selbstvertravens und der Selbsthilfeorganisation durch Basisarbeit in der Entwicklungshilfe: Ein Erfahrungsbericht aus der Arbeit von Zambia (1971–77).* Hohenheim: Universität Hohenheim Insitute für Agrarsoziologie, Landwirtschaftider Beratung und Angewandte Psychologie, Diplomarbeit zur Erlangung des Grades eines Diplom-Agrariengenieurs.

Cernea, Michael M.
(1988) *Involuntary Resettlement in Development Projects: Policy Guidelines in World Bank–Financed Projects.* Washington, D.C.: World Bank.
(1999) [editor] *The Economics of Involuntary Resettlement: Questions and Challenges.* Washington, D.C.: World Bank.

Cernea, Michael M. and Scott E. Guggenheim [editors]
(1993) *Anthropological Approaches to Resettlement: Policy, Practice and Theory.* Boulder, CO: Westview.

Cernea, Michael M. and Christopher McDowell [editors]
(2000) *Risks and Reconstruction: Experiences of Resettlers and Refugees.* Washington, D.C.: World Bank.

Clark, Samuel J.
(2001) "An investigation into the impact of HIV on population dynamics in Africa." Ph.D. dissertation. University of Pennsylvania, Philadelphia.
(forthcoming) "Gwembe DSS, Zambia." in *Population, Health and Survival in INDEPTH Sites*, vol. 1, *INDEPTH Network Monograph Series: Demographic Surveillance Systems for Assessing Populations and Their Health in Developing Countries*. Ottawa: IDRC Press.

Clark, Sam, Elizabeth Colson, James Lee, and Thayer Scudder
(1995) "Ten thousand Tonga: A longitudinal anthropological study from southern Zambia, 1956–1991." *Population Studies* 49:91–109.

Cliggett, Lisa
(1997a) "Economic and social components of migration in two regions of Southern Province, Zambia." Working paper. Bath: Center for Development Studies, University of Bath.
(1997b) "My mother's keeper: Changing family support systems for the elderly in the Gwembe Valley, Zambia." Ph.D. dissertation. Indiana University, Bloomington.
(2000) "Social components of migration: Experiences from Southern Province, Zambia." *Human Organization*: 59(1):125–135.
(2002) "Male wealth and claims to motherhood: Gendered resource access and intergenerational relations in the Gwembe Valley, Zambia." In Gracia Clark (editor), *Gender in Economic Life: Annual Readings in Economic Anthropology*. Walnut Creek, CA: AltaMira Press.
(n.d.-a) "Ambivalence of grandsons and rescue by daughters: One story of aging in the Gwembe Valley, Zambia." In Linda Walbridge and April Sievert (editors), *Personal Encounters in Anthropology*. Palo Alto, CA: Mayfield Press.
(n.d.-b) "Carrying capacity's new guise: Folk models in anthropology and the longitudinal study of environmental change." *Africa Today*.
(n.d.-c) "Gender, subsistence, and residential arrangements for the elderly in the Gwembe Valley, Zambia." *Journal of Cross Cultural Gerontology*. Submitted March 2000.

Colson, Elizabeth
(1954) "The intensive study of small sample communities." Pp. 43–59 in Robert F. Spencer (editor), *Method and Perspective in Anthropology*. Minneapolis: University of Minnesota Press.
(1960) *Social Organization of the Gwembe Tonga*. Manchester: Manchester University Press.
(1962) "Trade and wealth among the Tonga." Pp. 601–616 in Paul Bohannan and George Dalton (editors), *Markets in Africa*. Evanston, IL: Northwestern University Press.
(1963) "Land rights and land use among the Valley Tonga of the Rhodesian Federation: The background to the Kariba resettlement program." Pp. 137–156 in Daniel Biebuyck (editor), *African Agrarian Systems*. London: Oxford University Press.
(1964a) "Social change and the Gwembe Tonga." *Human Problems in Central Africa* 36:1–10.
(1964b) "Land law and land holdings among the Valley Tonga of Zambia." *South-*

western Journal of Anthropology 22:1–8.

(1966) "The alien diviner and local politics among the Tonga of Zambia." Pp. 221–228 in Marc Swartz, Arthur Tuden, and Victor Turner (editors), *Political Anthropology*. Chicago: Aldine.

(1967) "Competence and incompetence in the context of independence." *Current Anthropology* 8:92–100, 108–109.

(1969) "Spirit possession among the Tonga of Zambia." Pp. 69–103 in John Middleton and John M. Beattie (editors), *Spirit Mediumship and Society in Africa*. London: Routledge and Kegan Paul.

(1970a) "The assimilation of aliens among the Zambian Tonga." Pp. 33–54 in Ronald Cohen and John Middleton (editors), *From Tribe to Nation in Africa*. San Francisco: Chandler.

(1970b) "Converts and tradition: The impact of Christianity on Valley Tonga religion." *Southwestern Journal of Anthropology* 26:143–56.

(1971a) "Heroism, martyrdom, and courage." Pp. 19–35 in Thomas O. Beidelman (editor), *The Translation of Culture*. London: Tavistock.

(1971b) *The Social Consequences of Resettlement*. Manchester: Manchester University Press.

(1976) "From chief's court to local court: The evolution of local courts in Southern Zambia." *Political Anthropology* 1:15–29.

(1977) "A continuing dialogue: Prophets and local shrines among the Tonga of Zambia." Pp. 119–139 in R. Werbner (editor), *Regional Cults*. London: Academic Press.

(1980) "The resilience of matrilineality: Gwembe and Plateau Tonga adaptations." Pp. 359–374 in Linda Cordell and Stephen Beckerman (editors), *The Versatility of Kinship*. New York: Academic Press.

(1995) "The contentiousness of disputes." Pp. 65–82 in Pat Caplan (editor), *Understanding Disputes: The Politics of Argument*. Oxford: Berg.

(1996) "The Bantu Botatwe: Changing political definitions in southern Zambia." Pp. 61–80 in David Parkin, Lionel Caplan, and Humphrey Fisher (editors), *The Politics of Cultural Performance*. Oxford: Berghahn.

(1997) "Places of power and shrines of the land." *Paideuma, Mitteilungen zur Kulturkunde* 43:47–57.

(1999) "Gendering those uprooted by 'development.'" Pp. 23–39 in Doreen Indra (editor), *Engendering Forced Migration: Theory and Practice*. Oxford: Berghahn.

(2000) "The father as witch." *Africa* 70(3):333–358.

Colson, Elizabeth and Conrad Kottak

(1996) "Linkages methodology for the study of sociocultural transformation." Pp. 103–134 in Emilio Moran (editor), *Transforming Societies, Transforming Anthropology*. Ann Arbor: University of Michigan Press.

Colson, Elizabeth and Thayer Scudder

(1975) "New economic relationships between the Gwembe Valley and the line of rail." Pp. 190–210 in David Parkin (editor), *Town and Country in Central and Eastern Africa*. London: Oxford University Press.

(1988) *For Prayer and Profit: The Ritual, Economic, and Social Importance of Beer in Gwembe District, Zambia, 1950–1982*. Stanford: Stanford University Press.

Copestake, James
(1990) "Report of a demographic census of the area of operation of the Gwembe Valley Agricultural Mission in southern Zambia." Unpublished manuscript. Telford, U.K.: Harvest Help.

Crowley, Sara
(1985) *An Evaluation of Gwembe South Development Project: With Special Reference to Siatwinda*. Brussels: Commission of European Communities, DG VIII Evaluation Department.

DeWet, Chris
(1993) "A spatial analysis of involuntary community relocation: A South African case study." Pp. 321–350 in Michael M. Cernea and Scott E. Guggenheim (editors), *Anthropological Approaches to Resettlement: Policy, Practice and Theory*. Boulder, CO: Westview.

Dzingirai, V. and M. F. C. Bourdillon
(1997) "Religious rituals and political control in Binga District, Zimbabwe." *African Anthropology* 4(2):4–26.

Gillett, Rhonda M.
(1995a) "Growth and physical status: Biocultural measures of long-term underdevelopment among the Gwembe Tonga of Zambia." Ph.D. dissertation. Indiana University, Bloomington.
(1995b) "Development of a dental emergence aging standard applicable to Zambian populations: A comparison of the accuracy of three methods." *American Journal of Physical Anthropology*, Supplement 20:98–99 (Abstract).
(1996) "Growth status of adolescent school children in Choma, Zambia." American Association of Physical Anthropology Meetings. *American Journal of Physical Anthropology*, Supplement 22:112 (Abstract).
(1997) "Dental emergence among urban Zambian school children: An assessment of the accuracy of three methods in assigning ages." *American Journal of Physical Anthropology* 102:447–454.
(1998) "Permanent tooth emergence among Zambian schoolchildren: A standard for the assignment of ages." *American Journal of Human Biology* 10:45–51.

Gillett, Rhonda M. and P. V. Tobias
(In Press) "Human growth and development in southern Zambia: A first study of Tonga children predating the Kariba Dam, as baseline for comparison with contemporary Zambians." *American Journal of Human Biology*.

Gsanger, Hans, Ulrike Muller-Glodde, Thomas Selzer, and Gunther Taube
(1986) "Strengthening local linkages for socioeconomic development at regional level: A study on the rural economy of the Gwembe District, Zambia." Berlin: German Development Institute.

Haantobolo, G. H. N.
(1990) "Ecology, agriculture and proletarization: A study of the Sinazongwe Area in the Gwembe Valley of Southern Province of Zambia, 1900–1989." M.A. thesis. University of Zambia, Lusaka.

Habarad, Jonathan
(1988) "Neighborhood and nation in Gwembe District, Zambia." Revised and expanded paper presented at the Annual Meeting of the African Studies Association.

International Labor Office (ILO)
(1981) *Basic Needs in an Economy Under Pressure*. Addis Ababa: International Labor Office.

Jarman, P. J.
(1968) "The effect of the creation of Lake Kariba upon the terrestrial ecology of the Middle Zambezi Valley; with particular reference to large mammals." Ph.D. dissertation. University of Manchester.

Kamwanga, Jolly
(1997) *An Assessment of the Demographic and Health Situation in the Gwembe Valley*. Lusaka: Institute for Economic and Social Research, University of Zambia, for the World Bank.

Kamwanga, Jolly and Chosani A. Njobvu
(1997) *Development Strategies and Rehabilitation Programs for the Peoples Affected by the Construction of the Kariba Dam*. Lusaka: Institute for Economic and Social Research, University of Zambia, for the World Bank.

Kasimona, V. N. and J. Musiwa
(1997) *The Use of Meteorological and Hydrological Data in Recession Agriculture in the Gwembe-Valley Study*. Lusaka: Institute for Economic and Social Research, University of Zambia, for the World Bank.

Kasonde, C. K.
(1991) *Farming Systems Research Survey in Gwembe Valley North: A Case Study of Lusitu Sub-Boma and Simamba*. Lusaka: University of Zambia.

Klausen, Anne-Lise
(1987) *The Gwembe Valley Tonga Museum and Craft Project: Project Document 1987–1990*. Denmark: Mannerup Management and Marketing for Ministry of Foreign Affairs, Government of the Netherlands.

Lancaster, Chet S.
(1966) "Reciprocity, redistribution, and the male life cycle: Variations in Middle River Tonga social organization." *African Social Research* 2:139–157.
(1971) "The economics of social organization in an ethnic border zone: The Goba (Northern Shona) of the Zambezi Valley." *Ethnology* 10:445–465.

THAYER SCUDDER AND ELIZABETH COLSON

(1974a) "Brideservice, residence and authority among the Goba of the Zambezi Valley." *Africa* 44:46–64.

(1974b) "Ethnic identity, history, and 'tribe' in the Middle Zambezi Valley." *American Ethnologist* 1:707–730.

(1977) "The Zambezi Goba ancestral cult." *Africa* 47:229–241.

(1981) *The Goba of the Zambezi: Sex Roles, Economics, and Change.* Norman: University of Oklahoma Press.

(1987) "Political structure and ethnicity in an immigrant society: The Goba of the Zambezi." Pp. 102–120 in Igor Kopytoff (editor), *The African Frontier.* Bloomington: Indiana University Press.

Luig, Ulrich

(1992) *Es ist heiss in Zambia: Partner in der Entwicklungsarbeit.* Erlangen: Der Verlag der Ev.-Luth. Mission Erlangen.

(1997) *Conversion as a Social Process: A History of Missionary Christianity among the Valley Tonga, Zambia.* London: Transaction Publishers.

Luig, Ute

(1992) "Besessenheit als Ausdruck von Frauenkultur in Zambia." *Peripherie* 47/48:111–128.

(1993a) "Besessenheitsrituale als historische Charta: Die Verarbeitung europäischer Einflüsse in sambianischen Besessenheitskulten." *Paideuma, Mitteilungen zur Kulturkunde* 39:343–356.

(1993b) "Gesellschaftliche Entwicklung und ihre individuelle Verarbeitung in den affiltiven Besessenheitskulten der Tonga." *Tribus* 42:109–120.

(1995a) "Gender relations and commercialization in African possession cults." Pp. 33–50 in Mechthild Reh and Gudrun Ludwar-Ewe (editors), *Gender and Identity in Africa.* Münster/Hamburg: Lit-Verlag.

(1995b) "Naturaneignung als symbolischer Prozess in afrikanischen Gesellschaften." Pp. 29–50 in Ute Luig and Achim von Oppen (editors), *Naturaneignung in Afrika als sozialer und symbolischer Prozess.* Berlin: Das Arabische Buch.

(1996) "Wanderarbeiter als Helden: Zwischen kolonialer Entfremdung und lokaler Selbstvergewisserung." *Historische Anthropologie* 3(4)359–382.

(1999) "Constructing local worlds: Spirit possession in the Gwembe Valley, Zambia." Pp. 124–141 in H. Behrend and Ute Luig (editors), *Spirit Possession and Power.* Madison: University of Wisconsin Press.

Matthews, T. I.

(1976) "The historical traditions of the peoples of the Gwembe Valley, Middle Zambezi." Ph.D. dissertation. School of Oriental and African Studies, London University.

(1978) "The Tonga and the anthropologists: Essay review." *Rhodesia History* 9:115–122.

(1981) "Portuguese, Chikunda, and peoples of the Gwembe Valley: The impact of the 'Lower Zambezi Complex' on southern Zambia." *Journal of African History* 22(1):23–41.

(1988) *Tales of the Secret Valley.* Harare: Baobab Books.

Milimo, John
(1988) *An Analysis of the Experiences of Institutions Involved in the Development of the Middle Zambezi Basin.* Binghamton, NY: Institute for Development Anthropology.

Mudenda, Sylvia
(1990) *The Female Extension Programme of the Gwembe South Development Project.* University of Zambia: Institute for African Studies.

Mukwena, R. M.
(1998) "The role of local councils in rural development: A study of Gwembe and Kalomo District Councils, Zambia, 1981–1995." Ph.D. dissertation. University of Manchester.

Mwanza, Herbert M.
(1997) *The Land Use Study: Gwembe Tonga Rehabilitation and Development Study.* Lusaka: Institute for Economic and Social Research, University of Zambia, for the World Bank.

Njobu, C. A., E. T. Kasuta, and B. Siamwiza
(1997) *Participatory Strategies for the Rehabilitation and Development of the Peoples Affected by the Construction of the Kariba Dam.* Lusaka: Institute of Economic and Social Research, University of Zambia, for the World Bank.

Petit, Carine, Thayer Scudder, and Eric Lambin
(2001) "Understanding land-cover change processes from remote sensing operations." *International Journal of Remote Sensing.*

Price, N. L.
(1998) "Institutional determinants of high fertility in Gwembe Tonga society." *Social Sciences in Health* 4(1):25–44.

Reynolds, Barrie
(1968) *The Material Culture of the Peoples of the Gwembe Valley.* Manchester: University of Manchester Press.

Reynolds, Pamela
(1991) *Dance Civet Cat: Child Labour in the Zambezi Valley.* London: Zed Books.

Reynolds, Pamela and Colleen Cousins
(1989) *Lwano Lwanyika: Tonga Book of the Earth.* Harare: Baobab Books. (Reprinted 1993 by Panos Books, London.)

Schuthof, Arjan and Moniek Boerenkamp
(1991) *Spirits and Survival: Religion and Crisis Management within Tonga Society, Zimbabwe.* Utrecht: Utrecht University, Interfaculty Programme Society and Religion.

Scudder, Thayer
(1960) "Fishermen of the Zambezi." *Human Problems in British Central Africa* 27:41–49.

(1962) *The Ecology of the Gwembe Tonga*. Manchester: Manchester University Press.

(1966) "Man-made lakes and population relocation in Africa." Pp. 99–108 in R. Lowe-McConnell (editor), *Man-Made Lakes*. New York: Academic Press.

(1971) "Gathering among African woodland savannah cultivators. A case study: The Gwembe Tonga." Institute for African Studies, Zambian Papers No. 5.

(1972) "Ecological bottlenecks and the development of the Kariba Lake basin." Pp. 206–235 in M. T. Farvar and J. P. Milton (editors), *The Careless Technology: Ecology and International Development*. New York: Natural History Press.

(1973a) "The human ecology of big projects: River basin development and resettlement." *Annual Review of Anthropology* 2:45–55.

(1973b) "Summary: Resettlement." Pp. 707–719 in W. C. Ackermann, G. F. White, and E. B. Worthington (editors), *Man-Made Lakes: Their Problems and Environmental Effects*. Washington, D.C.: American Geophysical Union.

(1975) "Resettlement." Pp. 453–470 in N. F. Stanley and M. P. Alpers (editors), *Man-Made Lakes and Human Health*. London: Academic Press for the Institute of Biology.

(1976) "Social anthropology and the reconstruction of prehistoric land use systems in tropical Africa: A cautionary case study from Zambia." Pp. 357–381 in J. R. Harlan, J. M. J. De Wet, and A. B. L. Stemler (editors), *Origins of African Plant Domestication*. The Hague: Mouton.

(1983) "Economic downturn and community unraveling: The Gwembe Tonga revisited." *Culture and Agriculture* 18:16–19.

(1984a) "Economic downturn and community unraveling, revisited." *Culture and Agriculture* 23:6–10.

(1984b) "The development potential of new lands settlement in the tropics and subtropics: A global state-of-the-art evaluation with specific emphasis on policy implications, Executive Summary." U.S. Agency for International Development Program Discussion Paper No. 21. Washington, D.C.: USAID.

(1985) "A history of development in the Zambian portion of the Middle Zambezi Valley and the Lake Kariba Basin." Working Paper 11. Binghamton, NY: Institute for Development Anthropology.

(1986) "The Gwembe Valley Development Company in relationship to the development of the southern portion of Gwembe District." Unpublished report.

(1991) "A sociological framework for the analysis of new lands settlements." Pp. 148–187 in Michael M. Cernea (editor), *Putting People First: Sociological Variables in Rural Development*, revised and enlarged edition. London: Oxford University Press, for the World Bank.

(1993) "Development-induced relocation and refugee studies: 37 years of change and continuity among Zambia's Gwembe Tonga." *Journal of Refugee Studies* 60(2):123–152.

(1997a) "Resettlement." Pp. 667–710 in Asit K. Biswas (editor), *Water Resources: Environmental Planning, Management and Development*. New York: McGraw-Hill.

(1997b) "Social Impacts" Pp. 623–665 in Asit K. Biswas (editor), *Water Resources: Environmental Planning, Management and Development*. New York: McGraw-Hill.

Scudder, Thayer and Elizabeth Colson
(1968) "Memorandum for possible research workers in the Kariba Lake basin." *Bulletin of the Institute for Social Research, University of Zambia* 3:70–73.
(1971) "The Kariba Dam project: Resettlement and local initiative." Pp. 40–69 in H. Russell Bernard and Pertti Pelto (editors), *Technical Innovation and Cultural Change*. New York: Macmillan.
(1979) "Long-term research in Gwembe Valley, Zambia." Pp. 227–254 in George M. Foster, Thayer Scudder, Elizabeth Colson, and Robert V. Kemper (editors), *Long-Term Field Research in Social Anthropology*. New York: Academic Press.
(1980) *Secondary Education and the Formation of an Elite: The Impact of Education on Gwembe District, Zambia*. London: Academic Press.
(1982) "From welfare to development: A conceptual framework for the analysis of dislocated people." Pp. 267–287 in Art Hansen and Anthony Oliver-Smith (editors), *Involuntary Migration and Resettlement: The Problems and Responses of Dislocated People*. Boulder, CO: Westview Press.

Scudder, Thayer and Jonathan Habarad
(1991) "Local responses to involuntary relocation and development in the Zambian portion of the Middle Zambezi Valley." Pp. 178–205 in J. A. Mollett (editor), *Migrants in Agricultural Development*. London: Macmillan.

Seidman, Ann
(1979) "The economics of eliminating rural poverty and the distorted growth of import substitution industry." Pp. 100–128 in Ben Turok (editor), *Development of Zambia: A Reader*. London: Zed Press.

Siamwiza, Bennett
(1993) "Hunger in Gwembe Valley: A case study of Mweemba chieftaincy, 1905–1987." M.A. thesis. University of Zambia, Lusaka.

Simweemba, M.
(1989) *Report on the Sinazongwe Women's Clubs for the 26th to 30th Skills Courses*. Lusaka: Ministry of Labour and Social Services and World Vision International.

Soils Incorporated in association with Chalo Environmental & Sustainable Development Consultants
(2000) *Kariba Dam Case Study: Zambia and Zimbabwe*. Cape Town: World Commission on Dams.

Tremmel, Michael and the River Tonga People
(1994) *The People of the Great River*. Gweru: Mambo Press.

Weinrich, A. K. H.
(1977) *The Tonga People on the Southern Shore of Lake Kariba*. Gweru: Mambo Press.

Wood, Adrian P. and Violet Nanchengwa
(1985) *Evaluation of ZRC Disaster Relief in the Gwembe Valley, 1984 and Recommendations for Disaster Prevention*. Lusaka: Zambia Red Cross.

World Bank
(1980) "Social issues associated with involuntary resettlement in Bank-financed projects." Operational Manual Statement 2.33. Washington, D.C.: World Bank.

Wunder, Matthew Bruce
(1998) "Of elephant and men: Crop destruction, campfire and wildlife management in the Zambezi Valley, Zimbabwe." Ann Arbor: UMI Dissertation Services.

Zambezi River Authority
(1997) *Kariba Dam's Operation Noah Re-Launched*. Lusaka: Zambezi River Authority.

Zaucha, Grazyna
(1998) *Batonga Across the Waters*. Choma: Choma Museum.
(ms.) *The Gwembe Tonga*.

CHAPTER NINE

MULTIGENERATIONS AND MULTIDISCIPLINES: INHERITING FIFTY YEARS OF GWEMBE TONGA RESEARCH

Lisa Cliggett

Introduction

In March 1994, a month before leaving to begin eighteen months of dissertation research in Zambia, I made a decision to shift my field site from Zambia's Eastern Province to the Gwembe Valley in the Southern Province. Ted Scudder, crawling on his hands and knees around a ten-foot-square lab table covered with detailed maps of the Gwembe Valley, acted as the catalyst in my decision. It remains unclear whether it was Ted's show alone or the combination of his animated persuasion, his description of the Gwembe project history, and the opportunity to "jump-start" my research with forty years of data on the village where I would work that led to my decision. The specific reasons for turning my research gaze to the southern border of Zambia no longer seem important; the outcome of that decision, however, remains one of the most important forces in both my professional and personal life.

That decision of March 1994 was only one of many twists on my long and circuitous path toward establishing a research focus and site for my dissertation, which is not such a new story for many anthropologists. Tales abound in the discipline of doctoral research plans gone awry, and of chance happenings and resulting transformations in focus, region, and scholarship. In my case, the meandering path included initial graduate training focused on Caribbean anthropology, including religion and ethnomusicology, but eventually crystallized around household economy and social organization in Haiti. Political upheavals in 1991, which reached a peak within a month of my return from preliminary research, made it clear that I needed to reframe my research plans to accommodate an alternative research site. At about the same time, one of my graduate advisors became involved in a collaborative research project on aging in Zambia. Since he was a demographer familiar with highly quantitative data, and his Zambian colleague was a sociologist specializing in public health, and they knew my anthropological research interests centered on aging and household economics, they asked if I would consider joining their project as an ethnographer, to provide the ethnographic context and qualitative data that would complement the survey research they were proposing.

Lisa Cliggett and Elizabeth Colson at the Choma Museum, 1998. Photo by Grazyna Zaucha.

After much reflection on the ramifications of "jumping the Haitian ship," I decided to join their project. Of course, this meant prolonging my graduate training to gain more background on Africa in general and Zambia more specifically, to learn a new language, and to "retool" for an African focus in my dissertation research. Little did I know then that I was training myself for joining one of the oldest and most comprehensive anthropological studies carried out on the African continent.

How Does One Become the Next Generation?

Two years after turning my research interests farther east and south from Haiti, I found myself funded with my own Fulbright Fellowship, while the survey project remained unfunded and in a holding pattern after two rounds of proposal writing. In my last month of preparing for departure to Zambia, with functional language skills for a region in the Eastern Province, on the Malawian border, I met Ted Scudder. Or rather, he tracked me down as I passed through Bloomington, where I was a graduate student at Indiana University, between a variety of prefieldwork trips. Ted had heard about my plans to do research on household decision-making and support systems for the elderly from Rhonda Gillett-Netting, one of my graduate school colleagues who had linked her own dissertation work to Gwembe data (she is now one of the three members of "the next generation" of the Gwembe Tonga Research Project). When Ted learned about my planned dissertation research, he thought that my theoretical interests and topical focus meshed well with the Gwembe project and that my own work could benefit from the vast quantity of data he and Elizabeth Colson had collected over the years.

In fact, Rhonda had been trying to convince me to shift my Zambian regional focus to the Southern Province since I had first decided to work in Zambia, partly so that we could collaborate on certain aspects of our research. By telling Ted about my research interests, she gained a solid comrade with unmatched persuasive skills. Although Ted enthusiastically encouraged me to conduct research in the Gwembe, there was no discussion at that time about my becoming any kind of "project member." I would benefit from shifting my dissertation field site to the Gwembe through access to data, to which Ted and Elizabeth agreed, as well as the ease of "setting up shop" in a location where locals have previously lived with anthropologists. The project would benefit from my presence in the Gwembe in terms of the field notes and data I would share with Elizabeth and Ted, through my help in maintaining contact with communities and individuals during my stay, and simply by having another researcher show interest in the region. At the time, I saw the gains for both me and the project as short term: I could contemplate a timely completion of my dissertation, while the project would have a researcher in the region for a significant period of time.

Now—seven years, four field trips, and two research projects later—I am one of three social researchers comprising the next generation of the Gwembe Tonga Research Project (Cliggett 1997a, 2000). I feel deep gratitude for Ted's persuasive tendencies, Elizabeth's patience and insight, and their openness and encouragement. The benefits of joining a long-standing, systematic, and respected research program are immense, but the challenges can be daunting. In reflecting on my experience with long-term fieldwork, I highlight some of the benefits and challenges by considering the future of our project research among the Gwembe Tonga specifically and in anthropology generally.

Inheriting Relationships: Arriving in the Field as the Next Generation

As any social scientist conducting research among peoples already accustomed to our odd behaviors, activities, and incessant questions will point out, the ease of starting fieldwork in such a setting cannot be taken for granted. In the Gwembe Valley, I lived in the homestead of a man and his family who have been Elizabeth Colson's hosts since the early 1960s. Kaciente's familiarity with the anthropologist's need to spend a few hours every day writing in solitude (and most Americans' general preference for periods of privacy), without any explanation on my part, greatly facilitated my settling into Sinafala village. As soon as I said, "after eating, I will go to my house to write for a little while," Kaciente would appoint himself official greeter for any potential visitors and inform them that I could not be disturbed at the moment. Prior to conducting my field research, I never would have thought of the value of such "protection." Arriving into a system already in place (including my need to filter or boil water and other such peculiar behaviors) was one of the unanticipated, but extremely valuable, benefits of linking myself to the Gwembe project. These pragmatic and logistical details may appear somewhat superficial, but they can make a significant difference in how quickly a researcher can dive into the business that brought her to the field in the first place.

Of course, the value of the immense data resources, and especially detailed information on the group of people with whom a researcher will work, is one of the biggest draws to collaborating on a long-term research project. Aside from Ted's persuasive "table performance," it was the detailed histories of households, families, and individuals that made me forsake my earlier intentions to work in Zambia's Eastern Province and instead work in the Gwembe Valley. Even prior to my departure for Zambia, Ted provided me with a "checklist" (one of our Gwembe project terms, meaning a printed and bound book with detailed histories of all the households and their members) for the village where I planned to establish my home base and for the village I planned to use as my comparison site. Within the covers of these checklists, I had all the baseline demographic, genealogical, and educational information I needed to identify the ninety-two elderly individuals and their families with whom I would work during my year and a half living in the Gwembe. To identify, prior to setting foot in the region for the first time, not only a village site but also the individuals with whom a researcher will work, reduces the confusion common at the start of new research projects when there is so much to do, but no clear place to start.

Settling into a previously established research site also includes access to an established social infrastructure. Over their forty years of continuing research, Elizabeth and Ted have established close friendships, excellent working relationships, and good reputations for themselves as caring, committed, and generous individuals not only in the Gwembe Valley but throughout Zambia. Stepping into this social infrastructure was rewarding, though sometimes frustrating. Mentioning my association with Elizabeth and Ted almost always brought forth welcoming smiles, invitations to sit and talk, and a level of trust that would have been hard to establish during a first field season in a "virgin" field site.

I became acutely aware of the trust issue when I began working in a frontier migrant community, in search of individuals and families who had left the Gwembe to pioneer new farms in a region with better agricultural potential. Whenever I found a family from one of the Gwembe communities, they immediately smiled, greeted me in their distinctive style by asking many questions about me (including my body, my day, and my family), and brought me a wooden stool so that we could sit and have a good chat. In our ensuing conversations, though they had not met me before, they answered sometimes-delicate questions with little or no hesitation and willingly shared sensitive information. They did this simply because they understood that I worked with Elizabeth and Ted.

In contrast, when I went to ask about migration issues among the frontier region's non-Gwembe Tonga local leaders and residents, they did not try to conceal their suspicion of me. Presenting my official letters of introduction from the University of Zambia and letters from my home institution did nothing to allay their fears that the government might have sent me to inform on their activities—perhaps related to nonsanctioned land transfers, the boundaries for the nearby national park, or other of their many activities that they prefer to conduct without outside interference. Even my research assistant's attempts to build alliances and reduce suspicions did nothing to further the openness of our conversations. This type of interaction occurred at least five times during my first extensive fieldwork. From these encounters I became deeply aware of my good fortune in having the legacy of Elizabeth's and Ted's good reputations to help open doors, and lines of communication, with people I had never met. These encounters also emphasized to me the importance of participant observation and living close to people with whom we hope to gain trust.

One of the Gwembe project's well-established protocols is a commitment to continue gathering information about all the individuals and families whom Ted and Elizabeth first met in 1956. This not only serves our research purposes, but also fulfills local expectations. For many people, the primary purpose of our project is the detailed recording of their social history. Whenever I arrive in any community where Elizabeth and Ted have worked, a steady stream of visitors flows in my direction—to greet me, ask about their old American friends, and update me on their lives. This "updating" has become one of the primary research activities for Elizabeth and Ted on their return visits and is increasingly the responsibility of the next generation.

Upon my first arrival in the Gwembe, I was not aware of the significance of this updating activity. Neither Ted nor Elizabeth had charged me with the duty of doing an update of the checklists. Once I had identified the elderly individuals and their families with whom I expected to work—both in the village and wherever they might have migrated—I hoped to focus on this fairly large research population, containing close to 250 adults whom I planned to interview at least once. However, I quickly learned that all the people living in any of the research villages expected that I should work equally with each member, and family, of the village. They were not prepared for me to define a research problem and then limit my intensive work to a subset of their community. I, on the other hand, already felt daunted by the main research task ahead of me.

The local people's resistance to my focused research plan did not take the form of aggression or overt attempts to control my work. Rather, people simply demanded my time, attention, and, in some cases, resources. Unanticipated visits, during which people expected me to update their entries in the checklist, were one way that people forced me to realize that my involvement in the Gwembe project included a commitment to working with everyone in the village, not just a group on my particular research agenda.

Additionally, it became important that I recognize and reward close relationships that Elizabeth and Ted had established, even if I had very little contact with the particular individuals. In many cases I eventually developed friendships out of those contacts, but initially I felt put upon to engage in relationships for which I had little basis. In Gwembe society friendships and close relationships, whether between local community members or distant relatives, inherently include gift giving and exchange of material things. Additionally, their belief system that the inheritance by one individual of a deceased person's spirit, and all of the rights *and* responsibilities of the deceased, creates a context in which people expect an inheritor to fulfill obligations of those who came before her.

Although Elizabeth is still alive and well, and although she continues to return to the Gwembe for months at a time and writes frequent letters to her Gwembe friends, local people believed me to be Elizabeth's inheritor—at least for the period during which they had access to me. This meant that they expected me to honor their friendships with Elizabeth not only through my time and attention, but also through an exchange of some material goods. Since I conducted my research during a severe multiyear drought, assistance with food (whether cash to purchase, or actual packages of maize) was a primary request. I managed to acknowledge these relationships whenever possible and did what I could to assist people in coping with the drought, but I also struggled with feelings of being exploited and frustrations over attempting to establish relationships on my own.

Of course, over time I did build my own friendships and working relationships, but at times it felt (and sometimes continues to feel) that I bear a double burden—the desire to fulfill responsibilities to my own cohort of relationships and the obligation to fulfill responsibilities to the "Ted and Elizabeth" generation, without whose patience, acceptance, and friendship the Gwembe project would not exist.

Beyond the First Research of the Next Generation: How Does a Longitudinal Project Survive?

Conducting my dissertation research within the context of the Gwembe project most certainly benefited me in the short term. I settled into my field site quickly, began collecting data on my study population almost immediately upon arrival, and supplemented the data collected on my own with a storehouse of forty years' ethnographic observations. All this resulted in a relatively fast write-up of the dissertation and completion of my doctoral program (Cliggett 1997b). But what led me to stick with the project beyond the dissertation phase?

In fact, the process of my more formal incorporation into the project began *during* my first year and a half in the Gwembe. Just two months prior to the end of my dissertation fieldwork, the National Science Foundation awarded Ted a grant for a continuation of the Gwembe project. The major thrust of this grant involved systematizing the demographic component of Elizabeth's and Ted's data, instituting formal demographic data collection methods, training village research assistants to update the checklists throughout the year, and handing over the project to a new generation of social researchers. In attempting to hand over the most onerous work of the project (the detailed and regular updating of each person ever included in the original study population, and their descendants), Ted wrote three new colleagues into the grant to perform various duties. Sam Clark, previously Ted's undergraduate student at CalTech and later a graduate student in demography at the University of Pennsylvania, was brought in to develop the demographic database and data collection system. Ted included Rhonda Gillett-Netting (then a visiting professor at the University of Arizona) and me to participate in training the local research assistants and to conduct a resurvey of secondary school students whom Elizabeth and Ted had interviewed in the 1970s, as well as to continue collecting ethnographic and biocultural data that complemented the quantitative data.

As my earlier plan to work on the aging survey project in the Eastern Province demonstrates, I already had an interest in collaborative projects, and multidisciplinary studies in particular. I liked the idea of sharing perspectives and data, and what I perceived to be the benefit of examining questions from the view of different intellectual backgrounds. The opportunity to work in such a project, even temporarily (which is how I viewed my tie to the Gwembe project at that point), appealed to me, simply as a way to gain experience in collaboration. The grant also provided funds for field trips over the following three years, which obviously appealed to me because I would have a chance to return to my dissertation field site to fill in the inevitable gaps and update information.

By the end of my year and a half in the Gwembe, I had developed strong ties with many of the community members where I worked and also had a strong affection for the region and Zambia in general. I had also met and become friends with a number of other scholars from Europe and the United States who frequently conducted research in Zambia. During our chance meetings, as we passed through the Research Affiliation Office of the University of Zambia in Lusaka, we shared stories of our experiences and often had useful and provocative discussions about our ideas and interpretations. One of these scholars, an agricultural economist with whom I had discussed my exploration of the relationship between migrant relatives and elderly people in home villages, later offered me a consultancy on one of his projects examining the effects of migration on agricultural labor (Cliggett 1997a, 2000). Through that consultancy and the NSF grant, I was able to return to Zambia for three-month field visits during three consecutive years (1996 through 1998). The consultancy also allowed me to begin a new research project while remaining connected to the Gwembe project.

By the end of my doctoral research, I had begun to feel a growing sense of membership within both the Zambianist scholarly community and within the local communities where I did fieldwork. The three return field trips solidified this feeling and also helped me develop my self-perception as a professional anthropologist.

LISA CLIGGETT

The Transition from "Employee" to "Manager"

The turning point in how I viewed my association with the Gwembe project came after completing my dissertation, during the final year of the NSF grant for which Ted was the principal investigator. Until then, I had seen myself somewhat like an employee of the project—carrying out a variety of tasks that did not necessarily link to my own work. I saw my dissertation research and consultancy work as independent from the project obligations, and thus I had a dual identity at times—independent researcher and project employee.

However, as I began to think about my next big research project, and consequently to consider in more specific terms the process of systematically incorporating the now close to fifty years of Gwembe data, I began to see those decades of data as a frontier for investigation. My increasing recognition of the importance, and potential for my own research interests, of the Gwembe materials came about through my own intellectual development. In addition to the village checklists that they had given me at the start of my doctoral research, Elizabeth and Ted hold vast quantities of data on innumerable topics. The opportunity to draw from that data, not only at the outset of my research career but, more importantly, as time has moved on and I develop more subtle lines of inquiry, has been one of the greatest benefits of joining this longitudinal study. In fact, during my dissertation write-up, I did not draw as extensively as I might have on the thousands of pages of ethnographic field notes that Elizabeth and Ted made available to me. At the time, I was struggling with learning to interpret my own field notes and data. To attempt systematic interpretation of forty years of someone else's data seemed daunting, and posed the risk of "dissertating" for decades.

With time, however, I felt a greater sense of "ability" in understanding Gwembe life, and with that I developed more confidence to read my colleagues' field notes, reflections, interpretations, and thoughts, and to make my own sense of their views and their data. Indeed, the cognitive process of learning to trust yourself can be a never-ending challenge in collaborative longitudinal fieldwork. Especially during my dissertation write-up, I often felt that I could not say anything useful or new because Elizabeth and Ted already had written on all the important topics and had made all the meaningful interpretations of Gwembe life to which my work would speak. Indeed, Elizabeth and Ted already had published on aging (Colson and Scudder 1981) and on the relationship between rural populations and their migrant relatives (Colson and Scudder 1975; Scudder and Habarad 1991)—the two areas of my research at that time. I felt that all I could do was make a statement about how things are now compared to their earlier writings.

Part of working through those mental barriers meant having Elizabeth and Ted read what I had written. The first time I had them read my work was one of the most intellectually vulnerable moments in my young career. However, their detailed reading, commentary (almost like a conversation with my writing), and critical praise allowed me to continue writing, even with a bit more confidence. Although in comparison to Elizabeth and Ted I still feel rather like a child in my knowledge of the Gwembe, I now have greater confidence to attempt interpretations. This may be due, in part, to internalizing what Elizabeth has said about writing and publishing when working on long-term studies. She suggested that there is an inherent sense that our work is always "in process" when you engage in longitudinal studies—each publication is more like a "status report" than some kind of definitive statement (Colson 1999). Thus, unlike the case of those anthropologists who do "one-shot" studies, with each new article or book we have the chance to clarify (or correct) earlier statements.

With greater confidence in my skills of interpretation, even of someone else's field notes, I began to have a strong desire to work closely, and systematically, with the five decades of Gwembe materials, not just to use selected anecdotes and incidents from those years. I began to see the Gwembe data as a foundation on which to develop potentially more significant findings than I could produce through summer field studies as I pursued tenure at an academic institution.

Tied to the data were the ideas that drove Elizabeth and Ted to collect such detailed information in the first place. The intellectual framework inherent to the Gwembe study—a concern for community continuity, change, and adaptation—also was my own general area of interest. When I recognized that those fifty years of field notes, surveys, diaries, field maps, and so forth provided ways to examine these important questions, it became clear that taking some responsibility for the Gwembe project not only benefited the project, but also would benefit my own career.

At that turning point in my self-perception from employee to something more, I also knew that, at this stage in their careers, Elizabeth and Ted were unlikely to take responsibility for finding funding to manage data that they had already analyzed for their particular concerns. I realized that, in order to make the half century of data accessible and meaningful to me and my colleagues, I would need to take some responsibility for planning how that data should be processed, coded, and stored. Suddenly, I saw myself as a decision maker in the project, not merely as an employee.

Multigenerations and Multidisciplines: Synthesizing for the Long Term

Making the fifty years of qualitative data more easily accessible has become a primary concern for me and my other next-generation colleagues. By computerizing those data and, ultimately, linking them to the demographic database, we will create a unique and massive data resource that has applications not only for anthropology, but also such fields as comparative economics and political science, public health, ecology, demography, and development studies, to name only a few.

The challenge at this stage in the Gwembe project's life cycle is the tension between the next generation's desire aggressively to pursue support for continued data collection, data management, and fieldwork and our individual needs to establish ourselves within our disciplines and subdisciplines. In the spirit of the "publish or perish" tradition, we need to balance our work on these diverse opportunities so that we *can* remain committed to the broader project goals.

All three of us in the next generation of the Gwembe project face similar publishing and research requirements for tenure track positions at research universities—multiple articles in top-tier journals, a published book by the tenure review year, and external grants demonstrating an active research agenda. Of course, in the early years of being assistant professors, we also have commitments to develop, prepare, and teach new courses at our institutions. The pressures of all of these (and other) job components make these pre-tenure years a difficult time for sustaining our collaboration and our stewardship of the Gwembe project.

At times, any one of us may feel a need to carve out a particular research question of our own. We may feel a need to have "first rights" to publish on that topic and thus ensure recognition for "new and significant research activity" from our universities and tenure review committees. This same individualism also may emerge in terms of access to and control over portions of the data. Over time, particularly as we move beyond the tenure hurdle, tendencies toward individualism surely will give way to the cooperative and collaborative styles that led us to join this project in the first place.

My particular coping strategy for the stress of the tenure process includes planning smaller and more easily defined research projects from which I can publish articles relatively quickly. In one case, analyzing a small data set of diaries written by Gwembe research assistants offers the opportunity to explore a number of themes, including domestic violence and theft (Elizabeth initiated the analysis on this latter topic, and we are currently collaborating on a manuscript). In this sense, the Gwembe project remains active and relevant, but in some cases more in the form of an archive.

While many social scientists and scholars in the humanities conduct research that makes use of primary and secondary databases, anthropologists typically rely on collecting their own data through fieldwork. One of the great benefits of a longitudinal study is that, even when there is no time or funding for fieldwork, there always are data awaiting analysis. In the case of the Gwembe project, the data sets are too vast to analyze in their entirety (which is why we plan to computerize the data sets to render them more accessible), so pieces will need to be assembled, analyzed, and published in numerous separate articles—a strategy perfectly compatible with getting tenure.

During the moments when my next-generation colleagues and I can look beyond the immediate future of our careers, we do see a long-range and ambitious plan for the Gwembe Tonga Research Project. Recently, Rhonda Gillett-Netting and I, on behalf of the Gwembe team as a whole, submitted a proposal to a new program for infrastructure development for multidisciplinary social science projects at the National Science Foundation. If funded, this grant would have provided the necessary funding to computerize the fifty years of qualitative data and to create an interactive database linking the ethnographic data to the demographic information. Unfortunately, the grant proposal was turned down, partly because it was very ambitious (particularly given our "junior" status in our disciplines), and partly because multidisciplinarity means different things to different people (and disciplines) and consequently is difficult to achieve. Since hearing the outcome of that round of proposal submissions, we have decided to break the proposal into smaller sections and attempt funding for various components through different foundations. This approach will be much slower, and the ability to make the links between the ethnographic and quantitative data will be significantly delayed, but we are learning that, in longitudinal studies, time plays a role even in the search for funding.

The question of how to achieve multidisciplinarity plays out not only in our search for funding, but also in the collaboration among our project members. All five of us have differing strengths and research interests. Four of us have training in anthropology, although within the discipline we each tend toward different emphases. Sam Clark comes to the project with a background in computer science and demography, both of which are extremely valuable to the project as it now stands. Since the end of 1995, when we began the more formal collaboration under the NSF grant Ted secured, all of us have been learning the process of seeing research goals through other researchers' lenses. In some cases, this has been a long and difficult lesson. I have had to struggle with ideas, methods, and jargon from quantitative perspectives to which I have not been accustomed. At the same time, other team members consider the ethnographic emphasis on participant observation and narrative field notes too vague, subjective, and anecdotal to be of comparative value. Despite these differing viewpoints, we continue to discuss what data are so crucial that they *must* be collected regularly and systematically. After long and repeated discussions, we agreed on the need for maintaining detailed demographic records, a core of socioeconomic data, and diaries kept by village-research assistants. In addition, insofar as possible, we are committed to continuing local ethnography.

In the end, we believe that our work benefits from the collaboration. We have been forced to rethink our views regarding data, methods, and research questions. We have become more critically aware because we must explain, clarify, and sometimes justify our desires and research plans to each other long before our ideas reach a grant review panel or peer reviewers for publication. In short, we have better data, better analysis, better interpretations, and better answers for important questions about the human condition than if we worked within the traditional solitary framework of most anthropologists.

LISA CLIGGETT

Individual Personalities and Project
Results: Toward a Conclusion

At the outset I suggested that deciding to join the Gwembe Tonga Research Project significantly influenced both my professional and personal life. Pushing myself to handle different kinds and vast quantities of data has made me into a much different anthropologist than I would have been using my own field notes collected over a much shorter time frame. Remaining committed to one field site and study population, and to the questions that matter most within that context, helps to define how my individual research interests will develop. Learning to communicate effectively across disciplines, and within a team of individuals, challenges me not only to resist the temptations of individualism often associated with the anthropological persona, but also to make my research relevant beyond the discipline of anthropology.

But how does long-term research affect our personal lives? Certainly, it provides a sense of having an additional home and an additional family. I know that many fieldworkers feel their research sites to be like a second home. In my case, Zambia really is a second home, in the sense that I feel obligated to return. At times I love this obligation, but at times I resent it (much like I have felt about my home in the United States). I have responsibilities—both social and material—in Zambia that require my presence on a fairly regular basis. The project, and I, have numerous possessions (including household supplies, bedding, clothing, and equipment) that we must care for in Zambia. We also have social relationships that need regular nurturing through our presence if we expect to maintain them.

Although I feel close to some of my Tonga friends and research assistants in the Gwembe, they are *not* the second family of which I speak. Somewhat to my surprise, the Gwembe project "team," in a fascinating transformation from coworker to relative, has become like a new family. I say this not to suggest that we have bonded into a harmonious domestic group, but to recognize that, in family relationships, people remain connected despite conflicts and individual desires that at times might push nonfamily members away from each other. Individuals within families and households work together and remain linked because of what they achieve through their collaboration (Netting, Wilk, and Arnould 1984; Wilk 1989). The five team members—Colson, Scudder, Gillett-Netting, Clark, and myself—in the Gwembe Tonga Research Project find that the sum of our research efforts far outweighs the work we do alone, even when we find struggles in our collaboration. By working together, we also ensure the continuation of the project, something that we could not achieve as individuals.

Of course, there are many other ways that my association with the Gwembe Tonga Research Project has influenced my personal life, including my aesthetic tastes and dietary preferences, the way I think of seasonality and time, how I create a social life and friendships, and even my changing ideas of what is important in life. Anthropologists tend to merge our personal selves with our professional selves; it goes with the job. The inverse may also be true: individuals willing to blend their personal and professional lives can more easily become successful as anthropologists. We can say something similar about long-term anthropological studies. Individuals, working together and apart, shape and ultimately determine the direction, focus, results, and longevity of long-term projects. When a field research enterprise like the Gwembe Tonga project is sustained over decades, it is because individuals become committed to making it work. Only when we are willing to take on the challenges of longitudinal research can its professional and personal rewards accrue to us as individuals, to our discipline and to science in general, and to the people whose social history we preserve through our fieldwork among their households and communities.

References Cited

Cliggett, Lisa
    (1997a) "Economic and social components of migration in two regions of Southern Province, Zambia." Bath, UK: Center for Development Studies.
    (1997b) "My mother's keeper: Changing family support systems for the elderly in the Gwembe Valley, Zambia." Ph.D. dissertation. Indiana University, Bloomington.
    (2000) "Social components of migration: Experiences from Southern Province, Zambia." *Human Organization* 59(1):125–135.

Colson, Elizabeth
    (1999) "Passing the mantle: A discussion on long-term research projects." Paper read at the Annual Meeting of the American Anthropological Association, November 17–21, Chicago, IL.

Colson, Elizabeth and Thayer Scudder
    (1975) "New economic relationships between the Gwembe Valley and the line of rail." Pp. 190–210 in David Parkin (editor), *Town and Country in Central and Eastern Africa*. London: Oxford University Press.
    (1981) "Old Age in Gwembe District, Zambia." Pp. 125–153 in Pamela T. Amoss and Stevan Harrell (editors), *Other Ways of Growing Old*. Stanford: Stanford University Press.

Netting, Robert, Richard Wilk, and Eric Arnould
    (1984) *Households*. Berkeley: University of California Press.

Scudder, Thayer and Jonathan Habarad
    (1991) "Local responses to involuntary relocation and development in the Zambian portion of the Middle Zambezi Valley." Pp. 178–205 in J. A. Mollett (editor), *Migrants in Agricultural Development*. London: Macmillan.

Wilk, Richard [editor]
    (1989) *The Household Economy*. Boulder, CO: Westview.

CHAPTER TEN

A HALF CENTURY OF FIELD RESEARCH IN TZINTZUNTZAN, MEXICO: A PERSONAL VIEW

George M. Foster

Introduction

On January 5, 1945, as a Smithsonian Institution visiting professor at Mexico's National School of Anthropology, and in the company of four students from the school, I arrived in Tzintzuntzan, Michoacán, Mexico, charged with the responsibility of training the students in ethnographic field research methods. Thus began a study—now in its fifty-seventh year—that has become the longest *intensive* field research project in the history of the discipline. Except for the period from 1947 to 1951, at least one anthropologist has gathered data in the village every year since 1945. In my own case, I have regularly visited the village since 1958, usually twice a year, with my most recent (and perhaps last) visit in July 2000.[1]

More than half a century of field research in Tzintzuntzan offers a distinctive perspective for considering methodological problems in social anthropology. In this chapter, I focus on the importance of time depth for assessing changes in the community, on colleagues and myself as ethnologists, and on our relationships with the people we study. The nature of a community, the behavior of its people, and the processes of change can best be understood when a good historical record exists. On this score, Tzintzuntzan was a fortunate choice for a research enterprise that was to develop into an intensive longitudinal study, for its written historical record goes back nearly five centuries, while the archaeological record carries us back several centuries more. Today, Tzintzuntzan is a Spanish-speaking community of about 3,600 people, on the east shore of Lake Pátzcuaro, on a paved highway 230 miles west of Mexico City. The lake, justly famed for its beauty, lies at an elevation of 7,000 feet, surrounded by extinct volcanic peaks rising to 12,000 feet. When the Spaniards arrived in Mexico in 1519, Tzintzuntzan was the capital of the Tarascan Indian Empire,[2] the most powerful political group west of the Aztecs. Its precontact importance is still attested to by five circular pyramids (*yácatas*) standing on an immense artificial platform on the east side of the village. For a short time during the early colonial period, Tzintzuntzan seemed destined to become the seat of the bishopric for west central Mexico, but the church fathers soon thought better of this plan, first moving the seat 10 miles south to

Mariano Cornelio, a Tarascan fisherman. Photo by George Foster.

Pátzcuaro and subsequently to Valladolid (modern Morelia), 30 miles eastward. In spite of this loss, a major Franciscan monastery functioned there for well over two centuries, and colonial church buildings continue to cast their distinctive stamp on the village.

From the mid-1530s Spaniards and their Mexican-born descendants—increasingly mixed with the indigenous peoples of the area—lived in the village; well into the nineteenth century, church registers distinguish entries as *Ciudadano*

(Spanish speaking, and of presumed Spanish descent) or *Yndio* (Indian, Tarascan speaking). Although Tarascan appears to have been the dominant language until the late nineteenth century, for more than one hundred years Spanish has been the principal language. Today, the 10 percent of the population that can speak Tarascan—a figure that has held fairly constant since 1945—represents recent migrants from adjacent Indian villages. Few of the children of Tarascan speakers reported in the 1945 census today speak their parents' language, and few of the children of subsequent Tarascan-speaking immigrants will, as adults, speak the language. All Tarascan speakers are equally fluent in Spanish.

Traditional Tzintzuntzan was a pottery-making, fishing, and trading village, in which farming was of secondary importance, best characterized as mestizo by race and peasant in cultural typology. Although still mestizo, it can no longer be described as peasant. Some of the changes that have removed it from the peasant typology are described in later pages.

The First Visit

Although my wife, Mary, and I first passed through the village as tourists in early 1940, at a time when I was engaged in doctoral research among the Popoluca Indians in southern Veracruz State, the thought that I was being given a prescient glimpse of a large chunk of my professional career did not cross my mind. In the spring of 1944, Julian Steward, founder and director of the Smithsonian Institution's new Institute of Social Anthropology, sent Donald Brand, a geographer, and me to Mexico City to teach at the National School of Anthropology. The formal agreement between the Smithsonian Institution and Mexico's National Institute of Anthropology and History (the parent body of the school) specified that during half of each year we would meet classes and during the other half we would train students in field methods. It was further specified that the field training was to take place in the Tarascan area, thus carrying on "The Tarascan Project" (Rubín de la Borbolla and Beals 1940) initiated in 1939, and in 1944 still a high research priority in Mexican anthropology. Thus, I had no choice in selection of the research area; acceptance of the Smithsonian appointment committed me to work in Michoacán.

In June 1944, Brand and I visited the Tarascan area to pick a site to which to return with students. We visited Tzintzuntzan but did not seriously consider it, in spite of its historical importance, because clearly it was no longer Tarascan. Instead, we selected Ihuatzio, an extremely conservative Tarascan community three miles to the south. When we arrived, Brand and I, accompanied by six students, learned an important lesson. Although we were on an official government mission, had cleared our research with the appropriate state and local authorities, had visited the village, and had secured a pledge of cooperation from the priest, we were greeted with a reserve that verged on hostility. After three days we found it prudent to leave. Eight strangers dropped into a conservative community were seen as a major threat, and no official authorizations or orders would induce people to accept us. Consequently, we split our group so that, on January 5, 1945, I found myself in Tzintzuntzan with Gabriel Ospina (a Colombian), Pablo Velásquez (a native Tarascan from the sierra to the west of the lake), Remy Bastien (a Haitian), and Chita de la Calle (a Mexican).[3]

Bastien and de la Calle returned to Mexico City in February, when the spring term of the Escuela began, while Ospina, Velásquez, and I lived and worked together in Tzintzuntzan for the first six months of 1945, Velásquez concentrating his attention on the adjacent Tarascan-speaking hamlet of Ichupio, leaving the village for Ospina and me. In June, Velásquez and I returned to Mexico City, he to continue with his classes and I to resume my teaching obligations. Ospina remained in Tzintzuntzan until March 1946. During these additional eight months, I returned for about a week each month. Later, he and I revisited the village on several occasions, the last in September 1946, so that our observations spanned a twenty-month period. Ospina's continuous presence in the village for fourteen months and his superb qualities as a fieldworker spelled the difference between average and exceptionally good baseline data.

Tzintzuntzan proved to be a much better choice than Ihuatzio would have been. As *cabecera*, or chief administrative town of the *municipio* of Tzintzuntzan, the village is the site of the municipal archives and of most political activity as well. As the first Christian community in Michoacán, because of the long residence of Franciscan monks, and because of the continuous presence of priests since the Franciscans' departure in November of 1766, Tzintzuntzan, in 1945, had a more complex religious and ceremonial life than Ihuatzio. Again, with a major home-based pottery industry, as well as farming, fishing, muleteering, and tule reed weaving, Tzintzuntzan had a much more varied economic base than the latter village, whose economy was based largely on agriculture and fishing. Finally, Tzintzuntzan conformed more nearly than Ihuatzio to the type of community that shortly thereafter anthropologists would come to call "peasant." Consequently, my thinking about the nature of peasant society was stimulated well beyond what would have been the case had my theoretical orientation continued to be traditional, Tarascan Indian, and historical, as would certainly have proven true had we remained in Ihuatzio. The bulk of our findings on this initial project are found in Foster and Ospina (1948, 2000).

Return in 1958

In 1946, I did not seriously contemplate maintaining research continuity in Tzintzuntzan. Long-term field research was not an option that occurred to most anthropologists at that time. Today, it is hard to realize that fifty years ago anthropologists still thought in terms of the urgency of completing the inventory of "primitive" and "folk" societies around the world. In that intellectual and disciplinary context, a restudy was viewed as a luxury hard to justify, a squandering of scarce resources.

In my case, a return to Washington, D.C., in 1946, succeeding Julian Steward as director of the Institute of Social Anthropology; a year of field research in Spain during 1949–1950; a move to Berkeley in 1953; and applied anthropological consulting activities in other parts of the world in 1952, 1955, and 1957 all turned my mind away from continuing research in Mexico. Then, during the summer of 1958, Mary and I made a leisurely trip through Mexico to identify a site not only for our own research, but one also suitable for field training of Berkeley doctoral candidates. By then, the possibilities of a restudy of a community where good baseline data had earlier been gathered had been made clear by Robert Redfield's (1950) return to Chan Kom and Oscar Lewis's (1951) restudy of Tepoztlán. Consequently, Tzintzuntzan was a top candidate among the possibilities we considered.

When we arrived in the village in July 1958, we found that in spite of a twelve-year absence we were remembered in positive terms. The obvious pleasure expressed by old friends, and the presence of Gabriel Ospina and other professional colleagues at UNESCO's CREFAL (Fundamental Education Training Center for Latin America) at nearby Pátzcuaro, quickly tipped the scale in favor of a return to Tzintzuntzan.

Although I returned to Tzintzuntzan in 1958 with Redfield's restudy of Chan Kom and Lewis's restudy of Tepoztlán as my models, I did not realize that I was embarking on a very different type of project, a longitudinal study with frequent repeat visits more comparable to Kluckhohn's work among the Navajo (see Lamphere's chapter in this volume). In the 1950s, the distinction between a restudy and a longitudinal, or long-term, study had not yet emerged. Methodologically, this distinction is important. A restudy, particularly if the time spent in the field is relatively brief, inevitably draws attention to change. This is true, for example, of the Chan Kom restudy, *A Village That Chose Progress*, which is based on a return visit of only six weeks. In contrast, longitudinal study affords opportunity both to study change *and* to delve more deeply into the culture itself.

The twelve-year gap between my early and later observations suggests that my Tzintzuntzan research resembles both a restudy and a longitudinal study. To a certain extent, this is true. Actually, however, the gap is much less than the dates suggest, for Gabriel Ospina had returned to Pátzcuaro in 1952 as one of the first staff members of the newly established CREFAL. Because of his earlier residence in the village, his friendship with the people, and his knowledge of the local scene, Tzintzuntzan became a major community for CREFAL's training programs and planned culture change projects. Rare was the week from late 1952 until his departure from CREFAL in 1960 that Ospina did not spend several days in Tzintzuntzan. From long discussions with him, from CREFAL censuses and other records (e.g., Ospina 1954), and from reports of shorter studies by other anthropologists (e.g., García Manzanedo 1955; Willner 1958), I obtained a very good picture of what had transpired during the second half of the period I was absent, leaving a span of less than six years with no firsthand information other than from villagers themselves.

Living Arrangements

Where will I live? This is the first question facing all of us when venturing into the field. During the initial study, the students and I lived first in the school building (during the long winter vacation) and then in a small house at the pyramids built as a museum, our cooking and cleaning needs taken care of by *compadres* and other close friends. In both places we were physically in the village, but slightly removed from the center of things. We were unable to look out into the street and see who passed by, who interacted with whom; and we were unable quietly to observe from within how a household functioned. In beginning our new work, Mary and I were anxious to live in a village home, to be able to observe life from inside a family, in a way that previously had not been possible.

Here it was that an old friend, Doña Micaela González, her second husband Melecio Hernández, and her grown daughters, Dolores and Virginia Pichu, rose to the occasion. With great apprehension, Micaela subsequently told us, but in response to Ospina's assurance that we were really not difficult people, she agreed to accept us into her home, to put a glass window and a cement floor in a room for our use, to prepare our meals, to wash our clothing, and to answer our many questions.

The arrangement has proven immensely satisfying to all parties, and since 1959 we have lived with Doña Micaela on all of our visits. With each succeeding year, we found ourselves accumulating more and more field equipment, file boxes, local arts and crafts, and clothing, so that by 1970 we had outgrown our small room. Simultaneously Micaela—one of the first villagers to abandon traditional noncompetitive behavioral forms—had reached the point where she felt compelled to add a second story to her home to keep up with two or three neighbors doing the same thing. Here again our interests coincided: we designed and paid for a second-story apartment which we furnished and where we kept sufficient field equipment and clothing so that we could arrive with no more than an airplane carry-on bag and still live at a level of comfort enjoyed by few field researchers. We have no equity in this property; when we no longer need it, it reverts to the family. Meanwhile, we have comfortable and attractive quarters, loving care from the family members while we are in residence, and superb informants within hailing distance.

The research advantages of living with a family, and of observing it on a daily basis over many years, can scarcely be overemphasized. Serendipitously overheard chance remarks, and chance events observed—"trigger mechanisms," I call them—have been important sources of my theoretical ideas. My ideas about the perception and manipulation of social distance and about cultural responses to expressions of envy (discussed later in this chapter) illustrate this point.

Occasionally, such events simply bring delight to the research experience and enrich the texture of the ethnographer's data. For instance, one evening we were seated in the kitchen after our *café con leche* supper, reflecting on the day's happenings. Melecio and Micaela were quietly talking to each other when I overheard him ask, "When did Christ walk on this earth?" Without a moment's hesitation Micaela replied, "The Virgin of Guadalupe appeared on December 12, 1531. It was before then, perhaps 150 years earlier." She turned to me: "*Doctor*," she asked, "When did Christ walk on this earth?" In my best Socratic classroom manner I countered with, "What year is it now?" "Nineteen sixty-five," she promptly replied, puzzled as to what my question had to do with when Christ walked on earth. "And what happened in year one?" I continued. She reflected a moment, and then replied, with perfect logic, "I suppose that's when we began counting." She and Melecio were both astonished to learn that Christ was born so long before the appearance of the Virgin of Guadalupe, and that his birth provided the baseline from which we count passage of the years. This little episode gave rise to no startling theoretical formulations, but it gave us a meaningful insight into Micaela's and Melecio's perception of time depth, as well as the relative importance to them of the birth of Christ vis-à-vis the appearance of Mexico's patron saint.

Of course, there are many field situations in which it is not feasible to live intimately with informants; when it *is* possible, there is no substitute for it. The rich data obtainable in this fashion simply cannot be duplicated in any other way.

Change and Modernization in Tzintzuntzan

The ability to monitor in detail change and modernization in a community is certainly one of the chief justifications for long-term research. In the case of Tzintzuntzan the six comprehensive project censuses taken in 1945, 1960, 1970, 1980, 1990, and 2000 and the prices of representative staple goods recorded annually over a period of fifty-six years provide unparalleled information on precisely how a typical peasant community has, in the post–World War II years, ceased to conform to the classic peasant typology. The changes have been breathtaking. Had anyone in 1945 told me that what occurred during the following thirty years would in fact transpire, I would have laughed at such naïveté. Yet during this period, the community changed from a very "closed," "uptight," fearful, suspicious traditional community into an "open" community, very much a part of modern Mexico. Kemper and Foster (1975) describe in some detail the magnitude of changes during the first thirty years of research in Tzintzuntzan.

Since 1975, the changes have been even more dramatic. Increasing numbers of young people attend universities and technological institutes in Morelia and Mexico City, taking degrees in medicine, dentistry, nursing, law, engineering, computer science, and the like, and more than two hundred have become schoolteachers. Parents make great sacrifices to help their children obtain an education, a striking contrast to the 1940s when few were encouraged—or even permitted— to attend primary school. In 1942, the first graduating class in the new primary school numbered just six! Most of today's well-educated young people, of course, are lost to the local community, since they must seek jobs in larger centers, but many remit part of their earnings to help educate younger siblings, as well as to aid aging parents. Emigration likewise has become more marked, both to Mexican cities and to the United States (where Washington State has emerged as the current Mecca). The U.S. amnesty law of 1986, designed to impede illegal migration, has had little if any effect in slowing the traffic. To the contrary, whereas in earlier years most legal and illegal migrants were men, today entire families, children included, routinely make the move. Most emigrants, whether to other parts of Mexico or to the United States, significantly improve their standard of living. But within the village, too, the standard of living for a great many people has risen greatly (table 10.1).

Significant additions to standards of living have taken place since the February 1990 census, but the impact of these changes often is at the whim of external forces. Consider these two tales. In 1993, the village manual telephone switchboard, which for many years had frozen the numbers of subscribers at 50, was replaced by a direct-dialing system. Immediately, the number of subscribers rose to 75 or more, and now there are nearly 130 telephones in Tzintzuntzan. Residents

Table 10.1. Tzintzuntzan Material Possessions, 1945–2000 (Percent of Households)

Year of Census	1945	1960	1970	1980	1990	2000
Total Population	1,231	1,877	2,253	2,649	3,349	3,610
No. of Houses	248	319	358	448	580	738
Electricity	14%	52%	65%	81%	91%	99%
Raised bed	57%	69%	77%	94%	96%	99%
(Inner-spring mattress)	(0%)	(3%)	(24%)	(60%)	(62%)	(80%)
Piped water	22%	50%	62%	71%	81%	96%
Television	0	0	11%	54%	78%	92%
Propane stove	0	(two)	14%	49%	79%	87%
Electric blender	0	(two)	4%	34%	75%	83%
Radio	2%(?)	41%	70%	85%	94%	80%
Sewer	0	0	0	30%	66%	80%
Flush toilet	0	0	1%	10%	25%	62%
Refrigerator	0	0	0	11%	30%	50%
Hot-water shower	0	(one)	5%	10%	19%	43%
Videocassette machine	0	0	0	0	8%	40%
Washing machine	0	0	2%	5%	12%	33%
Stereo	0	0	0	21%	28%	29%
Truck or car	0	(one)	7%	13%	17%	25%
Telephone	0	0	0	9%	7%	17%
Microwave oven	0	0	0	0	0	12%
TV satellite dish	0	0	0	0	0	9%
Computer	0	0	0	0	0	2%

Note: When written out inside parentheses, "one" and "two" indicate the number of households possessing an item.

can make local and long-distance calls with virtually the same facility one enjoys in the United States. As of June 1998, more than 100 homes had large parabolic (satellite dish) television antennas; eight years earlier there had been none. Up until 1999, satellite dish owners could access, without additional fees, all the Mexican TV signals carried on the nation's Morelos II satellite. By the February 2000 census, the number of active satellite dishes in Tzintzuntzan had dropped to 68! What happened? Because of the privatization of telecommunications in Mexico, domestic access to satellite signals was no longer open and free, but required a decoder box and a monthly subscription fee. About a third of the local satellite dish owners responded by disconnecting their satellite systems (for which they had paid as much as US$2,000) and reinstalling their rooftop antennas.

Comparing the picture of today with that of 1945, it is tempting to believe that Tzintzuntzan has become a consumer society. As the tales of telephones and satellite TV demonstrate, even relatively affluent villagers may not be willing to commit their limited resources to consumer goods and services. Other families—a decided minority, however—still live at a poverty level, bypassed by most of the good things in life that have come to their fellow villagers. Less and less can the traditional fiction be maintained that "here we are all equal." Although Tzintzuntzan in no sense is a class society, the gap between the well off and the poor is far greater than in 1945.

Standards of living in Tzintzuntzan have risen, and so have prices. During most of the post–World War II period, Mexico enjoyed remarkable monetary stability compared to much of the Third World. Then, toward the end of the 1970s, a severe economic crisis occurred that continued until the early 1990s. The peso was continually devalued, and in some years inflation surged past 100 percent. Then, with economic recovery apparently well under way, effective January 1, 1993, the last three zeros were lopped off Mexican currency, so that 1,000 pesos became one "new peso," with an exchange rate of three pesos to one dollar. And, with the implementation in January 1994 of the North American Free Trade Agreement (NAFTA), the future looked increasingly bright. Then, in December of that same year, economic disaster struck Mexico. The peso was devalued 40 percent or more, capital fled the country, interest rates rose to more than 50 percent annually, and in spite of massive loans from the United States and European countries, social and economic pessimism grew significantly. The future is uncertain, but as I write in May 2001, Tzintzuntzeños continue to feel great economic pressure, and more and more they seek to solve their problems by emigrating to *el norte*. Table 10.2 shows the effect of inflation on Tzintzuntzan prices from 1945 to 2001.

In earlier statements (cf. Foster 1967), I have described Tzintzuntzan as a "peasant" community, using the term in the standard anthropological sense of a "part society" existing in a symbiotic relationship with urban centers, where the presence of the state is manifest in political domination of rural communities. Marginality has been noted as one of the primary characteristics of peasants, who

Table 10.2.   Prices of Staples in Tzintzuntzan, 1945–2001 (in Pesos)

Year	1945	1960	1970	1980	1991	2001
Maize, 4 liters	0.90	1.25	3.00	20	2,000	6.50
Beans, kg	1.30	1.50	3.50	350	4,000	14.00
Sugar, kg	1.00	1.80	2.50	16	1,700	6.00
Lard, kg	3.80	8.00	10.00	30	4,000	12.00
Beef, kg	2.00	10.00	20.00	120	16,000	45.00
Whitefish, kg	5.00	20.00	30.00	160	80,000	120.00
Milk, liter	nd	nd	1.80	9	1,400	5.00
Quaker Oats, pkg.	1.20	2.00	2.30	30	2,300	10.50
Bolillos (bread)	0.05	nd	1.50	3	250	1.00
Beer, bottle	0.40	0.60	2.00	7	1,000	5.50
Soft drinks, bottle	0.15	0.50	1.50	8	600	4.50
Cigarettes, pack	0.20	0.70	0.70	8	450	12.00
Hot sauce, bottle	0.60	nd	1.40	18	1,000	7.00
Laundry soap, bar	0.50	nd	1.10	28	1,300	5.00
Band-Aid	0.05	0.15	0.25	2	200	1.00
Flashlight battery	0.42	1.20	2.30	12	1,300	5.50
Lead glaze, kg	1.05	3.20	4.20	30	5,000	14.00
Propane gas, tank	nd	nd	34.00	200	23,500	176.40
Pátzcuaro, bus to	nd	nd	1.00	7	900	7.00
Mexico City, bus to	nd	nd	28.00	120	66,000	190.00
Mason, daily wage	5.00	nd	nd	300	50,000	200.00
Day laborer	2.00	nd	nd	150	20,000	100.00
Pesos to the US$	4.85	12.50	12.50	26	2,940	9.50

Note: In 1993, 1,000 pesos became 1 new peso.
nd = No data.

are seen as psychologically isolated from a culturally distant and little understood world. In Tzintzuntzan, throughout its colonial history and until about 1965, the gap between city and village in almost all aspects of life—occupation, education, clothing, access to health care and to news—was very real. Today, this is no longer the case. By no stretch of the imagination can the villagers be described as "isolated" peasants. Table 10.1 indicates how the standard of living has risen in recent decades.

Today, Tzintzuntzeños are best described as Mexicans who reside in a rural area which is itself an urban hinterland for the nearby city of Pátzcuaro, for the state capital Morelia, for the national capital Mexico City, and for diverse metropolitan areas in the United States. More and more, the residents of Tzintzuntzan are like their urban compatriots: their schooling is based on curricula set by the national government, they have access to the same kind of medical care (although in lesser degree, and often at greater cost), they drive the same motor vehicles, they watch the same television programs, they root for the same national sports teams, and they hold similar hopes for their children's future. Some anthropologists have used the expression "post-peasant" to describe communities like Tzintzuntzan. The term is awkward, but I know of no better one. In any event, if we can extrapolate Tzintzuntzan's transformation during the past generation to the rest of the world, the term *peasant* is about to join *feudal* as appropriate only to historical discussions.

Hypothesis Formulation

What theoretical or other considerations have guided me in asking questions and gathering data? Why have I emphasized some areas, and perhaps neglected others? Formulation of hypotheses in my office, to be tested by data specifically gathered to test these hypotheses, has played a very minor role in guiding my work. This is not to say that I work without a sense of problem. When I returned in 1959, I assumed—with the "restudy" model in mind—that the principal justification for continued research was to exploit a detailed cultural baseline to measure subsequent developments to learn more about processes of change. Consequently, I spent much time identifying innovators and noting how—in education, travel experience, work, and the like—they differed from less innovative personalities. I have maintained this interest and, in addition to systematic updating of censuses, vital statistics, and similar data, I have taken pains to note the growing numbers of young people who leave the village to continue higher education; the numbers and destinations of emigrants; the widespread acceptance of television, of cars and trucks, gas stoves, and other signs of "modernization." Emigration has, of course, become a major research topic in its own right (see Kemper, this volume).

But as time passed, I realized that the original Tzintzuntzan research barely scratched the surface and that in all areas of life there was still much to be learned. As a student of Kroeber and Lowie at the University of California (Berkeley), I was taught that all forms of behavior—all data—have meaning and are relevant to interpretation and explanation, even if this relevance is not apparent at the time they are noted or recorded.

Consequently, I have been happy in Tzintzuntzan to continue with my earliest research habits of recording as many data as possible on everything that occurs to me. When I become aware of data "out there," I want them, even if I have no plans for their immediate use, and even knowing that their real significance may never be revealed to me. I began recording dreams, for example, quite by accident. One day a neighbor told a complex and colorful dream he had had the night before, and it dawned on me that a collection of dreams would constitute a rich lode of information about many aspects of village life. It was not a topic that had previously interested me, and I felt deficient in the training in psychology necessary for the interpretation of dreams. Still, I felt that through content analysis I should be able to learn a good deal about personality, worldview, and perhaps other things. So, without definite plans, I plunged into the task, asking friends to tell me their dreams. I simply assumed that I was a sufficiently good anthropologist to be able to draw something meaningful—to recognize basic patterns—from a sizable collection of dreams. The result was "Dreams, Character, and Cognitive Orientation in Tzintzuntzan" (Foster 1973). Recording of twenty-two Thematic Apperception Test (TAT) protocols came about in a similar, largely unplanned, fashion. Monograph-length treatment of these data remains to be done, almost certainly by someone else.

The amassing of data alone, no matter how detailed, does not in itself lead to important theoretical formulations. Something more is needed. In reflecting on the origins of my theoretical hunches, I am impressed by the way in which anomalies in my data have been thrown into relief by chance observations, leading me to formulate new interpretations. Thomas Kuhn's paradigmatic model, which stresses the importance of anomaly in scientific breakthroughs, is relevant here. "Discovery," he writes, "commences with the awareness of anomaly, i.e., with the recognition that nature has somehow violated the paradigm-induced expectations that govern normal science" (Kuhn 1962:52). In my case, this awareness has been triggered by serendipitous—that is, lucky, unplanned—observations. Long ago, the sociologist Robert Merton recognized the "serendipity component" in qualitative research, a pattern that "involves the unanticipated, anomalous and strategic datum which exerts pressure upon the investigator for a new direction of inquiry which extends theory" (Merton 1948:506). "An unexpected and anomalous finding," he continues, "elicited the investigator's curiosity, and conducted him along an unpremeditated by-path which led to a fresh hypothesis" (1948:509). I illustrate the role played by serendipitous observations in clarifying anomalous data in my research with several examples.

(1) While doing doctoral research among the Popoluca Indians of southern Veracruz State during 1940–1941, I was intrigued to note that travelers—Indians and mestizos alike—when approaching each other on a jungle trail, would greet one another from a distance with *adiós* ("good-bye") rather than with some form of "hello." Subsequently, I learned that this is a common Mexican practice, not limited to any group or geographical area. Still, I puzzled over this anomalous (to me) linguistic form: why should "goodbye" be used as a greeting?

In Tzintzuntzan another linguistic anomaly puzzled me: why were friends, when separating, always careful to say "We will not say goodbye," when a straightforward "goodbye" seemed appropriate to me? A serendipitous observation provided the key to the puzzle. One evening I noted that Micaela, in kicking the dog out of the kitchen, addressed the animal with the respectful *Usted* form. Since children and other "social inferiors" are addressed with the informal second person singular, *tú*, I was again faced with an anomaly: why such courtesy to a bothersome animal? This time something clicked: I recalled speakers addressing other adults whom they regarded as social inferiors with the respectful form *Don* (or *Doña*, depending on sex). Formal address, I recognized, can be used to maintain social distance. Earlier observations on verbal interaction, including *adiós* and "We will not say goodbye" quickly came to mind, and almost immediately it dawned on me that perceived and desired social relationships are expressed and manipulated through an elaborate system of verbal forms. The dog clearly was being reminded that it was not human and was not to take liberties in the house. *Adiós*, I reasoned, is a way one conveys the message that "I see you, I respect you, I bear you no ill will, but I am busy and must be on my way; I have no time to talk." In contrast, "We will not say goodbye" conveys just the opposite message. An unadorned "goodbye" sounds abrupt; it suggests that perhaps the speaker has no desire to continue the relationship. To emphasize that the parting is not really "goodbye" counters this danger. Within half an hour I assembled from my notes most of the illustrations found in "Speech Forms and the Perception of Social Distance" (Foster 1964a).

(2) A serendipitous observation of what seemed to me to be anomalous behavior also "triggered" the line of thought that led to "Cultural Responses to Expressions of Envy in Tzintzuntzan" (Foster 1965a). Over the years I had recorded odd bits of behavior: the universal rejection of compliments, the *remojo* gift given to friends by someone who acquires something new of value, the concealment of pregnancy, the *bolo* (copper coins thrown by the godfather to village children immediately after the baptism of an infant), and the like. Then, on one occasion, fifty or more children came to Micaela's house for a "school breakfast." To my astonishment, they ate in absolute silence. "They're taught to eat in silence," was Micaela's response to my question as to why. That children would eat noisily in a group was as astonishing to her as that they could eat quietly was to me. Something whispered to me "envy!" and these and other behavioral forms quickly rose to a conscious level in my mind. I recalled how Micaela would become uneasy when, during mealtimes, we occasionally became animated in our discussion, raising our voices more than ordinarily. "Quiet!" Micaela would plead. "They will know on the street that we are eating." Once, daughter Lola was dispatched outdoors to check noise levels. Micaela breathed a sigh of relief when she returned with the report that our boisterousness could not be noted by passersby.

These forms of behavior quickly fell into what now seem like predestined places, and within an hour the paper was blocked out. Eating in silence, I realized, and many other seemingly unrelated forms of behavior, have one important thing in common: symbolically or in fact, they are devices useful in reducing the likelihood of envy from persons not fortunate enough to have sufficient food, a new possession of value, or a healthy new descendant.

(3) "The Validating Role of Humoral Theory in Traditional Spanish-American Therapeutics" (Foster 1988b) is also the product of anomaly-cum-serendipity. In conventional accounts of humoral theory the "principle of opposites" model (a metaphorically Hot remedy for an illness believed to stem from cold, or to be cold, and a metaphorically Cold remedy for a hot illness) is viewed as prescriptive, as a guide to therapy. With this paradigm accepted by all anthropologists researching humoral medicine, the task was seen to be to determine the basis for classification of foods and remedies and to explain away the inconsistencies that were commonplace. Eventually the paradigm came under such strain that it was, in Kuhn's terms, "in cri-

sis." No longer was it possible to force all of the contradictory data into the prevailing prescription model.

Meanwhile, I was increasingly puzzled by two anomalies in my data. The first was the striking differential agreement and disagreement among informants about the humoral values of herbal and other remedies. For many common remedies informants were in unanimous or near-unanimous agreement, while for other equally common remedies they were in wide disagreement. The second, and related, anomaly was the extent to which common therapies failed to conform to the principle-of-opposites prescription. Often, I found, they *did* conform, but equally often they did not. Theory that explains only part of the time is of dubious value; it cries out for a new paradigm.

I hit upon the new paradigm one afternoon while walking the streets of Pátzcuaro, pondering the problem. By chance, I passed by the Farmacia Moderna, its name belied by the hundred or more nineteenth-century porcelain pharmacy jars resting on wall shelves. Several years earlier I had recorded the labels of all jars, so I knew they represented a time when humoral remedies were establishment medicine. But this time the significance of these museum pieces dawned on me: when patients go to pharmacies, I mused, they complain of symptoms, asking the pharmacist for something to relieve these symptoms. They don't say, "I'm suffering from a hot illness, please give me something Cold for it." In other words, pharmacists (and *curanderos* as well) prescribe commonly accepted remedies for well-known symptoms, without thought of humoral consistency. Knowing I had pushed the principle-of-opposites prescriptive paradigm to the breaking point, that the accumulated inconsistencies could no longer be accommodated by it, and thinking over my data, I recalled constant question-and-answer interchanges like the following: "What is the quality of salamander?" "Cold." "How do you know?" "Because it is given to children suffering from *ético* (hectice fever)." In other words, a new paradigm—validation of empirical treatments—better accounts for the humorally inconsistent data than the prescriptive paradigm, since the anomalies created by the latter simply disappear.

(4) The model of Limited Good (Foster 1965b) represents a combination of a serendipitous "trigger" and a slowly growing awareness of how behavior conforms to a cognitive outlook. From the time of my first Tzintzuntzan work, I had speculated that the economic worldview of the villagers, and perhaps that of peasants in general, was marked by what I called the "Image of the Static Economy." The "economic pie," I argued, quite realistically was seen as constant in size and unexpandable. Consequently, "If someone is seen to get ahead, logically it can only be at the expense of others in the village" (Foster 1960–1961:177; see also 1961a, 1964b). I saw the problem, however, only in economic terms. The integrating theme of "implicit premises," central to the complete argument, developed in 1962 during a six-month community development assignment in Northern Rhodesia (now Zambia; Foster 1987a). There

I was struck by how different were Britishers' assumptions about people, character, and culture from my own and how different both of our assumptions were from those of people in Tzintzuntzan. I began thinking about the static economy in the wider context of implicit premises, but still I did not have the final key to Limited Good. This came—the idea was triggered—when I chanced to read an article by John Honigmann about a village in West Pakistan. Three sentences in a footnote caught my eye: "One dominant element in the character structure [of the villagers] . . . is the implicit belief that good of all kinds is limited. There is only so much respect, influence, power, and love in the world. If another has some, then somebody is certainly deprived of that measure" (Honigmann 1960:287).

This serendipitous reading of Honigmann caused all of the elements in the model (including such diverse things as treasure tales and the nonregenerative quality of blood) to fall into place. Limited Good thus owes its formulation to three major activities or events: the slow accumulation through field research and reading about peasant economic behavior; my exposure to a drastically different culture (British colonial society) that contributed an element critical to the model; and a trigger, a serendipitous event, the chance reading of the published observations of a colleague. The lesson I draw from this is that anthropologists, however strongly committed to a single community or people, should actively seek out other cross-cultural experiences as a source of pertinent ideas and that general, as well as specialized, reading is essential for the widest exposure to potential stimuli.

In other instances, I have been unable to identify the precise moment and manner in which new hypotheses or models first occurred to me beyond recognizing that masses of data slowly acquired made them possible. The "dyadic contract" articles (Foster 1961b, 1963) are illustrative. The ideas in the first paper developed in an unplanned fashion, as I was drawn into village reciprocity networks. Eventually, I realized that there was a significant pattern in exchange relationships. Only after writing the first paper did it occur to me that people interact with patrons, including supernatural beings, in essentially the same manner as with fellow villagers.

If, in 1945, I had realized that my commitment to Tzintzuntzan was to be lifelong, would I have done things differently? Are there additional kinds of data, and other approaches to gathering data, that I would have sought or used? In hindsight, I feel fortunate that I emphasized data rather than theory in the initial study. My regrets have to do, not with hypotheses that I failed to develop or test, but with data I failed to gather. Theories come and go but good data are timeless, grist for the anthropologist's mill when least expected. And, clearly, one of the advantages of repeated visits to a research site is that, as our data accumulate and we have time to ask questions about their meanings and their anomalies, we *can* write with confidence on theoretical matters, as I did in my second book on Tzintzuntzan (Foster 1967, and its two updates, 1979c, 1988a).

Methodological Problems: The Time Factor

In carrying out research in the same community for more than half a century, I have found that models which seemed appropriate at the time the data were gathered may require renewed scrutiny when, in later decades, conditions have changed. A second problem arising from the passage of time is that research tasks that initially seemed straightforward have become increasingly problematic. A third time-related problem is the question of anonymity.

The Limited Good model illustrates the first point. The model is accurate, I believe, for traditional Tzintzuntzan, perhaps to about 1965, although with a decreasingly good fit during the years immediately preceding that date. But changes in behavior, in attitudes, and above all in relations with the outside world—due particularly to radio and television, education, and emigration—have significantly modified the traditional Limited Good outlook and masked many of its manifestations that still survive. In other words, the kinds of evidence that led to my initial formulation of the model, while by no means gone, are much less obvious than they were two generations ago. It is possible that, had I begun my research in Tzintzuntzan in 1970, the idea of Limited Good would never have occurred to me. It would be entirely possible for young anthropologists to study Tzintzuntzan today, search for evidence of Limited Good, and, on the basis of their findings, argue that the Limited Good hypothesis is inappropriate. To a degree they would be correct: for contemporary Tzintzuntzan, it explains behavior much less satisfactorily than for traditional Tzintzuntzan. But such an argument, because of its lack of time depth, in no way destroys the model. It merely confirms what we already know: worldviews can and do change. A model is a function of specified factors, and if these factors change with the passage of time, the fit of the model may become less and less good.

Census taking illustrates the second point: changed conditions create anomalies that complicate research techniques. Colleagues and I have taken six 100 percent censuses of the village, in 1945, 1960, 1970, 1980, 1990, and 2000. Although these censuses cover a great deal of personal information and data on standards of living, I am here concerned with the single question of population: who is to be counted? In 1945 and 1960, and to a great extent 1970, there was little problem. People either were at home, or they were away for a predictable period of time, and it was known that they would return, or that they had emigrated and were no longer considered residents. I have no difficulty in saying what the population was in 1945, 1960, and 1970.

By 1980, it was impossible to report population figures in these simplistic terms. More and more people with lifelong ties to the community were away for long periods, their ultimate return uncertain. How does one treat men who may spend nine months a year working in the United States, returning once a year to be at home with their wives and children? They remain taxpayers, voters, and recognized members of the community, yet their status is quite different from that of husbands who remain in the village the year around. Again, a large number of schoolteachers, born and raised in the village, have jobs fifty to a hundred miles from Tzintzuntzan. Many of them have built homes in the village, to which they return, almost always for long vacations, often once a month and sometimes for weekends. Should they be counted? A similar pattern holds for high school and university students studying in Morelia, an hour and a half away by bus. They move from boarding house to boarding house, or stay with relatives, but often return home on weekends, and they remain dependent on their parents for support. And, with substantially increased migration of Tzintzuntzeños to the United States, one can never be sure about who will be present one day and gone the next, who should be counted as a permanent emigrant, and who is likely to return.

What all of these people have in common is that they are away from the village much more than they are in it, and their eventual relationship to the community is uncertain. In preparing for the 1980 census, we decided to deal with this residential anomaly by making two counts: a "core" population, which, apart from short trips, normally resides in Tzintzuntzan, and an "extended" population of commuters and those who travel even great distances to work or study but always with the expectation of coming home. An important criterion in determining whether persons were counted as part of the core population or the extended population was the attitude of the affected individuals and their families toward their residential situation. This long-term trend, and the different attitudes Tzintzuntzeños have toward emigration, means that it is no longer possible to give a straightforward answer to the question, "What is the population of Tzintzuntzan?"

In this context, table 10.3 presents our best estimate of the core population residing in Tzintzuntzan plus the extended population who felt that they should be included in the village count for census purposes. The great growth of Tzintzuntzeño migration to the United States in the 1990s created in its wake more than two hundred "empty" or "abandoned" houses. Instead of leaving a spouse and some children at home as in previous decades, during the 1990s household heads often went to *el norte* with as many family members as they could arrange (and afford) to take along. Consequently, the number of persons counted in 2000 as extended dropped dramatically compared to 1990, when the move of many Tzintzuntzeños to the United States was more tentative. This long-term trend is visible only through regular monitoring over several decades (see Kemper, in this volume).

The third problem—anonymity—reflects a changing norm in ethnographic writing. In my anthropological training, before World War II, I was taught to identify carefully informants by name and to tell something about them so that readers could evaluate their statements. Moreover, for North American Indian tribal research—the bulk of all research being carried out by U.S. anthropologists at that time—clear identification of places and people was an essential part of the

Table 10.3.   Tzintzuntzan Population: 1945–2000

	Tzintzuntzan Population		
Census Year	Core	Extended	Total
1945	1,231	na	1,231
1960	1,877	na	1,877
1970	2,253	na	2,253
1980	2,506	143	2,649
1900	2,999	350	3,349
2000	3,346	264	3,610

na = Category "not applied" to the census data.

record. Moreover, it was assumed that few if any informants would see, or be able to read, ethnographic accounts in which they appeared. During the intervening years, anthropologists increasingly have studied literate groups, whose members increasingly are concerned to see what the fieldworker has written. Consequently, the use of pseudonyms for community and informant, both within the United States and abroad, has become standard practice, a basic precaution to protect the people concerned.

When I first wrote about Tzintzuntzan in the late 1940s, this had not yet become common practice, and it never occurred to me to conceal the true name of Tzintzuntzan, nor to use other than the real names of informants. By the time I realized the ethical implications of my policy, it was too late to turn back. Calling Tzintzuntzan "Tarasca" (copying Oscar Lewis, who renamed Tepoztlán "Azteca" in his later works) would have fooled no one. Also, the villagers would have been furious. They are delighted to see my publications about Tzintzuntzan, some of which have been translated into Spanish (e.g., Foster 1972; Foster and Ospina 2000), to see their photographs, and to see their names in print. They would feel cheated if I had to tell them, "It says 'Informant B'; that's really you." Obviously, I do not use real names in every case; for example, in discussing criminal matters I change names and disguise circumstances. But my students have told me the principal criticism of those few villagers who have browsed through my works is that I have not given them and their families sufficient exposure.

Methodological Problems: The Ethnologist's Age

In "Encounters with Tikopia over Sixty Years," Raymond Firth (1990:241) succinctly stated the essence of long-term social anthropological research: "Anthropology has changed, I have changed, and the Tikopia have changed." Anthropology, he noted, had become less descriptively ethnographic than in earlier times, but he also saw signs that the discipline might "return to the notion of seeking as objective and dispassionate accounts as is possible of social institutions of people."

Firth also spoke of his changing statuses over the years, from young bachelor to married man, father and grandfather, moving professionally from a junior position "to one of some seniority and then one of retirement and less responsibility" (1990:241). The bulk of Firth's article, however, deals with sixty years of change for Tikopians, living both on and off the island. The magnitude of these changes, and the rapidity with which they came, was certainly impossible to predict when Firth began his research on this tiny, isolated island, but they are paralleled by the changes noted by all anthropologists engaged in long-term community-based field research. For "change," in the broadest sense of the word—social, cultural, economic, and political—is the common denominator in all longitudinal anthropological studies.

In the more than half a century I have known Tzintzuntzan, the village has changed dramatically, and the changes it has experienced have had important impacts on the research enterprise. I, also, have changed greatly, and these changes likewise have been reflected in the research I have carried out. I was thirty-two years old and only three years out of graduate school when I arrived in Tzintzuntzan. I was young, energetic, and gung-ho, like a puppy for whom all the world is an exciting new experience. My most recent—and perhaps last—visits to the village were at Christmas 1999 and in July 2000 when, at eighty-six years of age, and suffering from a debilitating neurological disease that severely limits my mobility, I felt anything but energetic and gung-ho. The village and its people, while still interesting, failed to excite me as in earlier years.

Little by little age takes its toll. Beginning about the time of my eightieth birthday party in 1993 in the village, I recognized that I no longer had the physical stamina to be present at all of the events—fiestas, baptisms, burials, town meetings, and the like—that I routinely would have attended in an earlier period. It had become more difficult, too, to strike up the kinds of new friendships with younger people—the bulk of the Tzintzuntzan population—that result in rich field data. The "young" people with whom I have most contact are, I realize, better described as middle aged. They are the children and grandchildren of close friends from my early years in the village, and I have kept in touch with them because these early associations have made it easy. My age mates, too—friends for half a century—are dropping off, so that the pool of informants to whom I can easily turn is diminishing. Even those who survive are less good informants than in earlier years: Their minds wander, they forget, and they are no longer central to the life of the community.

Again, in my last years in the village I have had fewer fresh ideas and insights than formerly; the point of diminishing returns has been reached, and the trigger seems rusty. This is due to at least two factors. The first is, as just noted, decreasing stamina, a lack of energy and drive, a reduced compulsion to make sure I am seeing everything that is going on. And the second is familiarity with the community. I have already identified and written about some of the most striking aspects of life in the village, such as the dyadic contract, Limited Good, manipulation of social distance, envy, the validating role of humoral theory, and the like. Does that mean that there are now fewer new themes to be found? Are theoretical ideas to be garnered from a single community themselves a limited good, their progressive identification gradually reducing the remaining pool? I think not. Brandes and Kemper, certainly, have not lacked for research topics. And Peter Cahn's recent doctoral research on Protestant conversions in the Tzintzuntzan region has opened a vast area crying out for attention (Cahn 2001). But I suspect that, for a single researcher, the passage of time diminishes the frequency of serendipitous observations that lead to fresh theoretical formulations.

Yet recent years have not been without great research satisfaction. During this time, I have devoted much effort to recording health and illness beliefs and practices. Thirty years ago I thought I knew all there was to know on the subject. In reality I knew almost nothing. Since 1978, I have published one book (1994) and a series of papers that collectively provide the most detailed picture to date of humoral medicine in Latin America (1978, 1979b, 1981, 1982, 1984a, 1984b, 1985, 1987b, 1988b). The last two—on the origin of humoral medicine in the Americas, and on the validating (rather than the prescriptive) role of humoral theory in therapy—I consider to be among my theoretically most important papers. Old age is a time when one learns to count blessings, and I am grateful that I have been able to continue productive field research, even though at a reduced pace as compared to earlier years.

Advancing age presents still another problem for anthropologists who have amassed a sizable corpus of field notes: what provision should we make for these materials for the time when we are no longer around to take responsibility for their safekeeping and proper use? I am fortunate that Stanley Brandes and Robert Kemper, both of whom first went to the field with me in 1967 as students, continue a lively interest in studying and publishing on the villagers, both in and away from the community (e.g., Brandes 1968, 1979a, 1979b, 1981a, 1981b, 1983, 1984, 1988, in press; Kemper 1974, 1977, 1979a, 1979b, 1981, 1994a, 1994b, 1995, 1996a, 1996b). They expect to continue monitoring developments during their active careers. While all my field notes (as well as personal correspondence) will ultimately go to the University of California's Bancroft Library, the Tzintzuntzan materials will do so only when Brandes and Kemper (and perhaps their students, such as Peter Cahn) feel they no longer have an active interest in them. Until that time, they will care for the data files, continuing to make them available to other scholars interested in Tzintzuntzan.

Integrating Students and Colleagues into the Project

The *raison d'être* for beginning fieldwork in Michoacán was, of course, to train students, and those students who were with me in Tzintzuntzan during the winter and spring of 1945 all completed master's degrees (the highest then offered) at the National School of Anthropology. During the twenty-year period from 1959 until my retirement in 1979, a dozen Berkeley graduate students accompanied me to the field, some more than once. I placed most of them in nearby communities where we had easy access to each other, but where they were largely on their own. I favored this arrangement not only because I was apprehensive about cluttering up Tzintzuntzan with outsiders (I remembered how too many students had forced our departure from Ihuatzio fifteen years earlier), but also because students enjoy having a community to themselves. Consequently, only five spent significant amounts of time in the village, and, as matters turned out, only Kemper (1971) completed a doctoral dissertation involving Tzintzuntzan. Brandes's predissertation Tzintzuntzan experiences, he tells me, were very helpful in the Spanish research on which his dissertation was based. He continues to visit and do research in Tzintzuntzan and has published a critically acclaimed book on ritual life in the village (Brandes 1988). Five more of the dozen students completed dissertations on other nearby communities, while a sixth did so on a Greek island.

My students and I never really worked on joint projects in the field, so we had no problem with integration of, or rights to, field data. The only joint publication is Kemper and Foster (1975), and that developed as an afterthought, when we found that our independently gathered data lent themselves to a specific problem. With all students I had a formal, written agreement that spelled out our mutual rights and expectations. All gave me copies of their field notes. If dealing with comparative topics where their data were pertinent, I had permission to cite their findings, with appropriate credit. The data, however, belonged to them and could be used in any way they wished. Students, in turn, had full access to my files with comparable reciprocal rights. As matters worked out, we drew very little on each other's materials. In more recent years, however, Brandes and Kemper (former students now become long-term colleagues) and I have freely made use of each other's materials and expertise.

The principal "colleague" (apart from Kemper and Brandes, whose roles changed following completion of their doctoral studies) integrated into research in Tzintzuntzan has been my wife, Mary, who has been with me most of the time in Tzintzuntzan since 1958. We have lived the same life in Tzintzuntzan, attended the same fiestas, heard the same things, and observed the same behavior. She has noted points that have escaped me and has had access to situations from which I, as a male, have been excluded. The discussions we have had in the field, the speculations about the significance of this or that act or event, and her perceptions as a woman have played a major role in my research and writing. While her interests have been primarily linguistic—her doctoral dissertation, a grammar, was based on data obtained in the nearby Tarascan-speaking village of Ichupio (M. L. Foster 1969)—she has also published significant ethnographic papers on the village (e.g., M. L. Foster 1983, 1985, 1989).

I have wondered why ethnologists—markedly individualistic in their behavior—would want to undertake research in communities already apparently well researched. The answer, I believe, lies in the fact that many specialized topics benefit from a preexisting database. In archaeological research, even the back dirt of previous excavations can sometimes yield important results with new research procedures. So, too, in ethnological fieldwork. Building on existing work, new researchers can make significant contributions in previously neglected cultural domains or can use new research methods to resolve old problems. For instance, Kemper's (1971) dissertation focused on the adaptation of Tzintzuntzeños to life in Mexico City, while Cahn's (2001) recent dissertation sheds new light on the convergence of evangelical Protestants and traditional Catholics in Tzintzuntzan and its region. Brandes's (1988) symbolic interpretation of ritual behavior and his forthcoming study of Alcoholics Anonymous (in press) likewise reveal the rich texture possible when new research begins with a solid database.

Personal Relationships with the Villagers

There are moral and ethical questions surrounding the relationships between anthropologists and informants that must be addressed. Clearly, I have profited greatly from this relationship. In a considerable measure, my reputation as an anthropologist is due to the people of Tzintzuntzan. If the village had the equivalent of a United Crusade, it would be easy to assign royalties from books to it. But Tzintzuntzan has no mechanism whereby money can be given for the benefit of the community at large. I contribute substantially to such things as public lighting and school funds, and my name routinely is found on the list of contributors to any village function for which individual citizens make donations. Each year I leave with the village priest a substantial sum of money to be distributed at his discretion among the village needy. Altogether, my continuing contributions have far exceeded any monetary profit to me from publications. Some people obviously have benefited more than others; others, whom I feel have little real call on my resources, have also benefited.

In a wider sense, and for the village as a whole, I think our (Kemper, Brandes, and Cahn included) major impact has been to give villagers a sense of *esprit* that otherwise would be lacking. Traditionally they have looked upon themselves as humble people, undervalued and ignored by their own more elevated countrymen. Prior to our arrival, no one had shown interest in their daily lives. The fact that we return year after year and are obviously delighted to be there has led to a feeling that Tzintzuntzan must be something special. After all, no other Michoacán village can boast several resident anthropologists. "*Qué bueno que no nos olviden*" is the standard greeting of villagers each time we return, "How nice that you don't forget us." And when we leave, it is always "*¿Porqué se vayan tan pronto?*" ("Why are you leaving so soon?") The phrases are ritual, but I believe they express the feeling that the presence of *El Doctor*, Mariquita, Roberto (Kemper), Tani (Brandes), and Pedro (Cahn) is tangible evidence that Tzintzuntzan is not an ordinary village.

Impact on the People Studied

Mary's and my impact (and that of students and colleagues) on Tzintzuntzan has been varied and significant. I believe no one is worse off for our presence, and I know that some are better off. A few, without our monetary intervention in medical crises, would almost certainly have died. Although we have hired local people to help in taking censuses, we have never directly paid informants for information. There have, however, been important material advantages for those people with whom we have worked most closely and to whom we have felt most indebted. These material advantages have taken the form of gifts, educational support, and even help with medical care.

The members of Doña Micaela's family are those to whom we have been most indebted, and in order to repay them in some small measure, we have brought them as tourists to the United States, in 1976, 1979, 1984, 1987, 1990, and 1993. On one or more of these trips they have visited my sister in Washington, D.C., my brother in San Diego, my son in Colorado, and the Kempers in Dallas. In turn, all of these people and their families have visited in Tzintzuntzan. The reactions of these visitors to what they see in the United States is always fascinating: so many American flags flying on government buildings, so few people walking in residential areas, home delivery milk bottles and newspapers lying untended on doorsteps, long-distance calls so easily made from airport telephones, and the like. Daughter Virginia found our automatic garage door opener to be the most intriguing of all: "*Es muy obediente,*" she said, "It's very obedient," just as if it were a dog obeying its master's command.

Just as living with the members of this family in Tzintzuntzan has provided rich insights into how villagers view the world and cope with life, so does having them as guests in our home add to our understanding of how their world, for all its similarities, differs from ours. With English-speaking guests one assumes that both they and hosts will welcome an occasional quiet hour, to read the morning newspaper or to continue with an interesting book. This is not the case, we learned, with all "literate" people. One morning Mary and I awakened about six-thirty to find, to our astonishment, that Micaela and her daughters were busy weeding the garden. An important truth dawned on us: to be literate, in the strict sense of the word of being able to read and comprehend legal and commercial documents and to write simple letters, is quite distinct from using literacy for pleasurable activities. Action, in the form of gardening, and not reading for pleasure, seemed to them to be the appropriate early morning activity. Micaela and her daughters are fully literate in the narrow sense of the word, but apart from a fleeting glance at a newspaper it never occurs to them to read for the sheer joy of reading or to fill an idle hour. Light reading is not found on their bedside tables nor is it packed in their travel luggage.

It is gratifying to make life a bit easier and more interesting—as I think we have done—for small numbers of friends. But there are also negative aspects to a policy of substantial help given to relatively few people. This help has affected relationships for the worse between some of the families that have benefited most from our presence and other families that likewise would have appreciated medical, educational, and other forms of aid. We are, after all, a limited good and our largesse, although considerable, is not inexhaustible. Just as village families traditionally see themselves in competition for scarce "good" of all kinds, so do those who benefit, or aspire to benefit, from us see themselves as competing for our favors. The resulting envy and jealousy are fairly well suppressed during our stays, but in at least a few instances they have resulted in strained relationships among village families.

Micaela and her family are probably the most envied people in the village. Their remarkable economic progress since we came to live with them is seen by fellow villagers as due almost entirely to our help, a perception wide of the mark. Nonetheless, it can be argued that, had we not come to roost with Micaela, she and the other members of her family would have more intimate ties with villagers than is now the case. It can also be argued that there would be little difference, for other families that have made major economic progress during the same period also find themselves increasingly distant from those who have progressed less.

Conclusions

In summary, I turn to the question of why long-term research? What can anthropology learn from it that goes beyond the results of intensive studies of a year or two? Should all anthropologists be encouraged to continue to monitor their field sites, or are the advantages of this type of research outweighed by the costs? The answer, obviously, depends on the interests and temperament of the individual anthropologist—as well as, perhaps, the attractiveness of the people and the natural environment. Scudder and Colson, for example, point out that although the Middle Zambezi Valley is beautiful, Gwembe settlements along the line of rail "are not places we would choose to vacation" (Scudder and Colson 1979:251). In contrast, Lake Pátzcuaro does not suffer by comparison to the Vale of Kashmir.

Insofar as the contributions to anthropology are concerned, I find two basic reasons to encourage long-term research. The first is the quantity and quality of the basic data that can be obtained, and the second is the dynamic view obtained of communities impacted by national and world trends and events. In addition to these scientific justifications there is the personal satisfaction and emotional fulfillment that comes from the relationships formed with people in an exotic society who start out as informants and gradually are transformed into close personal friends.

As to quantity and quality of data, it should be apparent that there is a direct correlation between time spent in the field and the information gathered. In theory, three or four years of research either in one block, or spread over twenty years, should produce comparable amounts of data. I doubt that this is true. After some months of steady research intellectual fatigue sets in; the researcher *must* get away to recharge the mind's batteries. In my case, I have found that, after my initial 1945–1946 session, relatively short repeat visits to the field—from one to four months—made possible highly efficient use of time. I would arrive in the field, charged up with questions and ideas that I had formulated and mulled over since my preceding trip, with the energy to work intensively until time to return home.

As pointed out previously, theoretical insights do not come to me in one massive package; they develop slowly, over time, often triggered by serendipitous observations, as I turn from one theme to another. The pattern of relatively unhurried repeat visits that has characterized my Tzintzuntzan research has vastly widened the spectrum of serendipitous behavioral situations to which I have been exposed; consequently, I have written about a much wider variety of topics than would have been possible had I limited myself to one or a few widely separated visits. Examples of the varied topics I have dealt with may be encountered in Foster 1960, 1966a, 1966b, 1968, 1969, 1970, and 1989, as well as Maccoby and Foster 1970.

My data are "thick." The patient accumulation of masses of data, the lack of a sense of urgency, the luxury of being able to hold off on a "hot" idea, secure in the knowledge that another field season will permit gathering of additional critical data—all have been advantageous to me. Moreover, repeat visits make it possible to correct errors, which are more common in all anthropological reports than we like to believe. One of my most blatant early errors was to describe the Hot-Cold syndrome in Tzintzuntzan as Mexican Indian in origin (Foster and Ospina 1948:51). But after discovering Hippocratic-Galenic humoral medicine and realizing that I was dealing with a paradigm (in Kuhn's terms) at least 2,500 years old, I was able on return visits to gather data to provide readers with an accurate and comprehensive account of this popular medical system and to place it in historical context (Foster 1994).

With respect to the second of the two major justifications for long-term research—the dynamic view obtained of a society or community—two themes are apparent. The first is that simply observing the magnitude of change over the period a community has been under observation reminds the researcher of the inevitably static bias of even the best classic studies, studies that portray a slice in time of a year, or two, or three.

The second theme has to do with prediction. The observation of the behavior of the members of a community over a number of years ought to provide the insights and hypotheses necessary to predict with a fair degree of accuracy future changes. This is a hope as yet largely unrealized. Perhaps with a growing number of long-term studies in hand, anthropologists will do better in the future, but certainly our record to date is not impressive. In my case, after my 1945–1946 research in Tzintzuntzan, I made only a few modest predictions. In the 1940s, process was still a topic little understood by ethnographers; I was more concerned to reconstruct the past and record the present than to tinker with the future.

In retrospect, I am relieved that I paid little attention to the future, for my major predictions turned out to be largely wrong. In 1948, I estimated that an annual family income of US$400 to $500 at 1945 price levels should "provide a reasonable standard of living in terms of local and national levels" (Foster and Ospina 1948:289). Few families enjoyed such income at the time, and I felt that existing techniques of production made such a goal for a majority of families extremely unlikely. I pointed out that, although increased efficiency in farming and pottery making and distribution were possible, the cost in labor redundancy would be high. Growing demand for labor in cities, I felt, might for a time draw off surplus rural population—as it has, in fact, done. But, in spite of the wartime *bracero* program whereby Mexican men came to the United States under contract for specific periods of time, I completely failed to foresee the role legal and illegal migration ultimately would play in providing work opportunities.

To compound my failure as a prophet, in 1967 I continued to emphasize "the fundamental factors which hold back the village" (Foster 1967:350) rather than the factors favoring progress. With respect to migration to the United States, I wrote that the 1964 termination of the Bracero Program surely would have deleterious effects on the community:

> The end of the *bracero* program is almost certain to cause a major economic (and perhaps social) crisis in Tzintzuntzan, and in the thousands of similar Mexican villages which, over a twenty-year period, have grown accustomed to this outside source of aid. Standards of living will fall, people will eat less well, new clothing will appear more rarely, and home necessities and luxuries will become scarce. (Foster 1967:287–288)

All this on the eve of Tzintzuntzan's most dramatic rise in standards of living! My most accurate prediction had to do with health care seeking. In 1948, I believed that *curanderos* already were on their way out and that modern biomedicine would be adopted increasingly by Tzintzuntzeños. On this point I was correct; for many years, people have preferred to consult medical doctors for illnesses deemed to be in any way serious. Traditional curers, while still present in small numbers, play a decidedly secondary role in meeting the health needs of most people.

What conclusions about prediction can be drawn from more than fifty years of contact with Tzintzuntzan? The most important, I believe, is that change in a twentieth-century village is intimately tied to the political, economic, and social events that occur in the country of which it is a part. When the country prospers, the developing infrastructure provides support for local progress. A high degree of Tzintzuntzan's relative well-being today has depended on state and national programs: a hard-surfaced road, electricity, potable water, a sewer system, primary and secondary schools and their teachers, a health center, and much more. The accident of geographical proximity to the United States also makes

Mexico a special case in development. Recognizing the negative as well as positive aspects of this fact, there is no doubt that legal (and illegal) employment in the United States has acted as a social and economic safety valve, relieving the pressure of a burgeoning population and raising standards of living from remittances sent back from *el norte*.

Obviously, ethnologists must know a great deal more than the local picture to comprehend changes that occur in communities under their observation. What is *not* obvious from the macro perspective is the behavior of individuals which, en masse, add up to change. The reason for the shift from *curanderos* to physicians, for example, becomes clear only when informants tell us that they find more satisfactory results when they consult the latter. And the patient accumulation of case studies gives insight as to why some people chose to emigrate, tentatively or permanently, and why others do not.

In the first version of this chapter, I commented on the personal satisfaction and sense of fulfillment that resulted from a long-term commitment to Tzintzuntzan and its people (Foster 1979a:182–183). This sense of familiarity (literally, feeling part of a family) has only grown over the passing years. Not only did the extended Foster family come to Tzintzuntzan to celebrate my eightieth birthday in 1993, we also gathered on January 5, 1995, to celebrate the fiftieth anniversary of my arrival in the community. Then, on June 28, 2000, we assembled once again, this time to celebrate the long-awaited translation into Spanish of *Empire's Children: The People of Tzintzuntzan* (Foster and Ospina 1948). At an academic ceremony held at the Colegio de Michoacán in Zamora, a two-hour drive from Tzintzuntzan, the biggest round of applause came for Doña Micaela González, the ninety-four-year-old matriarch of our Tzintzuntzan family.

The next day, many longtime Tzintzuntzan friends came to her home for a second celebration. We ate the traditional fiesta fare of pork *carnitas*, rice, and beans; drank our beers and soft drinks; and danced to the music of Pedro Dimas. We told stories about the people (many long deceased) staring out at us from the black-and-white photographs that grace the pages of the handsome new edition of *Los Hijos del Imperio* (Foster and Ospina 2000), and recalled the good times and difficult days shared throughout more than half a century.

Little did we suspect that, the very day we returned home to Berkeley, Micaela would die (of heart failure) in a Morelia hospital. For me, the coincidence of the book publication and Micaela's death marks the end of a long and very special era. With the ethnological mantle passed to Kemper, Brandes, and Cahn, research in Tzintzuntzan surely will go on for decades to come, but for all those who ever knew Doña Mica it can never be quite the same.

Notes

1. In the first edition of this volume, under the title "Fieldwork in Tzintzuntzan: The First Thirty Years" (Foster 1979a), I related my experiences up to 1975.

2. Were I beginning my writing on Tzintzuntzan today, I would use the word *Purépecha* rather than *Tarascan*, for that is the term the indigenous population of Michoacán uses to identify itself. This is also the official designation employed by Mexican government agencies. However, since the term *Tarascan* is much better known among historians, anthropologists, and the public at large, it seems appropriate to continue its use here.

3. Brand settled in Quiroga with José Corona Núñez, who became a distinguished Mexican specialist on Tarascan culture and history, while the sixth student, Angélica Castro (also Mexican) elected to work in a small settlement across the northeast arm of the lake opposite Tzintzuntzan.

References Cited

Brandes, Stanley

(1968) "Tzintzuntzan wedding: A study in cultural complexity." *Kroeber Anthropological Society Papers* 39:30–53.

(1979a) "Dance as a metaphor: A case from Tzintzuntzan, Mexico." *Journal of Latin American Lore* 5:25–43.

(1979b) "The household developmental cycle in Tzintzuntzan." *Kroeber Anthropological Society Papers* 55–56:13–24.

(1981a) "Cargos versus cost sharing in Mesoamerican fiestas, with special reference to Tzintzuntzan." *Journal of Anthropological Research* 37:209–225.

(1981b) "Fireworks and fiestas: The case from Tzintzuntzan." *Journal of Latin American Lore* 7:171–190.

(1983) "The posadas in Tzintzuntzan: Structure and sentiment in a Mexican Christmas festival." *Journal of American Folklore* 96:259–280.

(1984) "Animal metaphors and social control in Tzintzuntzan." *Ethnology* 23:207–215.

(1988) *Power and Persuasion: Fiestas and Social Control in Rural Mexico.* Philadelphia: University of Pennsylvania Press.

(in press) *Staying Sober in Mexico City.* Austin: University of Texas Press.

Cahn, Peter S.

(2001) "When conversion is convergence: Evangelicals and Catholics in Tzintzuntzan, Mexico." Ph.D. dissertation. University of California, Berkeley.

Firth, Raymond

(1990) "Encounters with Tikopia over sixty years." *Oceania* 60(4):241–249.

Foster, George M.

(1960–1961) "Interpersonal relations in peasant society." *Human Organization* 19:174–178.

(1960) "Life-expectancy of utilitarian pottery in Tzintzuntzan, Michoacán, Mexico." *American Antiquity* 25:606–609.

(1961a) "Community development and the image of the static economy." *Community Development Bulletin* 12:124–128.

(1961b) "The dyadic contract: A model for the social structure of a Mexican peasant village." *American Anthropologist* 63:1173–1192.

(1963) "The dyadic contract in Tzintzuntzan II: Patron-client relationship." *American Anthropologist* 65:1280–1294.

(1964a) "Speech forms and the perception of social distance in a Spanish-speaking Mexican village." *Southwestern Journal of Anthropology* 20:107–122.

(1964b) "Treasure tales and the image of the static economy in a Mexican peasant community." *Journal of American Folklore* 77:39–44.

(1965a) "Peasant society and the image of limited good." *American Anthropologist* 67:293–315.

(1965b) "Cultural responses to expressions of envy in Tzintzuntzan." *Southwestern Journal of Anthropology* 21:24–35.

(1966a) "Euphemisms and cultural sensitivity in Tzintzuntzan." *Anthropological Quarterly* 39:53–59.

(1966b) "World view in Tzintzuntzan: Reexamination of a concept." Pp. 385–393 in *Summa Anthropologica en homenaje a Roberto J. Weitlaner*. México, D.F: Instituto Nacional de Antropología.

(1967) *Tzintzuntzan: Mexican Peasants in a Changing World.* Boston: Little, Brown.

(1968) "El cambio cultural planificado y la irrigación en la cuenca del lago de Pátzcuaro." *Anuario Indigenista* 38:45–51.

(1969) "Godparents and social networks in Tzintzuntzan." *Southwestern Journal of Anthropology* 25:261–278.

(1970) "Character and personal relationships seen through proverbs in Tzintzuntzan, Mexico." *Journal of American Folklore* 83:304–317.

(1972) *Tzintzuntzan: Los campesinos mexicanos en un mundo en cambio.* México, D.F.: Fondo de Cultura Económica. (Translation of 1967).

(1973) "Dreams, character, and cognitive orientation in Tzintzuntzan." *Ethos* 1:106–121.

(1978) "Hippocrates' Latin American legacy: 'Hot' and 'cold' in contemporary folk medicine." Pp. 3–19 in Ronald K. Wetherington (editor), *Colloquia in Anthropology*, vol. 2. Dallas: Fort Burgwin Research Center.

(1979a) "Fieldwork in Tzintzuntzan: The first thirty years." Pp. 165–184 in George M. Foster, Thayer Scudder, Elizabeth Colson, and Robert V. Kemper (editors), *Long-Term Field Research in Social Anthropology*. New York: Academic Press.

(1979b) "Methodological problems in the study of intracultural variation: The hot/cold dichotomy in Tzintzuntzan." *Human Organization* 38:179–183.

(1979c) *Tzintzuntzan: Mexican Peasants in a Changing World.* Revised edition, with a new Epilogue. New York: Elsevier.

(1981) "Old age in Tzintzuntzan, Mexico." Pp. 115–137 in J. L. McGaugh and S. B. Kessler (editors), *Aging, Biology and Behavior.* New York: Academic Press.

(1982) "Responsibility for illness in Tzintzuntzan: A cognitive-linguistic anomaly." *Medical Anthropology* 6(2):81–90.

(1984a) "The concept of 'neutral' in humoral medical systems." *Medical Anthropology* 8:180–194.

(1984b) "How to stay well in Tzintzuntzan." *Social Science & Medicine* 19:523–533.
(1985) "How to get well in Tzintzuntzan." *Social Science & Medicine* 21:807–818.
(1987a) "Colonial administration in Northern Rhodesia in 1962." *Human Organization* 46:359–368.
(1987b) "On the origin of humoral medicine in Latin America." *Medical Anthropology Quarterly* 1:355–393.
(1988a) *Tzintzuntzan: Mexican Peasants in a Changing World.* With a new Afterword. Prospect Heights, IL: Waveland Press.
(1988b) "The validating role of humoral theory in traditional Spanish-American therapeutics." *American Ethnologist* 15:120–135.
(1989) "Change and continuity in world view in Tzintzuntzan, 1945–1985." Pp. 187–195 in Yólotl González (editor), *Homenaje a Isabel Kelly.* México, D.F.: Instituto Nacional de Antropología e Historia.
(1994) *Hippocrates' Latin American Legacy: Humoral Medicine in the New World.* Langhorne, PA: Gordon and Breach.

Foster, George M. and Gabriel Ospina
(1948) *Empire's Children: The People of Tzintzuntzan.* Smithsonian Institution, Institute of Social Anthropology, Publication No. 6. México, D. F.: Imprenta Nuevo Mundo.
(2000) *Los hijos del imperio: la gente de Tzintzuntzan.* Zamora, Michoacán, Mexico: El Colegio de Michoacán. (Translation of Foster and Ospina 1948).

Foster, Mary L.
(1969) "The Tarascan language." *University of California Publications in Linguistics,* Vol. 56. Berkeley: University of California Press.
(1983) "Tzintzuntzan marriage: An analysis of concordant structure." Pp. 127–153 in J. Oosten and A. de Ruitjer (editors), *The Future of Structuralism: Papers of the IUAES-Intercongress Amsterdam 1981.* Göttingen: Edition Herodot.
(1985) "Structural hierarchy and social good in Tzintzuntzan." *International Journal of Psychology* 20:617–635.
(1989) "Toward interpretation of ancient Tarascan terminology." Pp. 149–160 in Yólotl González (editor), *Homenaje a Isabel Kelly.* México, D.F.: Instituto Nacional de Antropología e Historia.

García Manzanedo, Hector
(1955) "Informe sobre la cerámica de Tzintzuntzan." Serie Mimeográfica, No. 7. México, D. F.: Instituto Nacional Indigenista.

Honigmann, John J.
(1960) "A case study of community development in Pakistan." *Economic Development and Cultural Change* 8:288–303.

Kemper, Robert V.
(1971) "Migration and adaptation of Tzintzuntzan peasants in Mexico City." Ph.D. dissertation. University of California, Berkeley.

(1974) "Tzintzuntzeños in Mexico City: The anthropologist among peasant migrants." Pp. 63–91 in George M. Foster and Robert V. Kemper (editors), *Anthropologists in Cities*. Boston: Little, Brown.

(1977) *Migration and Adaptation: Tzintzuntzan Peasants in Mexico City*. Beverly Hills, CA: Sage Publications.

(1979a) "Compadrazgo in city and countryside: A comparison of Tzintzuntzan migrants and villagers." *Kroeber Anthropological Society Papers* 55–56:25–44.

(1979b) "Fieldwork among Tzintzuntzan migrants in Mexico City: Retrospect and prospect." Pp. 189–207 in George M. Foster, Thayer Scudder, Elizabeth Colson, and Robert V. Kemper (editors), *Long-Term Field Research in Social Anthropology*. New York: Academic Press.

(1981) "Obstacles and opportunities: Household economics of Tzintzuntzan migrants in Mexico City." *Urban Anthropology* 10:211–229.

(1994a) "Extendiendo las fronteras de la comunidad en teoría y práctica: Tzintzuntzan, Mexico, 1970–1990." *Estudios Michoacanos* 5:119–129.

(1994b) "Migración sin fronteras: el caso del pueblo de Tzintzuntzan, Michoacán, 1945–1990." Pp. 67–82 in *XXII Mesa de Antropología de la Sociedad Mexicana de Antropología*. Tuxtla Gutiérrez, Chiapas: Gobierno del Estado de Chiapas.

(1995) "Comunidad y migración: El caso del pueblo de Tzintzuntzan, Michoacán, 1988–1994." *Relaciones* 61/62:133–148.

(1996a) "La comida en Tzintzuntzan, Michoacán: Tradiciones y transformaciones." Pp. 365–395 in Janet Long (editor), *Conquista y Comida: Consecuencias del Encuentro de dos Mundos*. México, D.F.: Universidad Nacional Autónoma de México.

(1996b) "Migration and adaptation: Tzintzuntzeños in Mexico City and beyond." Pp. 196–209 in George Gmelch and Walter P. Zenner (editors), *Urban Life: Readings in Urban Anthropology*. Third Edition. Prospect Heights, IL: Waveland Press.

Kemper, Robert V. and George M. Foster
(1975) "Urbanization in Mexico: The view from Tzintzuntzan." *Latin American Urban Research* 5:53–75.

Kuhn, Thomas S.
(1962) *The Structure of Scientific Revolutions*. Chicago: University of Chicago Press.

Lewis, Oscar
(1951) *Life in a Mexican Village: Tepoztlán Restudied*. Urbana: University of Illinois Press.

Maccoby, Michael and George M. Foster
(1970) "Methods of studying Mexican peasant personality: Rorschach, TAT, and dreams." *Anthropological Quarterly* 43:225–242.

Merton, Robert K.
(1948) "The bearing of empirical research upon the development of social theory." *American Sociological Review* 13:505–515.

Ospina, Gabriel
(1954) "Plan de rehabilitación cultural y económica de Tzintzuntzan." Mimeographed manuscript. Pátzcuaro: Centro Regional de Educación Fundamental para la América Latina (CREFAL).

Redfield, Robert
(1950) *A Village That Chose Progress: Chan Kom Revisited.* Chicago: University of Chicago Press.

Rubín de la Borbolla, Daniel and Ralph L. Beals
(1940) "The Tarascan project: A cooperative enterprise of the National Polytechnic Institute, Mexican Bureau-Indian Affairs, and the University of California." *American Anthropologist* 42:708–712.

Scudder, Thayer and Elizabeth Colson
(1979) "Long-term research in Gwembe Valley, Zambia." Pp. 227–254 in George M. Foster, Thayer Scudder, Elizabeth Colson, and Robert V. Kemper (editors), *Long-Term Field Research in Social Anthropology.* New York: Academic Press.

Willner, Dorothy
(1958) "Report on an evaluation of a community development project of CREFAL in Tzintzuntzan." Mimeographed manuscript. Pátzcuaro: Centro Regional de Educación Fundamental para la América Latina (CREFAL).

CHAPTER ELEVEN

FROM STUDENT TO STEWARD: TZINTZUNTZAN AS EXTENDED COMMUNITY

Robert V. Kemper

Introduction

On February 16, 2001, the front page of *The Washington Post* newspaper featured a story written by Mary Jordan about Tzintzuntzan and its migrants. This story provided millions of readers and Internet users with background for the first meeting between U.S. President George W. Bush and Mexican President Vicente Fox, both greatly concerned with the "problem" of Mexican migrants flowing into the United States without proper documentation and without adequate protections for their human rights. In preparation, Jordan called me in Dallas from Mexico City, then went to Tzintzuntzan where she interviewed several migrants, finally settling on Remigio Morales as the central figure for her article. When I began my involvement with the migrants of Tzintzuntzan more than thirty years ago, I would never have expected to see such a story published, much less to be quoted as the anthropologist "who has been studying the migration and demographic patterns of this town since 1969."

I first visited Tzintzuntzan in 1967, while doing summer ethnographic training in nearby Pátzcuaro's regional marketplace, studied first in 1945 by my advisor George M. Foster (Foster and Ospina 1948:132–137), then again in 1958 by David Kaplan (1960:175–232).[1] In addition, because Foster had placed a Mexican graduate student in anthropology with me in Pátzcuaro, I also encountered the daily delights and difficulties of collaborating with local scholars. So, instead of being sent out on my own in the classic "sink-or-swim" approach to fieldwork, I was nurtured in a "collaborative restudy" setting.

That summer determined my future as an anthropologist. On a hot August afternoon in Morelia, Michoacán's state capital, Foster and I sat waiting in the brown Ford station wagon provided to our summer project by the University of California, while Virginia and Lola Pichu set about making their weekly purchases at the "*Independencia*" wholesale market. Never a person to avoid an opportunity to move forward, Foster asked me at one point in the conversation, "And what do you plan to do for your dissertation research?" Having only just

Aerial view of Tzintzuntzan. Photo by Robert V. Kemper.

completed the first year of graduate studies at the University of California at Berkeley, I hardly had a good answer. I mumbled something about being interested in the effects of urbanization on pottery-making towns like nearby Capula, Tzintzuntzan (on the edge of Lake Pátzcuaro), and Patamban in the distant Sierra Tarasca. Instead of encouraging me to pursue this variation on Robert Redfield's (1941) "folk-urban continuum," Foster asked if I might be interested in following Tzintzuntzan migrants to the national capital. He knew, as I would come to learn, that such a study had been suggested long ago by Oscar Lewis (1952:41), who had argued that follow-up investigations of migrants from well-studied villages like Tzintzuntzan would yield valuable comparative data on Mexican urbanization.

In 1969, when I began doing my dissertation fieldwork among Tzintzuntzan migrants in Mexico City, most anthropological thinking about Mexican peasant villages included critical assumptions about their "closed corporate" and "limited" characteristics (see Potter, Diaz, and Foster 1967). My theoretical and methodological frameworks were modeled after the prior studies of rural-urban migrants in Mexico City done by Oscar Lewis (1952) among Tepoztecans and by his student Douglas Butterworth (1962) among Tilantongans. Thus, from the outset, my objectives in studying migrant adaptation were both comparative (Kemper 1970, 1971b, 1987b) and longitudinal (Kemper and Royce 1979, 1983), framed first within the then-prevailing paradigms of acculturation and modernization (Kemper 1977, 1987a) and more recently in terms of broader political-economic relationships between city and countryside (cf. Kemper 1979c, 1994b, 1995b; Kemper and Rollwagen 1996).

This could have been just another one-shot field study leading to a dissertation, a monograph, and some articles. Instead, it became the basis for a continuing thirty-year-long investigation of the "extended community" of Tzintzuntzan. In retrospect, it is clear that I entered the field at a critical moment. The late 1960s were not only tumultuous times in Mexico City (e.g., the October 2, 1968, massacre of students at the Plaza de las Tres Culturas took place only six months before I entered the field), but also marked the transition out of the long-standing bilateral agreement known as the Bracero Program, through which a generation of Mexican laborers had been contracted to work in the United States.

The impact of the Bracero Program on towns in Mexico, and especially in Michoacán, was not lost on ethnographers of that era. In fact, in concluding his monograph on the Sierra Tarascan community of Cherán,[2] Ralph Beals (1946:211) had remarked, "Cherán, like many Indian communities of Mexico, is increasingly influenced by the town and the city. . . . Cherán is probably more influenced by Gary (Indiana, U.S.A.), Mexico City, and Morelia (possibly in diminishing order) than it is by Uruapan and Pátzcuaro."

Foster (Foster and Ospina 1948:149) also had noted the positive experiences of Tzintzuntzeños—almost 50 percent of the village's adult males—who had traveled north to work in the United States: "Most are very anxious to get back to the United States, either to live permanently or to work for an extended period." During the 1950s, from 50 to 150 men went to the United States each year, at a time when few Tzintzuntzeños ventured to work and live in Mexico City (cf. Foster 1967:275–277).

Because I approached the migration problem from a singular perspective— that of a community already well known ethnographically through Foster's work—I could define broadly the people and places relevant for questions such as "Who is migrating?" "Where are they going?" and "From where are they returning?" Thus, although my first fieldwork was concentrated in Mexico City, for my dissertation I also analyzed Foster's master data file of all individuals censused in 1945, 1960, and 1970 to determine the destinations of *all* Tzintzuntzan migrants throughout Mexico and the United States. In this way, I got a sense of the broader picture within which cityward migration took place—and I opened a Pandora's box in terms of dealing with the broader migration *system* in which the community of Tzintzuntzan was participating (Kemper 1996b).

Being a Student: Dissertation Fieldwork during 1969–1970

Mexico City was selected as the field site because, at that time, Tzintzuntzan migrants shared with many Mexican peasants, including those of Tepoztlán, a preference for settling in the capital. Thus, not only would I find enough migrants to make the study worthwhile, I would be able to compare my findings directly with those of

Lewis and other scholars, while avoiding the arduous task of locating Tzintzuntzeños in a number of Mexican cities. Under these conditions, I conducted fieldwork in Mexico City, with several brief trips to the village, from April 1969 to August 1970. The dissertation fieldwork among the Tzintzuntzan migrants in the capital fell into three phases, punctuated by short trips back to the United States to renew tourist papers every six months. In the first phase, I faced three main problems: finding accommodations for me and my wife, Sandra, locating a relatively small number of migrants in a city of over eight million people, and beginning the process of data collection. During the second phase, marked by a transition from "passive" to "active" research strategies (Freilich 1970:24), I conducted a detailed ethnographic census of as many migrant households as could be located. The concluding phase was devoted to gathering life histories, household budgets, and social network data and to administering projective tests and questionnaires about migrant experiences. Thus, as the fieldwork progressed, the problem orientation became more specific and the data collection procedures more structured.

Selecting a Place to Live

All anthropologists face the problem of finding accommodations compatible with their field situation. In my case, after two weeks of living in hotels and rooming houses, we finally found an affordable furnished apartment for rent near the center of the city. Having an apartment independent of all of the migrants had immediate advantages and disadvantages: on the one hand, it gave us a place away from the constant demands of fieldwork in an unfamiliar setting; on the other, it denied us the intimacy of participant observation common to anthropologists who work in small communities. As it turned out, this separation gave me a neutrality which preserved the opportunity for future research. If I had made a commitment to reside with a particular family during this first field trip, it might have adversely curtailed my future options (cf. Berreman 1962).

Studying a Dispersed Population

When I arrived in Mexico City, I had a list of about twenty migrants' names and just two addresses, which I had obtained in a hurried search through Foster's data files before my departure from Berkeley. My immediate goal was to locate as many migrants as possible, as quickly as I could, so that I might get on with the "real" fieldwork. However, it took about a year to develop a network that included nearly all of the migrants. Eventually, my network became so much wider than that of any of the Tzintzuntzeños that they would ask me where one of their fellows lived or worked. The migrants were spread among more than forty neighborhoods in the metropolitan area, mainly in the northern periphery where many of the men worked in factories. Although a few people, usually relatives or *compadres* (co-godparents), lived next door to one another, most were separated by miles of urban traffic. Nor did the Tzintzuntzeños have a village-based voluntary association to compensate for their geographical dispersion.

Had I known from the outset that the Tzintzuntzan migrants were so numerous (483 persons living in at least 74 households, rather than my original guess of about 100 persons in 20 households), so dispersed (spread over the metropolitan area, whereas I had hoped that they might live in one or two neighborhoods), and that I would log so many miles (9,000) doing the fieldwork, I would have thought about another dissertation topic. The initial fieldwork in metropolitan Mexico City was grounded in the reality that the migrants were dispersed over some 500 square miles! In these circumstances, the field methods associated with nucleated peasant villages seemed completely inadequate.

In mid-fieldwork, I had the good fortune to be able to attend the 1969 annual meeting of the American Anthropological Association in New Orleans. At the book exhibit, I happened to lay hands on a new book (Mitchell 1969) dealing with social network approaches to urban populations in central Africa. Skimming through the pages of the introduction that first time was an epiphany! Here was a serendipitous solution to my dilemma. Back in the field, I was able to design a simple social network survey that provided crucial data for understanding how the Tzintzuntzan migrants operated in their dispersed circumstances in Mexico City (Kemper 1973; cf. Foster 1969).

During that first period of some seventeen months of fieldwork during 1969–1970, I occasionally was introduced to migrants who turned out *not* to be from the village of Tzintzuntzan proper, but instead were from one of the eighteen hamlets located within the boundaries of the *municipio* (county) or *parroquia* (parish) headed by Tzintzuntzan. My initial reaction to discovering such migrants was to record data about them and then to put it into a different file—separate from that on the "real" villagers being studied. My problem was twofold: first, that I could not link directly the migrants from these hamlets to the large ethnographic database which Foster had established for the residents of Tzintzuntzan proper; second, that I was uncomfortable about "contaminating" the study of the migrants from Tzintzuntzan proper with information about their friends and relatives who also happened to be living in Mexico City.

In effect, my narrow definition of "community" as a specific place on the ground—rather than as a broader social and economic field—made it hard for me to see what was going on among the migrants in Mexico City. In the final analysis, I did include data on these migrants from the hamlets around Tzintzuntzan—but I always felt uneasy about it, because this seemed to violate the prevailing Lewis–Butterworth framework of origin–destination analysis.

Establishing a Satisfactory Role in the Field

My affiliation with Foster provided the credentials necessary for conducting the fieldwork and for participating in professional activities in Mexico City. Since most of the migrants were aware of his work in Tzintzuntzan, they were willing to accept me as a student interested in their past, present, and future. Especially in the beginning, Foster's name (and through his connections, the names of certain well-known villagers) opened doors for me which otherwise might have remained closed. In terms of my professional relations, Foster gave me letters of introduction to the directors of several anthropological institutions based in Mexico City. In addition, because the Society for Applied Anthropology was holding its 1969 meeting in Mexico City, he came down and introduced me to a number of leaders in Mexican anthropology. Later on, he sponsored my membership in the Sociedad Mexicana de Antropología. At his suggestion, I audited a course at the National School of Anthropology and History during my first months in Mexico City. Toward the end of the fieldwork, at the invitation of Professor Angel Palerm and with Foster's encouragement, I taught a graduate seminar on urban anthropology at the Universidad IberoAmericana.[3] In these ways, I made contacts with Mexican anthropologists that would be valuable throughout my career.

The implications of my role situation among the Tzintzuntzeños and among Mexican anthropologists are clear. Under the auspices of a well-known patron, whose guidance placed me on the right path to do the dissertation research, I was able to establish my own contacts among the migrants and with key individuals in the Mexican social science community so that my research could continue. Following Foster's lead, I maintained a neutral stance toward the political side of Mexican anthropology; as a result, I have had no difficulty in continuing fieldwork with the people of Tzintzuntzan.

Collecting Field Data

I adopted the widely used Human Relations Area Files (HRAF) system for coding and filing field notes that Foster had recommended in the "methods" seminar I had taken before going to Michoacán in 1967. Information was typed onto five-by-eight-inch sheets and filed in two sets: one arranged topically in the HRAF numerical categories; the other by households. A third copy was mailed periodically to Berkeley where Foster read the notes, wrote comments to me regarding points of special interest, and then filed them for safekeeping. I was spared a great deal of work, especially in dealing with genealogies, because these data already existed in Foster's files. Moreover, we were each sufficiently familiar with the HRAF system (which Foster also used) and with the specific information in the files that it was easy for me to ask for data and for Foster then to retrieve, photocopy, and mail it to me. In addition to making his data files available, Foster also made a point to follow up on any leads related to migration when he was in Tzintzuntzan doing his own research. In recognition of our common interests and in partial reciprocity for his efforts on my behalf, I collected some data on topics of special interest to Foster. For example, I administered Thematic Apperception Tests (TATs) to fifteen migrants to provide comparative data for his sample of about twenty respondents in the village. In addition, I also gathered extensive information on *compadrazgo* relations among the migrants. I used these comparative data to examine villager–migrant differences and similarities in my dissertation and in subsequent publications (cf. Kemper 1979a, 1982).

The most important common element in our research was the 1970 ethnographic census. We asked for almost identical information and gave the census at about the same time. Whereas Foster was able to obtain a 100 percent response rate in the village—and found that Tzintzuntzan was a community of 2,253 residents—I could census firsthand only about 70 percent (51 of 74) of the migrant households, although in nearly all of the remaining cases I was able to get reliable secondhand information. As a complement to my work among the migrants, Foster inquired about the whereabouts of all villagers who had been in the community at the time of the 1960 census but were no longer present.

It was fortuitous that I did my initial fieldwork among the migrants at the same time that Foster was administering a census in the village. As a result, we now have a good set of demographic and socioeconomic core data on the Tzintzuntzeños in the capital comparable to that on their families of origin in Tzintzuntzan. Moreover, because the Mexican national census was conducted in February 1970, our ethnographic census data for migrants and villagers can be related to broader regional and national situations.

Analyzing Field Materials and Data Files: 1970–1973

Upon returning to Berkeley in September 1970, I began to organize my field materials into a format suitable for a dissertation. In accord with my original plans, I also examined Foster's data files for background information on the migrants' situations before they had gone to Mexico City. I soon realized that, although Foster had done considerable analysis of his materials, the information I sought was not tabulated according to *my* needs. Therefore, we went to considerable effort and expense to convert his 1945, 1960, and 1970 census materials into a format amenable to computer processing techniques. After several months' work, I was able to generate a substantial set of cross-tabulations that showed how markedly Tzintzuntzan had changed during the twenty-five years of Foster's work there. This material not only was valuable for the dissertation, but also served as the basis for a joint article (Kemper and Foster 1975) on the impact of Mexican urbanization on Tzintzuntzan.

In addition to devoting considerable time to analyzing the village census data and comparing the results with those of my migrant census in Mexico City, I also counted on the individual data five-by-eight sheets kept on each person who had been censused by Foster in 1945, 1960, or 1970. By close examination of this data file, which at that time contained personal information on more than 3,000 individuals, I ascertained that more than 700 villagers had emigrated since the late 1930s. Furthermore, because of the systematic detail on these data sheets, I could specify the type (and often, the place) of destination for each emigrant. Then, by correlating these data with the computerized household census files, I was able to show that the migrants to Mexico City were "positively selected" (i.e., came from households with higher living standards, better educational levels, and more innovativeness than found in nonmigrant households), but that this selectivity had declined in recent years as the number of emigrants had increased. Thus, I was in a position to support the demographic hypothesis of migrant "regression toward the mean" (cf. Browning and Feindt 1969) through a combination of my census data on the migrants in Mexico City and Foster's data on the entire natal community. This is a use to which Foster would probably *not* have put his own data, since his interests were far removed from migration theory.

There are several lessons to be learned from my analysis of Foster's data files in conjunction with the analysis of my own field materials. First, comparability should be built into a study from the beginning, since it is difficult to agree on definitions of, say, household and family types after investigations are completed. Second, using another scholar's data files requires an understanding of what the data "mean"; that is, the ambiguities in the field notes and census materials must be explicable either by the original scholar's direct explanations or through annotations in the data files. Third, the most useful data from another anthropologist's field materials are often those of lesser importance to that person's current interests. If this is so, analysis of the files by a student or colleague may be a valuable service to the original investigator. Finally, there must be an agreement as to what data may be used and to what purpose they may be put; otherwise, the original fieldworker's plans for subsequent publications may be compromised.

After about ten months of analyzing my own field materials and those from Foster's files, I managed to write the dissertation in about ten weeks (Kemper 1971a), so that I could begin a National Endowment for the Humanities (NEH) postdoctoral fellowship on Mexican–American studies at Berkeley for the 1971–1972 academic year. During that year, Foster and I held a seminar with a number of anthropology graduate students writing dissertations based on urban fieldwork. This seminar led to our collaboration on a volume titled *Anthropologists in Cities*, from which our introductory chapter (Foster and Kemper 1974) and my chapter on the Tzintzuntzan migrants in Mexico City have been reprinted several times (Kemper 1974b). In these and other articles (Kemper 1973, 1974a, 1975), I realized that there was no "ethnographic present"; instead, constant changes in the villagers' and migrants' situations were rendering these publications obsolete even before they appeared.

By late 1973, my sense of frustration had reached a point that getting back to Mexico City and to Tzintzuntzan had become a top priority. To this end, I received a small grant-in-aid from the Wenner-Gren Foundation for Anthropological Research to carry out a ten-week ethnographic survey among the Tzintzuntzan migrants in Mexico City during summer 1974. This fieldwork provided important mid-decade information on the changing migrant population and on the urban conditions in which it lived.

No Longer a Student: Fieldwork in 1974 and After

The 1974 summer fieldwork involved reestablishing contact with those migrants whom I had known in 1969 and 1970, discovering which migrants had left Mexico City to return to the village or to settle elsewhere, and censusing those newly arrived in the capital since 1970. Of course, I did expect to gather additional data beyond the census itself, on such topics as family and household developmental cycles, socioeconomic mobility, and intrametropolitan geographical movements. All of these topics needed more study before I could transform the dissertation into a monograph about the migrants' adaptations to urban life during the early 1970s.

That summer, I accomplished almost as much in ten weeks as I had in as many months during my earlier period in Mexico City. The "costs" of the research, in both money and personal effort, were substantially reduced during this second field trip. Not only did I know much more about the population I was studying, I also was a more effective ethnographer. A number of circumstances made the 1974 research especially productive; I treat these in the same categories as previously.

Selecting a Place to Live

Unlike the situation in 1969–1970, when Sandra and I had rented a downtown apartment, on this occasion I went to the field alone. I had a room to myself in the home of Rafael Campuzano Hinojosa, half brother of Micaela González Hinojosa, matriarch of the household where Foster—and I, too—resided while in Tzintzuntzan. Rafael's family had been our closest friends among the migrants during 1969–1970. His wife, Felipa, took excellent care of all my needs and was a superb cook as well. In short, although their house was located somewhat inconveniently in the extreme northeastern section of the Distrito Federal, the situation was ideal for getting maximum work done in a short time.

More important than just having a place to live was the chance to observe firsthand, on a daily basis, interpersonal relationships within a migrant household. In addition, the family's entrepreneurship (they had opened two small stores) gave me an insider's view of how migrants try to improve their economic situation in the city. And, finally, the family served as willing key informants on a wide range of topics. Since the family and I both were pleased with the arrangement, we agreed that I should continue to stay there on future trips to Mexico City.

That summer I also went to Tzintzuntzan for my first comprehensive village survey of migration. Using key informants in different neighborhoods, I was able to check on the current location of all 2,253 persons listed in the 1970 ethnographic census. For the first time, I began to see the village as the central node of an extended social and economic field, which included the hamlets in the *municipio*, towns throughout the state, large cities such as Mexico City, and even places in the United States.

Studying a Dispersed Population

Based on my earlier fieldwork, I knew that it would be impossible, in ten weeks or in a hundred, to locate and survey every Tzintzuntzan migrant in Mexico City. I did hope to canvass, with some field assistance, about 75 percent of the population. In fact, we were able to gather firsthand data on more than 70 households and got reliable secondhand data on most of the remainder, for a total of some 600 persons in a total of about 110 households. I had expected that the older or more affluent migrants who owned homes would still be living where they had in 1969–1970, whereas the younger, poorer, more recent arrivals would be more geographically mobile. I discovered that, although about half of the migrants had changed residences at least once since 1970, and some were no longer in the capital, this proposition held true.

Since I had no car on this field trip, I depended on the excellent public transportation system of taxis, jitney cabs, buses, and subways. In addition, Rafael seemed to enjoy taking me to visit other migrant households on weekends and on his days off from his job with the telegraph office. Even with this assistance, I found that the large number of recent arrivals forced a strict rationing of time and effort. Although it would have been pleasant (and perhaps ethnographically profitable) to pass time with old friends, I was determined to gather core data on people not already in my files. I also visited Tzintzuntzan to check on the dozen or so "return migrants" and to ascertain who else had left the village since the 1970 census. In the process, I confirmed the emigration of 205 villagers from Tzintzuntzan between 1970 and 1974, with 28 percent going to Mexico City, 29 percent staying within the state of Michoacán, and 15 percent traveling north to the United States (Kemper 1977:53).

For studying a dispersed population, a series of visits has many advantages. This time I knew what faced me and how to plan my available time to see as many migrants as possible. I did not have to build a social network family by family; I already had one that enabled me to cope with the migrants' geographical distribution in the metropolis. Moreover, the second visit to the Tzintzuntzeños made me aware of continuities and changes not observed on the first field trip.

Changing Roles in the Field

Previously, I had entered the field as a student; now I was a professor. Nevertheless, because of my relatively young age (twenty-eight), I continued to introduce myself as "Roberto" and asked that people so address me. I continued to use the formal *usted* rather than the informal *tú* in all conversations except with age mates (and children), whom I knew well and who used it first in speaking with me.

When I had been a student, I could plead poverty when unusual requests for assistance arose. Now, this was more difficult, and as I continued the research my social obligations to the migrants and villagers have had to be repaid with interest. I continued to decline requests that I become the godparent of migrants' children, not only on the grounds that I was not available on a full-time basis but also because I was a Presbyterian instead of a Roman Catholic. Additional burdens of reciprocity accrued with professional colleagues in Mexico City. As an anthropologist hoping to carry out research in Mexico for the rest of my career, I felt responsible to lecture in local universities, to publish papers and books in Spanish in local journals, and to assist in training local students. Surely, my greatest coup was arranging to bring Fernando Cámara (then associate director of the National Institute of Anthropology and History) to Dallas as a visiting professor for the spring semester of the 1974–1975 academic year.

Collecting Field Data

Since my primary goal was to survey as many migrant households as possible, and since I knew that there would be more than I alone could visit, finding field assistants was one of my first tasks. One of the sons (Ramon) of Rafael and Felipa served as an interviewer; as did Claudio, the son of Larissa Lomnitz, an anthropologist at the National University. After several training sessions, both proved to be superb census takers.

The productivity of the 1974 field trip showed me that not only are revisits economical, they also encouraged me to go to the field with a set of specific queries. Turning over a share of the core data collection to assistants gave me time to concentrate on these topics of special interest. Having my field notes arranged topically by HRAF categories and also by family group meant that I could daily see the depth and breadth of my sample grow. Let me give a brief example.

During the 1969–1970 field research, I had gathered a substantial body of data on the *compadrazgo*. I had discussed these data briefly, in comparison with those gathered by Foster for Tzintzuntzan, in my dissertation, but had not analyzed them fully. In returning to the field in 1974, the gathering of additional data on *compadrazgo* was a high priority. I was particularly eager to find out the variety of occasions (e.g., baptism, marriage) for which compadres could be chosen, especially since the anthropological literature was very sketchy on how the institution of co-godparenthood operated in urban settings. Data collected in the summer of 1974 led to two papers (Kemper 1979a, 1982) in which I showed how urban migrants use the *compadrazgo* as a mechanism for improving their socioeconomic mobility, for strengthening ties with relatives and friends dispersed throughout the metropolitan area, and for maintaining ties with the village.[4]

The Wenner-Gren Symposium: Learning to Take the Long View

In summer 1975, I had the opportunity to participate, as the designated "junior" rapporteur and paper presenter, in a Wenner-Gren–sponsored symposium on "Long-Term Field Research in Social Anthropology." If I had had any doubts about maintaining my work among the Tzintzuntzan migrants, the senior people

I met at Burg Wartenstein and the subsequent editing of their papers convinced me of the necessity of longitudinal research for understanding urbanization and migration processes (Kemper 1979b). In the mid-1970s, I also had to face the academic hurdle of tenure and promotion. In our department, this meant publishing a monograph in addition to writing articles, doing book reviews, getting grants, receiving excellent teaching evaluations, and so forth. I was able to visit the migrants in Mexico City briefly in November 1974, when the annual meeting of the American Anthropological Association took place there, and then again briefly in November 1975, in the midst of preparing *two* versions of a monograph on the Tzintzuntzan migrants. The Mexican Secretariat of Education published the Spanish-language version (Kemper 1976) in the affordable SepSetentas series. This edition of thirty thousand copies was distributed without charge to the nation's schools and libraries and, over the years, has been frequently cited by Mexican social scientists. In lieu of royalties, I was able to acquire three hundred copies of the SepSetentas edition, nearly all of which I gave away to interested migrants and villagers during the following years. The English-language edition (Kemper 1977) appeared a year later, but was declared "out of print" three years later by its trade publisher and consequently made much less of an impact than did the Mexican edition.

I returned to Tzintzuntzan to repeat the village-level survey of migration and population changes in August 1976 and again in August 1978. By that time, I realized that these biennial surveys also provided excellent preparation for the upcoming decennial village and migrant censuses. So, through these rapid surveys, I was not only looking backward to the 1970 census, but also looking forward to the 1980 census and beyond.

Shifting Perspectives on Tzintzuntzan Migrants: The 1980 Census

In the academic year 1979–1980, with a university research leave and a Fulbright research award in hand, Sandra and I spent nearly fifteen months in Mexico. Most of the time, we were in Mexico City, where we continued to live with the same migrant family, although now in a new house which they had built in 1976 on a nearby lot where Felipa's mother had lived. Onto this new two-story house, I added a rooftop apartment financed with a $6,000 personal loan from the Dallas Teacher's Credit Union. The construction of this apartment—to which I had no legal title—reflected the strength of my long-term commitment to the research project *and* the willingness of Rafael and Felipa to have us living with them for the foreseeable future.[5]

In February 1980, I (and Stanley Brandes, another of Foster's former students who continues to work in Tzintzuntzan) helped Foster to conduct the 1980 village census. As we worked on the census, it became clear that the simple division of the population into residents and migrants was inadequate to represent a continually changing social and economic reality. A significant increase in four socioeconomic categories—that is, high school and university students, workers commuting daily to other localities, persons working full-time outside of Tzintzuntzan who returned from time to time to be with their families, and illegal immigrants to the United States—all combined to complicate the definition of who should be counted as "present" in the community.

Our solution to this ethnographic problem was to create an intermediate category that we called the "extended" population. These people share one important characteristic: they are beyond the village much more than in it, and their eventual ties to the community are uncertain. Thus, for 1980, we counted a "core" population of 2,506 persons in Tzintzuntzan and an "extended" population of another 143, for a total of 2,649 people.

The villagers of Tzintzuntzan provided us with a dramatic example of how they had "extended" their community when, in 1979, some forty-five families invaded a strip of land belonging collectively to their own *comunidad indígena* ("indigenous community"). Located about 2 kilometers south of the village along the road to Pátzcuaro, this new settlement soon took for itself the name "Colonia Lázaro Cárdenas" in honor of a former president of Mexico who, while governor of Michoacán state, had been instrumental in establishing the *municipio* of Tzintzuntzan in 1930. Not knowing whether this *colonia*, composed entirely of people from Tzintzuntzan, would long survive, we chose to count its residents as continuing members of Tzintzuntzan proper.

During the rest of 1980, I worked (again with some assistants, including migrants themselves) with the migrants in Mexico City to carry out a parallel ethnographic census. We gathered data on around 1,000 persons living in some 200 households dispersed around the metropolitan area (Kemper 1981a). In addition, Juan Zaldivar, a schoolteacher who, in 1975, had created and still served as the leader of the Tzintzuntzan migrant association, was eager to use the census for his purposes as well as for mine. Therefore, on our behalf, he visited his fellow middle-class migrants not only in Mexico City, but also in several other cities, including Toluca, Morelia, and other smaller cities in the Lake Pátzcuaro region.

I obtained a small Ford Foundation grant so that two students in the graduate anthropology program at the Universidad IberoAmericana could do summer fieldwork with the Tzintzuntzan migrants. One student did some censusing in Mexico City, while the other (Victor Clark Alfaro) returned to his home town, the border city of Tijuana, Baja California, and subsequently accompanied me throughout California in pursuit of Tzintzuntzeños. In addition, two European students—Beate Engelbrecht and Jorge Mächler—were doing fieldwork in 1980 in Tzintzuntzan as part of their professional training programs. Engelbrecht did a dissertation (Engelbrecht 1987) comparing the situations of pottery makers in Tzintzuntzan with those of the Sierra Tarascan village of Patamban, while Mächler did a brief study of the emerging Colonia Lázaro Cárdenas.

I expanded my own fieldwork to the United States, both to southern and northern California and to Illinois, especially to South Chicago and West Chicago. This additional fieldwork yielded information on about 700 people living in some 150 households beyond what we had found in Mexico City.

One new component to the village work in 1980 was the creation of an album of several hundred black-and-white photographs that contained shots of every street and virtually every building in Tzintzuntzan, as well as those in Colonia Lázaro Cárdenas. This album has proven useful as an historical benchmark for measuring changes in housing and commercial activities, especially when used in conjunction with the detailed maps drawn of every block in the town's grid plan. I have continued to take photographs on each visit to Tzintzuntzan to document changes in housing and commercial enterprises (cf. Royce, in this volume).

In August of 1982, 1984, 1986, and 1988, I continued the biennial village-based survey of local demographic changes. During the middle 1980s, I also worked with Ben Wallace, a colleague at Southern Methodist University (SMU), on an agricultural research project in Bangladesh. There, I had the opportunity to study village-level migration in a quite different social and economic setting. In fact, it was the research in Bangladesh that led me to develop the concept of the extended community (Kemper, Wallace, and Wilson-Moore 1989).[6]

By the end of the 1980s, my perspective on Tzintzuntzan migrants had shifted from Mexico City back to Tzintzuntzan, but also had expanded from rural-urban migration to international migration. My initial short-term preoccupation with dissertation fieldwork (and then dealing with tenure and promotion issues) had been transformed into a long-term dedication to understanding migration as a major theme in the lives of the people of Tzintzuntzan. I now conceived of the village as the central node (what some Tzintzuntzeños called el meollo, a word that literally refers to the brain, but which figuratively means the "essence" or "principal component" of something—in this case, a community) in a spatially and temporally complex social field and as a dependent node in an even more complex political-economic field. I felt, and Foster agreed, that the three categories—resident, extended, and migrant—were simply three points along a continuum through which individuals and family units might pass during their life careers.

Taking on More Responsibility: The 1990 Census

The municipal elections in late 1989 left Tzintzuntzan and many other communities in turmoil. Although no one was killed in Tzintzuntzan, the representatives of the Partido de la Revolución Democrático (PRD) laid siege to the municipal offices to protest the ruling PRI party's declaration of victory. When Foster and I arrived in town in early January 1990, followed soon thereafter by Stanley Brandes and one of his graduate students (Sarah Miller), there was no competent municipal authority whom we could inform about our plans for carrying out another ethnographic census, as Foster had always done in the past. Eventually, a "mixed commission" (composed of PRI and PRD members) was established to govern the Tzintzuntzan *municipio*, with the job of *presidente municipal* falling to a well-regarded Tzintzuntzeño who long had served as head of the local civil registry. When, eventually, he was replaced in the civil registry by an outsider, we discovered that we no longer had direct access to birth, death, and marriage records in the civil registry. Thus, since the early 1990s, we have had to rely on the records maintained in the parish church. Unfortunately, however, these archives do not record information on deaths, this being a civil and medical matter.

Beginning in January 1990, and continuing for two months, I worked with Foster and the rest of our team to carry out the fifth ethnographic census of Tzintzuntzan. Then, I continued with my own work on migrants in Mexico City, in southern and northern California, in Illinois, and—for the first time—in Washington State, an area with no Tzintzuntzeños in 1980 and more than sixty households in 1990. In the absence of Juan Zaldivar (who had been killed in a car crash in the mid-1980s), I organized and trained several local people to pursue migrants in the *municipio* and throughout the rest of the state of Michoacán; in other Mexican cities such as Toluca, Guadalajara, and Tijuana; and in southern California as well. At one time or another, three professional anthropologists (Foster, Brandes, and Kemper), six student anthropologists (Marianka Nathanson, from the University of Toronto; Sarah Miller and Matthew Gutmann, both from Berkeley; Socorro Torres Sarmiento, from UC-Irvine, plus Claudia Caro and David Diaz, both undergraduates from UC-Irvine), three nonanthropologist social scientists (arranged through a colleague at the Instituto de Investigaciones Antropológicas of the National University in Mexico City), and eight Tzintzuntzeños—a total of twenty individuals—helped with the census in the village and among the migrants.

Our collective efforts revealed that, in 1990, Tzintzuntzan had a core population of residents of 2,999 persons living in some 580 households, but also had 350 individuals (from 178 different households; i.e., 31 percent of the total) classified as extended population, for a total local population of 3,349. As in 1980, we counted the population of Colonia Lázaro Cárdenas as a component part of Tzintzuntzan, although its more than 200 residents might better have been thought of as part of the extended community. In 1991, another invasion occurred—across the road from the *colonia*—involving perhaps another 20 families (some of whom are the married children of *colonia* residents). By adding a second *colonia*, this one called Tzintzuntzita ("little Tzintzuntzan"), the villagers themselves continue to redefine the spatial boundaries of their community in ways that would be difficult to comprehend through a one-shot, short-term investigation.

Living Arrangements: Problems and Resolutions

Unlike 1969–1970 and 1979–1980, my first priority for the 1990 census was Tzintzuntzan itself rather than the migrants in Mexico City. So, I spent more time in the village than in the capital. As luck would have it, in the late 1980s,

Ramon Campuzano built a new house down the street from his parents' house. This permitted me to move back up to the rooftop apartment for the time of the decennial migrant census in 1990. It also meant that there would be space available to bring Sandra for the first time since 1980 and our six-year-old son, John, for the first time ever. They came during the summer of 1990 and again in the summer of 1991, staying at the Campuzano home in Mexico City and with Micaela González's family in Tzintzuntzan.

I continued to have the use of the rooftop apartment at the Campuzano home in Mexico City until January 1996, even though Rafael had died in December 1991 and Felipa had been taking care of two of her grandchildren, while their parents— her oldest son (Roberto) and his wife (Lupe)—had been in Santa Barbara, California, for several years as undocumented workers. Now, Lupe was returning to live at Felipa's house and to care for her children. This meant that there would no longer be a place for me, not even in the downstairs room—since Felipa's college-age grandson would need that room, while Lupe and her daughter would require all of the rooftop apartment. So, I left behind the furniture, transported clothes and supplies to Tzintzuntzan, and took the computer system back home to Dallas.

I was greatly saddened to think that, after more than a quarter of a century, I was being separated from one of my two field "families." Fortunately, this separation lasted less than two years. Felipa was diagnosed with cancer in September 1997, and soon afterward we had a tearful reconciliation when we both happened to be in Tzintzuntzan to celebrate Micaela's Saint's Day later in that month. As a result, I once again had a room downstairs, which I was able to use on my occasional visits to the capital throughout the year 2000 migrant census, in which Ramon and his two teenage boys and Ramon's sister, Edelmira, and her teenage children all played significant roles as census takers.

Unfortunately, we all suffered a great loss when Felipa died on February 9, 2001, just four days after her sixty-sixth birthday, from the effects of the cancer she had suffered for the past several years. Her children are preparing to sell the house and divide the proceeds according to the terms of her last will and testament. So, in March 2001, I traveled for one last time to the house that had become another home, once more gathering up all my clothes, supplies, and computer equipment and transporting them to Tzintzuntzan. If the children of Ramon and Edelmira grow up, get married, and move out over the coming decade, perhaps a space will open up for me in one of their homes in time to deal with the 2010 migrant census. But I know, as they too know, it will never be quite the same.

Maintaining the "Master" Data File: Challenges and Opportunities

During the 1960s, Foster realized that the data in the 1945 and 1960 ethnographic censuses could be combined with information from other sources (e.g., the civil registry, the parish registry, genealogies) to develop a master data file—which came to be known as the *fichero*, the Spanish word for file or archive. By the time I went into the field in 1969, the *fichero* was already a wonderful tool for checking all kinds of individual and familial information. After I returned to Berkeley in 1970, Foster manually updated the *fichero* to include the 1970 village census data. For my part, I worked to create simple codes that could be used with the available mainframe computer programs of that pre-SPSS era. I spent many late-night hours punching Hollerith cards at the campus computer center and generating vast quantities of green-bar printouts.

As a result of that work on the 1970, 1960, and 1945 village censuses, I began to see that managing the data for the Tzintzuntzan migrants had to be linked to the much larger issue of managing the huge quantities of information Foster was continuing to gather in the village. In the run-up to the 1980 census, we were able to make use of Foster's handwritten data extracted from the civil and church registers as well as biennial population surveys I did in 1974, 1976, and 1978. The 1980 census went well, but the problem of data coding and analysis remained to be faced. Foster continued with his manual updating of the *fichero*, while I used the mainframe computer at SMU to carry out basic statistical analysis of the household and individual data in the census. By the mid-1980s, the first personal computers with enough memory and hard disk storage to handle database and statistical programs began to come onto the market. Not long afterward, the first PC version of SPSS became available and I began to migrate the data files from the university mainframe to personal computers.

In preparation for doing the 1990 village census, I had a DOS version of the recently introduced Paradox database program loaded with the more than four thousand names in the master *fichero* as well as their basic sociodemographic data. Similar database files were created for all individuals and households censused in 1945, 1960, 1970, and 1980. After the 1990 census was completed, an updated Paradox version of the master *fichero* was created, now containing more than 5,200 individuals. Foster and I worked together for a week at his home in Berkeley to manually update the individual data sheets and to photocopy all of these into a bound eight-and-a-half-by-eleven-inch format more suitable for carrying around in the field than the legal-sized post binders that contain the original household census data sheets. Similar files were created for all persons and households in the migrant censuses.

Collecting Field Data: New Initiatives

During the 1990s, I returned to Tzintzuntzan on a regular basis and conducted the biennial census survey in August of 1992, 1994, 1996, and 1998, just as I had been doing since 1974, but with a new twist. I found that I could use printed lists from the Paradox database to do the biennial surveys much more easily than in earlier decades—when I had read name after name, household after household, to my key informants who listened patiently for hours on end as we worked together through the entire census volume. Now, I could leave a set of printed lists with spaces for my informants to fill in any changes that had taken place during the past two years. Then, we could work over all of the "changes" to see if I understood them completely. Then, back in Dallas, I had an assistant enter all of the changes into a census update file. So, when I was preparing for the 2000 village census, I had an update file with all of the survey results for 1992, 1994, 1996, and 1998 to supplement the previous decennial census.

With the assistance of a few talented local residents, I also developed a project in the parish church to enter all of the baptismal, confirmation, marriage, and death records into laptop computer databases (using Microsoft Works in Spanish).[7] This archival work, started in 1991 with the cooperation of the local priest, has been sustained until the present through continuing agreements with his three replacements. At this point, we are working to convert and combine a large number of Works databases into a handful of much larger Microsoft Access databases, including more than forty thousand baptismal records dating back to the late 1700s, plus confirmation records, marriage records, and death records (up until around 1960).

I plan to do a monograph on the historical changes in the local community, analyzing the parish records in the light of our ethnographic censuses, genealogies, and related information. At an earlier time, Foster discussed doing such a work himself, but the amount of manual data processing required then would have been enormously burdensome. As the capabilities of personal computers and database programs have improved steadily from the mid-1980s to the present, the analysis of the parish archives now seems much more feasible.

Collaborative Projects and Secondary Data Analysis

One small-scale collaborative project took place in the 1980s, when Gabriel Lasker requested some data sets from Tzintzuntzan in order to compare names used in this lakeside community with names used in the Sierra Tarascan community of Paracho (Lasker et al. 1984).

During the 1990s, several anthropologists and journalists worked with the community and people of Tzintzuntzan. Two dissertations were completed based on fieldwork in Tzintzuntzan or its migrants: the first, by Scott Anderson (1998) of the University of California (San Francisco), dealt with the problem of growing old in Tzintzuntzan; the second, by Socorro Torres Sarmiento (1999) of the University of California (Irvine), focused on the economic life of Tzintzuntzan migrants in southern California and in Washington. Michael Shott (Shott and Williams 1997, 1999), an ethnoarchaeologist, included Tzintzuntzan in a regional project on pottery making and pottery use. Each of these anthropologists requested and received special data sets related to their particular interests.

In addition, anthropologist–filmmaker Jack Rollwagen came to Tzintzuntzan in 1991 to do videotaped interviews with George Foster about the history of his research and transformations in Tzintzuntzan and with me about tourism. Later, we did videotaping of the Campuzano family in Mexico City, among migrants in Chicago, and with Stanley Brandes at his Berkeley office. All of these taped interviews were assembled into "modules" for a videotape called *Tzintzuntzan in the 1990s* (Rollwagen 1992). In 1993, Rollwagen returned to shoot additional footage on the February Señor del Rescate festival and then traveled with me to Tacoma where he videotaped migrants at work, at leisure, and in church.

For more than a decade, I have been collaborating with Professor Luis Alberto Vargas, a medical anthropologist at the National University in Mexico City. To date, only one paper (Vargas, Kemper, and Casillas 1993) has resulted, but we are optimistic that we will be able to carry out a major research project in Tzintzuntzan related to medical anthropology. At the same time, I have maintained an affiliation with several anthropologists at El Colegio de Michoacán, located two hours to the west of Tzintzuntzan in the city of Zamora. I serve as a member of the advisory board for their journal *Relaciones*, have given seminars and taught courses in the graduate anthropology program when I am in the area, have been invited to participate in workshops and symposia (Kemper 1994a, 1995a), have sought out colleagues there when publishing opportunities arise (e.g., Roth-Seneff and Kemper 1995), and have established a personal book exchange with their library so that, eventually, they will receive upward of one thousand volumes of books and journals from my collection.

In 1998, a special opportunity came to deal with some of the challenges inherent in the massive Tzintzuntzan data sets. Doug White, who previously had worked with Scudder and Colson on their Gwembe data, wanted me to collaborate with him and a Swiss demographer colleague (Eric Widmer) in applying White's social network analysis tools to the Tzintzuntzan data files. We have spent some two years working together and look forward to continuing with the collaboration in years to come (see the Tzintzuntzan Web site, currently available at www.santafe.edu/tarasco/Mexican.html).[8]

Becoming Steward of the Tzintzuntzan Project: The 2000 Census

To become a steward is *not* the same as being the master of one's own house. In taking over the full responsibility for doing the 2000 village and migrant censuses, I was always aware that Tzintzuntzan is still the place made famous among anthropologists by my mentor–colleague George Foster. Even though ill health prevented Foster from coming to the village, and Brandes's teaching responsibilities kept him away as well, the sixth ethnographic census of Tzintzuntzan went forward as scheduled.

I had been planning for this occasion since 1990–1991, when I had taken my last university research leave, and so had saved two semesters' research leave for the time of the 2000 ethnographic census. Actually, I had known since September 30, 1994, that the responsibility for the 2000 census would fall on my shoulders—for that was the day when Foster handed over to me the metal file cases containing the original set of the master *fichero*. Perhaps the moment was not as dramatic as when the Old Testament prophet Elijah passed his mantle to Elisha, as the story is told in 2 Kings 2:13, but I surely felt the "spirit" pass into my hands.

Taking up that calling in January 2000, I assembled a team of some thirty local residents, whose work with the census I would coordinate with help from Peter Cahn (see his chapter in this volume). In the next few months, our team visited more than 700 households, inhabited by 3,346 residents and another 264 extended individuals, yielding a total population of 3,610 for Tzintzuntzan proper and its *colonias* (Lázaro Cárdenas, Tzintzuntzita, and the newest one, called San Juan). After censusing the nearby hamlets of Ojo de Agua and Ichupio for the first time since 1945, team members moved on to find migrants throughout the Lake Pátzcuaro area, in Morelia, and in other towns and cities in Michoacán. We also gathered data on migrants in Mexico City and in Guadalajara, as well as in California, Illinois, and the state of Washington, which now claims the largest enclave outside of Mexico—with perhaps as many as 200 families!

With respect to people living beyond the boundaries of Tzintzuntzan, we again have censused more than 3,000 migrants (including spouses, children, grandchildren, and great-grandchildren) in dozens of different localities. Simply put, about half of the people of Tzintzuntzan are now living in and around the village and the other half are living temporarily or permanently removed from their natal community. This is a dramatic shift from the situation in 1970, and even more striking when compared with the circumstances in 1945, when Foster first did fieldwork in Tzintzuntzan.

Tzintzuntzan as Extended Community

There are certainly hundreds, if not thousands, of community studies in the anthropological literature. Most of these works, especially those from earlier times, are focused tightly on a single place in time and space. Our continuing long-term fieldwork among the people of Tzintzuntzan suggests that we need to rethink our notion of community (cf. Foster, in this volume, for a similar perspective).

First, I am struck particularly by how hard it has become to define who is and who is not a resident of Tzintzuntzan. As we have seen, a growing proportion—currently more than 30 percent—of the local households have one or more extended members away from the village at any given moment, yet the families tend not to think of these persons as being migrants. In addition, given the flow of individuals and families from and back to the village in accord with academic schedules, vacations, and the planting-harvesting cycles in U.S. fields, the population is always in flux.

Second, distance is no longer the significant factor that it used to be. The transportation infrastructure permits relatively inexpensive travel by bus, private car, or even airlines to all parts of Mexico and to the United States. In recent years, several young adults who died from car accidents in the United States have had their bodies sent back by air to Guadalajara, thence by bus or family-owned truck to Tzintzuntzan for funeral and wake services.

Third, the limited access to telephone service has been upgraded to fully automatic service (now that Teléfonos de México has been privatized) so that rapid voice communication is replacing the slower and somewhat unreliable postal and telegraph systems as a preferred means of contact between the village and elsewhere. A recent effort to sign up new subscribers for the automatic direct-dialing system has resulted in more than a hundred households being subscribers—although they are listed in the phone book of the state's capital city as if they resided in nearby Quiroga.

Fourth, the increased participation of the young people of Tzintzuntzan in the higher educational system of Mexico means that many of them are away from the village for several years, except for vacation periods or weekends. Still, they continue to return to the community even after settling in urban areas where their hard-won job skills can be applied. For instance, one medical doctor has his practice in the state capital of Morelia but insists (even over his non-Tzintzuntzan wife's objections) on maintaining a weekend practice in Tzintzuntzan. More than 150 persons from the village have become schoolteachers, which is remarkable enough, but more interesting is that most desire to practice their profession with Tzintzuntzan as a base of operation. Thus, they live in the village and commute daily to other localities or even come back just on weekends if the distance is too great for commuting. The local primary and secondary schools are currently staffed almost entirely by teachers living in Tzintzuntzan.

Fifth, earnings and remittances from persons beyond the immediate community have become vital to the continuing economic survival of Tzintzuntzan and hundreds of similar Mexican villages. Since 1970, the Mexican peso has gone from a fixed value of 12.5 to the dollar to about 3,000 to the dollar by 1990, then suffered a 1,000 to 1 "adjustment," and has continued to decline to more than 9.0 new pesos to the dollar at present. As a result, the shift of the extended community toward the United States—and away from Mexico City—has become marked. When men fail to send money or do not return after the fall harvest season in the United States, their spouses and children suffer serious deprivations. On the other hand, temporary movements away from the village can be used to supplement inadequate local wages. Even some schoolteachers travel to California or Washington to work in the fields during the summer vacation period. There they can earn the equivalent of their entire year's salary in a couple of months of hard labor.

Sixth, inheritance is an important issue for residents and their relatives living away from Tzintzuntzan. A number of older migrants—some away from the village for more than forty years—still own houses or land there. Will they leave this property to their children, some of whom have rarely traveled to

Tzintzuntzan, or will it pass to family members still living in the village? On the other side of the equation, many younger migrants are concerned to establish their claims to a share of the family lands by continuing to visit Tzintzuntzan on a regular basis.

Finally, Tzintzuntzan is well known for fiestas and religious celebrations (Brandes 1988). Many migrants—as well as thousands of other tourists—come back to the community to participate in these festivals. Especially at the February festival, in honor of the Señor del Rescate, many migrants return to baptize or confirm their children in the *parroquial* church. Often, they select compadres (co-godparents) from village residents or from other returned migrants, thus emphasizing their solidarity with their natal community. This sense of membership and affiliation also applies to the people of the hamlets surrounding the village proper. Conveniently, the main elements of the annual fiesta cycle occur at times when Tzintzuntzeños away from the village can return as participants or observers. For example, one of the villagers responsible for the Holy Week celebrations is currently living in Orange County in southern California. He takes his two-week vacation to coincide with his duties in Tzintzuntzan. But since so many migrants now live in the Tacoma area, and a considerable number cannot return yearly to Tzintzuntzan, these migrants have begun to celebrate their own version of the Señor del Rescate fiesta each February!

The concept of the extended community has emerged over several decades during our work with the people of Tzintzuntzan. When Foster began work in Tzintzuntzan in 1945, it had only 1,231 residents, nearly all of whom were born in and lived most of their lives in what then appeared to be a "closed corporate community." By comparison, since I began work there in 1969 more than four thousand individuals have been added to the master data file. Time has transformed who "counts" in the village population, just as it has changed the makeup of the research team involved with Tzintzuntzan and its extended community—all the people who consider themselves to be Tzintzuntzeños wherever they may be, whether in the town itself or as far away as Tacoma, Washington.

In Place of a Conclusion

This chapter is no more than an "interim report" on my role in the Tzintzuntzan project. What will the situation be like in the year 2010 and beyond? By then, we will be working with the grandchildren and great-grandchildren of adults known to Foster in 1945. At this point, Foster is no longer able—at age 87—to travel to the village, but Brandes and I maintain frequent contacts with the community, and a third generation of fieldworkers is represented by Peter Cahn, who has completed a dissertation (Cahn 2001) on religious change based on his recent yearlong study in Tzintzuntzan. His chapter follows this one and provides an appropriate continuation (and new beginning) to the story of Tzintzuntzan and its anthropologists.

If Tzintzuntzan continues to develop as it did during the 1970s, the 1980s, and the 1990s, the challenge to our theories and methodologies will be significant. What once was treated—by villagers and anthropologists alike—as if it were a "closed" system has become a spatially and temporally extended community whose changing characteristics cannot be ignored. Indeed, for the migrants and their children returning to what some of them have jokingly identified as "Tzintzun-landia" (a play on "Disneyland," of course), the community is both "home" and "re-creation" site where they, like other tourists, can encounter Purépecha (now the preferred term for Tarascan) and Spanish colonial culture in twenty-first-century dress. Even more important, they encounter their own cultural and social circumstances being transformed before their very eyes.[9] Through our long-term field research, we have seen how the concept of "community" involves not only the sense of physical place (*pueblo*) but also the commitment to common identity and values (*communidad indígena*) regardless of whether the people of Tzintzuntzan are physically resident in the town or living elsewhere. This is a community still tied to pre-Conquest legends and more than four hundred years of colonial and postcolonial history, caught up in government-sponsored tourist campaigns to retain its traditional facade, but also striving to cope with modern life in a global system represented by satellite dishes, border crossings, and transnationalism—a world in which the community of Tzintzuntzan finds itself on the front page of *The Washington Post*.

Notes

The initial fieldwork in Mexico City during 1969–1970 was funded through NIGMS Training Grant GM-1224, which also covered the earlier summer field training in Pátzcuaro as well as the analysis and write-up of field materials for the dissertation. Additional financial support was received from the Center for Latin American Studies (University of California at Berkeley) for dissertation write-up during the months of July through September 1971. The Wenner-Gren Foundation for Anthropological Research provided a grant-in-aid (no. 3027) for the summers of 1974 and 1976 and for preparation of the Spanish- and English-language monographs based on that fieldwork. In the periods July 1979 through June 1980 and July through December 1991, fieldwork was supported by Fulbright-Hays Advanced Research Awards (American Republics Program). The Ford Foundation (Office for Mexico and Central America) provided a small grant to support two Mexican graduate students on the project in 1980. I also have received continuing support from Southern Methodist University through Faculty Research Fellowships and Awards for the periods of August through December 1979, June 1986 through July 1987, January through June 1990, and August 1999 through May 2000. In addition to these "standard" sources, a few private individuals have provided the project with significant funding, which I have matched through my own personal financial contributions. To all of these institutions and individuals go my most sincere thanks for their continuing support.

Of course, there would be no Tzintzuntzan project at all if George Foster had not blazed the trail that I and others have traveled more easily because of his decades of dedicated work. He and his wife, Mary, their children, and grandchildren have been gracious, generous, and welcoming for more than thirty years. In fact, since 1967, I have spent more time with the Fosters in the home of our extended Tzintzuntzan "family"— with Doña Micaela González, her daughters Virginia and Lola, and their friend María Flores—than with the families of my parents, siblings, and in-laws! Perhaps, the people of Tzintzuntzan who ask me if I am "*un hijo de Foster*" ("Foster's son") understand something profound about our relationship and the sense of gratitude I owe to the only anthropologist in Tzintzuntzan who ever will be known, respected, and loved as El Doctor.

1. As I was completing my summer's research in Pátzcuaro, John Durston arrived on the scene with the intention of studying the regional economy. I shared with him some of my field notes and sketch maps. His monograph (Durston 1976) stands as the last point in the systematic study of the Pátzcuaro marketplace.

2. It is a curious coincidence that, at the time when I was studying the Tzintzuntzan migrants in Mexico City, the community of Cherán was the focus of an intentional restudy designed to examine acculturation and change since Beals's original study in 1940. In discussing the "adaptation" of this "traditional" community, Castile (1974:139–141) commented on the continuing importance of temporary labor migration to the United States.

3. Among the students in the urban anthropology seminar was Larissa Lomnitz (who earlier had taken undergraduate work in anthropology with Foster at Berkeley), who not only gave me valuable assistance with the Tzintzuntzan migrant project, but also provided me with numerous opportunities to meet the many Mexican and international anthropologists who also enjoyed her gracious hospitality in Mexico City.

4. These findings on *compadrazgo* have been widely disseminated through the *Annual Editions* volumes, *Global Studies: Latin America*, edited by Paul Goodwin (ninth edition, 2000, Guilford, Conn.: McGraw-Hill/Dushkin).

5. By 1983, Ramon Campuzano had married and needed a place to live. We worked out an arrangement by which I "sold" him my interest in the rooftop apartment. Thereafter, I was given the use of a room downstairs, whenever I happened to be in Mexico City. As a result, I took some furniture and equipment to Tzintzuntzan, sold Ramon other pieces, and spent increasingly more time in Tzintzuntzan than in Mexico City during the rest of the 1980s.

6. It is surely a curious coincidence that Foster recognizes the "trigger effect" of having read Honigmann's article about a village in West Pakistan in the formulation of the "Image of Limited Good" and that my ideas about the extended community were similarly inspired by fieldwork in Bangladesh (formerly East Pakistan) and the reading of relevant literature, including Morris Opler's classic article on "The Extensions of an Indian Village" (1956).

7. Back in the late 1960s and early 1970s, Foster had copied many of the church (and civil) records by hand or by carrying the large record books to Ajijic, located on

ROBERT V. KEMPER

Lake Chapala, in Jalisco State. There he had access to a photocopy machine. Unfortunately, the cost of processing these handwritten copies or photocopies into a computer database was prohibitive. It was much less expensive simply to enter all of the church records into a computer database program. After ten years of data entry, virtually all of the two hundred years of more than fifty thousand existing records have been logged into a computer by Lucila Marín (who also is an assistant to the priest in charge of the parish).

8. In addition, I have acquired and registered the domain name tzintzuntzan.org as the permanent home of the Tzintzuntzan Project on the Internet.

9. In addition to works focused on migration, I also have examined Tzintzuntzan's transformations in other domains, including tourism (Kemper 1979d), urbanization and development (1981b), the production, distribution, and consumption of foodstuffs (1996a), changes in the use of the Tarascan language (1998), and manipulation of ethnic identity (Royce and Kemper n.d.).

References Cited

Anderson, Scott T.
(1998) "Growing old in Tzintzuntzan." Ph.D. dissertation. University of California, San Francisco.

Beals, Ralph L.
(1946) *Cherán: A Sierra Tarascan Village*. Smithsonian Institution, Institute of Social Anthropology, Publication No. 2. Washington, D.C.: U. S. Government Printing Office.

Berreman, Gerald
(1962) *Behind Many Masks: Ethnography and Impression Management in a Himalayan Village*. Society for Applied Anthropology, Monograph No. 4. Ithaca, NY: Cornell University Press.

Brandes, Stanley
(1988) *Power and Persuasion: Fiestas and Social Control in Rural Mexico*. Philadelphia: University of Pennsylvania Press.

Browning, Harley L. and Waltraut Feindt
(1969) "Selectivity of migrants to a metropolis in a developing country: A Mexican case study." *Demography* 6(4):347–357.

Butterworth, Douglas
(1962) "A study of the urbanization process among Mixtec migrants from Tilantongo in Mexico City." *América Indígena* 22(3):257–274.

Cahn, Peter S.
(2001) "When conversion is convergence: Evangelicals and Catholics in Tzintzuntzan, Mexico." Ph.D. dissertation. University of California, Berkeley.

Castile, George Pierre
(1974) *Cherán: La Adaptación de una Comunidad Tradicional de Michoacán.* Serie de Antropología Social No. 26. México, D.F.: Instituto Nacional Indigenista y Secretaría de Educación Pública.

Durston, John W.
(1976) *Organización Social de los Mercados Campesinos en el Centro de Michoacán.* Serie de Antropología Social No. 52. México, D.F.: Instituto Nacional Indigenista y Secretaría de Educación Pública.

Engelbrecht, Beate
(1987) *Töpferinnen in Mexiko: Entwicklungsethnologische Untersuchungen zur Produktion und Vermarktung der Töpferei von Patamban und Tzintzuntzan, Michoacán, West-Mexiko.* Basler Beiträge zur Ethnologie Band 26. Basel: Ethnologisches Seminar der Universität und Museum für Völkerkunde (in Kommission bei Wepf & Co. AG Verlag).

Foster, George M.
(1967) *Tzintzuntzan: Mexican Peasants in a Changing World.* Boston: Little, Brown.
(1969) "Godparents and social networks in Tzintzuntzan." *Southwestern Journal of Anthropology* 25:261–278.

Foster, George M. and Robert V. Kemper
(1974) "A perspective on anthropological fieldwork in cities." Pp. 1–17 in George M. Foster and Robert V. Kemper (editors), *Anthropologists in Cities.* Boston: Little, Brown.

Foster, George M. and Gabriel Ospina
(1948) *Empire's Children: The People of Tzintzuntzan.* Smithsonian Institution, Institute of Social Anthropology, Publication No. 6. México, D. F.: Imprenta Nuevo Mundo.

Freilich, Morris
(1970) *Marginal Natives: Anthropologists at Work.* New York: Harper and Row.

Kaplan, David
(1960) "The Mexican marketplace in historical perspective." Ph.D. dissertation. University of Michigan, Ann Arbor.

Kemper, Robert V.
(1970) "El estudio antropológico de la migración a las ciudades en América Latina." *América Indígena* 30(3):609–633.
(1971a) "Migration and adaptation of Tzintzuntzan peasants in Mexico City." Ph.D. dissertation. University of California, Berkeley.
(1971b) "Rural-urban migration in Latin America: A framework for the comparative analysis of geographical and temporal patterns." *International Migration Review* 5(1):36–47.
(1973) "Factores sociales en la migración: el caso de los Tzintzuntzeños en la Ciudad de México." *América Indígena* 33(4):1095–1118.

(1974a) "Family and household among Tzintzuntzan migrants in Mexico City." Pp. 23–45 in Wayne A. Cornelius and Felicity M. Trueblood (editors), *Anthropological Perspectives on Latin American Urbanization*. Latin American Urban Research Vol. 4. Beverly Hills, CA: Sage Publications.

(1974b) "Tzintzuntzeños in Mexico City: The anthropologist among peasant migrants." Pp. 63–91 in George M. Foster and Robert V. Kemper (editors), *Anthropologists in Cities*. Boston: Little, Brown.

(1975) "Contemporary Mexican urbanization: A view from Tzintzuntzan, Michoacán." *Proceedings of XL Congresso Internazionale degli Americanisti* 4:53–65. Genova: Casa Editrice Tilgher-Genova, s.a.s.

(1976) *Campesinos en la Ciudad: Gente de Tzintzuntzan*. Ediciones SepSetentas No. 270. México, D.F., Secretaría de Educación Pública.

(1977) *Migration and Adaptation: Tzintzuntzan Peasants in Mexico City*. Beverly Hills, CA: Sage Publications.

(1979a) "Compadrazgo in city and countryside: A comparison of Tzintzuntzan migrants and villagers." *Kroeber Anthropological Society Papers* 55/56:25–44.

(1979b) "Fieldwork among Tzintzuntzan migrants in Mexico City: Retrospect and prospect." Pp. 189–207 in George M. Foster, Thayer Scudder, Elizabeth Colson, and Robert V. Kemper (editors), *Long-Term Field Research in Social Anthropology*. New York: Academic Press.

(1979c) "Frontiers in migration: From culturalism to historical structuralism in the study of Mexico-U.S. migration." Pp. 9–21 in Fernando Cámara Barbachano and Robert V. Kemper (editors), *Migration Across Frontiers: Mexico and the United States*. Latin American Anthropology Group Contributions No. 3. Albany, NY: Institute for Mesoamerican Studies, SUNY Albany.

(1979d) "Tourism in Taos and Pátzcuaro: A comparison of two approaches to regional development." *Annals of Tourism Research* 6(1):91–110.

(1981a) "Obstacles and opportunities: Household economics of Tzintzuntzan migrants in Mexico City." *Urban Anthropology* 10:211–229.

(1981b) "Urbanization and development in the Tarascan region since 1940." *Urban Anthropology* 10(1):89–110.

(1982) "The compadrazgo in urban Mexico." *Anthropological Quarterly* 55(1):17–30.

(1987a) "Desarrollo de los estudios antropológicos sobre la migración mexicana." Pp. 477–499 in Susana Glantz (editor), *La Heterodoxia Recuperada, en torno a Angel Palerm*. México, D.F.: Fondo de Cultura Económica.

(1987b) "Urbanization in Latin American development." Pp. 229–242 in Jack W. Hopkins (editor), *Latin America: Perspectives on a Region*. New York: Holmes & Meier.

(1994a) "Extendiendo las fronteras de la comunidad en teoría y práctica: Tzintzuntzan, Mexico, 1970–1990." *Estudios Michoacanos* 5:119–129.

(1994b) "Migración sin fronteras: el caso del pueblo de Tzintzuntzan, Michoacán, 1945–1990." Pp. 67–82 in *XXII Mesa de Antropología de la Sociedad Mexicana de Antropología*. Tuxtla Gutiérrez, Chiapas: Gobierno del Estado de Chiapas.

(1995a) "Comunidad y migración: El caso del pueblo de Tzintzuntzan, Michoacán, 1988–1994." *Relaciones* 61/62:133–148.
(1995b) "Migración y transformación de la cultura mexicana: 1519–1992." Pp. 533–547 in Agustín Jacinto Zavala and Alvaro Ochoa Serrano (editors), *Tradición e Identidad en la Cultura Mexicana*. Zamora: El Colegio de Michoacán y Consejo Nacional de Ciencia y Tecnología.
(1996a) "La comida en Tzintzuntzan, Michoacán: tradiciones y transformaciones." Pp. 365–395 in Janet Long (editor), *Conquista y Comida: Consecuencias del Encuentro de dos Mundos*. México, D.F.: Universidad Nacional Autónoma de México.
(1996b) "Migration and adaptation: Tzintzuntzeños in Mexico City and beyond." Pp. 196–209 in George Gmelch and Walter P. Zenner (editors), *Urban Life: Readings in Urban Anthropology*. Third Edition. Prospect Heights, IL: Waveland Press.
(1998) "Tarascan speakers in Tzintzuntzan, 1945–1990." Pp. 38–42 in Robert Rubenstein and Paul L. Doughty (editors), *Symbols, Social Action and Human Peace: Papers in Honor of Mary LeCron Foster*. [A special issue of *Human Peace* 11(4).] Gainesville, FL: IUAES Commission on the Study of Peace.

Kemper, Robert V. and George M. Foster
(1975) "Urbanization in Mexico: The view from Tzintzuntzan." *Latin American Urban Research* 5:53–75.

Kemper, Robert V. and Jack Rollwagen
(1996) "Urban Anthropology." Pp. 1337–1344 in David Levinson and Melvin Ember (editors), *Encyclopedia of Cultural Anthropology, vol. 4 (S–Z)*. New York: Henry Holt and Company.

Kemper, Robert V. and Anya Peterson Royce
(1979) "Mexican urbanization since 1821: A macro-historical approach." *Urban Anthropology* 8(3/4): 267–289.
(1983) "Urbanization in Mexico: Beyond the heritage of conquest." Pp. 93–128 in Carl Kendall, John Hawkins, and Laurel Bossen (editors), *Heritage of Conquest: Thirty Years Later*. Albuquerque: University of New Mexico Press.

Kemper, Robert V., Ben J. Wallace, and Margot Wilson-Moore
(1989) "The extended community in rural Bangladesh: Household formation and migration in Kalampur and Jalsha." *Urban Anthropology* 18(3/4):347–363.

Lasker, Gabriel, Robert V. Kemper, Ronald K. Wetherington, and Bernice A. Kaplan
(1984) "Isonomy between two towns in Michoacán, Mexico." Pp. 159–163 in Rafael Ramos Galván and Rosa María Ramos Rodríguez (editors), *Estudios de Antropología Biológica* (Segundo Coloquio de Antropología Física 'Juan Comas,' 1982), México, D.F.: UNAM, Instituto de Investigaciones Antropológicas, Serie Antropológica 75.

Lewis, Oscar
(1952) "Urbanization without breakdown." *Scientific Monthly* 75:31–41.

Mitchell, J. Clyde [editor]
(1969) *Social Networks in Urban Situations: Analyses of Personal Relationships in Central African Towns.* Manchester: Manchester University Press (published for the Institute for Social Relations, University of Zambia).

Opler, Morris E.
(1956) "The extensions of an Indian village." *Journal of Asian Studies* 16(1):5–10.

Potter, Jack M., May N. Diaz, and George M. Foster [editors]
(1967) *Peasant Society: A Reader.* Boston: Little, Brown.

Redfield, Robert
(1941) *The Folk Culture of Yucatan.* Chicago: University of Chicago Press.

Rollwagen, Jack R.
(1992) *Tzintzuntzan in the 1990s: A Lakeside Village in Highland Mexico.* Video Program #1992-TZ1. Brockport, NY: The Institute.

Roth-Seneff, Andrew and Robert V. Kemper
(1995) "Tarascans." Pp. 243–247 in James W. Dow and Robert V. Kemper (editors), *Encyclopedia of World Cultures, vol. 8, Middle America and the Caribbean.* Boston, MA: G. K. Hall & Co.

Royce, Anya Peterson and Robert V. Kemper
(n.d.) "Who is an Indian in Mexico: Perceptions and performances." 62 pp. ms.

Shott, Michael J. and Eduardo Williams
(1997) "Pottery ethnoarchaeology in Michoacán, Mexico." Paper presented at 96th Annual Meeting of the American Anthropological Association.
(1999) "Pottery ethnoarchaeology in Michoacán, Mexico: The third season's report." Paper presented at 98th Annual Meeting of the American Anthropological Association.

Torres Sarmiento, Socorro
(1999) "Buscando el Gasto, Tzintzuntzeño immigrant income-generating strategies." Ph.D. dissertation. University of California, Irvine.

Vargas, Luis A., Robert V. Kemper, and Leticia E. Casillas
(1993) "Réseaux migratoires et santé: le cas du Mexique," pp. 62–71 in *Vers un ailleurs prometteur . . . l'émigration, une réponse universelle à une situation de crise?* Paris and Geneva: Presses Universitaires de France and Cahiers de L'I.U.E.D.

CHAPTER TWELVE

BEING THE THIRD GENERATION IN TZINTZUNTZAN
Peter S. Cahn

B eing a member of the third generation of anthropologists to conduct fieldwork in Tzintzuntzan has indelibly marked the nature of both the data I collected and the conclusions I made. If I had attempted the same project in a field site unknown to the anthropological literature, my results would have differed in far more than geographical nuance. Ethnographic research in social anthropology training is still a solitary task, a rite of passage that separates seminar-taking graduate students from writing-up fieldworkers.[1] However, by undertaking research in a community already well studied by my main advisor (Professor Stanley Brandes) and his own academic mentor (Professor George M. Foster), I joined an ongoing dialogue that included my informants as well as those of my predecessors. Through this dialogue, an ethnography emerges that is both informed and inchoate.

Contributors in earlier chapters of this volume have written about the history of long-term research projects, the effect of continuing contact with a community on their theory and method, and passing the mantle to the next generation. My own vision is less expansive. From my vantage point at the end of a Ph.D. program, I can look back with clarity on the decision to choose my field site and topic, the experience of conducting research, and the process of analyzing and writing. But, until I begin an academic career and take on students of my own, it is difficult to predict how I will care for the mantle I have received. Therefore, in this chapter, I confine my comments to the advantages and disadvantages, the benefits and frustrations, of being a third-generation fieldworker in Tzintzuntzan. Using examples from my own dissertation project, I argue for the significant impact that receiving the mantle of long-term research has had on the ethnography produced. I further suggest how joining an ongoing research project enhances graduate training.

Joining a Long-Term Project

I did not enter the Ph.D. program in sociocultural anthropology at the University of California, Berkeley, with the intention of joining a fifty-five-year

Young members of a West Palm Beach, Florida, evangelical church dramatize the life of Jesus in Tzintzuntzan's plaza. Following the performance, a Mexican preacher invited the audience to accept Jesus as their personal savior and pray with the actors. Photograph by Peter S. Cahn.

longitudinal study of the mestizo community of Tzintzuntzan, Mexico. My particular research interest was religious change among Latin American indigenous groups. Given my broad topical and geographic focus, I found the Berkeley Department's size and theoretical variety attractive. I had also forged a relationship with a professor there who agreed to become my primary academic advisor.

In my first year at Berkeley, rather than hone my own dissertation project, I took wide-ranging seminars and assimilated graduate-level reading loads. The first-year cohort met twice a week in a seminar designed to introduce us to major ideas in the discipline. On one day, we would meet with the professor for structured discussion of the readings; on the other, we students met on our own. We also instituted a series of visits from current and emeriti faculty, who would recount their intellectual autobiographies and familiarize us with their ongoing research projects.

One week, George M. Foster was the guest professor in our seminar. I knew that Foster had directed my advisor's doctoral dissertation, when Brandes had been a graduate student at Berkeley in the late 1960s. I also knew that Foster's recent generosity had helped solidify support for the department library, which was renamed to honor him and his wife, Mary. Until his visit to our classroom, however, I knew very little about his work on peasant societies or his longitudinal research project in Tzintzuntzan, Mexico. He described for us his initial fieldwork in Tzintzuntzan and how he had unintentionally begun a long-term ethnographic project there, sending teams of students during the summers to research different aspects of life around Lake Pátzcuaro. Although he had not brought graduate student researchers to Tzintzuntzan since his retirement about twenty years earlier, he still felt that many issues and changes in the community remained to be studied.

At that point in the semester, I was thinking about a summer visit to Latin America, possibly a chance to scout out a site for my own yearlong fieldwork experience. Later, when I recognized Professor Foster at a department function, I broached the idea of spending the summer in Tzintzuntzan. He responded enthusiastically. We arranged to meet to discuss the details, which turned into a weekly reading course in the spring semester before my first visit to Tzintzuntzan. That February, Foster and Brandes traveled to Tzintzuntzan to celebrate the community's largest fiesta of the year. On that trip, they selected a family for me to live with and prepared them for my arrival in June. Back in Berkeley, I had access to the most recent ethnographic census data, so I immediately looked up the household where I would be living and memorized the names and ages of all the family members.

For my summer project, Foster and Brandes advised that I select a project that could be completed in a two-month period. Pursuing the theme of religion seemed unfeasible since I would be present for only one of the major fiestas of the liturgical calendar. Moreover, discussing issues of spirituality and conversion would require greater rapport than I could generate in a short visit. So, I prepared to focus on the marketing of pottery, a topic that intersected with the changing socioeconomic conditions in the community that influenced religious life as well. Tzintzuntzeño potters, for the main, still produced their ceramic ware using the same methods that Foster had documented when he first arrived in the community more than a half century earlier. However, improvements in transportation and tourism had modified the way artisans sold their goods.

The directed reading course with Foster and Brandes familiarized me with the literature on Tzintzuntzan. Anthropological researchers in Tzintzuntzan, though collegial, have tended to publish as single authors and in a range of scholarly journals and monographs. To construct my reading list, I included as many pieces about Tzintzuntzan as I could find. From the first generation of researchers, I read the original ethnography that detailed the ways of life in the community as observed in 1945 (Foster and Ospina 1948). The first-year theory course no longer included discussion on the nature of peasant societies, so I revisited the debate about Foster's (1965) formulation of the Image of Limited Good. From the second generation, I read Kemper's (1977) study on the migration of Tzintzuntzeños to Mexico City and Brandes's (1988) examination of the fiesta system, neither of which seemed directly relevant to pottery, but which later proved useful.

Entering the Field as the Third Generation

When the summer of 1998 arrived, George and Mary Foster accompanied me to Mexico. We traveled with a classmate of mine, who also planned to do research in Tzintzuntzan that summer and had participated in the reading course. Even with my advance preparation, I was taken aback by the physical beauty of the setting: white-washed adobe houses on the edge of a lake surrounded by jagged volcanic cones. The rainy season made the hillsides lush with vegetation and the air clear and moist. The Fosters escorted me to the house where I would be living, a wonderfully simple process compared to what I had heard from colleagues who had spent the initial months of fieldwork locating a suitable place to live.

The Fosters stayed for an entire week to make sure that we two novice researchers began our projects smoothly. Despite the diminished energy associated with being in their upper eighties, the Fosters still maintained lively friendships with nearly the entire community and included us in all their socializing. They took care to introduce us to both potters and merchants, who would be helpful resources in understanding how the artisanry market had changed. They gave us advice on how to conduct ourselves in the field as well as how to take assiduous yet unobtrusive notes. With their imprimatur of legitimacy, initial acceptance into the community came with unusual ease.

Unfortunately, the near-universal welcome I received did not translate into productive research. As it turned out, pottery marketing was such an uncontroversial subject that neither artisans nor sellers had many opinions about it. To the potters, their craft was simply an inherited occupation and one of the few money-making activities, however meager, on which they could rely. Beyond that, potters and nonpotters had little to say about their craft, how they sold their goods, or what pottery making meant to them.

But when a troupe of Florida evangelicals pulled into the town plaza one summer evening with clowns, puppets, and balloon animals, the whole town started talking. My first hint that something out of the ordinary was going to happen came during Mass the previous Sunday. After giving his sermon and communion, the parish priest announced that a free medical clinic would be held the next day in the town hall. On Monday, after visiting with some potters, I decided to go see how the clinic was going. When I arrived, I found a mob of people. A whole section of the second floor was given over to an optometrist, another office had become a gynecologist's consulting room, and the ground floor had been transformed into a bustling pharmacy. Outside, dentists operating in a mobile van would end up pulling forty-three teeth that day.

I quickly noticed that the nurses and doctors were North Americans, only some with a command of Spanish. One of them, wearing a polo shirt and taking a break from the clinic, noticed me and introduced himself in English. He explained that he was part of a team of physicians and nurses from West Palm Beach, Florida, who had been coming to Michoacán for several summers to offer free medical clinics. I asked him if they came with a particular organization. He answered, pointing to the logo on his shirt, "The Church of Christ."

During the daylong clinic, there was no overt or even subtle proselytizing. When they packed up the supplies and the building gradually reverted to its government functions, I thought it was the end. I went into my room to write up all that I had seen that day. My landlady, who was used to housing anthropologists and understood that my project was to see everything mundane and unusual, knocked on the door and announced: "Something's going on in the plaza."

From the entryway to our house, I saw flashes of movement and heard children's squeals coming from the normally sleepy town square. When I got closer, I saw a clown enticing small children with animal-shaped balloons and a school bus unloading blond teenagers. On the adjacent basketball court, they had set up a makeshift puppet theater, microphone stands, and loudspeakers. The clowns led the kids from the street back toward the basketball court, where other visitors in sequined costumes were encouraging the children to sit facing the stage. When a ring of kids had formed along with some rows of adults standing on the edges, the performance began.

Only a few of the performers spoke Spanish, but that did not matter since they mostly acted their routines to the words of a taped Spanish soundtrack. A group of women singers led the chorus while puppets and magicians entertained. The culmination of the event was the teenagers' allegorical retelling of the New Testament in which God appeared as a toy maker and Jesus as the doll sent to bring harmony to the workshop.

As soon as the play ended, the preaching began. A Mexican took the microphone. He talked dramatically about the importance of having a personal relationship with Jesus Christ and his own miraculous recovery from drug and alcohol addiction. He ended his sermon by calling forward all those interested in delivering themselves to Jesus tonight. Having read about the hostility evangelical faiths had received in Latin America and having witnessed Tzintzuntzan's own strong Catholic faith, I expected the preacher to have few takers. To my surprise, a woman came forward, then another, and then several more until a group of thirty or so circled the speaker. The Floridians joined hands around them in energetic prayer.

In the days following the visit, I tried to understand why so many people had responded to the preacher's call. One Catholic informant, who did not join the prayer circle but watched the event, told me, "It is a beautiful message that there is one God." Others complimented the "beautiful" music. The only outright skepticism I heard came from a sixteen-year-old girl who taught catechism to Catholic children: "They don't want us to love the Virgin. She is even greater than Jesus. She is His mother. I just let the message go in one ear and out the other." In the play, the mother of Jesus was dressed like a flamenco dancer. She stepped out of a group of toys to receive God's child, then faded back into the chorus of toys for the rest of the play. The topic of religion did not prove too sensitive for discussion, and it certainly roused the emotions of the community more than ceramics ever did.

A pastor/physician returned to Tzintzuntzan without the Florida crew the following Monday for a Bible study and medical consultation. There were about sixteen women present on the now barren basketball court. They listened quietly as he read passages from Scripture, then became animated when he closed his Bible and opened his medical kit. He came several more Mondays and even talked of renting a more permanent location for his consultations. By then, the summer had ended, and I was scheduled to return to Berkeley. Though I failed to discover anything remarkable about pottery marketing, I had honed my qualitative research skills, confirmed my interest in the topic of religion, and selected Tzintzuntzan as my primary fieldwork site.

Advantages and Disadvantages of Third-Generation Fieldwork

When I returned to Berkeley, I felt both energized and focused. My foray into fieldwork convinced me that I had a feasible dissertation project, which I could summarize succinctly whenever anyone asked me. I began formulating a research proposal and contacting faculty members for advice. Neither Foster nor Brandes had pressured me or even suggested that I return to Tzintzuntzan for my dissertation research, but I felt a definite urgency to return. For one thing, the religious landscape seemed to be mutating so rapidly that I was curious to document all the developments. In addition, being in Tzintzuntzan had been so enjoyable, a sheer bliss that rarely makes it into the write-up and analysis of field research. The community's acceptance of my presence extended to a constant stream of invitations for meals, parties, and even to serve as a godparent. Collecting data was arduous, tiring even, but never dull.

A year after I had returned from my first visit to Tzintzuntzan, I loaded my backpack with notebooks for another research trip. This time I would travel alone and remain in the community for a full year, from August 1999 to August 2000. I had arranged to stay with the same family as I had during the previous summer, since we had developed a good rapport and I had cultivated a taste for my landlady's cooking. My intuition proved true in that religion was a topic of great personal and communal interest in Tzintzuntzan. During the year I spent in Michoacán, I regularly visited a dozen different evangelical congregations around Lake Pátzcuaro while living with a Catholic family and participating in the Catholic rites that dominated local life. Although I was investigating a topic that no previous researcher had asked about, I became increasingly aware of how the preceding generations of anthropologists informed both how my interlocutors viewed me and how I interacted with them.

(1) The first advantage I noted in the field was the ease of access. While it was true that I would have had difficulties asking about sensitive religious issues on my initial arrival in Tzintzuntzan, it did not take long before I had reached a high level of comfort with many informants. Letters of introduction on official university stationery impressed no one as much as a verbal explanation that I was a student of "El Doctor," their affectionate nickname for Foster. Sometimes, if I presented myself as an anthropologist, but not specifically as part of a team of researchers, informants would ask if I knew El Doctor. When I would say "yes," they immediately became less guarded and more responsive to my questions.

The community had become so thoroughly familiar with anthropologists that I rarely had to explain the goals of the discipline or the purpose of my project. They took it as a given that outsiders would want to know about how they lived and felt it a point of pride to inform me of the facts as they saw them. It had been challenging enough justifying to my parents the role of an anthropologist, so I was relieved to find that my new neighbors felt perfectly comfortable with the idea. As one friend phrased it, while introducing me to an out-of-town relative, "He's an anthropologist. That means he's going to learn how we live, then go back to his country to help people understand Mexicans better." I did not know if she was repeating what another researcher had said or simply was stating her observations of anthropologists' roles. In either case, I saw no reason to contradict her.

Tzintzuntzan had not always been so accommodating of foreign researchers. In fact, some of the most repeated anecdotes that I heard from neighbors recounted how Foster had been mistreated during the early days of his stay in the town. They jokingly told how a man had duped the eager ethnographer into drinking water after tasting fresh mescal, a combination known to induce vomiting. Their laughter belied their embarrassment at how ignorant and closed-minded their parents and grandparents had been. Now, they have come to appreciate the interest of outsiders, which distinguishes their community from others and helps generate tourism.

The frequency with which I heard the story about Foster drinking mescal points to another way in which being the third generation enhances access to data. People in Tzintzuntzan not only made me feel at home, but also knew how to relate to me because they saw me as part of a lineage of previous researchers. Much of my daily activity in the field involved a sort of informal intimacy, that is, visiting informants and engaging in unstructured conversations that traversed several topics. Many times, we filled the potentially awkward transitions in our chats with gossip about other ethnographers. My predecessors had established godparenthood ties as well as personal friendships over the years. They had introduced their families to people in Tzintzuntzan. While I was living in the community, I had periodic access to electronic mail in nearby Pátzcuaro, so I acted as a conduit for news between Mexico and the United States. In this way, data gathering mixed with pleasant chats and became a true exchange of information. Note taking felt more congenial than extractive.

At the same time, the facility of acceptance comes with the danger of greater expectations. Jose Limón's (1991) description of "precursory" ethnographers resonated with me in the field. As Limón had experienced in his own fieldwork in south Texas, anthropologists must contend not only with the group studied, but also with the anthropologists who have preceded them. In my case, the working habits of precursory ethnographers shaped the expectations for how I should behave.

For instance, Foster scrupulously collected data on traditional remedies, often with a tape recorder. In my research, I did not find it as important to document exact details of folk prescriptions, nor did I use a tape recorder in my interviews. This occasioned some questions. An older informant would sometimes interrupt a train of thought to ask me, "Aren't you going to write this down?" Or, she would make a reference to how El Doctor used to record their conversations. Another time a potter remarked to me that El Doctor used to stay at his house until midnight watching how he fired his wares. For me, the unspoken implication was that going to sleep at 10 P.M. made me a sluggish fieldworker. Even though the specifics of the pottery process were not so useful for my investigations, the expectation existed that I, too, would study what those before me had investigated.

The researchers who preceded me also framed my social expectations. When Foster first arrived in Tzintzuntzan, he was already a Ph.D. with a salaried job. Other researchers who started in the field as students later returned as tenured faculty. As such, they have been able to help families in Tzintzuntzan pay medical bills and send children to school. They are generous with gifts from toys to televisions, even sponsoring visits of Tzintzuntzeños to the United States. During my dissertation research year, I was financially dependent on a fellowship stipend for all my expenses. Though I knew of families with great monetary need, I could offer little more than emotional support. While the expectation to help financially was never voiced, I nonetheless felt its pressure.

There also were examples of past researchers' misdeeds that influenced how I was received in the field. These *were* expressed. Chief was the accusation that I would never return after finishing my stint there. Despite some fifty years of regular anthropological visits, people in Tzintzuntzan clearly remembered the ones who never came back. They had befriended these researchers and patiently answered their questions, but then never saw them again. In some cases, this had happened before I was born, but it still weighed on the informants and, consequently, on me. Particularly in the case of the colleague who had accompanied me to Tzintzuntzan in the summer of 1998 and later left the Berkeley Ph.D. program, I found myself defending her motives as well as my own. Proving future intentions was impossible, so I am especially conscious of my obligation to return after completing my dissertation.

(2) Another advantage of working in Tzintzuntzan has been the availability of resources. Even before entering the field, I had read published accounts of the

community as well as boxes of field notes. I had seen slides of the festivals in which I would later participate. Yet, once in the midst of research, I discovered that the most useful resource of all was an office and small library that the Fosters maintained in the house of the family with whom they stayed when in Tzintzuntzan.

Usually I wrote up my notes in the room I rented near the plaza, but it was not a space for reflection. The reason I enjoyed my living situation was its constant stimulation—small children playing, roosters crowing, customers entering, music blaring. Having a separate office became increasingly necessary. The Fosters' apartment was a place without distractions and with comfortable chairs. There, I could escape with my notebook to write more thoughtful prose, or I could read through monographs and check census data in the files kept there.

On one occasion, a nongovernmental organization working with potters in Tzintzuntzan asked me to give a seminar to its engineers on the cultural explanations for local artisans' unwillingness to accept innovation. By their calculations, they were offering potters more energy-efficient ovens with the possibility of producing higher-quality wares. Yet families in Tzintzuntzan and other communities were reluctant to incorporate the new techniques into their pottery making. I remembered from reading Foster's publications that CREFAL (Fundamental Education Training Center for Latin America, a UNESCO organization based in Pátzcuaro) had attempted a similar project in Tzintzuntzan back in the 1950s, in hopes of stimulating artisan cooperatives. It had met similar failure. However, I had brought very few materials with me that I could use to prepare a talk that would be both historically accurate and useful for the engineers. In the Tzintzuntzan office, I found the relevant citations with which I wrote a presentation that provoked productive debate among the audience.

I also benefited from the availability of human resources. At some point during my fieldwork, I received visits from Foster, Kemper, and Brandes. As much as I could, I participated in the once-a-decade ethnographic census (coordinated by Kemper in the year 2000) while continuing my dissertation fieldwork. In addition to the oversight and troubleshooting I offered to Kemper and the team of local census takers, I profited from the chance to meet families from all neighborhoods in Tzintzuntzan. In the end, the resulting demographic data served me in the chapter of my dissertation that describes the community.

Another time, I encountered difficulty with a particular informant. As a self-styled historian of the community and former seminary student, his perspective could have been especially helpful to my research. However, he was also a pompous anti-Semite. In one discussion of the emergence of evangelical churches in Tzintzuntzan, he spun a conspiracy tale involving covert Jewish domination of the world. He ended by recommending that I read the racist tract, "Protocols of the Elders of Zion." I did not hide my Jewish roots from the community, so I found this accusation personally offensive. Moreover, I was unprepared to dislike an informant so intensely and worried that it would impair my ability to understand religious movements in Tzintzuntzan. In an electronic mail to Brandes, I explained my frustration, hoping for some general advice. His reply was perfectly tailored: it turned out that when he had been a graduate student, he also had found this man offensive and recommended that I not bother trying to engage him further.

The ready availability of resources also has its downside. Although the need for reflection during fieldwork was undeniable and the office an oasis, I found that it threatened to turn me into a passive researcher. For example, I had to learn to rely on the census data volumes *only* when I had a specific question about genealogy or household arrangements. When I investigated on my own and asked questions, the results were both richer and more up-to-date than I would find in the volumes in Foster's office. Similarly, I needed to balance using the library with being an involved participant observer. Since my time in the field was limited, I could not justify spending it reading what I could find later back in Berkeley. It proved helpful to have resources at hand to answer strategic questions as well as to highlight what remained to be answered, but I did not want that to detract from my own discoveries.

(3) Additionally, I benefited from sensing that I was making a contribution. It is axiomatic that beginning researchers will experience pangs of anxiety in the field over the relevance of their project or their own ability to complete it. When I was feeling most skeptical about the validity of my findings, I could console myself with the thought that at least I was adding to the body of knowledge about Tzintzuntzan. Thankfully, the moments of self-doubt came infrequently. Most of the time, the ease of access and the availability of resources instilled confidence in me that I could collect sufficient data to make claims in my thesis that would be significant to the discipline.

It helped me that my advisors gave me freedom to pursue the research questions that interested me. The means of passing the mantle to younger anthropologists in Tzintzuntzan is very informal. My initial foray into the realm of pottery was meant to familiarize me with ethnographic research, not to track me into a particular area of inquiry. When I decided to follow the potentially divisive emergence of evangelical groups in Tzintzuntzan, I received solid support from other researchers. As a result, I feel that I am conducting more than simply a restudy. I am setting new terms for the consideration of religion in Tzintzuntzan. I am part owner of the long-term project, and not just a graduate student for hire.

The frustration has come from not being sure of my own expertise. Before I can claim anything about Tzintzuntzan, there are boxes of notes, dozens of articles, and several books that can contradict me. The knowledge I have gained in fourteen months of fieldwork is considerable, but there are several others whose time in the community dwarfs my own. In such circumstances, it requires an inordinate amount of certainty to make any assertion with authority. When I do feel confident in describing, for example, a Catholic fiesta, I am likely to find it has already been said in print.

I saw an example of this undermining of authority when Professor Michael Shott, an archaeologist from the University of Northern Iowa, came to Tzintzuntzan to carry out a comparative survey of the longevity of ceramics in several communities in Michoacán. He had contacted Foster and Kemper in advance for advice and a list of possible informants. I was visiting one of the suggested potters when Shott appeared at the door. The potter invited him in and listened to his request for information on the age of various pottery pieces. When he finished, the potter looked up at him from his clay and asked, "Didn't Dr. Foster already write an article about that?" Shott quickly explained that Foster had indeed collected that data decades ago, but that he was interested in updating the information.

While it has helped me to have advisors intimately familiar with the field site where I studied, coordination between researchers has proved challenging. The informality I referred to earlier that gives each member of the team part ownership of the project can lead to disarray. There is no central storehouse of data, nor any single format for recording them. I do not know whether any of the other graduate students who came with Professor Foster for a summer in and around Tzintzuntzan recorded information on early religious converts. In addition, I have no access to material collected by researchers who left without completing their theses or publishing their findings. Even among those scholars with whom I have regular contact, our projects stand independent of each other. Kemper and I shared the field comfortably while he coordinated the year 2000 ethnographic census, but the intellectual intersection between our projects never became clear. Our common base seems more geographical than theoretical or methodological.

Writing in the Third Generation

In some respects, the added scrutiny from both informants and other researchers encourages more scrupulous scholarship. It increases the opportunities for collaboration and correction, making for a more informed ethnography. But it also produces what I consider "inchoate" ethnography since there always exists the possibility of future updating, modifying, or challenging of any of our findings. Any ethnographic work is open to restudy or reconsideration in light of new theoretical and socioeconomic developments. However, in long-term research projects, the possibility is nearly a certainty and thus becomes an intrinsic part of the writing process. In turning my data into prose, I find myself emphasizing the historically contingent nature of my conclusions.

There have been only a limited number of ethnographies of conversion in Latin America, and almost all have been situated in communities with a large evangelical presence.[2] In Tzintzuntzan, non-Catholic religious groups have arrived only in the past twenty years and have remained a fringe phenomenon. By focusing my study on a community where evangelicals make up only a tiny percentage of the population, I could study the interaction between evangelicals and Catholics rather than simply the process of conversion.

In contrast, Annis (1987) conducted research in an indigenous Guatemalan community where 20 percent of the population had become evangelical Christians. His study draws sharp distinctions between Catholics and converts in agricultural production, political behavior, and even textile designs. He attributes entirely different "logics" to members of these two antagonistic religions. Catholics adhere to a colonial-era dependence on the land and accept the communal use of wealth through the distribution of ceremonial expenses, while converts aim to be self-supporting and reject as "wasteful" the payment toward community rituals.

As evidence for an evangelical interest in personal over collective advancement, Annis cites statistics which show that evangelicals buy plots in the best locations, plant higher-yielding crops, and cultivate them more intensively. Evangelical weavers display more entrepreneurial traits in selling their textiles and purchasing others' textiles to resell. Significantly, he records that converts opted out of the "Catholic cultural tax," the fees requested from every household for the celebration of communal fiestas. "By all accounts," Annis (1987:85) concludes, "it is 'cheaper' to be a Protestant than a Catholic." I wondered if this held true for Tzintzuntzan—with a far smaller proportion of converts—as well.

In a mostly evangelical community, I would be inclined to focus on the ruptures converts have made from the Catholic Church. However, in Tzintzuntzan my perspective was wider. The depth of anthropological observation there allowed me to see how the Catholic Church itself had changed over time. I could also see how conversion, though recent, had deep-rooted causes. Working with a small number of convert families, I was awakened to the accommodations they must make as a religious minority. Due to the friendly welcome I received, I was able to elicit rich qualitative data on an often prickly topic.

In analyzing and writing up my results, I have come to realize that it would be more fruitful for me to consider how evangelicals and Catholics in Tzintzuntzan share many similarities. I did not find an ideological cleavage between the two religious traditions; instead, I noted how both groups valued personal advancement and the pursuit of profit. At the same time, I spoke with several evangelical families who continue to pay the "cooperations" to community-wide Catholic fiestas. Though they recognize that the money supports another church, they feel that the promotion of community harmony outweighs any harm. Many converts maintain Catholic traditions such as praying to the saints and participating in fiestas.

Unlike Annis, I found that the Catholic faith had adapted to modern life and did not remain linked to a moribund colonial mind-set. Minor celebrations in the 1940s have expanded and grown more elaborate by 2000. Migration to the United States, in particular, has infused the fiestas with additional money and given new reasons to seek the divine intercession of the saints. For their part, Catholic clergy acknowledged their ongoing educational mission by encouraging evangelical-like principles among their parishioners. They called for individual reading and interpretation of Scripture as well as the restriction of alcohol consumption.

The conclusions I reach in the dissertation suggest an alternative view of religious conversion in Latin America, one that does not posit clear distinctions between Catholics and evangelicals but rather highlights their peaceful cohabitation. I am aware, however, that future visits to Tzintzuntzan could undermine these findings if serious division were to occur in the community because of religious differences. I also must be careful to distinguish conditions in Tzintzuntzan from those in other locations in Mexico, where evangelical religion has achieved a large percentage of converts and, in some cases, engendered violence. Still, my data support a novel contribution to the study of religion in Latin America. With the decades-long ethnographic record of the Catholic Church in Tzintzuntzan, I was able to identify how it had changed over time in reaction to the emergence of competing religious institutions.

Conclusions

Not only did participating in a long-term research project have intellectual consequences for my graduate training, it offered me practical advantages as well. Ph.D. programs at large research universities require students to work with a few faculty advisors in a mentor–apprentice relationship. In departments like engineering and physics, graduate students carve out a smaller project from a professor's ongoing research. Since their intellectual and methodological interests align closely, advisors and students in those disciplines form close relationships. Moreover, faculty members have a direct interest in the success of their students' research. This has not been the case in social anthropology, where advisors may do research in an entirely different country and language from that of their students. Participating in a long-term project in which my main advisor also has a stake has strengthened our relationship and made possible a more fluid exchange of ideas.

My connection with a long-term research project also has multiplied my opportunities for professional development. National conferences such as the American Anthropological Association's annual meeting receive more applications to present papers than their schedules can accommodate. As a participant in fieldwork in Tzintzuntzan, I had the opportunity to appear at an invited session at the AAA meeting in Chicago in 1999, which focused on many of the same issues that this volume addresses. When the Phoebe Hearst Museum of Anthropology at the University of California, Berkeley, hosted an exhibit of Foster's photographs of Tzintzuntzan, I was invited to be a speaker at the public event accompanying the opening. In my slide presentation, I updated the audience about the life of the community since Foster's original visit and shared insights from my own recent fieldwork.

Choosing Tzintzuntzan as the site for my doctoral research greatly reduced the time it took to receive my degree, a concern both graduate students and faculty share. It eliminated the need for extensive pilot studies and field visits to determine an appropriate site for research. In the field, I enjoyed unparalleled access to individuals in Tzintzuntzan, nearly all of whom received me with instant intimacy and candor. In writing up, I benefited from a treasure trove of published sources on the community as well as the careful attention of my advisors. Throughout the process, I did not let self-doubt derail me, because I felt certain my results would be relevant to other scholars. All these benefits contributed to my completing my degree in a time significantly shorter than average.

My involvement with Tzintzuntzan so far has not been "long term" by the standards of the other scholars contributing to this volume, but I am acutely aware that I am participating in a study that transcends my individual effort. Being a member of a long-term research project has colored how I experience the field as well as the conclusions I draw. The topic of conversion from Catholicism has not been explored fully in the corpus of Tzintzuntzan data. Though evangelical families in the community remain few in number, their presence is strongly felt and growing. My research will place them in relation to the Catholic majority and consider how both religions are modified and strengthened by the interaction.

For all the advantages I have enjoyed as a third-generation anthropologist in Tzintzuntzan, I also have had to endure frustrations. It was a challenge to establish a research style and persona separate from that of my predecessors. There was a larger than usual temptation to rely on already-gathered material rather than to put my participant-observer skills to work. Moreover, I will not have the opportunity to introduce a new field site into the anthropological literature. Instead, I will have the sense of caution that my arguments could be easily questioned by a number of persons with research experience in Tzintzuntzan.

Throughout my year in the field, I sensed an extra set of eyes looking over me. I felt the responsibility to behave myself in Tzintzuntzan, and not only because many of my neighbors could easily inform my advisors of any misdeed. I am aware that my time in the field will affect how future anthropologists are received there. And just as I have benefited from the warm relations cultivated by Foster and others, I intend to make Tzintzuntzan an attractive place to those researchers who follow me. Having now completed my degree, I can state confidently that the positives of participating in a long-term research project outweigh the negatives. The environment in which I conducted my research has helped shape the theoretical stance I take. The dissertation that resulted may lack a splashy first chapter describing a "new" field site, but the remaining chapters offer a fresh analysis on why religion has remained strong in Tzintzuntzan over the years.

Notes

1. Rabinow's (1977) account of the division at the University of Chicago Department of Anthropology between magically transformed fieldworkers and earnest but naive prefieldworkers has held true for many graduate programs in the 2000s.

2. See Garma Navarro (1987), Rosenbaum (1993), Eber (1995), Carlsen (1997), Chesnut (1997), and Sullivan (1998).

References Cited

Annis, Sheldon
(1987) *God and Production in a Guatemalan Town.* Austin: University of Texas Press.

Brandes, Stanley
(1988) *Power and Persuasion: Fiestas and Social Control in Rural Mexico.* Philadelphia: University of Pennsylvania Press.

Carlsen, Robert S.
(1997) *The War for the Heart and Soul of a Highland Maya Town.* Austin: University of Texas Press.

Chesnut, R. Andrew
(1997) *Born Again in Brazil: The Pentecostal Boom and the Pathogens of Poverty.* New Brunswick, NJ: Rutgers University Press.

Eber, Christine
(1995) *Women and Alcohol in a Highland Maya Town: Water of Hope, Water of Sorrow.* Austin: University of Texas Press.

Foster, George M.
(1965) "Peasant society and the image of limited good." *American Anthropologist* 67:293–315.

Foster, George M. and Gabriel Ospina
(1948) *Empire's Children: The People of Tzintzuntzan.* Smithsonian Institution, Institute of Social Anthropology, Publication No. 6. México, D.F.: Imprenta Nuevo Mundo.

Garma Navarro, Carlos
(1987) *Protestantismo en una Comunidad Totonaca de Puebla, México.* México, D.F.: Instituto Nacional Indigenista.

Kemper, Robert V.
(1977) *Migration and Adaptation: Tzintzuntzan Peasants in Mexico City.* Beverly Hills, CA: Sage Publications.

Limón, José E.
(1991) "Representation, ethnicity, and precursory ethnography: Notes of a native anthropologist." Pp. 115–135 in Richard G. Fox (editor), *Recapturing Anthropology: Working in the Present.* Santa Fe: School of American Research Press.

Rabinow, Paul
(1977) *Reflections on Fieldwork in Morocco.* Berkeley: University of California Press.

PETER S. CAHN

Rosenbaum, Brenda
>   (1993) *With Our Heads Bowed: The Dynamics of Gender in a Maya Community.* Albany,
>   NY: Institute for Mesoamerican Studies, State University at Albany.

Sullivan, Kathleen
>   (1998) "Religious change and the recreation of community in an urban setting among
>   the Tzotzil Maya of Highland Chiapas, Mexico." Ph.D. dissertation. City University
>   of New York.

INDEX

ABOUT THE CONTRIBUTORS

Megan Biesele (Ph.D., Harvard University, 1975). A self-employed scholar who teaches at the University of Texas, Austin, and at Texas A&M University; in 1998 she cofounded and serves as president of the School of Expressive Culture, a non-profit organization dedicated to research and public education about indigenous expressive forms such as rock art and folklore. Her research interests include religion, belief systems, and verbal and visual art of hunting-gathering societies; cognitive systems and environmental resource use; and contemporary political, economic, and human rights of indigenous peoples. In 1973, she helped to establish the Kalahari Peoples Fund and currently serves as its coordinator. From 1987 to 1992, she was director of a nongovernmental organization, the Nyae Nyae Development Foundation of Namibia. She is an elected member of the Committee for Human Rights of the American Anthropological Association. In 2000, she was presented with the Lucy Mair Medal for Applied Anthropology by the Royal Anthropological Institute of Great Britain and Ireland.

Peter S. Cahn (Ph.D., University of California, Berkeley, 2001). After undergraduate studies at Harvard University and a master's degree in Latin American Studies at the University of Cambridge, U.K., he came to Berkeley with a National Science Foundation Fellowship. His dissertation research focused on the rise of evangelical congregations in Tzintzuntzan, Mexico, and the reaction of the dominant Catholic Church. While in the field, he served as a commentator for the Pacific News Service. As a postdoctoral fellow at the Humanities Research Institute at the University of California, Irvine, he will continue to investigate the role of religion in everyday modern life, particularly in Latin America. His next project will examine both historically and ethnographically the way fraternal orders such as the Freemasons and voluntary associations such as Avon Ladies adopt religious characteristics and organize social behavior.

Lisa Cliggett (Ph.D., Indiana University, Bloomington, 1997). Recipient of a Fulbright grant for her dissertation research on household economy and support systems for the elderly in Zambia, she was a research assistant at the Population

Institute for Research and Training at Indiana University in Bloomington before accepting a postdoctoral fellowship at the University of Pennsylvania. Currently, she is an assistant professor of anthropology at the University of Kentucky, where her research and teaching interests include ecological and economic anthropology, social organization, migration, aging, and anthropological demography, with a regional emphasis on sub-Saharan Africa and the Caribbean. Her recent research activities focus on links between migration and environmental change in Zambia.

Elizabeth Colson (Ph.D., Radcliffe College, 1945). Director of the Rhodes-Livingstone Institute (1947–1951), then faculty member at Manchester University, Goucher College, Boston University, Brandeis University, and Northwestern University before joining the anthropology department at Berkeley in 1964, she has been professor emeritus since 1984. A member of Phi Beta Kappa, she was a fellow at the Center for Advanced Study in the Behavioral Sciences between 1967 and 1968 and was elected to the National Academy of Sciences in 1977 and then to the American Academy of Arts and Sciences in 1978. Recipient of honorary degrees from Brown University, the University of Rochester, and the University of Zambia, she also has been honored with the Bronislaw Malinowski Award of the Society for Applied Anthropology (SfAA), the Rivers Memorial Medal of the Royal Anthropological Institute, and the Distinguished Africanist Award of the American Association for African Studies.

T. Scarlett Epstein (Ph.D., University of Manchester, 1958). A pioneer in the field of applied economic anthropology, she held positions at the Australian National University, Canberra, and at the Royal College of Advanced Technology, Salford, U.K., before becoming research professor at the University of Sussex, U.K., from which she retired in 1984. Since then, she has continued to be active in diverse social research and voluntary agencies, including PEGS (Practical Education & Gender Support, based in the United Kingdom), INTERVENTION (a social research agency in India), and SOMRA (Social & Market Research Agency, in Bangladesh). She has served in editorial roles for a series on "International Population Studies" (Pergamon Press) and a series on "Women in Development Studies" (Pergamon Press and Hindustani Publishing Corporation, India). A fellow at the Center for Advanced Study in the Behavioral Sciences in 1974, she was elected to Honorary Fellowship in the Indian Anthropological Association in 1983 and to Life Membership in the Association of British Social Anthropologists in 2000.

George M. Foster (Ph.D., University of California, Berkeley, 1941). Professor emeritus at UC-Berkeley, his major interests are peasant society and socioeconomic change, especially international health and community development, with a regional emphasis on Mexico and Spain. Director of the Smithsonian's Institute of Social Anthropology from 1946 until he returned to Berkeley in 1953, he later served as consultant for USAID and the World Health Organization (WHO) in Southeast Asia and Zambia. President of the AAA in 1970, he received its Distinguished Service Award in 1980. A Guggenheim fellow and fellow at the Center for Advanced Study in the Behavioral Sciences, a member of the National Academy of Sciences and the American Academy of Arts and Sciences, he received the Bronislaw Malinowski Award from the SfAA and a Doctorate of Humane Letters from Southern Methodist University. In 1999, Berkeley renamed its anthropology library the "George and Mary Foster Anthropology Library," and, in 2000, SMU founded the "George and Mary Foster Distinguished Lecture Series in Cultural Anthropology."

Ulla C. Johansen (Ph.D., Hamburg University, 1954). After a long career working in museums and universities, she is now retired from her position as director and professor of the Institute of Ethnology at the University of Cologne. In addition to her long-term interests in ethnohistory, shamanism, and the comparative study of religion, her current work focuses on the ethnography of Turkish-speaking peoples, Estonians, and foreign workers in Germany. She is an honorary member of the German Anthropological Association (Deutsche Gesellschaft für Völkerkunde) and president of the international Societas Uralo-Altaica.

Robert V. Kemper (Ph.D., University of California, Berkeley, 1971). Professor of anthropology at Southern Methodist University and urban ministry advisor at SMU's Perkins School of Theology, his current interests include applied anthropology, bilingual education, community ministry, migration, and urban development, especially in Mexico and among Hispanics in the United States. A member of Phi Beta Kappa and a fellow of the American Association for the Advancement of Science (AAAS), he has been a Woodrow Wilson fellow and twice held Fulbright awards. He has served as president of the Society for Latin American Anthropology and the Society for Urban Anthropology and has been on the executive boards of the AAA, the SfAA, and the Council for the Preservation of Anthropological Records. He has been an editor with the *American Anthropologist, Human Organization,* and *Urban Anthropology;* has served on the editorial boards of *Relaciones* (El Colegio de Michoacán, Mexico), the *Encyclopedia of Urban Cultures,* and the *Encyclopedia of World Cultures;* and co-edits the series "Contemporary Urban Studies" (Bergin & Garvey).

Louise Lamphere (Ph.D., Harvard University, 1968). Distinguished professor of anthropology at the University of New Mexico, she formerly was on the faculty at Brown University (1968–1975, 1979–1986). Her research interests include women's work and gender, urban anthropology, ethnicity and immigration, and Native North America. Her field research has been carried out in New England and the Southwest. She served on the editorial board of the *Annual Review* *of Anthropology* between 1991 and 1996. She was presented the Conrad Arensberg Award by the Society for the Anthropology of Work in 1994, the Prize for the Critical Study of North America by the Society for the Anthropology of North America in 1995, and the Squeaky Wheel Award by the AAA Committee on the Status of Women in 1998. She was president of the American Ethnological Society from 1987 to 1989, chair of the Association for Feminist Anthropology from 1995 to 1997, president-elect of the AAA from 1997 to 1999, and its president from 1999 to 2001.

Richard B. Lee (Ph.D., University of California, Berkeley, 1965). University professor of anthropology and past chair of the African Studies Program at the University of Toronto, he has taught at Harvard, Rutgers, and Columbia and has held research positions at the Center for Advanced Studies in the Behavioral Sciences, Stanford, and at the University of British Columbia. Currently, he is visiting professor of African studies at Kyoto University, Japan. A fellow of the Royal Society of Canada and a former president of the Canadian Anthropology Society, he is known for his studies of hunting and gathering societies, particularly the Ju/'hoansi-!Kung San of Botswana, with whom he has worked since 1963. Studies of foragers have also taken him to Tanzania, Namibia, Alaska, Australia, British Columbia, the Yukon, and Labrador. His film credits include documentary films with Richard Leakey, David Suzuki, and Yo-Yo Ma. In 1990, he was awarded an honorary Doctorate of Letters by the University of Alaska, Fairbanks, for his research and advocacy on behalf of foraging peoples.

Wade Pendleton (Ph.D., University of California, Berkeley, 1970). Professor of anthropology at San Diego State University, he has held positions at Witwatersrand University (1970), the University of Cape Town (1971–1972, 1974), the University of Hawaii (1981–1982), the University of Zimbabwe (1995, 2001–2002), and the University of Namibia (UNAM; 1991–1993, 1996–1998). He is a research associate with the Social Sciences Division of the Multi-Disciplinary Research Centre of UNAM. Since 1997, he has been a research associate with the Southern African Migration Project, recently coordinating the project's National Immigration Policy Survey Project in southern African countries. In 1996, he was the recipient of a Fulbright Scholar Award.

Anya Peterson Royce (Ph.D., University of California, Berkeley, 1974). Chancellors' professor of anthropology and comparative literature at Indiana University, Bloomington, she holds additional appointments in the School of Music, in the Department of Folklore, and in Latin American and Caribbean Studies. A pioneer in the anthropology of dance and performing arts, her research and teaching interests also include ethnic identity, virtuosity and artistry, and the ethnography of Mexico and the American Southwest. She has been president of the Society for Latin American Anthropology and has served on the executive board of the

American Anthropological Association and on the Editorial Board of the *American Anthropologist*. She received a Guggenheim Fellowship in 1980, was a Phi Beta Kappa Visiting Scholar in 1991 and 1992, and has had additional research support from the American Council of Learned Societies, the American Philosophical Society, the Bogliasco Foundation, the Delmas Foundation, the National Endowment for the Humanities, and the Social Science Research Council.

Thayer Scudder (Ph.D., Harvard University, 1960). Professor emeritus at the California Institute of Technology, he earlier held positions with the Rhodes-Livingstone Institute in Northern Rhodesia and at the American University in Cairo. In 1976, he was one of three founding directors of the Institute for Development Anthropology, a nongovernmental organization well known for its work in Africa, Asia, and Latin America. In 1998, he was named to the twelve-member World Commission on Dams and spent most of the next two years analyzing large-scale projects around the globe. A fellow of the AAAS, he has received numerous honors for his theoretical and applied work, including the 1984 Solon T. Kimball Award for Public and Applied Anthropology and the 1991 Edward J. Lehman Award, both given by the American Anthropological Association, the 1998 Lucy Mair Medal for Applied Anthropology, and the 1999 Bronislaw Malinowski Award.

Evon Z. Vogt (Ph.D., University of Chicago, 1948). Professor emeritus of anthropology and honorary curator of Mesoamerican Ethnology, Peabody Museum, Harvard University, he was a fellow of the Center for Advanced Study in the Behavioral Sciences (1956–1957) just before beginning the Harvard Chiapas Project. Awarded the Fray Bernardino de Sahagún Prize of the National Anthropology and History Institute (Mexico), he was decorated as Knight Commander in the Order of the Aztec Eagle (Mexico) in 1978. He is a member of the National Academy of Sciences and the American Philosophical Society of Philadelphia and a fellow of the American Academy of Arts and Sciences. He has served on the executive board of the American Anthropological Association.

Douglas R. White (Ph.D., University of Minnesota, 1969). Graduate director of the Social Networks program, a member of the Institute of Mathematical Behavioral Science, and professor of anthropology at the University of California at Irvine, he is also a member of multiple working groups at the Santa Fe Institute. His current work is on complexity theory and the effects of emergent structure on a large scale in social networks, including social class, large-scale cohesion, solidarity and exchange, elites, markets, and global processes. He does extensive collaboration on longitudinal social research projects in Europe, Latin America, Africa, and Asia. In 1990, he was awarded the Alexander von Humboldt Prize to Distinguished Senior U.S. Social Scientists to further his collaborative work on comparative social systems worldwide.